(WITHDRAWN

D1260650

Sacred Passions

Sacred Passions

The Life and Music of Manuel de Falla

CAROL A. HESS

OXFORD
UNIVERSITY PRESS

2005

OXFORD
UNIVERSITY PRESS

Oxford   New York
Auckland   Bangkok   Buenos Aires   Cape Town   Chennai
Dar es Salaam   Delhi   Hong Kong   Istanbul   Karachi   Kolkata
Kuala Lumpur   Madrid   Melbourne   Mexico City   Mumbai
Nairobi   São Paulo   Shanghai   Taipei   Tokyo   Toronto

Copyright © 2005 by Oxford University Press, Inc.

Published by Oxford University Press, Inc.
198 Madison Avenue, New York, New York, 10016

www.oup.com

Oxford is a registered trademark of Oxford University Press

All rights reserved. No part of this publication may be reproduced,
stored in a retrieval system, or transmitted, in any form or by any means,
electronic, mechanical, photocopying, recording, or otherwise,
without the prior permission of Oxford University Press.

Library of Congress Cataloging-in-Publication Data
Hess, Carol A.
Sacred passions : the life and music of Manuel de Falla / Carol A Hess.
p. cm.
Includes bibliographical references and index.
ISBN 0-19-514561-5
1. Falla, Manuel de, 1876–1946.   2. Composers—Spain—Biography.   I. Title.
ML410.F215H48 2004
780'.92—dc22   2004041472
[B]

Evocation *from* IBERIA SUITE: Volume I for Piano [IMC Edition 2075]
By Isaac Albéniz
© Copyright 1982 by International Music Company
All Rights Reserved. International Copyright Secured

1 2 3 4 5 6 7 8 9
Printed in the United States of America
on acid-free paper

In loving memory of my parents

John A. Hess Jr.

Emily Olga Hess

and the music in our home

Preface

A few practical matters on translations should be mentioned. Whenever a foreign-language source is readily available, I omit the original language in the interest of space; press reviews and correspondence in less accessible secondary sources appear in both languages.[1] Each secondary source has been checked against the original document. Unless otherwise indicated, all translations are my own, although I warmly thank Edgardo Raul Salinas and Carlo Caballero for proofreading my renderings of the Spanish and French texts, respectively. Given Falla's sometimes knotty prose, their task was not always an easy one. Any remaining errors, of course, are mine.

Another editorial issue is the inconsistent use of the particle *de* in the composer's name. He was christened Manuel María de los Dolores Falla y Matheu (Falla being his father's family name and Matheu his mother's). Around 1900, for reasons that are unclear, he began signing Manuel de Falla, that is, adding the *de* and dropping his mother's name, the use of which is optional in Spain.[2] Since in peninsular Spanish

1. Translations of many of Falla's own writings are found in David Urman and J. M. Thomson's *On Music and Musicians* (London and Boston: Marion Boyars, 1979). Several new writings have come to light since its publication, however. For an alternative translation of some of the letters cited here, see Jorge de Persia, ed., *Manuel de Falla: His Life and Works* (London: Omnibus, 1999).
2. Concha Chinchilla, "Cronología de Manuel de Falla," in *Manuel de Falla en Granada,* edited by Yvan Nommick (Granada: Publicaciones del Archivo Manuel de Falla, 2001), 155.

it is common to drop the *de* when referring to the composer by his last name (Falla versus Manuel de Falla), I have continued that format here, although some older English-language sources retain the *de*, as do some Argentine press articles. When deciding between Spanish and Catalan names I take the one more commonly used in Falla's time (Orquestra Pau Casals rather than Orquesta Pablo Casals), although admittedly this is a judgment call. Titles of Falla's works appear in the original language with the exception of the ballet *The Three-Cornered Hat* (known in the ballet world as *Le tricorne*), given here in English to avoid confusion with the nineteenth-century novel, *El sombrero de tres picos*, on which it is based. Names of organizations or publications with reasonably obvious cognates are left in the original language.

Since most biographies of Falla are by Spaniards (the French run a close second), I have tried to offer a North American perspective where appropriate. Thus, I consider the reception of Falla's music in the United States and the various loopholes in copyright law that made it so easy for unscrupulous editors to publish and sometimes alter his works. I also introduce a phenomenon other biographers have conspicuously avoided: the commercialization of Falla's music through movies and pop arrangements.

It is always a pleasure—no, a moving experience—to thank the many people who helped me with this project. First and foremost, there is Joaquín Nin-Culmell, Professor Emeritus of Composition at the University of California at Berkeley, who died months before this book went to press. The son of composer, editor, and musicologist Joaquín Nin and singer Rosa Culmell (their oldest child was author Anaïs Nin), Nin-Culmell studied with Falla in the 1930s and shared with me compositional drafts, notes, and vivid memories of that extraordinary experience. I was privileged to have him as a friend and mentor, and his insights will always guide my work in Spanish music. I have also had the honor of meeting María Isabel de Falla de Paredes, Falla's niece and president of the Fundación Manuel de Falla. Her daughter, Elena García de Paredes, is manager of the Archivo Manuel de Falla (AMF) in Granada (Spain), where, thanks to funding from the Program for Cultural Cooperation between Spain's Ministry of Culture and United States' Universities and Bowling Green State University, I have spent long and contented hours. I am deeply grateful to Yvan Nommick, current director of the AMF, who not only facilitated my access to a wide range of materials but has set a new standard for Falla research through his meticulous and musically sensitive scholarship. The AMF's attentive staff is headed by Concha Chinchilla, whose elephant's memory enables her to know its holdings inside and out. Indeed, the AMF itself inspires awe, for it lies at the foot of the Alhambra palace, the Moors' last stronghold in Spain. Each time I walk there from downtown Granada, trudging up the Cuesta de Gomérez through the sixteenth-century Puerta de las Granadas, I revel in the crisp morning air, and as shafts of light cut through the thick, leafy canopy I invariably find myself wondering if any research environment more closely resembles paradise.

Emilio Ros Fábregas and María Gemberro of the University of Granada have provided hours of lively conversation on Spanish and U.S. perspectives on Falla. Ana María Locatelli de Pérgamo (Catholic University of Buenos Aires) and Myriam Kitroser (National University of Córdoba) welcomed me warmly to Argentine academic life and Mónica Gorgas of the Jesuit Museum of Alta Gracia (Argentina) made my visits to Falla's final residence exceptionally gratifying. I also thank Barbara Hall and the staff of the Margaret Herrick Library of the Center for Motion Picture Study (Academy of Motion Picture Arts and Sciences) in Beverly Hills, California. Joyce Ford facilitated my research at the University of California at Berkeley, and William L. Schurk of Bowling Green State University has been extremely helpful in my work with that institution's popular music collection (Sound Recording Archives). Also from Bowling Green are Adam Zygmunt and my two research assistants, Jennifer Stephen and Edgardo Raul Salinas, whom I thank for performing tasks that were often less than enthralling. Hubert Toney Jr. introduced me to various marching band versions of Falla's "Ritual Fire Dance," and Russell Schmidt generously shared with me his copious knowledge of jazz styles and film music. For many years, my research has been enhanced though informal dialogue on Spanish culture with Dru Dougherty of the University of California at Berkeley, and this book is no exception. I also owe a special debt to Merna M. Thomas (Professor Emerita, College of the Holy Names, Oakland, California), who, in sharing with me her memories of the "Ritual Fire Dance" and its popularity in the United States during the 1940s, suggested the line of inquiry pursued in chapter 10.

Several people have read all or part of the manuscript and have offered helpful comments, including the anonymous readers for Oxford University Press, Richard Crawford, Walter Clark, Michael Christoforidis, Bonna Boettcher, Deborah Schwartz-Kates, and especially John Koegel. In addition to reading portions of the manuscript, Edgardo Raul Salinas lent a sympathetic ear to my frequent and often rambling monologues on this enigmatic composer. Maribeth Payne, formerly of Oxford University Press, initially suggested the project, and Kim Robinson shepherded it along with patience and wit. As always, I thank Dorothy Weicker, whose support has meant so much to me over the years; my sisters Judy, Nancy, and Bonnie; and many other friends and colleagues, whose encouragement and good humor I can never adequately acknowledge.

Figures

Musical Examples

Contents

    Defining Moments: *El retablo de Maese Pedro* and the
    Harpsichord Concerto * The Allure of the Lost Continent *
    Figurehead for Youth: Falla as Teacher

7. "Far above the Workings of Politics" *185*
    Falla and the Republic * "Spes Vitae" (Hope of Life)

8. Falla and the Spanish Civil War *213*
    "The Breath of God over Our Bayonets" * Evasion,
    Acquiescence, Enigma: Falla's Declaration

9. Seeking the Lost Continent *243*
    Argentina and Self-Imposed Exile * The Aftermath: *Atlántida*

10. Falla's Legacy *285*
    Falla and Spain * The Other Falla

    Appendix 1 Works and First Performances *303*

    Appendix 2 Overview of Spanish History, 1874–1981 *309*

    Bibliography *311*

    Index *333*

Enter by the narrow gate, since

the gate that leads to perdition is

wide, and the road spacious, and

many take it; but it is a narrow gate

and a hard road that leads to life,

and only a few find it.

MATTHEW 7:13

Sacred Passions

Chapter 1

Confronting Falla

"I am I and my circumstance."[1] This deceptively simple statement by the Spanish philosopher José Ortega y Gasset hovers in the background of any biographical narrative that posits a dialogue between self and surroundings.[2] For Ortega's contemporary and compatriot Manuel de Falla (1876–1946), "circumstance" encompassed vertiginous change in the arts and two world wars; phenomena particular to Spain included the cultural renaissance known as the Silver Age (*edad de plata*), which saw the modernist creations of Lorca, Buñuel, Dalí, and Miró.[3] Roughly spanning the period between Spain's ignominious defeat by the United States in the Spanish-American War (1898) and the outbreak of the Spanish Civil War (1936),

1. José Ortega y Gasset, *Meditaciones del Quijote*, edited by Julián Marías, 3d ed. (Madrid: Cátedra, 1995), 77.

2. As Rockwell Gray has observed, Ortega's famous dictum stemmed from frustration over what he saw as Spaniards' tendency to "split self from circumstance" by indulging in isolationist behavior and thus preventing Spain from realizing its full intellectual potential in the modern age. See Rockwell Gray, *The Imperative of Modernity: An Intellectual Biography of José Ortega y Gasset* (Berkeley: University of California Press, 1989), 96.

3. See José-Carlos Mainer, *La edad de plata (1902–1939)*, 5th ed. (Madrid: Cátedra, 1999).

the Silver Age also sustained an impassioned debate over national identity that struggled to define the "essence of Spain."[4]

As for "self," Falla's seems a bundle of contradictions. According to Stravinsky, he was insusceptible to "manifestations of humor."[5] Yet Falla loved a good joke, even if it was on him. He was furious when unscrupulous publishers altered his music, yet more than once he tinkered with Chopin's compositions. He lived as a monklike ascetic yet wrote some highly sensual music. He claimed to shun publicity yet expressed his convictions in print, sometimes at considerable personal cost. His agonies over such simple decisions as which shirt to put on in the morning sometimes bordered on neurosis, yet his unswerving faith in what he considered the one true religion, Roman Catholicism, afforded him the peace of conviction. A liberal during World War I, he halfheartedly supported the Right in the Spanish Civil War, largely out of frustration with the anticlericalism of the Second Republic, the government overthrown by the forces of Gen. Francisco Franco. So meek as to apologize for killing a cockroach, he nonetheless accepted the human costs of the Civil War.

As for his music, Falla's artistic path is a series of about-faces. He embraced and then rejected nineteenth-century salon music, Wagnerian chromaticism, impressionism, Spanish nationalism, and neoclassicism. Mainly it was his neoclassical works, admired by the international musical intelligentsia, that established his reputation as the musical leader of Spain's avant garde (*vanguardia*), which flourished during the Silver Age. Yet the catchy melodies, infectious rhythms, and "exotic" character of his nationalist works, which date from an earlier period, have been applauded by a mass audience, especially in the United States. Thanks to that country's formidable music industry, Falla's music has been featured in Hollywood musicals and in pop and jazz arrangements, and has been recorded by artists as diverse as the Harmonicats, Fred Waring and the Pennsylvanians, and Miles Davis.

All this—the political and artistic ferment that formed the backdrop to Falla's life, his richly variegated (albeit slender) oeuvre, the critical issues raised by his music, and his intensely guarded personality—invites any number of biographical approaches. Previous scholars have tended to emphasize self over circumstance. The first significant biography of Falla, published in 1930 by the French critic Roland-Manuel, emphasizes the composer's spiritual life and attaches a religious dimension to his music.[6] Jaime Pahissa, the Spanish composer and music critic,

4. This is the translation that is sometimes given for Miguel de Unamuno's defense of Spain's "eternal tradition," *En torno al casticismo*, of 1895. See, for example, Richard Herr, *An Historical Essay on Modern Spain* (Berkeley: University of California Press, 1971), 28.

5. Igor Stravinsky and Robert Craft, *Memories and Commentaries* (New York: Doubleday, 1960), 76.

6. Roland-Manuel [Alexis Levy], *Manuel de Falla* (Paris: Cahiers d'Art, 1930). An earlier study is the unsigned essay *Manuel de Falla: Miniature Essays* (London: Chester, 1922). Its author is Eric Blom, as confirmed by his letter to Falla of 19 December 1921 (AMF correspondence file 6778).

concentrates on Falla's activities as a composer, illuminating his works, selected performances, and professional relationships. Pahissa interviewed the composer in Argentina, where both resided in the aftermath of the Civil War; consequently, his authorized biography essentially tells us what the composer wanted us to know.[7] To be sure, Falla was an honest man (unlike his friend Stravinsky, a chronic prevaricator), but he sometimes saw things from an idiosyncratic perspective. Then there is the spate of Spanish-language biographies that appeared in the three decades after the composer's death, some of which reflect the grandiloquent tone of Franco-period rhetoric.[8] As for English-language studies, John B. Trend's lively *Manuel de Falla and Spanish Music* deserves mention, although the most widely read continues to be the 1968 translation of Suzanne Demarquez's *Manuel de Falla*.[9] Like many others, it derives largely from Pahissa.[10]

In recent decades, two events have breathed new life into Falla research. First, the advent of democracy in Spain after Franco's death in 1975 has helped dampen some biographers' unrealistically worshipful outlook while encouraging exploration of the complicated "circumstance" the Civil War and Spanish politics imposed during the composer's lifetime.[11] Second, the establishment in 1991 of the Archivo Manuel de Falla in Granada has centralized thousands of letters, press clippings, musical sketches, and drafts of prose articles, as well as the composer's heavily annotated personal library. As a result, a new generation of Falla scholars has produced a catalog of works and manuscripts, editions, sketch studies, musical analyses, reception studies, and biographical essays. My study, which seeks to integrate self, circumstance, and music, draws almost exclusively on this new material.

---

7. Jaime Pahissa, *Vida y obra de Manuel de Falla* (1947; 2d ed., rev. and enl., Buenos Aires: Ricordi, 1956). See also Pahissa's *Manuel de Falla, His Life and Works,* translated by Jean Wagstaff (1954; reprint, Westport, Conn.: Hyperion, 1979). Falla also worked closely with Roland-Manuel (see n6 within this chapter).

8. F. Adolfo Masciopinto, *El nacionalismo musical en Manuel de Falla,* Publicación de Extensión Universitaria, no. 75 (Santa Fe: Ministerio de Educación de la Nación, Universidad Nacional del Litoral, 1952). See also Ángel Sagardía, *Manuel de Falla* (Madrid: Unión Musical Española, 1946); Enrique Franco, *Manuel de Falla y su obra* (Madrid: Publicaciones Españolas, 1976); and Luis Campodónico, *Falla,* translated by Françoise Avila, Collections microcosme, solfèges, no. 13 (Paris: Éditions du Seuil, 1959).

9. John B. Trend, *Manuel de Falla and Spanish Music* (1929; reprint, New York: Knopf, 1934); Suzanne Demarquez, *Manuel de Falla,* translated by Salvator Attanasio (Philadelphia: Chilton, 1968).

10. See Antonio Campoamor Gonzálo, *Manuel de Falla, 1876–1946* (Madrid: Sedmay Ediciones, 1976); José Casanovas, *Manuel de Falla, cien años* (Barcelona: Ediciones de Nuevo Arte Thor, 1976); and Campodónico, *Falla.*

11. See, for example, Andrew Budwig and Gilbert Chase, *Manuel de Falla: A Bibliography and Research Guide* (New York and London: Garland, 1986); or Carol A. Hess, "Manuel de Falla's *The Three-Cornered Hat* and the Spanish Right-Wing Press in Pre–Civil War Spain," *Journal of Musicological Research* 15 (1995): 55–80.

How to achieve such a synthesis? Our image of Falla is colored by frequently repeated anecdotes that, when thoughtfully examined, reveal as much about his biographers as the composer himself. My purpose here is not so much to debunk these impressions (some are not without basis and others cannot yet be proven one way or another) but to invite the reader to reflect on their origins and motivations. Take, for example, the charge that Falla, who never married, was a misogynist.[12] Since there is no concrete evidence for this, the question is not so much whether Falla detested women as what the status of misogynist would have meant in the patriarchal social and religious climate of early twentieth-century Spain. There are also "accusations of homosexuality," to which several scholars uneasily refer, accusations that arose primarily in connection with Falla's friendship with the poet Federico García Lorca and the Madrid-based music critic Adolfo Salazar, both gay.[13] Rather than ask if Falla was a homosexual (or had homosexual inclinations or experiences), we might instead wonder why some have taken umbrage at the mere suggestion. In turn, these two issues—and biographers' ways of dealing with them—are linked to what we might call Falla hagiography. Further, although we might assume that this tendency originated during the *franquista* period, when Franco made Catholic identity a rallying point for the authoritarian Right, in fact the theme of "Falla as saint" surfaced well before the outbreak of the Civil War. In many respects, moreover, it was an essentially accurate, if extravagant, description: deeply religious and distrustful of wealth, Falla led a life of quietude and abnegation, especially in his later years. Reverential and fawning treatment at the hands of his biographers would have irked him no end, however, especially Federico Sopeña's uncritical acceptance of the "assurance" of Manuel Orozco, a medical doctor and Falla enthusiast, that the composer died a virgin.[14] Again, my task will be not so much to challenge the notion that Falla was a saint as to consider why some have sanctified him.

The trickiest point to reconcile between self and circumstance concerns Falla's political leanings. Here, post-Franco perspectives diverge: Andrew Budwig, for example, paints him as a "poor liberal," while Sopeña sees his "patriotic Catholicism" as evidence of his solidarity with Franco.[15] As I argue in detail here, neither assessment is precisely correct, and again these conflicting opinions say more about those

12. Tomás Marco, *Siglo XX*, Historía de la música española, no. 6 (Madrid: Alianza, 1989), 41.

13. Nancy Lee Harper, *Manuel de Falla: A Bio-Bibliography* (Westport, Conn.: Greenwood, 1998), 22; Federico Sopeña, *Vida y obra de Manuel de Falla* (Madrid: Turner Música, 1988), 135.

14. Sopeña, *Vida y obra*, 204n2.

15. Budwig and Chase, *Manuel de Falla*, 28. Orozco goes a step further by asserting that Falla was an "innate liberal" in *Manuel de Falla: Historia de una derrota* (Barcelona: Ediciones Destino, 1985), 206. See also Federico Sopeña, *Manuel de Falla y el mundo de la cultura española* (Madrid: Instituto de España, 1976).

interpreting the behavior—however ambivalent—of the biographical subject than about some reified historical "reality."

As much as possible, I have let Falla and his contemporaries tell their stories. An inveterate pack rat, the composer usually kept carbon copies and drafts of both his articles and his extensive correspondence. This affords the biographer access to sender and recipient and in several instances entry into Falla's thought process. I also rely on the press, weaving in reviews by international music critics and their Spanish counterparts; the personalities and politics of the latter I describe in *Manuel de Falla and Modernism in Spain, 1898–1936*, a reception study that can be read as a companion to the present biography. In addition, I seek to maintain "a posture . . . more dialogistic than analytic, more conversational than assertive and judgmental," an epistemological stance famously articulated years ago by Hayden White.[16] In probing the delicate and elusive links between self and circumstance, in weighing the perils and rewards of intuition, and in negotiating the interplay between artifact and memory, the biographer confronts head-on the paradoxical nature of our desire to fit human experience and historic events, often random or cataclysmic, into a coherent narrative. Still, as White acknowledges, there is an "apparently universal need not only to narrate but to give to events *an aspect of narrativity*" (emphasis added).[17] The fact that biographers so regularly marvel at inconsistencies in their subjects' personalities—as I have just done—surely exposes a collective ingenuousness about human behavior. As we satisfy our narrative urge by tracing Falla's complex and contradictory life, one stubbornly dedicated to the pursuit of perfection in a disappointing world, we may find our subject by turns exasperating, winsome, obdurate, or affectionate—that is, a decided threat to any "aspect of narrativity" we may be earnestly trying to create. I hope to demonstrate, however, that the richness of dialogue among self, circumstance, and music is well worth the occasional loose end or unresolved question. An enigma thoughtfully pondered is more rewarding than the so-called definitive answer with its false promise of nonambivalence and the misguided premise that history must present itself as either black or white.

16. Hayden White, *The Content of the Form: Narrative Discourse and Historical Representation* (Baltimore and London: Johns Hopkins University Press, 1986), 186. See also Carol A. Hess, *Manuel de Falla and Modernism in Spain, 1898–1936* (Chicago and London: University of Chicago Press, 2001).

17. White, *Content of the Form*, 4.

Chapter 2

The Waning of Romanticism:

A Composer Begins

The Atlantic port of Cádiz, founded by the Phoenicians around 1100 B.C.E. is redolent with myths and memories of the sea. Close by are the Pillars of Hercules, two limestone shafts that were joined until that mighty god supposedly separated them with his club.[1] In nearby Huelva Province is Palos de la Frontera. There Christopher Columbus, the hero of many an impressionable boy, set sail in August 1492, ultimately assuring that throughout Spain's period of colonial domination gold, silver, and other goods from the New World would be discharged in Cádiz. Ideas flowed freely as well: although the city fell to Franco's troops early in the Spanish Civil War, a tradition of liberalism and tolerance has shaped its collective memory. In 1812, months before Napoleon's occupation of Spain ended, a constitution known as the "liberal codex" was drafted in Cádiz, and today the city is known for its extravagant carnival celebrations and relaxed social mores.[2]

A "VERY STUDIOUS, VERY CONSCIENTIOUS YOUNG MAN"

When Manuel de Falla was born in Cádiz on 23 November 1876, calm and prosperity prevailed. The Bourbon dynasty had been recently reinstated after decades of

---

1. Earl Rosenthal, "Plus Ultra, Non Plus Ultra, and the Columnar Device of Emperor Charles V," *Journal of the Warburg Institute* 34 (1971): 204.
2. Raymond Carr, *Spain, 1808–1975*, 2d ed. (Oxford: Clarendon Press, 1982), 92–105.

foreign invasions, civil wars, and a fitful experiment in representative government known as the First Republic (February to December 1873).[3] To be sure, under Alfonso XII's constitutional monarchy this tranquility was due mainly to electoral manipulation, with the two main political parties regularly alternating in an arrangement known as the *turno pacífico*.[4] This contrivance underwent several ideological tests, one of which concerned the relationship between church and state. The 1876 constitution, while recognizing "the Apostolic Roman religion" as the official state religion, also required "tolerance" of other faiths, a point on which traditionalists dissented with liberal, radical, and often rabidly anticlerical elements.[5] In this and other ways, the Spanish Civil War, a defining moment for Spaniards of Falla's generation, was foreshadowed well before its outbreak in 1936.[6]

Such conflicts as simmered beneath this placid surface had little effect on Falla's parents, José María de Falla Franco (1849–1919) and María Jesús Matheu Zabala (1850–1919), both of Cádiz.[7] Of their five children, Manuel (Manolo) was the firstborn, and only two others survived: María del Carmen, six years younger than Manuel; and Germán, thirteen years younger. José María, born two years after Manuel, died at age seven when a cholera epidemic claimed over five hundred lives in southern Spain.[8] Servando, a boy born in 1889, died in infancy. Falla felt deeply this early and immediate experience of death, so much a part of childhood in that era. This awareness, coupled with his own delicacy of build and constitution undoubtedly shaped his subsequent preoccupation with contagion and disease.

3. See John Bergamini, *The Spanish Bourbons* (New York: Putnam, 1974), 282–91. On the First Republic and its effects, see Herr, *An Historical Essay on Modern Spain*, 108–10. On economic prosperity, see Carr, *Spain*, 390–93.

4. Carr, *Spain*, 347–79, esp. 356.

5. Frances Lannon, *Privilege, Persecution, and Prophecy: The Catholic Church in Spain, 1875–1975* (Oxford: Clarendon, 1987), 119–21. A lively account is in John David Hughey, *Religious Freedom in Spain: Its Ebb and Flow* (1955; reprint, Freeport, N.Y.: Books for Libraries, 1970), 74–76. Anticlerical sentiment in Spain prior to the Civil War is discussed in Timothy Mitchell, *The Betrayal of the Innocents: Desire, Power, and the Catholic Church in Spain* (Philadelphia: University of Pennsylvania Press, 1998), 32–62.

6. See Paul Preston, *The Coming of the Spanish Civil War: Reform, Reaction, and Revolution in the Second Republic*, 2d ed. (London and New York: Routledge, 1994). A still useful source on the foundations of the Civil War is Gerald Brenan, *The Spanish Labyrinth: An Account of the Social and Political Background of the Spanish Civil War* (1950; reprint, Cambridge: Cambridge University Press, 1990), esp. 1–86.

7. A family genealogy is in Javier Suárez-Pajares, ed., *Iconografía/Iconography: Manuel de Falla, 1876–1946—La imagen de un músico/the Image of a Musician* (Madrid: Sociedad General de Autores de España, 1995), 68–69.

8. "La epidemia de cólera del año 1885," *Diario de Cádiz*, 3 October 1976, cited in Andrew Budwig, "Manuel de Falla's *Atlántida*: A Historical and Analytical Study," Ph.D. diss., University of Chicago, 1984, 127.

Between José María's successful shipping business, his forays into the stock market, and María Jesús's generous dowry, the family lived in near luxury at no. 3 Plaza de Mina.[9] Entertainments included the yearly carnival, in which Falla, an imaginative child who delighted in games of make-believe, participated (see figure 1). As in most bourgeois homes of the day, the wife and mother oversaw cultural enrichment. María Jesús, whom the family called Jesusita, was a capable pianist who gave her eldest child his first music lessons. She also played Chopin, Beethoven, and operas for her family, and it was thanks to her impromptu performances that Falla was drawn to Gounod's *Faust.* When he was finally taken to see it, he protested bitterly when his parents refused to let him stay up for the final act.[10] Piano-vocal scores of *Manon Lescaut* and *La Bohème* later found in the adult composer's library were purchased in Cádiz, and as yet unidentified annotations in a score of *La Traviata* suggest that at least some member of the Falla family followed the 1895 performance of that work in Cádiz.[11]

Musical institutions in Falla's home city included the Teatro Principal and the Cómico, the latter completed when he was twelve. The Sociedad de Conciertos de Cádiz, modeled on the Madrid-based Sociedad de Conciertos (founded by the composer and musicologist Francisco Asenjo Barbieri) offered frequent performances. Three military bands, the Engineers, the Artillery, and the Córdoba Regiment, played on civic occasions. Among the opportunities for aficionados was private instruction at the Academia Santa Cecilia. Its founder, Salvador Viniegra, was an amateur cellist on whom Saint-Saëns presumably called during his travels in Spain. A close friend of the Falla family, Viniegra had an impressive music library and hosted chamber music evenings in his comfortable home, which Falla began attending as a boy.[12]

He was hardly a prodigy. But when he was nine his mother decided it was time for him to study the piano more rigorously. So he began lessons with a friend of hers, Eloisa Galluzo, whose method he later described as "very severe."[13] He obediently followed her instructions, however, and Galluzo seems to have been attached to her young pupil. In March 1889, when Falla was eleven, she gave him a Spanish translation of Berlioz's *The Symphonies of Beethoven* (Madrid: Antonio Romero, 1870), in which she wrote "an affectionate remembrance for my unforgettable stu-

9. Since Falla's birth, the square has undergone various name changes, including Espóz y Mina and Generalísimo Franco.

10. Pahissa, *Vida y obra,* 22.

11. Montserrat Bergadà, "La relación de Falla con Italia: Crónica de un diálogo," in *Manuel de Falla e Italia,* edited by Yvan Nommick (Granada: Publicaciones del Archivo Manuel de Falla, 2000), 21n11.

12. Antonio Gallego, *El amor brujo* (Madrid: Alianza Música, 1990), 21–23. See also Juan J. Viniegra (Salvador's son), *Vida íntima de Manuel de Falla* (Cádiz: Diputación Provincial, 1966), 47.

13. Letter, Falla to Georges Jean-Aubry, 28 August 1910, cited in Gallego, *El amor brujo,* 23n16.

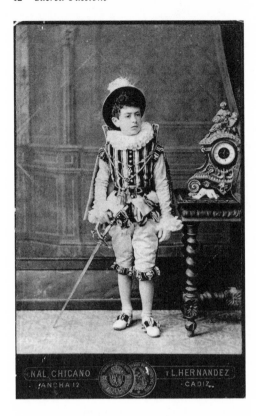

Figure 1. Falla, 6 March 1886, disguised as Count Raoul of Meyerbeer's *Les Huguenots* for a ball at the home of Ricardo González-Abreu, Cádiz. (Reprinted by kind permission of the Archivo Manuel de Falla)

dent and little friend Manuel de Falla." When Galluzo became a novice of the Sisters of Charity, Falla worked with Alejandro Odero, who had studied piano and harmony at the Paris Conservatory. After Odero's death, Falla studied with Enrique Broca. Other musical experiences included playing four-hand arrangements of Wagner and Mozart with a German woman, a family friend.[14]

Cádiz's most celebrated musical event was the yearly performance on Good Friday of Haydn's *The Seven Last Words of Our Savior on the Cross* (H. XX/1A) in the Santa Cueva (Sacred Cave) oratory below the church of the Rosario. The practice of meditating on Christ's final words, initiated by Jesuits in seventeenth-century Lima, was given new life in 1787 when Haydn composed his cycle of somber orchestral utterances for Cádiz.[15] The work ends not with a hopeful meditation on salva-

---

14. Michael Christoforidis, "Falla, Manuel de," in *Diccionario de la música española e hispanoamericana*, edited by Emilio Casares (Madrid: Sociedad General de Autores y Editores, 1999), 4:895. The Spanish edition of Berlioz's *The Symphonies of Beethoven* was published in Madrid by Antonio Romero.

15. Robert M. Stevenson, "Haydn's Iberian World Connections," *Inter-American Music Review* 4, no. 2 (1982): 8–12.

tion but with the depiction of an earthquake in agitated Sturm und Drang style. It was in such a service that Falla, at the age of nine, made his first public appearance, playing with his mother an arrangement for piano duet of the *Seven Last Words* in the church of San Francisco.[16] Both the religious drama and the music, with its dire conclusion in the dimly lit church, made a deep impression on the sensitive boy.

Initially, however, Falla favored literature over music. When he was twelve, he created his own magazine, *El Burlón* (The Wag), of which he was editor in chief and staff writer; that "publication" was followed by another called *El Cascabel* (The Rattle). With their whimsical hand-drawn covers, the two magazines complemented yet another journalistic effort, the newspaper *El Més Colombino* (The Messenger Pigeon).[17] All were destined for the readership of the imaginary city of Colón. Impressed with tales of exploration and adventure on the high seas, Falla greatly admired Christopher Columbus (Cristóbal Colón) and christened his metropolis accordingly; the idea of creating his own city had come to him when his parents denied his sudden request that the entire family move to Seville.[18] As shown in figure 2, he was also attracted to Paris, an interest cultivated by his reading and lively curiosity.

Urban planning for Colón included a theater, for which Falla may have composed a four-act *opera seria, El conde de Villamediana* (The Count of Villamediana). No score has survived. The libretto, however, was inspired by the romantic poet and dramatist the Duque de Rivas, two of whose sonnets appeared in earlier issues of *El Cascabel*, hand copied by the editor in chief. Although the project is briefly mentioned in Pahissa, it may be that Falla only sketched it (or just imagined it) for his make-believe theater. After all, his compositional technique was extremely limited at the time, and opera seems an improbable medium for an inexperienced fifteen-year-old. Whatever the truth of *El conde de Villamediana*, it is clear that the stage, which exerted a profound influence on Falla for the rest of his career, attracted him early on.[19] A likelier "opus 1" is the Gavotte and Musette for piano, which he probably composed around 1892, that is, when he was sixteen.[20]

In his seventeenth year, having outgrown his chimerical city, Falla decided to dedicate himself to music. According to a 1928 statement to his biographer and friend Roland-Manuel, he now realized that his early literary pursuits had been nothing

---

16. The piano four-hand arrangement performed by Falla and María Jesús was by Louis Winkler. See Jorge de Persia, ed., *Poesía*, Número monográfico dedicado a Manuel de Falla, nos. 36 and 37 (Madrid: Ministerio de Cultura, 1991), 21. Haydn himself arranged the *Seven Last Words* for string quartet (1788) and chorus (1796).

17. De Persia, *Poesía*, 23.

18. Pahissa, *Vida y obra*, 24–25.

19. Antonio Gallego, *Catálogo de obras de Manuel de Falla* (Madrid: Ministerio de Cultura, 1987), 11; Pahissa, *Vida y obra*, 24.

20. Gallego, *Catálogo*, 12; Pahissa, *Vida y obra*, 28.

Figure 2. Cover, *El Burlón*, one of Falla's childhood journalistic projects. (Reprinted by kind permission of the Archivo Manuel de Falla)

but a "childish whim" in which creative anxiety had been "totally absent." It was with some trepidation, however, that he opted for music:

> This [musical] vocation was so strong that it even made me fearful, since the hopes it awakened in me were well above what I felt capable of achieving. I don't say this from a purely technical standpoint, for I knew that with time and work technique can be acquired by anybody moderately gifted; but as for INSPIRATION, in the truest and highest sense of the word, that mysterious force without which—as we well know—nothing really useful can be realized . . . of that I felt incapable. Thus, without the great help of my religious convictions I would never have had the courage to pursue a path so filled with shadows. . . . In reality, unjustified fear has never dominated my character.[21]

21. "Et cette vocation est devenue si forte que j'en ai eu même peur, les illusions qu'elle évellait en moi étant trop au dessus de ce que je me croyais capable de faire. Je ne dis pas cela au point de vue purement technique, car je savais qu'avec le temps et le travail la technique peut être acquise par n'importe qui moyennement doué; mais c'est l'INSPIRATION, dans le vrai et plus haut sens du mot; cette force mystérieuse sans laquelle—comme nous le savons trop—rien de vraiment utile on peut réaliser, et dont je me croyais incapable. Or, sans l'aide puissante de mes convictions réligieuses je n'aurais en jamais le courage de poursuivre un chemin dont les ténèbres remplissaient sa plus grande partie. . . .

Even allowing for a degree of embellishment (he made these remarks to Roland-Manuel thirty years after the fact), Falla's account seems faithful. Less than brilliantly prepared, he had no reason to anticipate glory or fame as a composer. At the same time, that heady proximity to the sublime, that pull of "mysterious forces" to which he refers, were working in tandem with his burgeoning religious faith, one so strong that it would light the path "filled with shadows" and banish "unjustified" fear; this, evidently, was music's main attraction. Of course, we are entitled to wonder what Falla considered *justified* fear. As it turns out, doubt and hesitation—both of which could be debilitating—would at various intervals affect not only his "character" but his creative process as well.

The quest for "INSPIRATION, in the truest and highest sense of the word" began in earnest in the mid-1890s, when Falla was in his late teens. During intermittent trips to Madrid, he studied piano at the conservatory. Established in 1830 by Ferdinand VII's Neapolitan queen, María Cristina, this institution (known in Falla's times as the Escuela Nacional de Música y Declamación) initially reflected Italy's strong influence on Spanish music: for decades, the voice faculty was primarily Italian and much instruction was given in Italian.[22] Falla's piano teacher, José Tragó, had studied with a student of Chopin's and was highly respected in Madrid's pianistic circles. He also pioneered the solo piano recital, then uncommon in Spain, where pianists tended to intersperse solo works with vocal and/or instrumental selections.[23] Tragó thought highly of his pupil, writing Viniegra that Falla was "a very studious, very conscientious young man; of fine artistic talents, and for whom a rosy future in our difficult art is surely waiting."[24] A photograph of the slight, serious young man—but with vaguely dreamy eyes—bears out Tragó's impression (see figure 3).

Yet Falla's idyllic family life was deteriorating. By the late 1880s, the industrial and agricultural prosperity that undergirded the initial stages of the Bourbon Restoration had lapsed into economic depression, and by the mid-1890s José María's

---

D'ailleurs la crainte injustifiée n'a jamais dominé dans mon caractère" (letter, Falla to Roland-Manuel, 30 December 1928, AMF correspondence file 7521).

22. As Salter observes, this policy may have been intended to make Spanish singers competitive. Of course, Spanish nationals were also appointed. See Lionel Salter, "A Nation in Turbulence," in *The Late Romantic Era*, edited by Jim Samson (Englewood Cliffs, N.J.: Prentice Hall, 1991), 152.

23. Carlos Gómez Amat, *Siglo XIX*, Historia de la música española, no. 5 (Madrid: Alianza Música, 1984), 80. See also Montserrat Comellas i Barri, *El romanticisme musical a Barcelona: Els concerts* (Barcelona: Els Llibres de la Frontera, 2000); and, on an earlier period, Robert M. Stevenson, "Liszt in the Iberian Peninsula," *Inter-American Music Review* 7, no. 2 (1986): 3–22, and "Liszt at Madrid and Lisbon (1844–1845)," *Musical Quarterly* 65, no. 4 (1979): 493–512.

24. "Un muchacho muy estudioso, muy concienzudo; de muy buenas condiciones artísticas y que seguramente le espera un porvenir muy lisonjero en nuestro difícil arte" (letter, Tragó to Viniegra, 13 December 1899, AMF correspondence file 7755).

Figure 3. Falla as a young man, ca. 1896. (Reprinted by kind permission of the Archivo Manuel de Falla)

once-profitable business ventures had failed.[25] By late 1896, Falla was living full time in Madrid; the rest of his family soon joined him so as to depend on his scant earnings from private teaching. Graduating with highest honors from the conservatory in 1899 did little for his sudden shift in status to family breadwinner, however, and conditions at no. 70 Serrano were precarious. This is evident from records of items pawned, which included bedsheets and underwear.[26] Exacerbating this disastrous situation was Falla's lack of business acumen: according to one account, if a student complained about the fee at the moment of payment Falla would resignedly lower it rather than hold firm.[27]

At the same time, Spain was experiencing "disaster." At least, this was how Spaniards referred to the Spanish-American War, declared by the United States in April 1898 over the administration of Cuba. In a matter of months, Cuba, Puerto Rico, the Philippines, and other vestiges of the once-powerful Spanish empire were lost to the crushing military superiority of the *yanquis.* The two nations clashed, sometimes hysterically, on cultural grounds as well: as Spanish propagandists decried unbridled capitalism and work-obsessed Protestantism, North American journalists for the "yellow press" spewed out flashy and often exaggerated stories of Spaniards' misdeeds in Cuba.[28] In Spain, the disaster sparked debate over the elusiveness of national identity in an increasingly internationalized age. This matter engaged the Generation of '98, a loosely knit literary entity that included Miguel de Unamuno, Pío Baroja, Antonio Machado, Ramón del Valle-Inclán, Ramiro de Maeztu, José Martínez Ruiz (Azorín), and according to some scholars José Ortega y Gasset.[29] But the group failed to reach consensus, and polemics over Spanish identity would inform political and aesthetic discourse for decades.

25. Carr, *Spain,* 393–97.

26. Sopeña, *Vida y obra,* 28.

27. Mario Verdaguer, *Medio siglo de vida barcelonesa* (Barcelona: Editorial Barna, 1957), 181. The story is plausible enough, although Verdaguer's discussion of Falla contains several errors of fact.

28. For the Spanish perspective on the war, see Sebastian Balfour, "'The Lion and the Pig': Nationalism and National Identity in *Fin-de-Siècle* Spain," in *Nationalism and the Nation in the Iberian Peninsula,* edited by Clare Mar-Milinero and Ángel Smith (Oxford and Washington, D.C.: Berg, 1996), 107–17. American attitudes are treated in David F. Trask, *The War with Spain in 1898* (New York and London: Macmillan, 1981); and Ernest May's classic *Imperial Democracy: The Emergence of America as a Great Power* (New York: Harcourt, Brace, and World, 1961).

29. Donald Leslie Shaw, *The Generation of '98 in Spain* (London: E. Benn; New York: Barnes and Noble, 1975); E. Inman Fox, *Ideología y política en las letras de fin de siglo (1898)* (Madrid: Espasa Calpe, 1988). In addition to Unamuno's *En torno al casticismo,* see also Ángel Ganivet's *Idearium español* of 1896, discussed in H. Ramsden, *The 1898 Movement in Spain: Towards a Reinterpretation with Special Reference to En torno al casticismo and Idearium español* (Manchester: Manchester University Press; Totowa, N.J.: Rowman and Littlefield, 1974).

Music was affected, primarily in opera, since many considered the lack of a strong national presence in this genre an urgent matter.[30] The principal houses in Madrid and Barcelona, the Teatro Real and the Gran Teatre del Liceu, respectively, programmed mainly Italian and French works, along with a healthy dose of Wagner, the latter often for the intellectual set.[31] Asserting native talent were Emilio Serrano's *Doña Juana la Loca* (Joan the Mad) of 1890, Federico Chueca's *Cádiz* of 1897, and Tomás Bretón's *Los amantes de Teruel* (The Lovers of Teruel) of 1889. The first two received only five performances each at the Real, and the Bretón work, which, as a tribute to Italian hegemony, premiered as *Gli amanti di Teruel*, only three.[32] Instead, audiences clamored for Spanish-language operetta, or *zarzuela*, which has been upheld, often stridently, as the nationalist genre par excellence.[33] To be sure, *zarzuela* libretti were peppered with real street names or scenes of peddlers hawking local products such as *azucarillos* (a light, sugary pastry), as in Fernando Chueca's tale of summer nights in the Paseo del Prado, *Agua, azucarillos y aguardiente*, of 1897. Yet *zarzuela* abounds in hybrid musical features, many of which are international in origin. Especially conspicuous are Central European dances. The mazurka, popular in the Hispanic world (in his memoirs Pablo Neruda recalls hearing mazurkas in rural Chile around 1910) figured even in late *zarzuelas*, such as Federico Torroba Moreno's *Luisa Fernanda* of 1932, and waltzes such as "Yo te adoro, mi dulce ilusión" (I Adore You, My Gentle Hope) from Chueca's *Agua, azucarillos y aguardiente*, could pass for Lanner or Strauss.[34] There is also that highlight of the immensely

---

30. Attempts to forge a national Spanish opera has been called "the great unfinished business" of late-nineteenth-century Spain. See Belén Pérez Castillo, "Spain: Art Music, Nineteenth Century," in *The Revised New Grove Dictionary of Music and Musicians*, edited by Stanley Sadie and John Tyrell (London: Macmillan, 2001), 24:130.

31. In Barcelona, there was also a populist dimension to *wagnerismo*: the Sociedad Choral Euterpe, which first performed sections of *Tannhäuser* in 1862, was founded by Josep Anselm Clavé, who also established several workers' choruses. See Alfonsina Janés i Nadal, *L'Obra de Richard Wagner a Barcelona* (Barcelona: Fundació Salvador Vives Casajuana, Ajuntament de Barcelona, Serveis de Cultura, Institut Municipal d'Historia, 1983), 19–20. See also Xosé Aviñoa, *La música i el modernisme* (Barcelona: Curial, 1985), 40. On *wagnerismo* in Madrid, see José Subirá, *Historia y anecdotario del Teatro Real* (Madrid: Editorial Plus-Ultra, 1949), 631–55.

32. Gómez Amat, *Siglo XIX*, 193; Subirá, *Historia y anecdotario*, 803–5.

33. Gómez Amat, *Siglo XIX*, 131–32. *Zarzuela* was also popular in the United States and Latin America. See Janet Sturman, *Spanish Operetta, American Stage* (Urbana and Chicago: University of Illinois Press, 2000).

34. Pablo Neruda, *Confieso que he vivido* (Barcelona, Caracas, and Mexico City: Editorial Seix Barral, 1981), 20. Granados composed several mazurkas in the mid- to late 1880s, and in 1887 Isaac Albéniz wrote a *Mazurka de salón*. See Carol A. Hess, *Enrique Granados: A Bio-Bibliography* (Westport, Conn.: Greenwood, 1991), 115, 117, 123; and Walter A. Clark, *Isaac Albéniz: A Guide to Research* (New York and London: Garland, 1998), 127.

popular *La Gran Vía* of 1886, by Chueca and Joaquín Valverde, namely, the "Chótis [Schottische] del Eliseo Madrileño."

Still, "Spanishness" could be created through *andalucismo*, a catalog of musical gestures hailing from southern Spain that included Phrygian melodic turns, hemiola, rhythmically free *fioratura*, castanets, and hand clapping. The guitar was also suggestive: composers could base harmonies on its open strings, simulate various strumming techniques, or draw upon flamenco formulae such as (iv–♭ III–♭ II–I), known as the *seis con décima*.[35] National dances might figure, as in Barbieri's *El barberillo de Lavapiés* (The Little Barber of Lavapiés) of 1874, with its *Jota de los estudiantes* (Students' Jota).[36] So might Latin American genres, such as the witty "Tango de Menegilda" (Menegilda's Tango) in *La Gran Vía* or the *habanera* "¿Dónde vas con mantón de Manila?" (Where Are You Going in That Manila Shawl?) in Bretón's *La verbena de la paloma* (The Feast of Our Lady of the Dove) of 1894. Throughout, functional harmony (occasional flashes of "folkloric" modality notwithstanding), regular phrase lengths, closed forms, and occasional recitative à la Donizetti, supported by polished but conservative orchestration, presented few aesthetic challenges to common practice conventions. In the wake of the "disaster," moreover, *zarzuela*'s familiar diction and usually wholesome outlook were especially welcome. In much the same way that many Hollywood musicals would tranquilize audiences in the United States during World War II, *zarzuela* offered a troubled public an ambience in which "no one [could] be really wicked, or miserably poor, or irremediably unhappy."[37]

As for instrumental music, many critics in Madrid and Barcelona scathingly compared Spanish concert life to that of other European countries. It was not until 1882 that Beethoven's Ninth Symphony was performed in Spain, and orchestral and chamber music societies often operated on a shoestring.[38] Among native composers were Jesús de Monasterio, who wrote a violin concerto and a nationalistic *Fantasía característica española* for orchestra, and Pedro Miguel Marqués of Mallorca, known in some circles as the "Spanish Beethoven" for his dedication to the symphony.[39] Chamber and solo piano music flourished in the private homes of aristocrats such

35. Prisco Hernández, "Décima, Seis, and the Puertorican Troubadour," *Latin American Music Review* 14 (1993): 22.

36. Despite his generally lukewarm attitude toward the genre, one of the *zarzuelas* Falla admired was *El barberillo de Lavapiés*. See Manuel de Falla, "Nuestra música," in *Escritos sobre música y músicos*, edited by Federico Sopeña, 4th ed. (Madrid: Espasa Calpe, 1988), 55.

37. G. G. Brown, *A Literary History of Spain: The Twentieth Century* (London: E. Benn; New York: Barnes and Noble, 1972), 119.

38. Gómez Amat, *Siglo XIX*, 55. See John Edwin Henken, "Barbieri, Francisco Asenjo," in Sadie and Tyrell, *Revised New Grove Dictionary*, 2:700.

39. Luis Iglesias de Souza, "Monasterio y Agüeros, Jesús de," in Casares, *Diccionario de la música española e hispanoamericana*, 7:664–76. See also Ramón Sobrino, "Marqués García, Pedro Miguel," in 7:202–12 of the same work.

as Count Guillermo Morphy, amateur musicologist and patron of Isaac Albéniz and Pablo Casals. Much of the salon fare consisted of unpretentious character pieces such as mazurkas, waltzes, serenades, and caprices. (Albéniz's sonatas of the late 1880s, which incorporate sonata, scherzo, and rondo forms, are far from typical.)[40] Conspicuously lacking on the musical landscape at the turn of the century was a "great" composer who could shape an agenda for the future of Spanish music and secure its place in the international sphere.

"SELF-LOVE" AND THE WAYS OF ART

During his early years in Madrid, Falla tested his abilities in *zarzuela*. First, however, he completed several salon works. Around 1898, he composed a Scherzo in C Major, which, along with a Nocturne in F Minor (probably from 1899) and a Mazurka in C Minor, disclose his admiration for Chopin. His experiments in the late romantic idiom, worlds away from his mature style, throw an interesting light on his wry assessment of the nineteenth century, offered decades later, as an "enormous carnival."[41] Still, these early works are marked by constraint, in both harmonic language and emotional range. The Mazurka exploits conventional key relationships both at the level of its insistently regular eight-bar periods and at the level of its large-scale structure, which, with a threefold repetition of the A section, suggests a rondo with a plagal codetta. As shown in musical example 1, the multisectional Nocturne is also harmonically timid, although isolated "Spanish" features emerge in melodic figures containing augmented seconds (mm. 29–30) and an implied *seis con décima* in the bass on F (E♭) D♭ C (mm. 32–35), harmonized accordingly. Surface gestures are similarly conventional: dotted rhythms, drone accompaniments, and agogic accents on the second beat occur with steadfast regularity in the Mazurka, while the Nocturne's *cantabile* texture is only occasionally relieved by two-part writing (mm. 51ff.).

Although Falla modestly disparaged his pianistic abilities, he concertized intermittently throughout much of his adult life, especially during his first Madrid period.[42] Two of his recitals from 1899 reflect turn of the century tastes in programming: on 16 August at Cádiz's Salón Quirell, he played Grieg's *Au Printemps* (no. 6 of the Lyric Pieces op. 43), two movements of Mendelssohn's Fantasy in F♯ Minor op. 28 (*Sonate eccosaise*), *La Fileuse* by Joachim Raff, *La Castagnette* by Henri Ketten, his

40. Walter Aaron Clark, *Isaac Albéniz: Portrait of a Romantic* (Oxford: Oxford University Press, 1999), 63.

41. Manuel de Falla, "Notas sobre Ricardo Wagner en el cincuentenario de su muerte," in Falla, *Escritos*, 139.

42. He also recorded on occasion. Reissues can be heard on *Manuel de Falla, 1876–1946: Grabaciones históricas* (Almaviva DS–0121); *Composers in Person: Manuel de Falla, Enrique Granados, Federico Mompou, Joaquín Nin* (EMI Classics, CDC 7 54836 2); and *Manuel de Falla: Historic Recordings, 1928–1930* (EPM 150 112).

Musical Example 1. Falla, Nocturne, mm. 29–35. (Reprinted by kind permission of Ediciones Manuel de Falla)

own Nocturne, and other short salon works.[43] On 10 September at the Teatro Cómico (in Cádiz), he repeated the Mendelssohn Fantasy and added Schumann's well-known *Arabesque* op. 18, a Romance by the same composer, Chopin's hypnotic *Berceuse* op. 57, Saint-Saëns's *Allegro appassionato*, two movements of Grieg's Sonata in E Minor op. 7, and Benjamin Godard's Waltz in B Flat.[44] An anonymous critic for the *Diario de Cádiz* compared Falla's playing to that of the French pianist Francis Planté, observing that despite the "supercorrectness" of Falla's training, a distinct personality had emerged.[45] That he did not offer more details on that personality leaves tantalizingly open to question the nature of Falla's playing at this time.

Both concerts launched Falla's career as a composer of chamber music, a medium that proved to be a lifelong interest. For the August program, he performed with Viniegra the *Melodía* for cello and piano, perhaps in homage to the soirees in his old friend's home.[46] Harmonically richer than the Mazurka or the Nocturne, *Melodía* contains a German sixth chord, rare in Falla, which resolves in a cadence

43. AMF, program file no. 1.

44. Ibid. It is not clear if the Schumann Romance was that from *Faschingsschwank aus Wien* op. 26 no. 2, Three Romances op. 28, *Klavierstücke* op. 32 no. 3, or *Albumblätter* op. 124 no. 11.

45. V., "Manuel de Falla," *Diario de Cádiz*, reproduced in de Persia, *Poesía*, 30.

46. Two other works for cello and piano, the *Romanza* and a *Pieza en Do Mayor* (Piece in C Major), date from around 1898.

colored with modal mixture (mm. 56–62). An episode in the raised submediant area (B minor) is enriched through brief melodic interchanges between piano and cello, interrupting the piano's strictly accompanimental role throughout the rest of the piece and whose ongoing syncopation recalls Schumann's rhythmic insistencies. Featured on both programs were movements 2 and 3 of his Piano Quartet in G Minor, as well as Falla's only piece explicitly for violin and piano (i.e., not an arrangement), the *Serenata andaluza* (Andalusian Serenade). These works have disappeared.

Falla's late romantic leanings also surfaced in *Mireya*, his programmatic quintet for violin, viola, cello, flute, and piano based on a poem by Federico Mistral. This tale of ruin, death, and the spirit world takes place on the eve of the feast day of Saint Medardo, patron of the corn harvest and often depicted as "laughing inanely."[47] Falla set two episodes, the "Muerte de Elzear" (Death of Elzear) and "Danza fantástica" (Fantastic Dance). Shades of Saint-Saëns's *Danse macabre* or Liszt's *Totentanz*? Since both the quintet and Falla's subsequent transcription for piano solo of the "Danza fantástica" are lost, we have no means of discerning his youthful visions of death and the supernatural, nor how he realized these portentous topics musically.[48] But *Mireya*'s dramatic import must have been considerable: at the Teatro Cómico premiere, the composer overhead a woman remark from the first row, "It's just like being at the opera!" It was an anecdote he saw fit to repeat to Pahissa over four decades later.[49]

Falla was also inspired by poetic accounts of love's turmoils. Around 1900, he set Antonio Trueba's poem "Preludio: Madre, todas las noches" (Prelude: Mother, Every Night), in which a young girl confides to her mother her confusion over the attentions of the young man who pours out his lovesick heart nightly beneath her balcony, awakening in her both ecstasy and despair.[50] Declaring that such utterances are "the prelude to the greatest poem in all the world," the mother instructs her to seek the Virgin Mary's help. What is unclear is whether the mother believes that the Virgin will urge the girl to renounce her passions and transfer her love to God or to embrace the sanctity of married love, a matter Falla himself would soon confront. Set for voice and piano, "Preludio" requires the singer to "act" the roles of the three

---

47. Herbert Thurston and Donald Attwater, eds., *Butler's Lives of the Saints*, rev. and suppl. ed. (New York: P.J. Kennedy and Sons, 1956), 2:502.

48. A few pages of notes on instrumentation for *Mireya*, along with accounts of his personal expenses, are reproduced in Yvan Nommick and Francesc Bonastre, eds., *Manuel de Falla: Apuntes de harmonía y dietario de Paris (1908)* (Granada: Publicaciones del Archivo Manuel de Falla, 2001), 173–74.

49. Pahissa, *Vida y obra*, 28. Falla performed the piano transcription on 6 May 1900 at the Madrid Athenaeum.

50. As Gallego points out, the poem is from Trueba's own *Arte de hacer versos, al alcance de todo el que sepa leer* (Barcelona: Librería de Juan y Atonio Bastinos, 1881, 113–14), and is entitled "Preludio" (singular) (Gallego, *Catálogo*, 32).

protagonists. Unfolding in tripartite form, it begins in the tonic E minor, as the maiden describes her eager suitor (mm. 1–22). Dropping to the flat submediant, she then expounds on her "joys and sorrows" (alegrías y tristezas, mm. 23–39). The final section, which belongs to the mother, is in the parallel major, recalling, perhaps, the conclusion of another musical essay on the confusion between religious and romantic impulses, Schubert's "Die junge Nonne." Throughout, Falla's harmonies remain conservative, venturing only occasionally into modal mixture (e.g., C minor in the midst of an E major passage, m. 7) or savoring the fleeting color of a root-position Neapolitan chord (m. 20). He also exploits the tension of chromatic passing tones, as in the F✱ of the coda (m. 69), an unprepared chromatic upper neighbor of the dominant harmony. A weightless augmented sonority, B D♯ F✱ (mm. 69, 71, 72, 73), ultimately resolves upward.

Another early work for voice and piano was inspired by one of Spain's most important romantic poets, Gustavo Adolfo Bécquer. His signal achievement is the *Rimas*, a series of eighty brief, yearning verses, five of which inspired Albéniz, who published his *Rimas de Bécquer* in 1892. As with the works just discussed, the two *Rimas* that Falla set, "Olas gigantes" (Giant Waves) and "¡Dios mío, qué solos se quedan los muertos!" (My God, How Lonely the Dead Are!), describe emotional vulnerability. In "Olas gigantes," for example, the singer hopes only that the powerful waves will sweep him along in their foamy wake, the last stanza revealing that his desire to unite with nature stems from fear of being alone with his pain (tengo miedo de quedarme con mi dolor a solas). Repeated bass notes and accented chromatic passing tones evoke the crashing waves, and a thin-textured and harmonically stable coda that repeats "con mi dolor a solas" confirms the singer's resignation. "¡Dios mío, qué solos se quedan los muertos!" is on a slightly larger scale and contains isolated "Spanish" elements such as prominent augmented seconds (mm. 1–8 and reprises). Illuminating Bécquer's gloomy text is the occasional jolt of harmonic color, such as the augmented chord in "they covered his face with a white cloth" (taparon su cara con un blanco lienzo [mm. 14–16]) and the grating voicing in the French sixth chord in "some [mourners were] sobbing" (unos sollozando [mm. 16–17]). Still, Falla's harmonic language is generally pale and ill-suited to Bécquer's perfervid sentiments.

Over the next few years, Falla persisted with small-scale works (see appendix 1). A minor triumph was the publication in 1902 of *Vals capricho* (Capricious Waltz) and *Serenata andaluza*, both for piano. The former unfolds over a relentless oom-pah waltz accompaniment and resembles the Mazurka in its predictable periodicity (in the C section, one phrase is cranked out sequentially nearly three times). Still, it is Falla's most virtuosic composition prior to *Allegro de concierto* and as such is noteworthy for the glimpse it affords of a Falla unfamiliar to us today: a composer conversant with salon music's flashy priorities. The *Serenata andaluza*, with its bright, bell-like opening and left-hand leaps, requires considerable dexterity as well. Falla, who would later disparage these early works, seems to have harbored some fondness for the *Serenata andaluza*, for he performed it on 6 May 1900 at the Madrid Athenaeum and twice in Cádiz, in 1900 and 1902.[51] In the final weeks of his life, he became incensed upon discovering that, thanks to the rapacious North American music industry, the *Serenata* had circulated for years in altered form without his authorization.

These modest works could not begin to alleviate Falla's economic woes, however, and anxious for his family's well-being he decided to try his hand at *zarzuela*. As Tragó reported to Viniegra, Falla "expressed to me . . . his decision to throw himself into writing something for the theater, for which I could do nothing less than congratulate him, since this is the only path to a secure and real future for musicians in Spain."[52] To this end, Falla consulted José Jackson Veyán, also from Cádiz and the author of several libretti. Mainly, he encouraged expediency, urging Falla to compose "polkas, waltzes, marches that will be useful to us later on."[53] Next Falla met the well-established Chueca, who tried to help him secure performances. Most promising was his association with Amadeu Vives, eventually the composer of over one hundred *zarzuelas*, including *Los bohemios* (The Bohemians), *Maruxa*, and *Doña Francisquita*. In 1902, Vives and Falla undertook the admittedly ill-conceived plan to write *zarzuelas* together. They completed only three, none of which was performed.[54] Neither was Falla's earliest *zarzuela*, *La Juana y la Petra o La casa de Tócame Roque* (Juana and Petra or the House of Tócame Roque), which he wrote himself.[55]

In 1903, in the midst of his immersion in *zarzuela*, Falla returned to the intimacy of the solo song with "Tus ojillos negros" (Your Little Dark Eyes), an "Andalusian song" for voice and piano. Its sentimental text by the journalist, novelist, and poet Cristóbal de Castro bemoans the vagaries of frustrated love. Although some have

51. On the Athenaeum and music, see Hess, *Manuel de Falla and Modernism in Spain*, 49–51. Also on the program were Grieg, Preludium (Suite Holberg); Louis-Claude Daquin, *Le Coucou*; Weber, Rondo from Sonata no. 24; Chopin, Mazurka op. 17 no. 4; Moskowski, Waltz in E Major; Schumann, "Des Abends" and "Warum?" from the op. 12 *Fantasiestücke*; Chopin, Etude in C Minor op. 25 no. 12; Wagner-Liszt, "Spinning Chorus," from *The Flying Dutchman*"; Falla, *Vals capricho*, *Serenata andaluza*; and Liszt, Hungarian Rhapsody no. 12 (AMF program file no. 4).

52. "Me manifestó . . . su decisión de lanzarse a escribir algo para el teatro, de lo cual no pude menos de felicitarle, pues es el único camino de un porvenir seguro y material para los músicos en España" (letter, Tragó to Viniegra, 13 December 1899, AMF correspondence file 7755).

53. "Polkas, valses, marchas que nos servirán más adelante" (letter, Jackson Veyán to Falla, 4 December [probably 1900], cited in Gallego, *El amor brujo*, 25).

54. *El cornetín de órdenes* (The Bugle) and *La cruz de Malta* (The Maltese Cross) date from 1903 and are lost; *Prisionero de guerra* (Prisoner of War), from 1903–4, is unperformed and unpublished.

55. The manuscript, which dates from around 1900 and is on a libretto by Javier Santero (after a work entitled *La Petra y la Juana* of 1792 by Ramón de la Cruz), is lost.

attacked the modest work (Demarquez wonders whether she should "deplore this indiscreet publication"), "Tus ojillos negros" in fact raises some provocative questions.[56] According to a frequently cited letter from the Valencian soprano Lucrezia Bori to Castro, it was quite successful in America; in the 1920s, Hipólito Lázaro and Elvira Hidalgo recorded it, both with orchestral accompaniment.[57] Besides these recordings, for which Falla was never compensated, an altered version for violin and piano circulated as late as 1929. Leopoldo Matos, a lawyer and one of the composer's closest friends, described its impact: "It was 'your little dark eyes' and—horrors!— they were suffering from conjunctivitis, iritis or styes. Even you wouldn't have recognized it. I felt swindled, but they showed me the score and I had to keep mum."[58] Why this popularity? Certainly the song has all the earmarks of the typical "Latin" light classic. A multisectional, minor-key work, it contains the inevitable "maggiore" section (as does Agustín Lara's "Granada," for example) and various "Spanish" or "Latin pop" traits, such as the gently syncopated accompaniment figure of the A section (mm. 1–9 and reprises), the extended Phrygian cadence embellished with a G♮–G♯ fluctuation and concluding with a sixteenth-note triplet (mm. 10–12), and the prominent augmented second of the coda (mm. 79–83). Motivic predictability fortifies the regular phrase structure of Castro's verse, as in Falla's setting of the line describing the totality of the beloved's eyes, which reflect "noches muy obscuras, días muy serenos" (very dark nights, very serene days, mm. 36–42). Such parallelisms, formulaic but winning, would be perfectly at home in a Xavier Cugat movie (see musical example 2). In short, "Tus ojillos negros" exposes the tenuous boundary between nightclub and concert hall, one that popular "Latin" music often straddled in the early twentieth century and that later influenced Falla's legacy in the United States.

Not only that, but the passionately uncertain lyrics of "Tus ojillos negros" hint at a side of Falla's personality easily overlooked, given the austerity of his later years. Around 1904, he fell in love with his cousin, the attractive María Prieto Ledesma, who lived with her family in the Calle de Cubas. The courtship, if it can even be called that, is known to us almost exclusively through the letters of Falla's spiritual

56. Demarquez, *Manuel de Falla*, 17.

57. Reissue numbers RCA 74321 35634 2 and Almaviva DS 0121, respectively. Hidalgo recorded it again on Columbia 3901-M. See Justo Romero, *Falla: Discografía recomendada* (Barcelona: Ediciones Peninsula, 1999); and William Sewall Marsh, *Musical Spain from A to Z* (Provincetown, R.I.: Campbell Music, 1929), 19. The letter from Bori is cited in Ángel Sagardía, *Vida y obra de Manuel de Falla* (Madrid: Escelicer, 1967), 16.

58. "Fueron tus ojillos negros, y ¡horror! padecían conjunctivitis, iritis y orzuelos. Ni tú los hubieras conocido. Me creí estafado, pero me mostraron la partitura y tuve que callarme" (letter, Matos to Falla, 22 September 1929, AMF correspondence file 7263/2). Matos was one of the few acquaintances with whom Falla used the intimate form of address. In his response to Matos on 21 October 1929 (AMF correspondence file 7264), Falla seemed to take the whole thing as something of a joke, commenting: "Who would want to play that old thing?" (¿Pero a quien se le ocurre tocar ese vejestorio?).

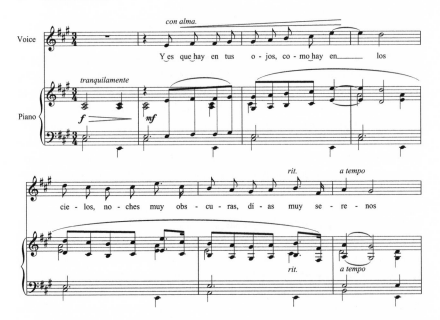

Musical Example 2. Falla, "Tus ojillos negros," mm. 36–42. (Reprinted by kind permission of Ediciones Manuel de Falla)

adviser, Fr. Francisco de Paula Fedriani. Back in Cádiz, Falla had attended Fedriani's meetings for young men, some of whom the priest also advised privately.[59] We can only speculate on the extent of his influence—and on how much psychological damage it may have inflicted. His customary salutation, "queridísimo hijo mío" (my dearest son), notwithstanding, Fedriani's letters are revealing for their frequency, vehemence, and often rabid insistence that Falla, hesitant in matters of the heart, act decisively. Condemning the timid young man's vacillations as "truly ridiculous and inappropriate," Fedriani exhorted Falla to "give up those manias and ridiculously childish behaviors of being this way and that."[60] Apparently—for we have only Fedriani's letters and none of Falla's—the composer summoned up his courage and declared himself, probably around April 1905. But the girl's parents were leery of Falla's financial condition, and María herself may have been lukewarm about her nervous suitor. The following November, now aged twenty-nine, Falla seems to have contemplated asking for her hand a second time, and again Fedriani lambasted him for his indecision. "If due to her character or whatever circumstance

59. Statement by Viniegra, AMF correspondence file 6962; see also Viniegra's *Vida íntima*, 55–57.
60. "Déjate de esas locuras y niñerías ridiculísimas de estar de este modo y del otro" (letter, Fedriani to Falla, 1905, month unknown, AMF correspondence file 6962).

she likes mysteries as you do," he sarcastically observed, "this won't work for you. Yes, you can wait to declare yourself. You can also do it now . . . as you wish. But silliness, suppositions, verifications, conjectures, quibbling and other things of an equally ridiculous and foolish nature, no, a thousand times no."[61] Thus, the bashful, infatuated Falla, who had reveled in poetic images of spiritualized love and passionate longing, digested the economic and emotional requirements of a middle-class marriage—and his inability to fulfill them.

As we have seen, Falla's religious faith influenced his decision to become a composer. So it is no surprise that in matters of the heart he required a solution acceptable to Roman Catholic teachings, and indeed to God himself, whose will Fedriani invoked more than once: "Be at peace and give up foolishness and stupidities, for if and when [love] comes from God, then so be it, and if it doesn't happen, it will be for your own good. So, tranquility and absolute indifference."[62] Surely Falla considered Fedriani as nothing less than God's representative; in fact, thirty-five years later, he remembered Fedriani in his will as "the one to whom I owe the most sacred and effective counsel and instruction to solidify my religion and to try to comply with the obligations that it imposes on all humble disciples of Our Lord Jesus Christ."[63] As a result, Fedriani's advice, however belittling, was law.

Perhaps for these reasons, some have seen this romantic episode as a harbinger of Falla's innate celibacy. Sopeña, for example, interprets the composer's early heartthrob as "clearly adverse, not only to a nonexistent priestly vocation but . . . to the other vocation, that of celibacy."[64] But other accounts reveal that the event left Falla neither "tranquil" nor "indifferent," as Fedriani had demanded, but with thoughts of suicide, a mortal sin in the Catholic Church. Years later, when he was living in Granada, he confessed as much to Emilia Llanos, a friend of the Lorca family.[65] That Falla offered these confidences so long after the fact (ironically, at a point

61. "Si por su carácter o cualquier circunstancia quiere misterios como tú, eso no te conviene. Puedes sí, dilatar el declararte. Puedes también hacerlo ahora . . . como quieras. Pero tonterías, suposiciones, averiguaciones, conjeturas, cavilaciones y demás del mismo jaez ridículo y necio, eso no y mil veces no" (letter, Fedriani to Falla, 14 November 1905, AMF correspondence file 6962).

62. "Tu estáte muy tranquilo y déjate de majaderías y tonterías que si está de Dios y cuando esté de Dios será y si no sucede para tu bien será. De modo que tranquilidad y absoluta indiferencia" (letter, Fedriani to Falla 14 November 1905, AMF correspondence file 6962).

63. The original text is reproduced in Budwig, "Manuel de Falla's *Atlántida*," 461. It is true that Falla named various individuals in his will, including Galluzo and Tragó. At this time, however, he was extremely meticulous about language (and its potential for "deformation," as he called it) and chose his words with requisite care. We can assume, therefore, that his gratitude to Fedriani was sincere.

64. Sopeña, *Vida y obra*, 28.

65. Personal interview, author and Joaquín Nin-Culmell (who was also a friend of Emilia Llanos), January 2000.

when his music was being hailed for its "abstemiousness," "purity," and lack of "guilty sensuality") suggests that the frustrated romance, with its fearsome mix of timidity and desire, marked him profoundly.

Not content to restrict himself to the young composer's emotional state, Fedriani also ventured into the artistic realm. His advice here centered on Falla's studies with Felipe Pedrell (1841–1922), the composer, critic, and musicologist who in 1900 moved to Madrid to teach aesthetics and music history at the conservatory. Pedrell was the first to articulate a program for national music, and his manifesto of 1891, *Por nuestra música* (For Our Music), exhorts Spanish composers to reject French and Italian influences and find their own voices.[66] Falla wasted no time in seeking lessons with him, which Melquíades Almagro, a friend from Fedriani's youth group from Cádiz days, offered to finance. To be sure, we sometimes have the impression that Pedrell's instruction consisted more of spontaneous philosophical discussions than rigorous training sessions in the composer's craft.[67] But Falla credited Pedrell with revealing to him the secrets of orchestration, and under his guidance the young composer pored over treatises by Berlioz and Gevaert. One of their first projects was reorchestrating *La casa de Tócame Roque*.[68] Pedrell also introduced Falla to the beauties of Spanish folk music, which, directly or indirectly, would inform the great majority of his future musical utterances.

Yet Fedriani was unimpressed. Although his understanding of the problems Falla and Pedrell were exploring was surely minimal, he informed Falla in no uncertain terms that struggling over the niceties of orchestration was a waste of time. He nagged

66. *Por nuestra música* (2d ed. [Barcelona: Henrich, 1891]) is the preface to Pedrell's operatic trilogy, *Los Pirineos* (The Pyrenees), *Els Pirineus* in Catalan. See also Federico Sopeña, "Pedrell en el Conservatorio de Madrid," *Anuario Musical* 27 (1972): 95–101; and Francesc Bonastre Bertran, *Felipe Pedrell: Acotaciones a una idea* (Tarragona: Caja de Ahorros Provincial de Tarragona, 1977). Despite errors, Pedrell's complete edition of the works of Tomás Luís de Victoria remains a landmark in Spanish Golden Age scholarship. See Robert M. Stevenson, "Tomás Luis de Victoria: Unique Spanish Genius," *Inter-American Music Review* 12, no. 1 (1991): 93–95.

67. Pedrell himself described his lessons with Albéniz as "simple chats between good friends" (simples charlas de amigos camaradas). See Felipe Pedrell, *Músicos contemporáneos y de otros tiempos* (Paris: Paul Ollendorf, 1910), 377.

68. Valuable insights into Falla's studies with Pedrell are in Begoña Lolo, "Las relaciones Falla-Pedrell a través de *La vida breve*," in *Manuel de Falla: La vida breve*, edited by Yvan Nommick (Granada: Publicaciones del Archivo Manuel de Falla, 1997), 121–46. On Falla's interest in the treatises of Eslava and Richter, see the *Apuntes de harmonía*. While working with Pedrell, Falla also studied *L'accoustique nouvelle, ou Essai d'application d'une méthode philosophique aux questions élevées de l'acoustique, de la musique et de la composition musicale* (Paris, 1854) by the polymath Louis Lucas. Although some of Falla's biographers consider the treatise to be fundamental to his evolution, mostly with regard to "harmonic generation from natural resonance," in fact Lucas barely covers that topic. See Chris Collins, "Manuel de Falla and *L'Acoustique Nouvelle*: A Myth Exposed," *Journal of the Royal Music Association* 128, no. 1 (2003): 71–97.

him toward expediency: "if it weren't for the fact that you know more than you yourself believe . . . there would be no way that after only one or two lessons Pedrell would have been satisfied."[69] Had Fedriani only known that despite the inglorious history of *La casa de Tócame Roque*, a portion of its discarded overture would endure—and in an especially witty orchestration—as the mincing "Dance of the Corregidor" in Falla's 1919 ballet, *The Three-Cornered Hat!* Additional advice was even sharper. "Take Pedrell with a grain of salt," Fedriani ordered. "He could be wrong and have bad faith, relative or absolute. . . . Besides, to compose *zarzuelas* that will bring in money, which is what you need right now, this much perfection is unnecessary."[70] Obviously Fedriani's aesthetic philosophy embraced neither the quest for the sublime, nor, as Falla would put it, "INSPIRATION in the truest and highest sense of the word."

If *La casa de Tócame Roque* had no immediate impact on Falla's career, another *zarzuela*, *Los amores de la Inés* (The Loves of Ines), did. On a libretto by Emilio Dugi, *Inés* premiered on 12 April 1902 at Madrid's Teatro Cómico and ran for some twenty performances in a production by the impresario-actors Enrique Chicote and Loreto Prado.[71] One critic noted its high comedy, writing: "In *Los amores de la Inés*, the character types are keenly observed, there are inspired verses, and comic situations that merited the audience's applause, and ingenious jokes. The second act especially entertained the public, which called Mr. Dugi to the proscenium in a scene . . . of much amusement. The music of maestro Faya [*sic*] was applauded."[72] Others, however, attacked the libretto for its hackneyed story line, which centers around romantic contretemps between two couples.[73] Nor did it help that the orchestra had only one

69. "Si tú no hubieras sabido más de lo que tú mismo creías . . . no es posible que con una o dos lecciones estuviera ya Pedrell satisfecho" (undated letter, Fedriani to Falla, AMF correspondence file 6962).

70. "No hagas a Pedrell sino un caso muy relativo . . . puede equivocarse y puede tener mala fe relativa o absoluta. . . . Además, para componer zarzuelas que te dejen el dinero que es lo que de momento necesitas, no es preciso tanta perfección" (undated letter, Fedriani to Falla, cited in Gallego, *El amor brujo*, 26). Fedriani had a more positive reaction to Falla's collaboration with Vives, writing that it "doesn't seem like a bad idea to me" (letter, Fedriani to Falla, 25 June 1903, AMF correspondence file 6962).

71. The libretto was published in 1902 by the Sociedad de Autores Españoles (Madrid: R. Velasco) and the entire score (piano-vocal) in 1965 (Madrid: Unión Musical Española). See Elizabeth Seitz, "Manuel de Falla's Years in Paris, 1907–1914," Ph.D. diss., Boston University, 1995, 72–79.

72. "En *Los amores de la Inés* los tipos están bien observado, hay versos inspirados y situaciones cómicas que merecieron los aplausos de la concurrencia y chistes muy ingeniosos. El segundo cuadro divirtió mucho al público, que llamó al proscenio al Sr. Dugi en una escena . . . de mucha gracia. La música del maestro Faya fue aplaudida" (G. B., "Teatro Cómico," *La Época*, 13 April 1902, 2).

73. Summarized in Sagardía, *Vida y obra*, 26; and Demarquez, *Manuel de Falla*, 15–16.

violist and no oboist and that its lone bass player had to be repeatedly coaxed out of the neighborhood bar.[74] Despite the reasonably healthy number of performances, Falla profited little from the venture, and shortly after *Los amores de la Inés* closed he complained to his friend José Rodríguez Fernández that he was "without a coat."[75] Another *zarzuela*, *Limosna de amor* (Alm of Love), from 1901–2 and on a libretto by Veyán, remains unperformed. But in one sense it was an important step for Falla, since in *Limosna de amor* he incorporated musical folklore from Asturias (in northwestern Spain).[76] This effort was followed with his setting of folkloric *villancicos* (Christmas carols) in the *Cantares de nochebuena* (Songs of Christmas Eve) for voice and guitar of 1903–4.[77] (The first song, "Pastores venir," also calls for rabel, a bowed instrument with gut strings, and *chicharra*, a friction drum.) Seeking a simple, natural style, Falla assigned the guitar only four or five chords. The minor melody of the fourth song, "Un pastor lleva un pavo" (A Shepherd Carries a Turkey), must have appealed to him, for he would use it ten years later in a far different guise in the *Siete canciones populares españolas* (see musical example 3).

Still burdened by family responsibilities, in late 1903, Falla presented his next composition in a piano competition organized by Bretón. A faculty jury of the Madrid Conservatory would award a prize of 500 pesetas to the best performer/composer of an *Allegro de concierto*, to be subsequently used as an examination piece. Falla's *Allegro de concierto* was his most substantive composition to date. Formally free, the work revolves around a dramatic and thick-textured main idea, which occurs three times, often with rich harmonies, such as the ninth chord enhanced with a chromatic passing tone in m. 66. Although the piece can be played convincingly, it could not compete with the elegant work of the same title by Enrique

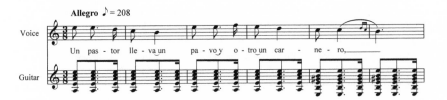

Musical Example 3. Falla, *Cantares de nochebuena*, "Un pastor lleva un pavo" (A Shepherd Carries a Turkey), mm. 1–6. (Reprinted by kind permission of Ediciones Manuel de Falla)

74. Pahissa, *Vida y obra*, 32.

75. Letter, Falla to Rodríguez Fernández, 22 May 1902, cited in Gallego, *El amor brujo*, 26.

76. Seitz, "Manuel de Falla's Years in Paris," 64–71. On Falla's sources, see Inmaculada Quintanal Sánchez, *Manuel de Falla y Asturias: Consideraciones sobre el nacionalismo musical* (Oviedo: Instituto de Estudios Asturianos, 1989), 13–27.

77. The most complete discussion of the *Cantares de nochebuena* is in the prologue to Antonio Gallego's edition of the same work (Madrid: Ediciones Manuel de Falla, 1992).

Granados composed for the same event, which, unlike Falla's, has remained in the repertory. Falla took a special mention, however, along with six of the twenty-four entrants in the contest. (The contestants were required to submit their works with pseudonyms, many of which were quite colorful, such as Cyrano de Bergerac or Juan Sebastian Bach, which Granados used. Falla contented himself with a mere "X.") Like much of the salon music discussed earlier, the surviving *Allegros de concierto* reflect the "European" outlook of many late romantic Spanish composers, as neither Falla's nor Granados's contain overtly "Spanish" gestures.[78]

All told, frustrated attempts at *zarzuela*, less than lucrative recital engagements, and a class of sluggish piano and harmony students added up to discouraging circumstances. It seems that Fedriani only exacerbated these difficulties. We have no indication, for example, that he ever patted Falla on the back for having assumed the role of breadwinner at a relatively young age or for trying to live a principled life. (On the other hand, he did not hesitate to ask Falla to buy him lottery tickets.) Fedriani also had ready labels for the causes of Falla's problems, the central one being "self-love." This condition, roughly equivalent to egoism, earned St. Augustine's harsh condemnation; antidotes proposed by various Roman Catholic authorities included mortification, obedience to the norms of monastic life, humility, or metaphorically leaving the self through charity, "and, through Jesus, to be in God."[79] For Fedriani, it was the sin of self-love that explained Falla's perfectionist streak, which in turn accounted for his failure to launch a career:

> Among other things, you need to have less self-love . . . Cheer up. And have faith in the Lord and work with a certain moderation and without self-love, scruples [or] desire for absolute perfection, because such perfection is impossible to acquire right away; rather, it will come as a natural consequence of studies and experiences. . . . Apart from the fact that for the success of the moment, you need neither more nor less. And keep all these instructions in mind so as to follow them exactly.[80]

78. The most complete discussion of the contest is in Jacinto Torres Mulas, "Efemérides: Cien años del Concurso de piano del Conservatorio: Los *Allegros de Concierto* de Granados y Falla," *Música: Revista del Real Conservatorio Superior de Música de Madrid* 10 (2003): 277–86. I wish to thank Professor Torres for making his work available to me prior to publication.

79. M. B. Schepers, "Self-Love," in *The New Catholic Encyclopedia* (New York: McGraw-Hill, 1967), 13:63–64.

80. "Entre otras cosas, necesitas tener menos amor propio, . . . Anímate. Y ten confianza en el Señor y trabaja con cierta moderación y sin amor propio, escrúpulos [o] deseo de absoluta perfección, porque esa perfección ni es posible adquirirla de pronto; sino que ella vendrá como consecuencia natural de estudios y experiencias. . . . Aparte de que para el éxito de momento, no necesitas tanto ni mucho menos. Y todas estas instrucciones ténlas presente para realizarlas con exactitud" (undated letter, Fedriani to Falla, AMF correspondence file 6962).

These were harsh words, though not completely off the mark. Nowadays, Falla's chronic hesitancy might be diagnosed as "scrupulosity," an obsessive-compulsive disorder rooted in fear of failure in the eyes of God coupled with the tendency to see sin where none exists. In his discussion of "the doubting disease," Joseph W. Ciarrocchi observes that the word *scruple* comes from the Latin *scrupulum*, meaning a "small sharp stone," which, if stuck in one's shoe, impedes comfortable walking.[81] Although at various points in his life Falla did act decisively, small but persistent doubts frequently assailed him. For example, scrupulosity may well have made the composer's romantic agonizing more tortured than was normal, even for one as shy as he. It could also account for his rigid attention to his toilette, which, as noted by many biographers, involved counting the strokes of his toothbrush. There was also Falla's exaggerated sense of contrition: at least once Fedriani encouraged him to confess *less* frequently. Since Falla's only immediate points of reference were his own hesitations and Fedriani's hectoring—coupled with the fact that the composer professed total allegiance to the belief system Fedriani represented—we should not be surprised by the crippling effects these doubts had, however earnest the composer's assertion to Roland-Manuel in his 1928 letter, that "unjustified fear . . . never dominated [his] character."

Of course, perfectionism is hardly uncommon among musicians: we need only think of Falla's future mentor Paul Dukas, who destroyed a good deal of what he wrote and published little. But, as we shall see, Falla's pursuit of perfection often caused him to lose perspective on his strengths and weaknesses as a composer, as his long battle with the scenic cantata *Atlántida*, a sprawling work to which he was temperamentally unsuited, attests. There is also the traditional Catholic concept that self-love often masquerades as self-abasement. Seen in this light, Falla's assessment in 1910 of his works prior to *La vida breve*, for example, takes on a whole new meaning. In it, Falla stated that "whatever I published before 1904 has not the slightest value. They are simply silly trifles. . . . A nocturne, for example, was written when I was practically a child. . . . Maybe in my unpublished works one could find things of a bit more interest, but among my published works, there is nothing, nothing."[82] Such a remark might strike us as utterly lacking in self-love. Yet in making it, Falla would probably have berated himself, mindful of Fedriani's view that the quest for "absolute perfection" betrays an *excess* of ego—and willingness to indulge it. (Inci-

81. Joseph W. Ciarrochi, *The Doubting Disease* (New York and Mahwah, N.J.: Paulist Press, 1995), 5.

82. "Ce que j'ai publié avant 1904 n'a pas la moindre valeur. Ce sont tout simplement des *betises*. . . . Un nocturne, par example, a été écrit quand j'étais presque un enfant. . . . Peut être dans mes travaux qui sont restés inédits on pourrait trouver des choses d'un peu plus d'intérêt; mais parmi les oeuvres publiés, il n'y a rien, rien" (letter, Falla to Jean-Aubry, 3 September 1910, AMF correspondence file 7132/1). Falla always considered *La vida breve* his "opus. 1." See Lolo, "Las relaciones Falla-Pedrell," in Nommick, *Manuel de Falla: La vida breve*, 128.

dentally, Falla indulged in exaggeration in this same statement: he was twenty-three when he composed the nocturne in question, not a "child.") Thus, however unsympathetic Fedriani's endless harangues may seem, we cannot overlook their convoluted power of persuasion and its effect on the sin-haunted composer.

FAREWELL TO JUVENALIA: *LA VIDA BREVE*

In summer 1904, Falla learned of a composition contest sponsored by the Madrid-based Real Academia de Bellas Artes de San Fernando. Founded in 1744, this august association, which still awards memberships to luminaries in Spanish arts and letters, announced several prizes: 1,000 pesetas for the best orchestral work, 300 pesetas for the best patriotic song, and 2,500 pesetas for the best one-act Spanish-language opera, of which the librettist would receive 30 percent.[83] In light of his previous experience (not to mention the considerable cash incentive), Falla found opera the most attractive category. There was also the possibility of a performance, for, as article 9 of the contest rules stated, "the Academia [will] try to assure that the prize-winning works will be publicly performed, with the appropriate brilliance, in one of Madrid's theaters. In this first performance, if it should take place, the Academia will be exempt from satisfying the authors' rights that, as such, are due them."[84] The operative word in that last sentence is *if*.

With Carlos Fernández Shaw, a minor playwright and author also from Cádiz, Falla immediately began casting about for a libretto. One idea was *Francesca da Rimini*, a topic that had inspired Tchaikovsky, and in Spain Granados and Conrado del Campo, each of whom composed symphonic poems entitled *La Divina Comedia*.[85] Falla and Fernández Shaw also considered Pedro Antonio de Alarcón's novel *El sombrero de tres picos* (The Three-Cornered Hat), later the basis of Falla's ballet. In August, Fernández Shaw sent Falla a libretto entitled *La vida breve* (Life Is Short). It was based on an earlier poem, "La chavalilla" (The Little Lass), which had appeared in the Madrid press.[86] Set in Granada, the Moorish city in southern Spain where Falla would eventually reside, *La vida breve* is one more tragic tale of deceit and class

83. The contest regulations are reprinted and translated in Seitz, "Manuel de Falla's Years in Paris," 331–33.

84. "La Academia habrá de procurar que las obras premiadas sean ejecutadas públicamente, con la debida brillantez, en un Teatro de Madrid. En esta primera representación, si se efectuara, la Academia quedaría exenta de satisfacer a los autores los derechos que, como tales, hubieran de corresponderles" (Seitz, "Manuel de Falla's Years in Paris," 332).

85. These works were composed in 1915 and 1908, respectively. See Hess, *Enrique Granados*, 116. On Conrado del Campo, see Miguel Alonso, *Catálogo de obras de Conrado del Campo* (Madrid: Fundación Juan March, Centro de Documentación de la Música Española Contemporánea, 1986), 25.

86. Details of Falla and Fernández Shaw's collaboration are in Guillermo Fernández Shaw (son of the librettist), *Larga historia de La vida breve* (Madrid: Ediciones de Revista de Occidente, 1972).

difference between lovers. Salud, an innocent gypsy girl, falls for Paco, the son of a wealthy landowner. Her grandmother and uncle (Tío Sarvaor) watch sympathetically as she agonizes over Paco's lateness for their daily tryst; once he arrives, however, he promises eternal devotion and Salud's peace of mind is restored. But when Salud learns that Paco will marry a woman of his own social standing she and her relatives show up at the elaborate wedding party posing as entertainers, and, confronting her feckless lover before the assembled guests, she abruptly dies at his feet. Throughout, workers in a forge sing resignedly of the inscrutability of fate, like the chorus in a Greek tragedy.

With the 31 March deadline looming, Falla set to work. If ever there were an exercise in overcoming his perfectionist tendencies, composing an opera in six months was it. Since he had never visited Granada, he asked some friends to rush him postcards of the Albaicín, its gypsy quarter, which he studied furiously. By February, he was setting down daily assignments for himself, as a memo discovered among the sketches reveals ("on Friday the 3rd, make a clean copy through the finale").[87] The same memo indicates that he planned to begin the orchestration only on 4 February, surely a risky procedure for one still uncertain about the nuances of orchestration and temperamentally unsuited to working at white heat. At the same time, he was preparing a demanding program for a competition sponsored by the Spanish piano manufacturer Ortiz y Cussó, the prize for which was a grand piano. As his dull and tightfisted students continued to consume his energies, his less than robust health reacted accordingly, and by 30 March *La vida breve* still required so much copying that Falla despaired of turning in the score on time. His brother Germán stepped in to help with the text underlay, but, unschooled in music, he inserted large chunks of text either under the wrong notes or, worse, under rests.[88] In the frantic final hours, Falla decided to submit the manuscript anyway, with an explanatory note to the committee. He even managed to do so on time.

What sort of work did Falla offer the *académicos*? Essentially, *La vida breve* rejects the facile workings of his earlier salon music and the simple folklore of *Cantares de nochebuena* in favor of a rich, even eclectic, musical language.[89] Falla's expanded harmonic palette includes added-note chords (10 mm. before Salud's first-act solo, "Vivan los que rien," page 22 of the piano-vocal score); modal coloring (the plagal cadence that concludes the forge singer's plaint on pages 10–11);

---

87. Gallego, *El amor brujo*, 28n36.

88. Pahissa, *Vida y obra*, 37.

89. Further discussion is found in Yvan Nommick, "*La vida breve* entre 1905 y 1914: Evolución formal y orquestal," in Nommick, *Manuel de Falla: La vida breve*, 11–118. This work is a collection of essays devoted to the opera. The musical discussion here is based on the piano-vocal score published by Eschig (which lacks rehearsal numbers). Differences between the 1905 version and subsequent reworkings are noted in chapter 3.

whole-tone sonorities, sometimes at moments of dramatic tension (Sarvaor's vow to kill Paco, page 39, or Salud's confrontation with Paco at the wedding party, page 118); and pedal tones. There are also frankly diatonic passages, usually in lighter moments. One of these is the *Intermedio*, in which a panoramic view of Granada inspires "ahs" from the collective anonymity of a six-part chorus, followed by oscillating V–I cadences (Scherzando, p. 48). Key areas are often third related, as in the movement from the luminous A♭ major chord, marked "calmo," to a *pp* B major, over which Salud floats her quiet confession, "I feel I'm about to die" (Yo me siento morir). Clashes of nonharmonic tones and winding chromatic lines also reinforce the forge singers' unhappy pronouncement on page 11, "Malhaya quien nace yunque en vez de nacer martillo" (Unhappy is he who is born an anvil instead of a hammer). Perhaps most palpable is the strong presence of chromatic harmony, which in several instances can be justly described as Wagnerian. Nommick, for example, has cited the passage in which Paco duplicitously vows never to forget Salud (p. 35). Certainly the ascending chromatic line rising out of a half-diminished chord, B–D–F–A, the accented chromatic passing tone resolving to a German sixth, along with other unresolved and unprepared nonharmonic tones, all vividly recall *Tristan und Isolde*.[90]

But *La vida breve*'s Wagnerian elements go beyond these instances of chromatic harmony. Salud's agitated entrance (see musical example 4), with its jagged contour, is only one example of a melody sculpted out of speech, that is, of Wagnerian aversion to symmetrical phrase structure. Further, although some discrete "numbers" were later extracted from the opera (see chapter 3), the bulk of *La vida breve* relies on the Wagnerian practice of continuous music. More often than not, Falla places voice and orchestra on an equal footing, another procedure common in the work of Wagner. He also approximates leitmotiv strategy. Among the many examples we could cite is the initial motive of Salud's act 1 meditation, "Vivan los que ríen" (Long live those who laugh), which reappears in various guises throughout, such as sequential treatment as it flits through the conversation between Paco and his bride (p. 112). The motive also insinuates itself into Sarvaor's pathetic offer to sing and dance for the wedding guests (p. 115) and marks Salud's death in the final four measures.[91] There is also a "love theme," whose agogically accented ascending major sixth is varied intervallically throughout, as on page 16, in which the grandmother notes Salud's lovesickness, or on page 78, where a fragment of the theme, now introduced by a minor sixth, B♭–G♭, is woven into the wedding celebration. Its

---

90. Yvan Nommick, interviewed by Sarah Walker for the program "Deep Song," British Broadcasting Company (BBC), 21 July 2002.

91. Manuel García Matos finds a parallel between "Vivan los que ríen" and the Andalusian *seguiriya*, along with folkloric resemblances (though no direct quotes) throughout *La vida breve*. See "El folklore en *La vida breve* de Manuel de Falla," *Anuario Musical* 26 (1971): 173–197.

Musical Example 4. Falla, *La vida breve*, act 1, sc 1. Salud's entrance. (Reprinted by kind permission of Ediciones Manuel de Falla)

sequential treatment on pages 88–89 is paired with *ff* statements of the "Vivan los que ríen" motive, gradually thinning out into bare octaves (see musical example 5). Ironically, the most forthright statement of the love theme is uttered by the two-timing Paco, who exuberantly proclaims to Salud, "Por ti yo desprecio las galas del mundo" (For you, I renounce the gains of the world).

Especially artful is Falla's manipulation of a brief motive that initially occurs on the words "¡Ay, amor!" (G–G♯–B), where it is harmonized in the Wagnerian style described above and is promptly followed by a thematic reference to the forge music; these five measures are then repeated a minor third higher (p. 9). The same motive introduces the disembodied lament of the anonymous forge singer (D♯–E–G), juxtaposing lovesickness and grinding poverty. After Salud's entrance, Falla again alludes to "¡Ay, amor!": when the grandmother halfheartedly assures her that Paco will indeed come that afternoon, C♯–D is stated, but the expected F is delayed for another bar and a half. A threefold repetition of the motive, slightly varied, then reinforces the grandmother's warning that "es dañoso tanto querer" (it's dangerous to love so much). When the third statement concludes with the leap of a tritone, however, it is clear that her words will not be heeded. (Incidentally, the tritone, prominent in *La vida breve*'s opening measures, occurs at other pivotal moments throughout the score; e.g., on p. 44 it punctuates the juncture between Paco's false of profession of love and a return of the forge music.) Also compelling are echoes of the motive in the *Tranquillo* section on page 10, where the inner voice, A–B–C, recalls "¡Ay, amor!" through intervallic contour and agogic accent. It is at moments such as these that Falla's ever surer sense of timing, color, and melodic invention is at its most evocative.

None of this, of course, is to say that Falla composed *La vida breve* deliberately intending to imitate Wagner, however much he studied and annotated the German master's scores during his formative years. Certainly he was aware of how Wagnerian techniques had been developed by the composer's followers in France; he also

Musical Example 5. Falla, *La vida breve*, act 2, sc 1. "Allegro furioso" ("Vivan los que ríen" and "love" motives). (Reprinted by kind permission of Ediciones Manuel de Falla)

acknowledged the influence of Charpentier's *Louise* in his work on *La vida breve.*[92] Other elements adding to the opera's expressive range include *verismo* (the unisons on p. 26 could have come straight from Mascagni's *Cavalleria rusticana*) and the marked presence of explicitly Spanish music. The first "Dance," for example, is a graceful balance of incisive rhythm and thematic ingenuity, as in the countermelody in the horns at the return of the principal theme.[93] Simple but gratifying bursts of harmonic color rush forth in sequences on page 69, and the fleeting primitivism of the B section, with its narrow intervallic range and Phrygian turns, is introduced by hemiola, itself a foreshadowing of the final cadence. Spanish character also emerges in the song of the *cantaor* (male flamenco singer), the highly realistic evocation of flamenco style—Falla's first—that opens act 2. With its title, "Yo canto por soleares" (a *soleá* being a mournful flamenco genre), guitar accompaniment, freewheeling vocal *fioritura* in Phyrgian mode, and mournful "¡ays!" the number announces itself as one of the more authentic moments in all of Spanish musical theater (see musical example 6). All told, Falla's first mature utterance reminds us that the category "hybrid" need not be pejorative.

Yet history has judged *La vida breve* a flawed work. This is not so much due to the music: apart from some flatfooted choral writing at the beginning of the second tableau and the grandmother's hooting "Salud!" via vocal *glissandi* worthy of a corny horror movie, the score is entirely satisfying. The libretto, on the other hand, falls short. To be sure, it concerns the stuff great plots are made of—jealousy, collective versus individual pain, class differences, obsessive love. Yet these timeless themes remain undeveloped, especially when crammed into the skimpy one-act format mandated by the Academia. Even once we have undergone the "willing suspension of disbelief" necessary in any number of operas, several aspects of the plot fail to convince, especially Salud's precipitous demise. Other operatic deaths occur for a plausible reason: Carmen is murdered, Violetta falls ill, and Madama Butterfly takes her own life. While we need not rule out the possibility that a sensitive and delusional creature like Salud *might* die of a broken heart, the abrupt swoon at her lover's feet occurs so carelessly and with so little dramatic preparation that we are likelier to react with surprise—or perhaps mild irritation—than compassion. Also, since none of the other characters are particularly vivid, the dramatic burden falls solely on Salud and her abject state. As we wonder what drew Falla to this libretto, it is tempting to suggest that its treatment of unrequited love and the defeat of an innocent heart reflected his own romantic frustrations. As he noted in a pencil sketch, his intention was to "evoke sentiments . . . of hope and torture, of life and death, of

92. I wish to thank Michael Christoforidis for this information.
93. The number is perhaps better known in its numerous transcriptions: for solo cello; for twelve cellos, guitar, piano solo, and piano four-hands; and Fritz Kreisler's version for violin and piano.

Musical Example 6. Falla, *La vida breve*, act 2, sc 1. "Yo canto por soleares." (Reprinted by kind permission of Ediciones Manuel de Falla)

exaltation and humiliation."[94] It is a shame that he did not find a libretto that more competently addressed this lofty goal.

Still, *La vida breve*'s strengths convinced the jury. By 13 November, when the unanimous decision to award it the opera prize was announced, Falla had already started revising his hastily completed score, undoubtedly hoping for a performance. Yet none materialized in the immediate aftermath of the contest, and Falla bitterly resented the fact that *La vida breve* seemed condemned to the same fate as his immature *zarzuelas*. In fact, it is difficult to know his understanding of the contest rules, which by no means guaranteed a premiere. In a press interview a few years later, for example, he insisted that "among the contest's conditions was that the winning work

94. "Procurar, ante todo y sobre todo, evocar sentimientos . . . de esperanza y de tortura, de vida y de muerte, de exaltación y de abatimiento" (cited in Antonio Gallego, "*La vida breve*," program booklet for *El sombrero de tres picos/La vida breve*, in *Teatro Real* [Madrid: Fundación del Teatro Lírico, Temporada 1997–98], 66).

would be staged at the Real."[95] Pahissa's biography, authorized by Falla, puts it even more bluntly: "But, although in the contest rules it was stated that the Academia would arrange the premiere, at the Teatro Real, of the prizewinning work, that institution did nothing to that end."[96] Subsequent biographers have perpetuated this tale of injustice, among them Demarquez, who describes the Real's refusal "to honor" the "promise" of a performance.[97] Yet it cannot be said that the Academia did nothing. Gallego notes that in November 1906 it passed an official motion to set aside 25,000 pesetas for musical support (probably thanks to one of Falla's allies, the music critic Cecilio Roda); this action was prompted by the failure to secure performances for the various prize-winning works, despite the Academia's best efforts.[98] In addition, Bretón and Serrano, both members, intervened on Falla's behalf, as he himself later acknowledged: "Difficulties came up everywhere . . . because right away in official spheres indifference, coldness, and bureaucracy arose. The Academia did nothing in any official capacity for my work to be premiered. Some Academia members, Bretón and Serrano . . . particularly mediated with the management of the Real so that *La vida breve* could be premiered. But a prejudice existed that it was written in Spanish."[99] So prejudice was also to blame? Certainly in the decade prior to the contest the Real mounted only a handful of Spanish-language operas, offering Bretón's *Raquel* (20 January 1900, based on Grillparzer's *Die Judin von Toledo*) and Montilla's *Venganza gitana* (5 March 1902), with five and three performances, respectively. The best-known Spanish-language opera from that period was Bretón's *La Dolores*, which, however, premiered at the Teatro de la Zarzuela (16 March 1895) and was taken up by the Real only in 1915. By then—well after the debacle of *La vida breve*—the Real had produced Ruperto Chapí's *Margarita la Tornera* (24 February 1909), Vives's *Colomba* (15 January 1910), and Conrado del Campo's *El final de don Álvaro* (4 March 1911).

In sum, the composer's understanding of the matter is confused. The Academia did *not* promise a performance, it *did* try to secure one, and at least a few other

---

95. "Entre las condiciones del concurso figuraba la de que la obra laureada sería puesta en escena en el Real" (Fernando Herce, "Ante el estreno de *La vida breve*," *La Mañana*, 14 November 1914, AMF press file).

96. "Pero, aunque en las bases del concurso se hacía constar que la Academia gestionaría el estreno, en el Teatro Real, de la ópera premiada, nada hizo, para ello, esa institución" (Pahissa, *Vida y obra*, 41).

97. Demarquez, *Manuel de Falla*, 33.

98. Gallego, *El amor brujo*, 28n39.

99. "Empezaron a surgir dificultades por todas partes . . . porque en las esferas oficiales despuntó en seguida la indiferencia, la frialdad y el reglamentarismo. La Academia nada hizo de un modo oficial porque mi obra se estrenase. Algunos académicos, Bretón y Serrano . . . particularmente, mediaron con la Empresa del Real para que se pudiese estrenar *La vida breve*. Pero existía el prejuicio de estar escrita en español" (Herce, "Ante el estreno de *La vida breve*").

Spanish-language operas *were* performed at the Real. Either Falla was simply unaware of all this (difficult to imagine, given his involvement in Madrid's musical scene) or resentment blinded him to reality. Ironically, *La vida breve* had to wait until 1997 for a performance at the Real when that theater reopened after one of the many closures that has marred its history.

With the piano competition, Falla had better luck. On 24 April 1905, exhausted and with a flask of the protein compound peptone at hand, he played so movingly that one of the judges, Pilar Mora, wept.[100] He performed the Bach-Liszt Prelude and Fugue in A Minor, the Scarlatti-Tausig *Pastoral e Capriccio*, Beethoven's Sonata in D Minor op. 31 no. 2 (the "Tempest"), Chopin's Ballade in F Minor op. 52, Schumann's *Fantasiestücke* op. 12, nos. 1–3, and Saint-Saëns's *Study in the Form of a Waltz*. As if this were not enough, the judges requested the third of Liszt's "Paganini" studies, *La Campanella*.[101] Falla was declared the winner, a fact that is particularly impressive given that he was competing against Frank Marshall, Granados's protégé and later Alicia de Larrocha's teacher. Clearly Falla's self-deprecating remarks about his own piano playing cannot be taken seriously, except perhaps as one more indicator of his perfectionist tendencies.

Besides the new grand piano, winning the contest secured Falla a few performances, some of which featured one of his favorite composers, Domenico Scarlatti.[102] His program on 15 May 1905 at the Madrid Athenaeum, for example, included his own *Allegro de concierto*, Liszt's Twelfth Hungarian Rhapsody, and two Scarlatti sonatas, albeit in "revised" editions by Carl Tausig. Although winning the contest must have lifted his spirits, by late 1905 Falla was thinking seriously of seeking his fortune in Paris, long a mecca for Spanish artists and musicians. Albéniz had moved there in 1894, largely to escape musical conditions in Spain, and Granados, saddled with domestic and administrative cares in Barcelona, also "dreamed of Paris."[103] Most persuasive was Falla's associate of several years, Joaquín Turina, a former Tragó student, who by 1905 was studying at the Schola Cantorum. Falla was motivated both by frustration with Madrid's musical establishment and a keen interest in French music. He knew, for example, Ravel's *Sonatine* of 1903–5, and in 1906 he began arranging for piano the harp part of Debussy's *Danse sacrée et danse profane*. He even wrote Debussy for clarification on some of its rhythmic nuances and received a courteous but open-

---

100. Pahissa, *Vida y obra*, 39; Gallego, *El amor brujo*, 28n37. As early as 1904, Fedriani had been advising Falla to mix peptone with "cherry extract" to "combat weakness" (letter, Fedriani to Falla, 20 January 1904, AMF correspondence file 6962).

101. AMF program file 5.

102. On Falla's lifelong admiration for Scarlatti, see Elena Torres Clemente, "La presencia de Scarlatti en la trayectoria musical de Manuel de Falla," in Nommick, *Manuel de Falla e Italia*, esp. 68n10, 94–97.

103. Letter, Granados to Vives, translated and cited in "Amadeu Vives, "N'Enric Granados i l'edat d'or," *Revista Musical Catalana* 13 (1916): 182, cited in Hess, *Enrique Granados*, 35.

ended response in which Debussy stated that he would be "quite happy to leave the performance to [Falla's] good taste."[104] On 4 February 1907, Falla performed his arrangement at the Teatro de la Comedia and repeated it on 11 April at the Círculo de Bellas Artes to reasonably positive reviews.[105]

Still, he saw no way out of Madrid. Now almost thirty-one, he had utterly failed in a popular-commercial genre (*zarzuela*), had been denied a production of his one "serious" opera, and had enjoyed only limited success as a concert pianist and composer of salon pieces. His main source of income was teaching and accepting whatever playing engagements came his way. Coming to grips with the perils of romantic attachment left its effects as well. As far as we know, Falla never loved a woman again nor was he tempted to define himself as a man through physical intimacy with a woman.

Given Falla's ambition to compose full time, this scenario offered small comfort. Yet all was not bleak, as the following recollection in Pahissa reveals. It also discloses a far different Falla from the humorless ascetic often portrayed: "In Falla's house friends gathered, Saturdays at night and Sundays in the afternoon, all of them young and cheerful. They talked, they argued, they sang, and played the piano with such enthusiasm—this was the concert grand won in the contest—that the floor vibrated. . . . Conversation and music were enhanced with beer from a keg someone brought, and they entertained themselves with cakes or *jamón serrano*."[106] One of these high-spirited individuals was Juan Carlos Gortázar, secretary for the Bilbao Philharmonic, who arranged a concert in that city for Falla and the Polish violinist Paul Kochanski in early 1907. One night, they dined there with Kochanski's agent, to whom Falla confided his dream of visiting France. The agent immediately promised him some concerts. After months of anxious waiting, during which Falla brushed up on his French, an offer came through. Despite its less than precise terms, that summer Falla boarded the train to Paris. Although he planned to stay for only a few weeks—and brought money for only a few days—he remained for seven extraordinary and decisive years.

104. Letter, Debussy to Falla, 13 January 1907, cited and translated in François Lesure and Roger Nichols, eds., *Debussy Letters*, translated by Roger Nichols (Cambridge: Harvard University Press, 1987), 176. Although it is possible that Albéniz informed Debussy of Falla's abilities, Debussy was probably simply giving Falla a polite, pro forma answer.

105. The performance is discussed in Hess, *Manuel de Falla and Modernism in Spain*, 30–31; for the status of Debussy in Spain, see pages 78–86.

106. Pahissa, *Vida y obra*, 42–43.

Chapter 3

In Paris on the Eve of the Great War

When Falla stepped off the train at the Quai d'Orsay in the summer of 1907, Kochanski's agent was nowhere to be seen. After taking a cab he could ill afford to that individual's squalid apartment, Falla learned that the promised engagements had fizzled and the only work to be had was with a touring pantomime company. It would travel through the Vosges and parts of Switzerland, presenting *L'enfant prodigue* (The Prodigal Son) by former Prix de Rome winner André Wormser. Falla had little choice but to accept. As it turned out, the tour agreed with him tremendously, even if it offered scant opportunity to show his true abilities. He wrote his family: "It wasn't possible for me to play concert pieces because the pianos were horrible, and on top of this . . . I had no time to practice, since the trip was a 'cinematographic' one. In Martigny, there was no orchestra for the overture and I had to play it on the piano [but with] such great success that the applause continued even after the play had begun.[1] Although the tour was a financial disaster, Falla was at least paid something. Back in Paris, he practiced at the Salle Pleyel, informing his family that "one of the house managers is awfully nice to me." To this he added, amazed: "Whoever would have thought years ago that I was ever going to practice at Pleyel, in Paris?"[2] Later that August, another tour came along, as did a booking with a singer, from which he expected to earn 1,500 francs. Eventually, Falla acquired

1. Letter, Falla to his family, 16 August 1907, cited in de Persia, *Poesía*, 51.
2. Letter, Falla to his family, 16 August 1907, cited in de Persia, *Poesía*, 51.

enough piano and harmony students to stay afloat in the French capital, writing Viniegra a few months later: "I rejoice more and more for having decided to leave Madrid. For me there was no future there. The piano and harmony lessons I gave there I have commenced here—where I'm better paid."[3] Perhaps he could even begin to forget the humiliation of feeling forced to lower a student's fee at the moment of payment.

"WITHOUT PARIS, . . . OBSCURITY"

The sensation that he had suddenly entered a dream world persisted as Falla hastened to present himself to Paris's leading musical figures. Debussy was away for the summer, as was Dukas, although Falla managed to catch the latter on one of his days in town. He played *La vida breve*, and Dukas promptly encouraged him to seek a performance at the Opéra-Comique; that May, Dukas's own *Ariane et Barbe-bleue* had premiered at the same theater. After his disappointments in Madrid, this struck Falla as nothing short of miraculous. Dukas, who in a few years would devote most of his energies to teaching orchestration at the Paris Conservatory, also offered to advise Falla on that subject, discouraging him from studying formally at the Schola Cantorum, which, in some circles, had a reputation for rigidity.[4] In that first meeting, so "unforgettable and transcendental," Dukas, ordinarily rather formal, also promised to introduce Falla to the colorful and gifted Albéniz, whom Falla had never met. During that first visit between the two compatriots, Albéniz regaled Falla with selections from *Iberia*, although by 1907, in the twilight of his life, Albéniz could only approximate that formidable knuckle twister. Albéniz, Dukas, and Falla then dined together and chatted, "as if they had known one another all their lives."[5]

Like Dukas, Albéniz proved both friend and professional ally. On 25 September, he gave Falla a signed copy of the third book of *Iberia* (soon to be premiered by Blanche Selva) and introduced him to one of that work's most brilliant interpreters, the Catalan pianist Ricardo Viñes, for whom Falla also had a letter of recommendation from Madrid. A pioneer of new piano music (e.g., Debussy's *Pour le piano* and Ravel's *Gaspard de la nuit*), Viñes introduced Falla to Ravel, initiating a long

3. Letter, Falla to Viniegra, 13 December 1907, cited in de Persia, *Poesía*, 52.

4. As Nommick observes, Falla had been steadily revising *La vida breve*, that is, before meeting Dukas, as Falla himself explained in a letter to Fernández Shaw dated 16 August 1907. See Nommick, "*La vida breve* entre 1905 y 1914," in Nommick, *Manuel de Falla: La vida breve*, 15. On the Schola in relation to the politicization of French music, see Jane F. Fulcher, *French Cultural Politics and Music from the Dreyfus Affair to the First World War* (New York and Oxford: Oxford University Press, 1999), 24–34, 48–55.

5. Falla's account of the meeting with Albéniz appears in a letter to Fernández Shaw dated 31 March 1910, cited in Nommick, "*La vida breve* entre 1905 y 1914," in Nommick, *Manuel de Falla: La vida breve*, 32. See also Pahissa, *Vida y obra*, 49–50.

and respectful association.[6] In Paris, Falla also reconnected with Turina, who recommended lodgings in the Avenue Kléber, off the Arc de Triomphe, where he was living himself. Falla, whose numerous address changes in Paris occasioned comparisons with Beethoven, remained there until the daily combat between his and Turina's rented pianos became unbearable.[7]

In October, Falla finally met Debussy. Having seen photographs in which the French composer's cheeks appeared sunken, Falla initially failed to recognize the robust figure who greeted him with a jovial "c'est moi, c'est moi-même!"[8] As with Dukas, Falla played *La vida breve* from beginning to end, ever mindful of the seemingly incredible nature of this encounter and, as he related later to Pahissa, a bit cowed by Debussy's sardonic humor. In fact, Falla's timidity sometimes puzzled his distinguished new colleagues. On one occasion, he called on Debussy and, after learning that he was out, was ushered by a servant to wait in a small, poorly lit storage area off the dining room, which happened to be filled with Chinese masks. Eventually Falla heard Debussy, his wife Emma Bardac, and a guest, whom he later identified as Satie, begin their lunch. Too timid to enter the dining room unannounced, Falla remained in the darkened room, lightheaded from hunger. The masks, with their ghoulish expressions, seemed to swim before his eyes. Finally, when the noise of conversation and the clatter of plates had ceased, Falla slipped out. As luck would have it, he collided head-on with Mme Debussy in the dim corridor, who let out a shriek. Although everyone urged Falla to stay and eat, he was so frazzled that he apologetically took his leave.[9]

Despite the thrill of living in Paris, Falla was occasionally discouraged, for he was still living very modestly and sometimes had to take on odd jobs. (At one point, he did translations for a feather catalog.)[10] Some engagements in northern Spain, at Oviedo and Bilbao, with the violinist Antonio Fernández Bordas and the cellist Víctor Mirecki came his way in January 1908. Besides the strain of travel, however, this meant preparing several piano trios, including Mendelssohn's demanding op. 49 in D Minor and Beethoven's op. 97 in B♭ major (the "Archduke"). Overcome with frustration, he confessed to Albéniz:

> Believe me, I'm desperate. I, who left Madrid because my teaching there left me no time for anything, am here . . . worse off, because all my hopes of working with you and with . . . Dukas have been dashed. Now, this business with

6. See Elaine Brody, "Viñes in Paris: New Light on Twentieth-Century Performance Practice," in *A Musical Offering: Essays in Honor of Martin Bernstein*, edited by Edward H. Clinkscale and Claire Brook (New York: Pendragon, 1977), 57–59.

7. Pahissa, *Vida y obra*, 48. By 1910, he was living in a *Hôtel* Kléber on the Rue Belloy. See letter of 28 April 1910, Fernández Shaw, *Larga historia de La vida breve*.

8. Pahissa, *Vida y obra*, 51.

9. Pahissa, *Vida y obra*, 53–54.

10. Pahissa, *Vida y obra*, 60.

Bilbao can give me a little relief maybe for two months, but afterward I'll have to continue as until now, taking whatever engagement presents itself in order to continue *vegetating*, which is the only thing one achieves with this way of life.[11]

Yet temporary relief was imminent. In the same letter, Falla hopefully asked about a subvention from the Spanish royal family that the generous Albéniz was trying to expedite on his behalf. When funding from the marquis of Borja finally materialized, Falla could dedicate himself to composing, at least for a few months.[12] Albéniz also saw to it that Falla met Paul Milliet, one-time secretary of the Society of French Authors, who would eventually translate *La vida breve* into French.[13]

No longer "vegetating," Falla completed his first significant piano work in spring 1908.[14] The *Cuatro piezas españolas* (Four Spanish Pieces), begun two years earlier, assert Falla's musical personality anew and without the distraction of *La vida breve*'s dramatic infelicities. Their scope, harmonic color, and pianism leave behind the *morceaux* of just a few years earlier, reminding us of the composer's own harsh assessment of his works composed before 1904. Like Albéniz's *Iberia*, each of the four movements evokes Spain, either through geography or genre; Falla himself explained to Cecilio Roda that the *Cuatro piezas* were to "express musically the soul and atmosphere of each of the regions indicated in their respective titles."[15] "Aragonesa" evokes the province of Aragón, famous for its lively dance, the *jota*; "Cubana" contains a mixture of 3/4 and 6/8 time, suggesting the swaying *guajira* of Cuba, the former colony; "Montañesa" quietly portrays the Asturian landscape; and "Andaluza" recalls the region whose musical language is most readily associated with Spain. Falla seems to have deliberately set himself thematic limitations, drawing on one or perhaps two principal themes per piece, some borrowed. "Montañesa," for example, draws on the Asturian song, "La casa del señor cura" (The House of the Priest) from José Hurtado's *100 cantos populares asturianos*, a source Falla had already used in *Limosna de amor*.[16]

11. Letter, Falla to Albéniz, 11 January 1908, cited in de Persia, *Poesía*, 55.

12. Falla wrote Albéniz on 17 January 1908 to express his gratitude. See Walter Aaron Clark, *Isaac Albéniz: Portrait of a Romantic*, 253.

13. See letter, 9 February 1908, Falla to Pedrell, cited in Lolo, "Las relaciones Falla-Pedrell," in Nommick, *Manuel de Falla: La vida breve*, 131–32.

14. Michael Christoforidis, "Manuel de Falla, Debussy, and *La vida breve*," *Musicology Australia* 18 (1995): 9n20.

15. "Expresar musicalmente el alma y el ambiente de cada una de las regiones indicadas en sus títulos respectivos" (typescript in the AMF's unnumbered *Cuatro piezas españoles* file). This explanation to Roda also appears in a letter Falla wrote Henri Collet on 4 April 1909. See Michael Christoforidis, "Aspects of the Creative Process in Manuel de Falla's *El Retablo de Maese Pedro* and *Concerto*," Ph.D. diss., University of Melbourne, 1997, 46.

16. Quintanal Sánchez, *Manuel de Falla*, 28–36. Hurtado's *100 Cantos* was published in Madrid by Antonio Romero in 1889.

Falla dedicated the *Cuatro piezas* to Albéniz, and certain echoes therein of his senior colleague's harmonic language have not gone unremarked. Ronald Crichton, for example, speaks of the similarity of "the basic musical language," and Demarquez notes "the slightly troubled sensibility of the second theme of the 'Evocation' [*Iberia*, book 1, no. 1]" in the "Tranquillo" section (m. 43) of "Aragonesa" in addition to "modulations prepared by altered chords in the manner of Albéniz" and "Albéniz-like chords" in "Andaluza."[17] To what extent does analysis confirm these reactions? Demarquez's first example, the middle section of "Aragonesa," contains several similarities with Albéniz's "Evocación," though principally with the section beginning in m. 115. In both, an ascending melodic line, stepwise in "Evocación" and nearly stepwise in "Aragonesa," stands in relief against a thicker harmonic underpinning (although Falla's textures tend to be more transparent). Both melodies are ornamented with sixteenth-note triplets, are preceded by a ritard, and are supported by long pedals. Also, each involves a key change and marks the dominant of the new key, the A♭ pedal in "Evocación" notwithstanding. The most significant parallel between the two passages, however, occurs in the balance of harmonic color and the internal rhythm of the melody: Falla launches his melody from a V13 chord, with the thirteenth (B♮) falling on the second beat. Albéniz's melody, although harmonized by a V9 chord (E♭ root), contains a passing thirteenth (C♮) on the second beat, agogically accented, a rhythmic pattern established at the outset (see musical examples 7a and 7b).

As for "Andaluza," its opening crushes, single-note melody, and narrow range dimly recall the drum roll of the opening measures of "El Corpus en Sevilla" (*Iberia*, book 1, no. 3). More significant is Falla's launching (m. 82) of a gradual progression of added-note chords, many spiced with minor ninths or major sevenths, which culminates in the "racimo de uvas" (bunch of grapes) style so associated with Albéniz (see musical example 8).

Soon Falla was playing the *Cuatro piezas* for his friends. Debussy heard it on 30 June 1908 and, along with Dukas and Ravel, recommended it to the publisher Durand, who, much to Falla's astonishment, offered the princely sum of 300 francs.[18] To Falla, then meticulously recording the cost of meals, metro tickets, cologne, and the inevitable cigarettes, this reward seemed like a gift from heaven.[19] Similarly marvelous was the premiere of the *Cuatro piezas* on 27 March 1909 at the Salle Érard by Viñes, who represented the new and the bold to Paris's musical public. We can only

17. Ronald Crichton, *Falla: BBC Music Guides* (London: British Broadcasting Corporation, 1982), 22; Demarquez, *Manuel de Falla*, 45, 46.

18. Christoforidis, "Manuel de Falla, Debussy, and *La vida breve*," 2; Pahissa, *Vida y obra*, 55.

19. See introductory commentary on pages 279–97 of Nommick and Bonastre, *Manuel de Falla*.

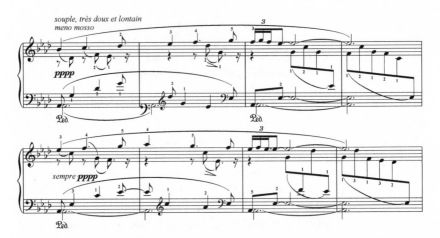

Musical Example 7a. Isaac Albéniz, *Iberia*, "Evocación," mm. 115–22. (Reprinted by kind permission of International Music Company)

Musical Example 7b. Falla, *Cuatro piezas españolas*, "Aragonesa," mm. 43–50. (Reprinted by kind permission of Ediciones Manuel de Falla)

wonder where pursuing such a harmonically dense style might have led Falla, who never again hinted so broadly at the language of his admired compatriot.

It was also thanks to Viñes that Falla began his association with Les Apaches. This spirited group of aesthetes (the name roughly translates as "young rowdies") had since 1902 been meeting weekly to discuss the latest aesthetic trends and perform new music, and Falla was glad to join. Members included the composers Maurice Delage, Florent Schmitt, and Ravel; the poet Tristan Klingsor; the critics Michel Calvocoressi and Émile Vuillermoz; and the conductor and composer D. E. Inghelbrecht.[20] They were especially taken with the latest Russian music, especially that of Stravinsky, and attended rehearsals of Sergei Diaghilev's Ballets

20. Jann Pasler, "Stravinsky and the Apaches," *Musical Times* 123 (1982): 403–7.

Musical Example 8. Falla, *Cuatro piezas españolas*, "Andaluza," mm. 87–89. (Reprinted by kind permission of Ediciones Manuel de Falla)

Russes, which was then taking Paris by storm. Stravinsky himself attended Apaches meetings beginning in 1910. This is probably when he met Falla: in his autobiography, Stravinsky recalls meeting him around the time of the *Firebird*, that is, around June 1910.[21] Although he found Falla "modest and withdrawn as an oyster" and with an "unpityingly religious" nature, they enjoyed a long and mutually respectful friendship.[22]

Another work, *Noches en los jardines de España* (Nights in the Gardens of Spain), was also on Falla's mind. As Yvan Nommick has demonstrated, the composer began this three-movement work for piano and orchestra in Paris, not Madrid, as is sometimes suggested.[23] On 13 January 1909, Falla asked his family to send him, "by rail or whatever means" *Jardins d'Espanya* (Gardens of Spain), a book by the Catalan artist and playwright Santiago Rusiñol.[24] Like Gustave Doré, Rusiñol, and Washington Irving, Falla was inspired by the Alhambra, the Moorish fortress that casts its imposing spell over half of Granada. While roaming the bookstalls in Paris, Falla also discovered *Granada: Guía emocional* by the Spanish playwright Gregorio Martínez Sierra, with whose name Falla's would shortly be linked.[25] Initially, the composer projected a four-movement work with the title *Nocturnos* (Nocturnes), which he hoped Viñes would premiere—or so he told that avid supporter of Spanish music, the critic Georges Jean-Aubry, whose long and fruitful association with

21. Igor Stravinsky, *An Autobiography* (New York: Norton, 1962), 30–31.

22. Stravinsky and Craft, *Memories and Commentaries*, 76. Falla also became one of Stravinsky's most loyal supporters in Spain. His role in Stravinsky's tours there in 1916, 1921, 1924, and 1925 is discussed in Hess, *Manuel de Falla and Modernism in Spain*, 98–104, 161–98.

23. Yvan Nommick, *Jardines de España: De Santiago Rusiñol a Manuel de Falla* (Granada: Ayuntamiento de Granada, 1996), 7–9.

24. Letter, Falla to his family, 13 January 1909, cited in Nommick, *Jardines de España*, 7.

25. Gregorio Martínez Sierra, *Granada: Guía emocional* (Paris: Garnier, 1910). See also Nommick, *Jardines de España*, 12.

Falla had begun two years earlier.[26] Falla worked only intermittently on *Noches* while in Paris, however, and it remained unfinished until 1916.

He did, however, finish the *Trois mélodies* (Three Melodies), a set of solo songs for voice and piano on texts by Théophile Gautier. Here it is worth noting that part of Falla's work in Paris involved accompanying singers; in fact, he dedicated the second of the *Trois mélodies* to one of his clients, a wealthy North American, Romaine Brooks. Once again, the work swerves stylistically from Falla's previous music, now with a marked French quality. In the first song, "Les Colombes" (The Doves), Falla draws on whole-tone sonorities and chantlike declamatory writing. The second, "Chinoiserie," pays homage to France's time-honored fascination with the Orient, one Debussy had acknowledged in "Pagodes," the first number of the piano suite *Estampes*, and Stravinsky in the *Three Japanese Lyrics* (written in the company of Les Apaches).[27] Most surprising is the third, "Séguidille," with its Frenchified approach to that sprightly Spanish dance. Not only do "Spanish" sixteenth-note triplets enliven its demanding piano part, but the subject matter is similarly conventional: Gautier's protagonist, a flirtatious *manola*, or "working girl," is little more than a wholesome version of Bizet's Carmen. (Recall the lively—albeit inauthentic—"Séguidille" from act 1 of Bizet's opera.) In sum, the *Trois mélodies* show Falla in yet another new light: as the cosmopolitan experimenter, unafraid of seeming to reinvent himself from a French perspective and, at least in "Séguidille," to indulge in a bit of playful irony.

The songs were premiered on 4 May 1910 at the Salle Gaveau by Ada Adiny (Paul Milliet's wife) with the composer at the piano. The event was significant in several ways. It was one of the first concerts of the Société Musicale Indépendante (SMI), which Ravel had spearheaded in 1909 largely out of enmity with Vincent d'Indy, who presided over the Société Nationale de Musique.[28] The SMI was determined to offer more imaginative programming than the Société Nationale, and to that end it represented a broad spectrum of international composers, including Vaughan Williams, Kodály, Schoenberg, Casella, and Malipiero. It also featured Spanish music, offering Conrado del Campo's *Caprichos románticos* (Romantic Caprices), Pedrell's "Canción de la estrella" (Song of the Star), Turina's *Rincones sevillanos* (Places in

26. They met at a concert at the Salle des Agriculteurs in June 1908. In 1910, Jean-Aubry organized an all-Spanish concert in Le Havre, at which Falla performed the *Cuatro piezas españolas*. See G. Jean-Aubry, "Manuel de Falla," *Revista Musical Hispano-Americana* (30 April 1917): 1. Falla briefly describes his initial conception of *Noches* in a letter to Jean-Aubry dated August 1901, cited in Nommick, *Jardines de España*, 8.

27. See Richard Taruskin, *Stravinsky and the Russian Traditions: A Biography of the Works Through Mavra* (Berkeley: University of California Press, 1996), 1:822.

28. Michel Duchesneau, "Maurice Ravel et la Société Musicale Indépendante: 'Projet mirifique de concerts scandaleux,'" *Revue de Musicologie* 80, no. 2 (1994): 260. See also Fulcher, *French Cultural Politics*, 161. Falla's account of the SMI's founding is in Pahissa, *Vida y obra*, 80.

Seville), and Falla's *Cuatro piezas españolas* on 6 April 1911.[29] Sharing the May 1910 concert with Falla and Mme Adiny was the Polish harpsichordist Wanda Landowska, who interpreted works of Bull and Purcell. Falla, who probably first met Landowska when she played in Madrid in 1903, must have been delighted to renew his acquaintance with her, even if at the time he could not have imagined the extent to which she would shape his career.[30]

Other projects never progressed beyond the planning stage but still give an idea of Falla's priorities at this time. An opera based on Eugène Demoldier's *Le jardinier de la Pompadour* (Mme Pompadour's Gardener), for example, was to have a libretto by fellow Apache Michel Calvocoressi, a critic for *La revue musicale* and *Comoedia*. Falla also contemplated a one-act sequel to Bizet's *Carmen*. Its projected title was *La muerte de Carmen* (The Death of Carmen), and it would follow Mérimée's novella, with its poignant conclusion, more closely than Bizet's opera did. This intriguing idea—of a Spaniard taking up the story that perhaps more than any other has imposed a Frenchified view of Spain on the international public—failed when Bizet's widow objected.[31] Falla then encountered a libretto called *Las flores* (The Flowers) by those masters of popular Spanish theater, the Álvarez Quintero brothers, and he briefly considered turning from his newfound cosmopolitanism to more familiar materials.[32]

Falla also reveled in Paris's early music scene. He heard Monteverdi's *L'incoronazione di Poppea*, with Jane Bathori and Émile Engel, on 8 May 1911; on the tenth, he applauded Landowska (who this time appeared with singer Marie de Wieniawska) in works by Giovanni Maria Bononcini and Alessandro and Domenico Scarlatti. He also met Alfredo Casella, with whom he would remain friends for decades. Casella promoted early music both in performance (Falla attended his concert of Cesti and Alessandro Scarlatti at the Salle des Agriculteurs on 23 February 1911) and in his own compositions, such as the Sarabande for piano, which Falla heard during the 1909–10 season.[33] For Falla, early music satisfied his yearning for cosmic order governed by the law of God. For his French contemporaries, who tended to favor Couperin and Rameau, there was another agenda, however. By upholding the values of the "French tradition"—taste (*goût*), balance, brevity, and wit—French composers could persuade themselves that they were resisting German musical hegemony, which had held sway since the end of the Franco-Prussian War in 1871. Rejecting the gargantuan orchestras of Mahler or Strauss, many French composers now began to write for smaller forces and to draw on baroque and classical forms, as in Debussy's Sarabande of 1901 (from the suite *Pour le piano*) or Ravel's Sonatine of 1905. They

---

29. Duchesneau, "Maurice Ravel et la Société Musicale Indépendante," 276.
30. Christoforidis, "Aspects of the Creative Process," 174.
31. Pahissa, *Vida y obra*, 117–18.
32. Christoforidis, "Manuel de Falla, Debussy, and *La vida breve*," 4.
33. These activities are covered in Bergadà, "La relación de Falla con Italia," in Nommick, *Manuel de Falla e Italia*, 23n17.

and their supporters became increasingly convinced of a "Latin" musical identity, one that comprised France, Italy, Spain, and even Russia—it was an admittedly elastic concept. Whether they hailed it as "Latinité" or "Latino-Slav art," its proponents felt they could stand up to "Teutonic" domination.[34] In effect, some of the same geopolitical tensions that precipitated the outbreak of World War I made themselves felt in musical circles.

None of these polemics was very much on Falla's mind, however, for unfortunately his financial situation had worsened again. After his grant from the marquis of Borja ran out, he sought funding from the Madrid-based Junta para Ampliación de Estudios e Investigaciones Científicas (Council for the Enhancement of Scientific Study and Research), whose board of directors included histologist Santiago Ramón y Cajal and painter Joaquín Sorolla. Given the Junta's progressive outlook and its goal of promoting study abroad, it is difficult to know why Falla, who applied twice, was turned down both times.[35] His funds were so depleted that when the opportunity to perform in London arose in May 1911, he had to ask his uncle, Pedro Matheu, chargé d'affaires in France for El Salvador, for a loan of 100 francs.[36]

For his London debut, Falla participated in a concert of Spanish music organized by the pianist Franz Liebich. It was less than brilliant: the anonymous critic for the *Times* observed that "the concert given in the Aeolian Hall by Mr. Franz Liebich failed to make much effect, partly owing to the intrinsic dullness of much of the music . . . and partly because the performance of it was not accomplished."[37] This harsh judgment was largely without foundation, for the program included André Caplet's two-piano arrangement of Debussy's "Ibéria," works by Cabezón, the second book of Albéniz's *Iberia*, and selections by Granados, which the critic censured as "dull little dances." Alas, a similar reaction awaited the *Cuatro piezas españolas* and *Trois mélodies*:

> The younger Spanish school was represented mainly by Señor Turina's suite *Sevilla* and a set of pieces by Señor de Falla, played by the composer. Both men have studied in Paris—the former under d'Indy; the latter under Debussy—and the French influence has kept their technique clear. Señor de Falla's pieces, however, are too monotonous in rhythm and weak in melody to be really interesting, and his experiements in tonality are indecisive. Señor Turina's Suite is stronger melodically and shows more originality in every way, but the music is quite slight. . . . The songs of both these composers were less forced than

34. Scott Messing, *Neoclassicism in Music from the Genesis of the Concept through the Schoenberg/Stravinsky Polemic* (1988; reprint, Rochester, N.Y.: University of Rochester Press, 1996), 38–43.

35. See letter, Falla to Fernández Shaw, 28 April 1910, cited in Gallego, *El amor brujo*, 30n43. On the Junta, see Gray, *The Imperative of Modernity*, 50.

36. Gallego, *El amor brujo*, 30n44.

37. "Concert of Spanish Music," *Times* (London), 26 May 1911, 10.

the instrumental music, but they were not particularly attractive, nor were they well sung.[38]

Whatever his low opinion of Falla's music, this reviewer can at least be grudgingly credited with one of the few explicit statements in the literature on Falla's relationship with Debussy. As we shall see in the rest of this chapter, Debussy's influence on Falla was significant and unique enough that it prompted conductor Ernest Ansermet to declare that "Debussy had hardly any immediate descendants except Falla."[39]

Despite some low moments, Falla never seriously considered returning to Spain, and he seemed content to carry on, always in wide-eyed appreciation of his adopted home. Summing up the difference between musical life in Madrid and Paris years later, he offered a damning comparison. "Without Paris," he asserted, "I would have remained buried in Madrid, submerged and forgotten, scraping by in obscurity, living miserably on teaching, and saving, like a family heirloom, my framed prize [for *La vida breve*] and, in a closet, the score of my opera."[40] In fact, it was *La vida breve*, which had made so little impact in Spain, that now earned Falla his first moment of glory on the international musical scene.

A CAREER IS LAUNCHED

Ever since his first encouraging visit with Dukas, Falla had continued to revise *La vida breve*, and by mid-1908, the same year in which Milliet completed the French translation, he had divided it into two acts. On 3 July, a reading was held for Albert Carré, director of the Opéra-Comique.[41] Afterward, surely in anticipation of a performance, Falla confided to Fernández Shaw that he "would give anything" for Mary Garden (the only Mélisande, incidentally, to win Debussy's unequivocal approval) to play Salud.[42]

An intriguing speculation is the extent to which Debussy influenced *La vida breve*'s gradual transformation. Certainly Falla's fascination with Debussy's music intensified during his Paris years. In April 1908, he purchased a score of *Pelléas et Mélisande*, and that June he heard the opera three times,[43] which probably explains his enthusiasm for Mary Garden. Eventually his library included *La mer, Prélude à l'après-midi*

38. "Concert of Spanish Music," p. 10.

39. Ernest Ansermet, *Les fondements de la musique dans le conscience humaine* (Neufchâtel: Langages, 1987), cited in Michael Christoforidis, "De *La vida breve* a *Atlántida*: Algunos aspectos del magisterio de Claude Debussy sobre Manuel de Falla," *Cuadernos de música iberoamericana* 4 (1997): 15.

40. Cited in Pahissa, *Vida y obra*, 43.

41. Christoforidis, "Manuel de Falla, Debussy, and *La vida breve*," 2.

42. Letter, Falla to Fernández Shaw, 11 July 1908, cited in Fernández Shaw, *Larga historia de La vida breve*, 87.

43. Christoforidis, "Manuel de Falla, Debussy, and *La vida breve*," 2.

d'un faune, the Quartet, and many other Debussy works, and he eagerly attended performances of *Nocturnes*, *La mer*, *Prélude à l'après-midi d'un faune*, and, from the orchestral *Images*, "Ibéria" and "Rondes de printemps."[44] Falla also sought Debussy's musical counsel, and their friendship became sufficiently close that the older composer, who had initially intimidated the timorous Falla, came to address his younger colleague in their correspondence as "cher ami" (rather than "cher monsieur").[45]

Starting on 10 October 1911, Falla began recording in his diary some of Debussy's advice under the heading "observations to be used in the next opera." For example, he noted Debussy's view that the harp was "not an instrument of *assistance*, nor [one] . . . to augment the sonority," but one that gives "color, though nothing more" and "used badly . . . can produce an effect of *poverty*."[46] Falla's own partiality for the harp would blossom not in "the next opera" but in *Psyché*, his latter-day impressionist vocal chamber work, which features prominent yet subtle harp writing and is in effect an homage to Debussy's Sonata for Flute, Viola, and Harp of 1915, which Falla considered "music for paradise."[47] He also used the harp in the "Soneto a Córdoba" of 1927 but with a wholly different set of aesthetic priorities.

Falla also jotted down suggestions specific to *La vida breve*.[48] These included cutting the barrage of imprecations just before the final curtain ("Cursed be your father! Cursed be your mother! Cursed be the children you have! May God curse them! May God curse you!"). Debussy felt this would "accelerate the coda" and heighten the tragic element.[49] Having eliminated these, Falla added twelve intensely chromatic measures just before Salud's death. Debussy also advised joining without interruption the end of the first act to the Intermedio, which Falla did. He did

44. For an inventory of Falla's library, see Michael Christoforidis, "A Composer's Annotations to His Personal Library: An Introduction to the Manuel de Falla Collection," *Context* 17 (1999): 48–68.

45. Use of the new form of address seems to have begun in the fall of 1911. See Christoforidis, "Manuel de Falla, Debussy, and *La vida breve*," 2.

46. Christoforidis, "Manuel de Falla, Debussy and *La vida breve*," 5. Christoforidis summarizes and translates many of Falla's notes.

47. Cited in Marcel Dietschy, *A Portrait of Claude Debussy* (Oxford: Clarendon, 1990), 183.

48. The most complete discussion of Falla's revisions to *La vida breve* is in Nommick, "*La vida breve* entre 1905 y 1914" in Nommick, *Manuel de Falla: La vida breve*; see also the same author's "De *La vida breve* de 1905 à *La vie brève* de 1913": Genèse et évolution d'une oeuvre," *Mélanges de la Casa de Velázquez* 30 (1994): 71–94. A semiotic exploration of Debussy's influence on Falla is Anna Rita Addessi, *Claude Debussy e Manuel de Falla: Un caso di influenza stilistica* (Bologna: Cooperativa Libraria Universitaria Editrice Bologna, 2000).

49. Christoforidis, "Manuel de Falla, Debussy, and *La vida breve*," 3–4. Nommick notes, however, that the curses were erased from the autograph manuscript of Fernández Shaw, that is, ms. XXXV C1 ("De *La vida breve* de 1905 à *La vie breve*," 82 n44). They can be seen in ms. XXXV A1, a vocal score that includes the French translation above the Spanish text, an addition that, according to Christoforidis (private communication with author, 2000) Falla probably made around 1908.

not, however, follow Debussy's advice to shorten the Intermedio. He also transposed "Vivan los que ríen" down half a step. As for orchestration, we cannot be sure of Debussy's influence here since we have no point of comparison: the orchestral version of 1905 has disappeared, leaving only the piano-vocal score of the same year.[50] We can assume, however, that *La vida breve*'s final version reflects the new coloristic language Falla absorbed in Paris.

As Gallego has noted, several of Falla's alterations arose out of the more expansive two-act format.[51] Most significant in fleshing out the new second act was the addition of another dance number. This was the suggestion of conductor André Messager, who wished to satisfy the dance-loving Parisian public. Another avowedly Spanish number, the second "Dance" includes hand clapping, shouts of "¡Olé, olé!", choral interjections filled with half-step grace notes, and hemiola. With its prominent second-beat accents, it complements the wedding reception of Paco and his bride, thus furnishing the final moment of gaiety before *La vida breve*'s abrupt and tragic conclusion.

By September 1912, the revised *La vida breve* was far enough along that Falla traveled to Milan to discuss a possible contract with the publisher, Tito Ricordi. But the visit was fruitless: Ricordi doubted *La vida breve*'s theatricality and believed it to be "too exclusively Spanish."[52] As Pahissa tells it, Ricordi argued that "for the theater one must compose music of the universal sort," and offered *Cavalleria rusticana* and some of Puccini's operas as examples, a less than objective stance typical of that era of intensifying nationalisms.[53] Ricordi did, however, offer Falla a contract to set *Anima allegra*, a still unfinished libretto based on a work by the Álvarez Quintero brothers, one Puccini had turned down for lack of familiarity with Spain.[54] Stubbornly but politely, the uncompromising Falla rejected the offer, despite the absence of other possibilities for *La vida breve*.

Back in Paris, a different fate awaited him. Milliet, aware of Ricordi's reaction, now introduced Falla to the publisher Max Eschig. What followed probably seemed like a dream: after hearing *La vida breve*, Eschig offered him a contract for both it and *Noches*, along with a monthly salary. The contract also helped effect the opera's hard-won premiere, now set for 1 April 1913 at Nice's Casino Municipal in Milliet's translation. It is telling that before leaving for Nice Falla, so confident with Ricordi, now surrendered to his perfectionist tendencies and met one last time with Dukas

50. Based on a thorough examination of sketches and Falla's evolving priorities as an orchestrator, Nommick suggests several possible alterations. See "*La vida breve* entre 1905 y 1914," in Nommick, *Manuel de Falla: La vida breve*, 23–37.

51. Antonio Gallego, "*La vida breve*," 62–63.

52. Letter, Falla to Milliet, cited in Bergadà, "La relación de Falla," in Nommick, *Manuel de Falla e Italia*, 24.

53. Pahissa, *Vida y obra*, 64.

54. Luigi Motta, "*Anima allegra*, Puccini e Cilea," *L'opera* 2, no. 2 (January-March 1966): 64–67.

and Debussy to resolve lingering doubts about orchestration. He must have been exceptionally nervous, for they both had to repeatedly assure him that every note was in place. Dukas even remarked, perhaps with faint exasperation, "Do you think I don't know how to read a score?"[55]

Reviews of Falla's opera in the Nice press, though positive, draw attention to two issues that have dogged *La vida breve* since its creation. One is the libretto, which some critics judged as little more than an excuse for "la belle musique." Another is length: clocking in at around an hour, the work must be performed with either another short opera or additional music. Nice's solution to this problem bordered on variety show format. The evening began with a *Marche Solenelle* (Solemn March) by Parès, followed by a *saynète, La Peur d'Aimer* (Fear of Love), by Émile Boucher, after which *diseur* M Leroy recited "L'histoire d'un Crime" (History of a Crime). Following this "fête littéraire" were two selections by Massenet: an aria from *Le jongleur de Nôtre Dame* and Salomé's air from *Hérodiade* sung by Félia Litvinne, who also obliged with the "Hopack" from Musorgsky's incomplete opera, *The Fair at Sorochintsï.* Concluding the program's first half were the "strophes émouvantes" of Nadaud's *Trois Hussards.*[56] Only then did the curtain rise on *La vida breve*, which, despite these lengthy preliminaries, received a warm welcome.[57] Several reviewers gloated that France had the honor of presenting *La vida breve*, with the anonymous critic for *La Comédie Niçoise* magnanimously complimenting a work that could stand up to the "Spanish" music of Bizet and Chabrier.[58] Other critics drew on long-held views of Spain, sometimes equating these impressions with the composer himself. For example, Georges Avril, the Paris correspondent for *Comoedia*, commented that Falla was "linked to his Iberian origins and his work, very coloristic, very evocative of a Spain that is amorous, violent, melancholy, joyous, and tragic [and] has a beautiful and ardent bearing."[59] In other words, Nice's critics were eager to praise a Spanish composer for creating a work that corresponded to a view of Spain largely engineered by Frenchmen.

Falla was delighted by this experience. First, he had never really heard his music performed by an orchestra (we can hardly count the lamentable ensemble that performed *Los amores de la Inés* in 1902). Second, the Nice premiere generated more

55. Pahissa, *Vida y obra*, 66.

56. L. D., "La matinée du 'Figaro,'" *L'Éclaireur de Nice*, 2 April 1913, AMF press file.

57. See, for example, J.-A. May, "Les avant-premières au Casino Municipal: *La vie brève*," *Le Petit Niçoise*, 1 April 1913; May, "La belle création de *La vie brève*," *Le Petit Niçoise*, 3 April 1913; Montsalvat, "Casino Municipal: *La vie brève*," *Le Phare du Litoral*, 3 April 1913; Ph.-Emmanuel Glaser, untitled article in *Le Figaro* (Paris), 4 April 1913; and M. D. Calvoccoressi, "Nice," *Musica*, April 1913. All can be found in the AMF press files.

58. "Semaine théatrale," *La Comédie Niçoise*, 10–17 April 1913.

59. "Falla est lié a ses origines ibériques et son oeuvre très colorée, très evocatrice de l'Espagne amoureuse, violente, mélancolique, joyeuse et tragique est de belle et ardente tenue" (Georges Avril, "Au Casino Municipal de Nice: *La vie brève*," *Comoedia* [Paris], 3 April 1913).

press coverage than any of his previous works. When news of the performance reached Spain, Falla could only have felt vindicated. In *La Correspondencia de España*, an anonymous reviewer dedicated a sympathetic half-column to *La vida breve*'s tortured history in its native land.[60] In *Nuevo Mundo*, Alejandro Míquis went further, delivering a blistering attack on the Spanish musical establishment and complaining that "while Spanish impresarios run like a bat out of hell from operas by our compatriots, foreign impresarios make hay with them."[61] An even more powerful voice was Pedrell's. In the Barcelona daily *La Vanguardia*, the composer-critic cited verbatim extended portions of Míquis's diatribe and addressed the broader issue of Spanish character in music and the disconcerting ease with which it normally inspired *andalucista* clichés. For Pedrell, however, *La vida breve* contained not the slightest hint of "that false and annoying *andalucismo* of the corrupt *género chico* [one-act *zarzuela*], equivalent to the degenerate tavern repasts that have assaulted many stages today."[62] As in France, defining what constituted Spanishness depended far more on local perception than specifically musical content, corroborating Carl Dahlhaus's assertion of many years later that "what does and does not count as national [music] depends primarily on collective opinion."[63]

After his triumph in Nice, Falla returned to Paris, where he made the acquaintance of two compatriots, the husband and wife theatrical team of Gregorio and María Martínez Sierra. By any standard, theirs was an unusual union. Gregorio had married María in 1900 and allowed her to support him while he established himself as a playwright. As he gradually realized that his real talents lay in directing and entrepreneurship, María took over the writing of the plays he produced. The result was that most of the fifty-odd plays Gregorio mounted between 1908 and 1930 are hers, even though he passed them off as his own.[64] They include several commer-

60. "Nuestro arte en el extranjero," *La Correspondencia de España*, 12 May 1913, AMF press file.

61. "Mientras los empresarios españoles huyen como alma que lleva el diablo de las óperas de nuestros compatriotas, los empresarios extranjeros hacen con ellas sus fiestas mayores" (Alejandro Míquis, "En plena paradoja," *Nuevo Mundo*, n.d., AMF press file).

62. "Ese falso andalucismo latoso de género chico corrompido, propio de las cuchipandas golfescas tabernarias que han asaltado hoy las tablas de muchos escenarios" (Felipe Pedrell, "Quincenas musicales, *La vida breve*," *La Vanguardia*, 29 May 1913, AMF press file).

63. Carl Dahlhaus, "Nationalism and Music," in *Between Romanticism and Modernism*, translated by Mary Whittall (Berkeley: University of California Press, 1980), 87–88.

64. An overview of Gregorio's career is in Julio Enrique Checa Puerta, "Los Teatros de Gregorio Martínez Sierra," in *El teatro en España entre la tradición y la vanguardia, 1918–1939*, edited by Dru Dougherty and María Francisca Vilches de Frutos (Madrid: Consejo Superior de Investigaciones Científicas, Fundación Federico García Lorca, and

cial hits, such as *Canción de cuna* (Cradle Song) of 1911, which has been described as "the greatest international success in modern Spanish theater prior to [Lorca's] *La casa de Bernarda Alba*."[65] A striking element in this arrangement is María's desire—apparently genuine—for anonymity.

In her memoirs, María described the couple's first meeting with Falla, which took place during a trip they took in the spring of 1913. She observed that he lived in "one of those dismal, sordid, repellent hotels . . . in which Paris has sheltered so many artistic dreams and so much hopeful promise of future glory."[66] When she and Gregorio entered these depressing quarters, Falla was poring over the score of *The Rite of Spring*, the infamous premiere of which he surely heard that May.[67] Whatever his immersion in Stravinsky (his "idol," as María put it) and however much he sensed himself standing on the threshold of bold, new ideas, Falla's own absorption of Stravinsky's modernist musical language (and subsequent abandonment of the "Spanish" idiom Nice had so warmly applauded) was still years away.

By early November, rehearsals for the Paris production of *La vida breve* were in full swing at the Opéra-Comique. This was the site of the unfortunate premiere of Bizet's *Carmen* in 1875, at which some critics had railed against "Andalusians with sun-burned breasts, the kind of women . . . found only in the low cabarets of Seville . . . vomitted from Hell."[68] In fact, prior to *Carmen* the theater had had a tradition of emphasizing edifying or sentimental family entertainment. Plots might offer virtuous female role models for daughters of the bourgeoisie to emulate, such as Anna and Jenny, the selfless heroines of François Adrien Boieldieu's *La dame blanche*, which Bizet heartily detested.[69] After *Carmen*, however, with its daring treatment of a sexually liberated female, the Opéra-Comique began to address class difference (e.g., in Charpentier's *Louise*, performed in 1900), sexual license (Ravel's *L'heure espagnole*, performed in 1911), and Jewish identity, which was especially compelling in the wake of the Dreyfus affair (Camille Erlanger's *Le juif polonais* of 1900 and

---

Tabacalera: 1992), 121–26. See also Ian Gibson, *Federico García Lorca: A Life* (New York: Pantheon, 1989), 87–88. Gibson's definitive biography has recently been updated under the title *Vida, pasión, y muerte de Federico García Lorca, 1898–1936* (Barcelona: Plaza and Janés, 1998). Two studies of María's works are Patricia O'Connor, *Gregorio and María Martínez Sierra* (Boston: Twayne, 1977); and Antonina Rodrigo, *María Lejárraga: Una mujer en la sombra* (Madrid: Vosa, 1994).

65. Arturo del Hoyo, prologue to Rodrigo, *María Lejárraga*, 16.

66. María Martínez Sierra, *Gregorio y yo* (Mexico City: Biografías Gandesa, 1953), 120.

67. Although factual precision is sometimes lacking in María's account of her friendship with Falla, here she could be referring to the piano four-hand version of the *Rite of Spring*, which was published that year.

68. Jean-Pierre-Oscar Comettant, *Le Siècle*, cited in Mina Curtiss, *Bizet and His World* (New York: Knopf, 1958), 403.

69. Susan McClary, *Carmen* (Cambridge: Cambridge University Press, 1992), 15–16, 36.

Albéric Magnard's *Bérénice* of 1911).[70] The influence of Wagner also simmered, as the conflicted reception to Debussy's *Pelléas et Mélisande* in 1902 shows.[71] *La vida breve*, with its emphasis on marginality and class difference, thus offers the following irony: if we take the domesticated women of *La dame blanche* and the defiant protagonist of *Carmen* as opposite extremes of female behavior, Salud, created by a Spaniard, is far closer to Boieldieu's Anna and Jenny than to the sexually uninhibited Andalusian created by the Frenchman Bizet. As it turned out, *La vida breve*'s emphasis on Salud's innocence, a trait considered inimical to Andalusian gypsies, introduced fresh insight into the tired theme of "Spanish" fatalism and reckless passion.

First, however, one complication had to be worked out. Falla was irked when Milliet, as the translator, wanted to take credit for authorship of the libretto. Weeks before the *répétition génerale*, or public rehearsal, on 30 December, Falla's mood was such that he sent Pedrell a dire prediction: "It's enough for me to say that, unless circumstances require it, *La vida breve* will be my last dramatic work, since, as I said before, I'm suffering a great deal, and not because of the theater, where, until now, the rehearsals are going very well, but rather on account of a serious matter related to the translation and another thousand or so intrigues that cloud the satisfaction I would otherwise enjoy."[72] Luckily, Falla proved less than competent as a prophet. Moreover, his optimism about rehearsals was justified, since during them "the singers, the orchestra, and the choruses applaud frequently." So he reported to Fernández Shaw's widow, Cecilia de Yturralde (the librettist died in June 1911), adding that such applause was "a very good sign, especially given that people here are very reserved in rehearsal."[73]

Of course, a work to accompany *La vida breve* had to be found. Paris's solution, an improvement over Nice's, was to pair it with the one-act *Francesca da Rimini* (the theme of which Falla and Shaw had considered in 1904) by the London-based Italian composer Franco Leoni, who was best known for his one-act *L'oracolo* (The Oracle) of 1905. Yet *Francesca* disappointed. At the official premiere on 7 January

70. On *Louise*, *Le juif polonais*, and *Bérénice*, see Fulcher, *French Cultural Politics*, 77–97, 104, 208–9. On *L'heure espagnol*, the libretto of which Gaston Carraud called a "mildly pornographic vaudeville" (he later retracted this statement), see Arbie Orenstein, *Ravel: Man and Musician* (New York: Columbia University Press, 1975), 57.

71. Jann Pasler, "*Pelléas* and Power: Forces behind the Reception of Debussy's Opera," *19th-Century Music* 10 (1987): 259–62.

72. "Me basta decirle por mi parte que, a no exigírmelo las circunstancias, *La vida breve* será mi última obra dramática, pues, como le he dicho antes, estoy sufriendo mucho, y no a causa del teatro, donde, hasta ahora, marchan muy bien los ensayos, sino por un grave asunto relacionado con la traducción y otras mil majaderías que me nublan las satisfacciones que pudiera tener por otros motivos" (letter, Falla to Pedrell, 5 December 1913, cited in Lolo, "Las relaciones Falla-Pedrell," in Nommick, *Manuel de Falla: La vida breve*, 132).

73. Fernández Shaw, *Larga historia de la vida breve*, 55.

1914, one of its more generous critics commented laconically that it was "no better, no worse . . . than a hundred other Italian works from modern Italy"; other critics were similarly lukewarm.[74] Clearly, the coupling of *La vida breve* and *Francesca* did not begin to approximate the happy and seemingly indissoluble marriage of, say, *Cavalleria rusticana* and *I Pagliacci.*

As in Nice, some critics complained about the weaknesses of *La vida breve*'s libretto. Isidore de Lara of *Gil Blas* tactlessly noted that "from the viewpoint of the drama itself, there would be much to say about the choice of libretto. 'Unhappy is he who is born an anvil instead of a hammer,' says the text. Frankly, in regard to this poem, the public is the anvil, because the dramatic vicissitudes whack them on the head, as hard as the blow of a cudgel."[75] Others, such as Henri de Curzon, praised Falla's score but described the book as "very banal and very ordinary."[76] Some, however, proposed that Marguerite Carré's performance as Salud, with the "intensity of her accentuation and her highly intelligent acting," compensated for its flaws.[77] Yet, as in Nice, most critics were not especially troubled by the plot's "simplicity" or "banality." Rather, they reveled in *La vida breve*'s compelling evocation of Spain, with some drawing broader conclusions about national character in music. A starting point was the mise-en-scène, the detail and exactitude of which won lavish praise.[78] Émile Vuillermoz, a fellow Apache, described it as a series of "windows opened onto the agitation of a Granadine street"—little imagining that the composer had never set foot in Granada.[79] Others alluded to the "truth" of Falla's musical utterances, with the critic for *Autorité* commending his sensitivity in "sing[ing] forth the

---

74. "Ni meilleure, ni pire . . . que cent autres oeuvres italiennes de l'Italie moderne" (Charles Koechlin, "Chronique musicale," *La Chronique des Arts*, 4 January 1914). See also Jean Prudhomme, "Opéra Comique," *Comoedia*, 18 January 1914; Paul Abram, "Opéra Comique," *Le Petite République*, 2 January 1914; and Isidore de Lara, "*La vie brève*," *Gil Blas*, 1 January 1914. All reviews of *La vida breve* cited here are in the AMF press file.

75.   "Au point de vue du drame même, il y aurait beaucoup à dire quant au choix de livret. 'Malheur à qui nait enclume au lieu d'être né marteau,' dit le texte. Franchement, en ce qui regarde ce poème, c'est le public qui est l'enclume, car le péripéties dramatiques s'abattent sur sa tête, dures comme coups de trique" (De Lara, "*La vie brève*").

76. Henri de Curzon, "*La vie brève* de Manuel de Falla," *Le Guide Musicale*, 4 January 1914, 6.

77.   De Lara, "*La vie brève*." See also "La Vie Théâtrale et Artistique," *Courrier del Argentine*, 15 January 1914.

78.   "Théâtre National de l'Opéra Comique: Répétition générale de *La vie brève*," *Autorité*, 31 December 1913.

79.   Vuillermoz's review is from *La Revue Musicale, S. I. M.*, 1 February 1914, 39–40, cited in Christian Goubault, *La critique musicale dans la presse française de 1870 à 1914* (Geneva and Paris: Éditions Slakine, 1984), 474.

Andalusian soul with fervor . . . with truth."[80] Applauding Falla's "sincere evocation of the race and mentality," Henri de Curzon also noted the presence of fatalism, a trait long associated with Spain, and for him manifest in the "only interesting
character . . . the young Salud."[81] Yet he found in Salud's fatalism "all the original-
ity of the work, [which] distinguishes it from anecdotes of death and vengeance to
which Spain has accustomed us in the theater. It is this that lends character to the
score."[82] Thus, Salud was "interesting" because her naive (rather than "vengeful")
fatalism not only challenged a persistent stereotype but affected the way the music
sounded.

In short, critics hailed Falla as the leader in current Spanish music. Jean Prudhomme, who had previously considered Spain a "country of popular music" long
indifferent to "la musique pure," upheld him as the heir to the "robust" modern
school established by Albéniz.[83] Ravel, Jean-Aubry, and Charles Koechlin concurred,
although it must be admitted that they did so largely because they saw Falla as one
of their own. Ravel, for example, maintained that of all modern Spanish composers
"Falla offers the closest affinity with present-day French musicians."[84] Jean-Aubry,
who feared that the dull, two-hour *Francesca da Rimini* might cause the public's
enthusiasm for *La vida breve* to cool, defended French art against "foreign impor-
tations," of which he considered the Leoni work an unfortunate example. Falla,
though "foreign," had studied with Debussy and Dukas. Thus, he proffered tasteful rather than trashy *verisme*, utterances devoid of filler (*remplissage*), and "harp
glissandi and stopped horns" that were "without grandiloquence, without frills
(*tarabiscotage*)"; as such, Falla's music bespoke natural restraint and *goût*, both

80. "Théâtre National de l'Opéra Comique." Léon Vallas described the work's *veriste*
subject matter, "realized with perfect musicality," in the *Revue Française de Musique*,
10 January 1914, 97–98, cited in Goubault, *La critique musicale*, 474. See also Pierre Lalo,
Le Temps, 6 March 1914, cited in Demarquez, *Manuel de Falla*, 59.

81. De Curzon, "*La vie brève*," 7.

82. "Ce fatalisme est toute l'originalité de l'oeuvre, et la distingue des anecdotes de
meurtre et de vengeance auxquelles l'Espagne nous a habitués au théâtre. C'est lui que
donne son caractère à la partiture [partition?]" (De Curzon, "*La vie brève*," 7).

83. Prudhomme, "Opéra-Comique." On the various ways in which "la musique
pure" might differ from the German ideal of "absolute music" (as defined by d'Indy,
Marnold, Déodat de Sévérac, and Vuillermoz, among others), see Brian Hart, "The
Symphony in Theory and Practice in France, 1900–1914," Ph.D. diss., Indiana University, 1993, 150–51.

84. Maurice Ravel, "À l'Opéra-Comique: *Francesca da Rimini* et *La vida breve*,"
Comedia Ilustré, 20 January 1914, 390–91, cited in Arbie Orenstein, comp. and ed., *A
Ravel Reader: Correspondence, Articles, Interviews* (New York: Columbia University Press,
1990), 373.

notable French qualities.[85] Ever the crusader for national identity through music, Jean-Aubry considered *La vida breve* solid evidence that music was "particular to [a] race" rather than a "universal" art.[86] Both Jean-Aubry and Falla would address this issue after the outbreak of the war, when such matters assumed far greater urgency.

On that point, in fact, Koechlin was explicit. Echoing the anti-German sentiment then brewing in French musical circles, he noted the often overwhelming influence of an art "still charged with the infinite pessimism of *Tristan* and superhuman mysticism of *Parsifal*," that is, German art. As for its baleful effects on French music, he noted that "The 'savvy' critics vilify without respite the musical simplicity of a Delibes, of a Massenet . . . the Chabriers, the Debussys, the Faurés were not stricken with the malady of today . . . the d'Indys, the Chaussons . . . had only a partial case of the invasive virus. But their followers!"[87] The Spanish school, however, had remained impervious to the Teutonic blight:

> Albéniz had a horror of this false sublimity, this false profundity, this obligatory sadness, repulsive and conventional, of an art that stubbornly confuses Beauty with the gloomy translation of suffering. . . . He was not in the least afraid of fine good humor, nor to light his familiar, tender route with the healthy clarity of popular songs of his country: truly Mediterranean art for its clean contours, for its rhythms of short and diverse waves, and for the harmonious light of its cloudless melodies.[88]

85. *"La vie brève* par M Manuel de Falla," *L'Art Moderne*, 11 January 1914. Jean-Aubry was careful to add, however, that "il ne faut pas oublier que *La vie brève* a été écrite en Espagne il ya plusieurs années, alors que son auteur ignorait la plupart des oeuvres françaises d'aujourd'hui" (One shouldn't forget that *La vida breve* was written in Spain several years ago, when its author was unaware of most French works of today).

86. *Race* in romance languages—*raza* in Spanish—approximates more closely "stock" or "people" than its more limiting English equivalent. Some terminological ambiguities are discussed in James G. Kellas, *The Politics of Nationalism and Ethnicity*, 2d ed. (New York: St. Martin's, 1998), 3–6.

87. "Les critiques 'avertis' vilipendaient sans relâche la simplicité si musical d'un Délibes, d'un Massenet . . . Les Chabrier, les Debussy, les Fauré n'étaient atteints de la maladie du jour, ô paradoxe, que pour y puiser des forces nouvelles; les d'Indy, les Chausson . . . ne souffraient qu'à demi l'envahissant microbe. Mais les disciples!" (Koechlin, "Chronique musicale").

88. "Albéniz avait en horreur ce faux sublime, cette fausse profondeur, cette tristesse obligée, rébarbative et conventionelle, d'un art que s'obstinait à confondre la Beauté avec la morne traduction de la souffrance. . . . Il ne craignait point la sainte bonne humeur, ni d'éclairer sa route familière et tendre à la bonne clarté des chants populaires de son pays: art véritablement méditerranéen par la netteté de ses contours, par ses rhythmes aux lames courtes et diverses, et par l'harmonieuse lumière de ses mélodies sans brouillard" (Koechlin, "Chronique musicale").

The metaphor of Germanic fog, which was also attractive to Ortega y Gasset and the polymath Marcelino Menéndez Pelayo, prompted Koechlin to advocate "Mediterraneanizing" music; indeed, his review quotes Nietzsche's famous dictum "il faut méditerraniser la musique." By placing Spain under the elastic rubric of Mediterranean or Latin, Koechlin deftly linked *La vida breve* to the French spirit through the "refinement," *goût*, and "nobility [inherent] in all [of Falla's] attitudes." And if Nietzsche had praised Bizet's "African" qualities, Koechlin found that *La vida breve* defied Spain's habitual status as an unspoiled preserve of naturalness.[89] Its composer was "not at all a maladroit or a primitive" but rather a musical "aristocrat," who approached his raw materials with the simplicity and restraint so conspicuously lacking in the *veristes*.[90]

What could be better for *La vida breve*'s career in France than the fact that it invited French critics to proclaim the virtues of "Latinité"? Although Falla must have been elated by their enthusiasm, to Pedrell he only reported modestly that the press "had behaved very nicely with [him]."[91] Some of his compatriots, however, saw fit to throw cold water on this happy moment. The critic "Daniel" carped about the Paris production in the *Heraldo de Madrid*, insisting that the work suffered in translation.[92] Critic and composer Vicente Arregui (also a prize winner in the Academia contest of 1905 but for orchestral music) went further, finding in *La vida breve* scant evidence of Falla's "personality."[93] Least sympathetic of all was Ignacio Zubialde, whose review of the piano-vocal score in the *Revista Musical* notes an excess of generic *andalucismo*. "There are too many songs, funereal in the first act and jubilant in the second," he argued. Moreover, he found "all of them [to be] of the same Andalusian lineage."[94] For Zubialde, the inescapable conclusion was that *La vida breve* belonged on the *tablao* (stage) of a flamenco café, not the opera house. His reaction, which smugly combines elitism and nationalistic bias, seems to have been the first example of the sort of two-pronged attack Falla would suffer throughout his career: either critics questioned his expression of national identity or they considered him incapable of distinguishing between popular and "serious" genres.[95] Some, like Zubialde, found him guilty on both counts.

89. See Friedrich Nietzsche, *The Case of Wagner*, translated from the German by Walter Kaufmann (New York: Vintage, 1967), 158.

90. Koechlin, "Chronique musicale."

91. Letter, Falla to Pedrell, 13 January 1914, cited in Lolo, "Las relaciones Falla-Pedrell," in Nommick, *Manuel de Falla: La vida breve*, 136.

92. Daniel, "Vida escénica en París," *Heraldo de Madrid*, 7 January 1914.

93. Vicente Arregui, *Revista Musical Hispano-Americana*, 2d ser., 6, no. 1 (January 1914): 6.

94. "Hay demasiadas canciones, fúnebres las del primer acto y jubilosas las del segundo . . . todas ellas son de la misma cepa andaluza" (Ignacio Zubialde, "*La vida breve*," *Revista Musical* [Bilbao] 5, no. 9 [September, 1913]: 202).

95. As with the Nice premiere, Alejandro Míquís (primarily a theater critic) defended Falla. See his "Una ópera española en París: *La vida breve*," *Diario* [?], 3 January 1914.

Falla's response was to write another explicitly "Spanish" work. Thanks to his contract with Eschig, he could work full time on the *Siete canciones populares españolas* for voice and piano, which he finished in mid-1914. As Michael Christoforidis has speculated, this is "the most popular set of Spanish songs ever written," a claim substantiated by their widespread performance, both in the original format and in versions for violin and piano (under the name *Suite populaire espagnole*, arranged by Paul Kochanski), for cello and piano (arranged by Maurice Maréchal), for voice and orchestra (arranged by Ernesto Halffter in 1951 and Luciano Berio in 1978), and for other combinations.[96] Even more than in *La vida breve*, Falla affirms his musical personality in this polished, ingratiating work. This may be due in part to his melodic blueprints: the melodies come from late-nineteenth- and early twentieth-century printed sources, including José Inzenga's *Ecos de España* (songs 1, 2, 4, 6), José Hurtado's *100 cantos populares asturianos* (song 3), Eduardo Ocón's *Colección de aires nacionales y populares* (song 7), and an unidentified lullaby reproduced at the end of the play *Las flores* by the Álvarez Quintero brothers (song 5).[97]

Subtlety and simplicity are the songs' most appealing features. All unfold in two strophes, sometimes with the second varied, as in song 1, "El paño moruno" (The Moorish Cloth), in which the second strophe begins in the relative major. Especially remarkable is Falla's elegant reinterpretation of his sources and the way in which he illuminates their essential qualities. For example, song 2 ("Seguidilla murciana") is little more than a succession of dominant pedals, with "added notes" piled on. Harmonic resolutions occur in each of the two strophes (mm. 7 and 19 in strophe 1 and mm. 39 and 51 in strophe 2) only to be swept up in the next dominant pedal (see musical example 9) This internal working against harmonic closure is in fact a witty commentary on the final lines of text ("for your fickleness, I compare you to a peseta that passes from hand to hand, and is finally erased, so that, thinking it fake, no one will take it!"), emphasizing the agitated circularity of romantic frustration. By comparison, the final resolution, announced with a ♭ 3–2–1 cadential motion in the bass, asserts itself audaciously, and the insistence on "nadie la toma" (no one will take it) suggests a chin-up acceptance of sober reality.

Dominant pedals are less prominent in song 1 ("El paño moruno"), although added notes in mm. 16–23 simultaneously include the lowered second degree along

96. Christoforidis, "Folksong Models and Their Sources: Manuel de Falla's *Siete canciones populares españolas,*" *Context* 9 (1995): 14. Ronald Crichton observes that Berio's orchestra is the same as that of the 1925 version, *El amor brujo*, minus the piano. See Crichton, *Falla*, 29.

97. Sources and their publication information are given in Christoforidis, "Folksong Models." On page 14, Christoforidis notes Falla's use of "El zorongo" (Inzenga, 102) as a probable source for the last movement of *Noches en los jardines de España*. A pioneering study is Manuel García Matos, "Folklore en Falla, I," *Música* 2, nos. 3–4 (1953): 41–68; and "Folklore en Falla, II," *Música* 2, no. 6 (1953): 33–52.

Musical Example 9. Falla, *Siete canciones populares españolas*, "Seguidilla murciana," mm. 1–9. (Reprinted by kind permission of Ediciones Manuel de Falla)

with a raised and lowered third, variable notes in some flamenco scales (F♯G A A♯ D E as V in B minor). Another artful use of tension and resolution is in song 4, "Jota," the song with the most exuberant piano part. Poised on a dominant harmony, a full thirty-seven bars elapse before a resolution to the tonic (the fleeting E-major root-position I chord in m. 35 has no staying power) before finally arriving at a solitary E in the bass. In song 3 ("Asturiana"), on the other hand, a subdominant introduction (B♭ minor) abruptly shifts to the dominant in m. 7, giving the false relation between E♭ (mm. 2 and 4) and the singer's initial E♮ a jarring poignancy. Falla recalls these same gestures in that song's terse postlude, drawing on modal mixture for a luminous B♭-*major* chord and, again, a prominent E♮ (m. 37), now repeated against a tonic harmony without resolution, echoing the plaint of the dejected lover languishing in the shade of a weeping willow.[98]

Falla also uses motivic play to charming effect. In song 4 ("Jota") the motive E–D♯–E–C♯–B dominates the piano prelude, eventually gathering momentum with a sixteenth-note triplet (mm. 18–32) before showing up more discreetly in the bass in the thicker textured middle section (mm. 51–53 and 55–57; see also the parallel section mm. 109–11 and 113–15). It also serves as a hinge for the common-tone modulation to G major, that key having been anticipated in m. 34. Finally, it appears in canon (starting m. 125) but peters out so that the singer can address in a state of dreamy defiance the beloved's mother, the principal obstacle to the couple's happiness. As in several of the other songs, hemiola abounds in "Jota."

Although they are not customarily viewed as a song cycle, the *Siete canciones populares españolas* are usually performed as an integrated set. Perhaps this is because subtle narrative links unify the discrete numbers, several of which involve wry appraisals of infidelity. The Andalusian preoccupation with premarital virginity—for women—surfaces in the second strophe of song 1 ("El paño moruno"): the words "now [the Moorish cloth] sells for a lower price" burst out in the relative major (mm. 46–53), only to immediately revert to minor "because it has lost its value" (m. 53) before an eight-bar "¡Ay!" (one of Falla's few interpolations to the original source) clinches the matter. Song 2 ("Seguidillas murciana"), with its metaphor of the coin that "passes from hand to hand," embellishes the same topic more frantically, whereas the unprepared dissonances of song 3 ("Asturiana") suggest real despair. Song 4 ("Jota") offers a flash of hope in that an external obstacle, the young woman's mother, rather than innate fickleness, impedes true love. To be sure, song 5 (the lullaby "Nana") breaks the narrative of frustrated love. Yet with its hypnotic accompaniment and subtle exploitation of scant materials, it could perhaps be read as a dream of procreation with the beloved, however unrealistic. "Canción" returns abruptly to the uncertainties of romantic disillusionment; then, with the final song, "Polo," with its relentless repeated notes and pounding percussive effects, we descend into full-blown torment.[99]

A photograph taken around the time of *La vida breve*'s Paris premiere gives an idea of Falla's sense of well-being (see figure 4). In it, we see a diminutive but healthy man of thirty-seven with his customarily serious expression and calm, penetrating

---

98. *Pino verde* is a common term in Asturias for "weeping willow," information that was kindly provided by Alejandro Enrique Planchart.

99. As noted in chapter 2, the melody of "Un pastor lleva un pavo" is a minor-key version of "Canción." In fact, Falla vacillated between major and minor in composing "Canción." See Christoforidis, "Folksong Models," 16. In 1931, Encarnación López Júlvez (known as "La Argentinita"), accompanied by Lorca at the piano, recorded another version called "Romance pascual de los pelegrinos" (also known as "Los pelegrinitos"), a charming, multistrophic tale of two young pilgrims who marry in Rome with the Pope's blessing (*Colección de canciones populares españoles,* Sonifolk 20105).

Figure 4. Falla in Paris around the time of the premiere of *La vida breve* at the Opéra-Comique, December 1913. (Reprinted by kind permission of the Archivo Manuel de Falla)

eyes. Thanks to Eschig, he could finally enjoy financial stability and freedom from teaching and odd jobs, as his dapper attire attests. Though naturally reserved, he nonetheless liked socializing and discussing music with various friends and associates, especially now that his work was gaining recognition. In fact, he was so optimistic about his future in Paris that he even considered bringing his parents and sister to France (by then, Germán was in the French capital studying architecture). On 20 June 1914, he wrote Matos of his hope that his parents and María del Carmen would join him "not in Paris, but a healthy, quiet village, cheerful and picturesque, within an hour of the Gare Saint-Lazare."[100]

We may never know how seriously Falla and his family considered this hopeful plan. Eight days later, the Archduke Francis Ferdinand was assassinated by a Slav nationalist, and in a month Austria had declared war on Serbia. The elaborate complex of alliances and secret agreements crafted over the past three decades now unfolded in its terrible inevitability: in the first days of August, Germany supported Austria by declaring war on France, Russia backed Serbia, and Britain declared war on Germany on behalf of France. As evening fell in London on 4 August, the British foreign secretary, Sir Edward Gray, predicted in words as poetic as they were true that "the lamps are going out all over Europe; we shall not see them lit again in our lifetime."[101]

Suddenly Paris mobilized for war. We can get an idea of the prevailing mood from the Spanish novelist Vicente Blasco Ibáñez, whose 1923 novel *Los cuatro jinetes del apocalípsis* (The Four Horsemen of the Apocalypse), while not a historical document, compellingly describes "street cars, automobiles and cabs roll[ing] by with crazy velocity . . . the Reserves . . . donning old uniforms which presented all the difficulties of suits long ago forgotten" and "the clash of steel and the rhythm of clanking metal."[102] There were also the processions of various foreign legions, "saluting France in her hour of danger with hearty spontaneity."[103] Although Spain remained neutral during what would be known as the Great War, some Spaniards fought for France in legions such as these. Even Falla briefly contemplated volunteering.[104] But as there was still his family to support, brutal self-assessment may have persuaded him that his talents might be better employed in some nonmilitary capacity and he decided to return to Madrid. The exact date of his return is not known. On 9 August, after the exodus of foreigners from the Quai d'Orsay had begun, Falla was still in Paris. On that day, aware that his recent good fortune was

100. Letter, Falla to Matos, cited in de Persia, *Poesía*, 77.

101. Quoted in Birdsall S. Viault, *Modern European History* (New York: McGraw-Hill, 1990), 384.

102. Vicente Blasco Ibáñez, *The Four Horsemen of the Apocalypse*, translated by Charlotte Brewster Jordan (New York: Dutton, 1918), 151–52, 186–87.

103. Blasco Ibáñez, *The Four Horsemen of the Apocalypse*, 185.

104. Gallego, *El amor brujo*, 31.

dissolving around him, he wrote Matos and asked him to find him work, piddling if necessary, any "productive occupation, such as scribe, salesperson, clerk in an office or store . . . something that will enable me and my family to live."[105] By mid-August, foreigners were leaving Paris in droves, Falla among them.[106] Exiting proved complicated: a series of articles for the Madrid daily *ABC* noted that while on certain days trains were set aside for foreigners, at other times none were available.[107] The journey to the border, which included a stop in Bordeaux, lasted forty-two hours. In the crowded cars, passengers perched on their luggage in the aisles; Falla would have observed military trains filled with men, horses, and war materials passing ominously on parallel tracks. In San Sebastián, he had to take another train to Madrid to complete the long and disheartening journey. Whatever his regret at leaving Paris, however, it was surely with relief that he arrived home, where his parents and sister embraced him and war no longer swirled around him.

105. Letter, Falla to Matos, 9 August 1914, cited in Gallego, *El amor brujo*, 31n50.

106. This is according to a later report on an unrelated matter. See "Una ópera española: *La vida breve*," *ABC*, 14 November 1914, AMF press file.

107. These fascinating articles are by Juan José Cadenas, who was also a theatrical impresario. See his "Impresiones de París," *ABC*, 8 August 1914, 9–10; and "Impresiones de París: Dos jornadas," *ABC*, 9 August 1914, 11–12.

Chapter 4

In Neutral Spain

Even back home, the war made itself felt. From Madrid, Falla would have mourned the crushing Allied defeats at Charleroi and Mons and felt encouraged in early September when the Germans failed to take Paris in the battle of the Marne. Not all Spaniards shared his pro-French sentiments, however. Supporters of Germany (*germanófilos*) tended to be political conservatives, upper-class industrialists, military officers, and Carlists.[1] Much of the Spanish Catholic clergy also favored Germany, for despite a long tradition of anti-Protestant sentiment in Spain the Church preferred Lutheranism to the secularism of the French Third Republic.[2] Defenders of the Allies (*aliadófilos*) were mainly liberal intellectuals, members of the Republican Party, regionalist bourgeoisie (Catalans and Basques), and workers.[3]

1. Carlists were the traditionalist and ardently Catholic supporters of Don Carlos (brother of Ferdinand VII, r. 1808–33), the pretender to the throne, who denied the legitimacy of all subsequent Spanish monarchs. See Martin Blinkhorn, *Carlism and Crisis in Spain, 1931–1939* (Cambridge: Cambridge University Press, 1975).

2. Gerald H. Meaker, "A Civil War of Words: The Ideological Impact of the First World War on Spain, 1914–18," in *Neutral Europe between War and Revolution, 1917–23*, edited by Hans A. Schmitt (Charlottesville: University Press of Virginia, 1988), 12.

3. Carr, *Spain*, 499. On *aliadofilismo* and *germanofilismo* in Spanish literary circles, see Mainer, *La edad de plata*, 145–47.

FALLA AND THE "IDEALIZED FEMALE ARCHETYPE": *EL AMOR BRUJO*

Although Falla would eventually speak out on the war, first he had to reestablish himself in Madrid. His parents were now in their mid-sixties, and at thirty-one María del Carmen remained unmarried. Although Germán could be expected to contribute to the household, it was still important to act quickly. Luckily, the Teatro de la Zarzuela decided to mount *La vida breve* in November. That theater was presenting a series of Spanish lyric dramas: *Maruxa* by Vives, *Margot* by Turina, *La Culpa* (Guilt) by del Campo, and *Becqueriana*, by María Rodrigo, one of twentieth-century Spain's few women composers. Before the curtain went up on his opera, Falla gave two interviews, one with Fernando Herce of *La Mañana* and another with F. Martín Caballero of *El Noticiero Sevillano*. Since he was still convinced that the Real had cheated him out of a performance, neither interview minces words. The *La Mañana* interview, for example, has Falla "laughing deprecatingly" while explaining, "when I mentioned in Paris that to premiere a work by a Spanish composer in our foremost lyric theater, it was a liability if it weren't written in Italian, they couldn't believe it."[4] The composer also railed against the Real's "indifference, coldness, and slavish adherence to the rules." Critics, too, took his part. According to Luis Astrana Marín of *El Radical*, "the Real closed its doors to [Falla], as did all the venues in which absurd productions of *género chico* were ruling the roost . . . it seems that they had connived against premiering it. Falla realized that in Spain one wouldn't earn a peseta with serious art."[5]

Even as they bashed Spain's musical institutions, critics hailed the Madrid premiere of *La vida breve* precisely as a beacon for "serious art." Not only that, but it also offered tangible proof that Spanish opera was a perfectly viable concept, thus challenging skeptics who subscribed to the view of the distinguished critic Antonio Peña y Goñí (1846–96), who had argued that no legitimate national lyric art had ever been realized in Spain.[6] A. B. of *La Esfera* was especially convinced that *La vida breve* had achieved this long-awaited goal:

> All the conventionalities and all the routines . . . of Spanish lyric theater are
> now bravely excised . . . with all the resources of modern technique as a means
> for expressing sentiments, for depicting atmospheres and situations; and while
> realizing the work of art, luminous, intense, powerfully emotional, the music

4. "Cuando yo conté en París que para estrenar en nuestro primer teatro lírico una obra de un compositor español es un inconveniente el hecho de que no esté escrita en italiano, no lo querían creer." (Herce, "Ante el estreno de *La vida breve*").

5. "El Real le cerró sus puertas, y todos los coliseos, en los que predominaban las producciones absurdas del género chico . . . parece que se habían dado de mano para no estrenarla. Comprendió Falla que en España no ganaría una peseta con el arte serio" (Luis Astrana Marín, "*La vida breve*," *El Radical*, 14 November 1914, AMF press file).

6. See Pérez Castillo, "Spain: Art Music, Nineteenth Century," in Sadie and Tyrell, *Revised New Grove Dictionary*, 24:130.

does not depart except for the briefest of instants from the fixed agenda proposed: to make Spanish art, but without lending it a vain and ephemeral appearance of life by inserting and freely taking advantage of popular folklore, but rather by realizing something of a far superior merit, which is to . . . engender a genuine being, investing in it the entire spirit of a race.[7]

The anonymous critic for *ABC* also alluded to the difference between superficial folklorism and "the spirit of a race," labeling *La vida breve* as "purely Spanish" (castizamente española).[8] Still, although *La vida breve* was considered completely new, modernism was not its central concern, nor was the opera so "advanced" that the average listener was put off. In this vein, Astrana Marín noted only that the orchestration was "enriched with modern procedures," while Juan Fala referred to "exquisite and elegant modernism."[9] Fernando Herce expressed relief that it surpassed the efforts of many "unmelodic" contemporary composers, "unbearable and soporific virtuosos who, in exchange for providing us with an arduous and complicated instrumentation, don't even offer the slightest homeopathic dose of melody."[10] Resistance to undue complexity was evidently compatible with the "spirit of the race."

Yet we should not overlook the irony that the Spanish critics tended to apply to *La vida breve* the very labels foreigners have habitually attached to Spain, many of which are nowadays considered clichés. The reviewer for *La Época*, for example, held that *La vida breve* was "fierce, cruel and endlessly sweet, bitter and dreamy, heartrending, desolate . . . and mystical all at once: it's made with sun and sorrow, with love and death, which, thanks to I don't know what prodigy of bedeviled alchemy,

7. "Se extirpan ya, valientemente, todos los convencionalismos y todas las rutinas . . . de la escena lírica española . . . con todos los recursos de la técnica moderna como medio para la expresión de los sentimientos para la pintura de ambientes y de situaciones, y al realizar la obra de arte, luminosa, intensa, poderosamente emotiva, la música no se aparta, sino por brevísimos instantes, de la línea inflexible que se propuso: hacer arte español, pero no dándole una vana y efímera apariencia de vida, con la inserción y libre aprovechamiento del *folk-lore* popular, sino realizando algo de muy superior mérito, que es . . . engendrar un ser propio, poniendo en él el entero espíritu de una raza" (A. B. "Crónica teatral: Estreno de *La vida breve* en Madrid," *La Esfera*, n.d., AMF press file). The writer could be Luis Viladot, who wrote at least one *sainete*. See P. P. Rogers and F. A. Lapuente, *Diccionario de seudónimos literarios españoles, con algunas iniciales* (Madrid: Editorial Gredos, 1977), 36.

8. "Una ópera española: *La vida breve*," *ABC*.

9. Astrana Marín, "*La vida breve*"; Juan Fala, "Los estrenos de anoche: *La vida breve*," 15 November 1914, newspaper unidentified, AMF press file.

10. "Insoportables y soportíferos virtuosos que a cambio de facilitarnos una instrumentación árdua y complicada no nos sirven ni la más homeopática dósis de melodía" (Fernando Herce, "Crónicas madrileñas:" *La vida breve*, day unknown, November 1914, AMF press file).

is redolent of incense and smacks of fatality."[11] Another noted "languorous nights and blood-stained twilights."[12] Although these time-worn constructions—mysticism, fatalism, sensuality—have sometimes conferred upon Spanish scores the status of "glorified and tasteful picture-postcards" in the international community, clearly Madrid's critics were as prepared to link them to *La vida breve* as their foreign counterparts were.[13]

If the Madrid premiere confirmed Falla's ability to reconcile Spanish identity with modernist techniques (albeit less than radical ones), his next projects in dramatic music were not as successful. They were undertaken with María and Gregorio Martínez Sierra, whose 1913 visit to Falla's threadbare Paris apartment now probably seemed as if it had taken place aeons ago. Incidental music he composed for several of María's plays met with indifference, and the *gitanería*, or "gypsy ballet," *El amor brujo* (Love, the Magician) of 1915 occasioned bickering over the very question of Spanishness. The following pages consider all of Falla's collaborations with the Martínez Sierras except the pantomime *El corregidor y la molinera* (better known in its ballet version, *The Three-Cornered Hat*) and two unfinished works, which are addressed in chapter 5.

We may never know the exact distribution of literary labor between Gregorio and María. María herself was vague on this point: sometimes she claimed full authorship for certain works but later contradicted herself.[14] Nor have witnesses clarified the matter, for some maintain that her role was largely editorial while others credit her with every play Gregorio produced. The theater critic Pedro Gonzalo Blanco, for example, states:

> Gregorio Martínez Sierra never wrote anything that circulates under his name, whether novel, essay, poetry or theater. . . . This is something that . . . I know well. . . . Falla knew it—the directions for the ballets for *El sombrero de tres picos* and *El amor brujo* are by María. . . . But those who knew it best were the actors, who were always nervous when they left Madrid and especially when they were traveling around America: "The third act that Doña María has to send hasn't arrived yet, and we'll have to suspend the rehearsals." "I hear there's a cable from Doña María saying that she has mailed the play," etc.[15]

11. "Es bravía, cruel y dulcísima, áspera y soñadora, desgarrada, desolada . . . y mística a un tiempo: está hecha con sol y llanto, con amor y muerte, que merced a no sé qué prodigio de alquimia endemoniada, huele a incienso y sabe a fatalidad" ("Una ópera española: *La vida breve*," *La Época*, 14 November 1914, AMF press file).

12. Eduardo Muñoz, *El Imparcial*, cited in Demarquez, *Manuel de Falla*, 67.

13. Constant Lambert, *Music Ho! A Study of Music in Decline* (London: Faber and Faber, 1934) 170–71; cited in Hess, *Manuel de Falla and Modernism in Spain*, 1.

14. O'Connor, *Gregorio and María Martínez Sierra*, 54–55.

15. "Notas," n.d., n.p., cited and translated in O'Connor, *Gregorio and María Martínez Sierra*, 49. Similar contemporaneous accounts are on pages 45–51.

Much of Gregorio's correspondence, in which he prods María to "hurry up" and complete this work or that, confirms Gonzalo Blanco's account.[16] Yet a notarial document of 1930 is maddeningly unspecific, for it states only that all Gregorio's theatrical works were written "in collaboration" with María.[17] Her anonymity also had a personal dimension. She departed from the Spanish custom that a married woman will retain her family name (in her case, Lejárraga) and instead took Gregorio's, desiring that "the children of [their] intellectual union . . . not carry other than the father's name."[18] The strength of this "intellectual union" was sorely tested when Gregorio became romantically involved with his lead actress, Catalina Bárcena (for whom, incidentally, María wrote several compelling roles). Ever the optimist, María remained on friendly terms with Gregorio even after 1922, when he began living openly with Catalina. Falla, a firsthand witness to this arrangement, could hardly have approved of Gregorio's behavior. But he seems to have kept a discreet silence on "la Bárcena," probably in accordance with María's wishes.

Whatever her personal self-effacement, María was a crusader for women's rights. She published numerous essays on feminism—all under Gregorio's name—and later served the liberal Second Republic as a Socialist representative for Granada Province. Her plays also reflect this outlook.[19] Unlike the bored or passive society women of many sentimental dramas, María's protagonists confront pressing social issues. In *Cada uno y su vida* (To Each His Own) of 1919, a female medical student earns better grades than her male peers, a daring stance in a society in which "education" for women emphasized catechism and needlework.[20] The same can be said for Rosario, a married woman in *Sueño de una noche de agosto* (Dream of an August Night) of 1918, who, "tired of being a parasite," concludes that relations between the sexes are more gratifying when women develop skills beyond the domestic realm and achieve

16. O'Connor, *Gregorio and María Martínez Sierra*, 43; see also 61–64.

17. O'Connor, *Gregorio and María Martínez Sierra*, 60.

18. Other reasons have been given for this, including a desire to imitate English custom and the possibility that for personal reasons she wished to reject her family name. O'Connor, *Gregorio and María Martínez Sierra*, 52–53.

19. Her writings include *Cartas a las mujeres de España* (Madrid: Clásica Española, 1916); *Feminismo, feminidad, españolismo* (Madrid: Renacimiento, 1917); *Nuevas cartas a las mujeres* (Madrid: Ibero-Americana de Publicaciones, 1932); and *Cartas a las mujeres de América* (Buenos Aires: Renacimiento, 1941). She also published *La mujer española ante la República* (Madrid: Ediciones de Esfinge, 1931), a series of speeches she presented at the Madrid Athenaeum, under her own name. See O'Connor, *Gregorio and María Martínez Sierra*, 148–49. María's political career is treated in Rodrigo, *María Lejárraga*, 273–79.

20. Mary Nash, *Defying Male Civilization: Spanish Women in the Spanish Civil War*, Women and Modern Revolution (Denver: Arden, 1995), 17–23.

financial independence.[21] María's public, of course, knew a different world: the Civil and Penal Code stipulated that the wages of working women be controlled by their husbands and that a wife must secure her husband's permission to work.[22] This character type recurs so frequently in María's plays that Patricia O'Connor has dubbed it the "idealized female archetype." She also notes that María sought to persuade rather than shock her public: the typical Martínez Sierra heroine is "intelligent but not pedantic, independent but not rejecting, pretty but not vampish, positive but not domineering, strong but not overbearing."[23] This moderate tone probably accounts for the plays' ready acceptance in that patriarchal society.[24] Falla's best-known collaborations with the Martínez Sierras promoted this progressive yet tempered feminine ideal.

The first, *La pasión*, opened on 30 November 1914 at Madrid's Teatro Lara. Falla's music has never surfaced, nor do press reviews mention his name. The only eyewitness account of his participation is that of Gregorio's lover, Catalina Bárcena, who was to sing Falla's *soleá*, a mournful flamenco song. Lacking confidence in her vocal abilities, "la Bárcena" protested to the composer. He insisted she sing, offering a helpful tip: "The moment you feel you can't go on . . . just burst into tears."[25] Other incidental music for the Martínez Sierras included Falla's score for *Otelo, o Tragedia de una noche de verano* (Othello, or Tragedy of a Summer Night) from 1915, the same year as his score for *Amanecer* (Dawn). In the latter, a once frivolous debutante challenges social mores by assuming economic responsibility for her mother and siblings when the father abandons the family under a cloud of embezzlement charges. Falla's score has not survived, nor is it mentioned in reviews.[26]

Besides incidental music, Falla composed two solo songs with piano accompaniment on María's texts. In December, he finished "Oración de las madres que tienen a sus hijos en brazos" (Prayer of Mothers Who Hold Their Children in Their Arms). He subtitled it "Villancico" (Christmas Carol), perhaps with the sad reality of Christmas 1914 in mind. With its winding accompanimental lines, frequent tempo changes, and understated final resolution, "Oración" packs into a minia-

---

21. As O'Connor observes, Rosario's diatribe is practically identical to one of the addresses in María's cycle of five speeches given at the Madrid Athenaeum in 1931, later published under the title *La mujer española ante la República* (*Gregorio and María Martínez Sierra*, 127–130).

22. Nash, *Defying Male Civilization*, 16.

23. O'Connor, *Gregorio and María Martínez Sierra*, 122.

24. It also may account for the fact that María's writings are not universally praised by present-day feminist scholars. See Geraldine M. Scanlon, *La polémica feminista en la España contemporánea, 1868–1974*, translated by Rafael Mazarrasa (Madrid: Akal, 1986), 197–98, 262–63.

25. Valentín de Pedro, "Catalina Bárcena y Martínez Sierra recuerdan al Maestro Falla," *¡Aquí está!* 11, no. 1098 (1946), 3, cited in Gallego, *Catálogo*, 112.

26. An overview of *Amanecer*'s scant musical requirements is in Gallego, *Catálogo*, 115.

ture tripartite structure the anguish of a mother who prays that her son will not become a soldier. It premiered on 8 February at Madrid's Ritz Hotel on a concert that also included the *Siete canciones populares españolas* (introduced on 15 January 1915 at the Madrid Athenaeum), Turina's Piano Quintet in G Minor op. 1, various Granados works, and J. S. Bach's Concerto in C for Three Harpsichords and Orchestra, played on three pianos by Turina, Falla, and Miguel Salvador and conducted by Bartolomé Pérez Casas.[27] This was the inaugural concert of the Sociedad Nacional de Música (National Society for Music), an organization formed while Falla was still in Paris. Through it, Falla worked closely with Adolfo Salazar (1890–1958), the society's secretary between 1915 and 1922. Also a founding member of the Société Française de Musicologie, Salazar studied composition with Ravel and wrote several books. But he is best known as a newspaper critic, and his columns illuminate the events, aspirations, and frustrations of musical life in Spain before the Civil War, perhaps the richest period in twentieth-century Spanish music. He would early on become one of Falla's strongest allies in the composer's frequent brushes with the Madrid press.

Another song for voice and piano was "El pan de Ronda que sabe a verdad" (The Bread of Ronda is the Real Thing). María originally conceived it as part of a stage work, *Pascua florida* (Easter Sunday), which she began sketching in Cádiz. She and Falla had stopped there on a trip they took through Andalusia in the spring of 1915, presumably so that Falla could orchestrate *El amor brujo* far from the distractions of the capital.[28] On 27 March, María attended a concert of sacred music in Falla's native city and sketched the various acts of *Pascua florida* on the back of her program. Then she dedicated the fragment to "Maestro Falla, devotee of hoarding old papers." (This was certainly accurate: like many sufferers of scrupulosity, Falla saved everything from bus tickets to censorious reviews of his music.)[29] Of *Pascua florida*, only "El pan de Ronda que sabe a verdad" saw the light. A paean to life's simple pleasures, it praises the delicious bread baked in Ronda, a town about seventy-five kilometers northeast of Gibraltar. This delicacy, which María and Falla would munch while roaming the streets of small Andalusian towns, inspired her to jot down a few lines; these Falla set with the subtitle, "Canción andaluza." A far simpler affair than any of the *Siete canciones populares españolas*, "El pan de Ronda" contains repeated Phrygian seconds and the *seis con décima* formula, sometimes elaborated (mm. 5–6). It also exudes a slapdash quality and is therefore not one of Falla's more significant utterances. Still, he copied the song onto a parchment roll, which he tied with a silk

---

27. On the Athenaeum concert, see Gallego, *El amor brujo*, 31n53.

28. The song was not published until 1980, however. The most detailed account of the trip is in Gallego, *El amor brujo*, 17–20.

29. Concert program cited in Gallego, *El amor brujo*, 19n6. The information about bus tickets (!) was gleaned in a personal interview with Joaquín Nin-Culmell, January 2000. On hoarding and scrupulosity, see Ciarrocchi, *Doubting Disease*, 24.

ribbon and presented to María as a souvenir of their travels. Flattered ("why not admit it?" she later wrote), she displayed the copy in her home.[30]

Although Falla's traveling alone with a married woman might strike us as odd behavior for one so bound to Catholic morality, the friendship between Falla and María seems to have been purely platonic, whatever their fondness for private jokes or the intimate tone of their frequent correspondence (which at no point, incidentally, contains the intimate form of address, *tú*, but, as in the great majority of Falla's letters, relies on the more formal *usted*). Given María's pleasing appearance, wit, and competence—the similarity with her own heroines is obvious—Falla may even have been vaguely attracted to his collaborator (see figure 5). But María, though fond of Falla, commented more than once on his fussiness and "obsession" with sin. While such differences could be negotiated or even overlooked between friends, they would have quickly sabotaged any deeper involvement.

One of their stops was Granada, which, thanks to his friends' hastily mailed postcards, Falla had evoked in *La vida breve* but had never seen for himself. In her memoirs, María describes their visit to the Alhambra. Proposing that Falla close his eyes "until she advised him to open them," she led the composer by the hand through the Patio de los Arrayanes (Patio of the Myrtles) and then to the Palacio de Comares (Hall of the Ambassadors), with its magnificent dome, under which Boabdil, the last of the Moorish rulers, signed away his kingdom to Ferdinand and Isabella, the Catholic monarchs, in January 1492. Then María gave the word:

> He opened his eyes. I won't forget the "Ah!" that came out of his mouth. It was almost a cry. Simple admiration? The pleasure of having guessed through the pages of a book an enchantment previously unknown? . . . The rejoicing of the artificer for having succeeded in refining in rhythm and sound the marvel of the unknown? Perhaps all at once. I think that moment of total happiness— his cry left no room for doubt—was one of those ecstasies that compensated for the torment of his existence, diminished by so much small-mindedness and, at times, unnecessary fretting. . . . The emotion wouldn't let him feel anything else. And we returned home, leaving for another occasion the visit to the rest of the palace.[31]

For María, Falla's "ecstasy" was merely temporary relief from his customary "torment" and "unnecessary fretting." But how relevant, really, were fits of scrupulosity in that eloquent moment? After all, it was during this first visit to Granada that the charming city, with its winding streets, whitewashed walls, miniature gardens, Moorish echoes, and elegiac beauty first took hold of Falla. The visit to the Alhambra only confirmed his belief in perfection. As for María's tender game of blindman's bluff, it recalls poet F. A. de Icaza's immortal words, "There is no worse affliction

30. Martínez Sierra, *Gregorio y yo*, 133.
31. Martínez Sierra, *Gregorio y yo*, 135.

Figure 5. María Martínez Sierra. (Reprinted by kind permission of the Archivo Manuel de Falla)

than to be blind in Granada." That the tourist industry has emblazoned this phrase on ashtrays, keyrings, and other souvenirs in no way diminishes its aptness.

In Seville, Falla caught the train for Madrid, where he would attend the opening of *Amanecer* (7 April) and then the final rehearsals of *El amor brujo*, whose premiere was the following week. Both Falla and Gregorio Martínez Sierra sensed generalized curiosity about their latest project, although it was impossible to tell if *El amor brujo*'s uniqueness would work for or against them. Especially unusual was the presence of Pastora Imperio, a Seville-born gypsy then popular in Madrid's flamenco bars, who would "authentically" sing the principal female role.[32] Gregorio, who took full credit for the idea of transferring the popular idiom to the concert stage, declared to the Madrid daily *La Patria* that "the concept of *El amor brujo* was born in me . . . to see to what point the exceptional abilities of Pastora Imperio could reach

32. José Blas Vega believes that Pastora herself was only 50 percent gypsy. See his "Falla y el flamenco," *La Caña* 14–15 (fall–winter 1996): 11–14.

in a repertory until now new to her.[33] He added, however, that "maestro Falla, sharing with me the dramatic vision that we experienced together, has surpassed my idea by writing just the right music for that pantomime."[34] Was the idea for *El amor brujo* "born" in Gregorio? In Falla? In María? As usual, the breakdown between inspiration, labor, and end result is confused. What *is* clear, however, is that María's contribution was substantive. The literary scholar Antonina Rodrigo has argued in favor of her authorship on the basis of handwriting,[35] and Gallego, confirming the handwriting, rather cautiously describes María as "at least a coauthor."[36] Undoubtedly both Gregorio and Falla also volunteered their suggestions for the story line; thus, *El amor brujo* was "born" from the three-way brainstorming typical of Falla and the Martínez Sierras, a process that would later prove impossible to unravel in terms of both authors' rights and interpersonal rapport.

Not surprisingly, María's "idealized female archetype" takes center stage in *El amor brujo*. This time, however, she represents Spain's underclass. Like Salud of *La vida breve*, Candelas is a young gypsy woman in love with a philanderer. But unlike Salud, who dies helplessly at her lover's feet, Candelas exorcizes her unhealthy attachment and ultimately wins her lover's admiration. For a woman of María's social class, this challenge to the sexual double standard would have been atypical: in Spain at that time, no criminal charges could be leveled against a man who committed adultery unless he kept a mistress in his house, while women who had extramarital affairs were imprisoned from two to six years.[37] In Andalusia, with its ingrained cult of machismo, such plucky determination from an economically disadvantaged female would have been nearly unthinkable.[38] The musical idiom for Candelas's self-realization was flamenco, the voice of Andalusia's downtrodden and the artistic validity of which many in Falla's audience disputed.[39]

In his own way, Falla promoted *El amor brujo*. He told Rafael Benedito of *La Patria*, that Pastora, though musically illiterate, had learned her part with the ease of a "consummate solfègist." He also credited her with furnishing several musical ideas and helping to guide his compositional process in the "eminently gypsy" work,

33. Fernando Izquierdo, "En Lara, hablando con Martínez Sierra," *La Patria*, 14 April 1915, cited in Gallego, *El amor brujo*, 38–39.

34. Gallego, *El amor brujo*, 38.

35. Rodrigo, *María Lejárraga*, 164.

36. Antonio Gallego, *Conciertos de inauguración: Archivo Manuel de Falla* (Granada: Archivo Manuel de Falla, 1991), 120.

37. Nash, *Defying Male Civilization*, 16.

38. Timothy Mitchell, *Passional Culture: Emotion, Religion, and Society in Southern Spain* (Philadelphia: University of Pennsylvania Press, 1990), 36–37. See also Stanley Brandes, *Metaphors of Masculinity: Sex and Status in Andalusian Folklore* (Philadelphia: University of Pennsylvania Press, 1980), esp. 87–92.

39. Timothy Mitchell, *Flamenco Deep Song* (New Haven and London: Yale University Press, 1994), 160–77.

"the authenticity of whose [melodic] ideas no one could deny."[40] Energetically defending the idea that the musical language of Spain's underclass was compatible with the more rarefied world of lyric theater, Falla even ventured to assert his kinship with that very underclass, declaring that with *El amor brujo* he had "tried to live it" as if "a gypsy himself . . . employing only those elements [he believed] to express the soul of the race."[41] Although Falla's assertions verge on the hyperbolic (at least as they appear in Benedito's account), they are not insincere, for he greatly respected gypsy music. Still, we should note that more than half the music of *El amor brujo* has little to do with genuine flamenco sources.[42]

Indeed, was it really possible to express "the soul of the race" in what is essentially a concert work? The following synopsis illuminates *El amor brujo*'s hybrid nature. We first encounter Candelas's struggle against obsession in the *fuego fatuo* (will-o'-the-wisp) theme. Presented in the introduction, its persistently recurring E, embellished by upper and lower neighbor notes, will punctuate the work (see musical example 10). The lower strings then enter with a persistent tremolo at the interval of a tritone (m. 24), and terse, unevenly spaced melodic fragments surface in the brass, one of which (mm. 35–39) will later be linked to Candelas's moral victory. Then the curtain rises on a gypsy cave in Cádiz, where several women are consulting the cards, as in act 3 of Bizet's *Carmen*. The depiction of this exclusively female activity is redolent of Andalusian fatalism in that the *echadora* (the reader of the cards) seeks only to know God's will, which is impossible to change.[43] Accordingly, the women in *El amor brujo* observe the sea, which "says nothing, neither good nor bad," but "makes a noise because it is moved by the wind: like the damned, it talks

Musical Example 10. Falla, *El amor brujo*, "Introduction," mm. 1–4. (Chester Music Ltd. International copyright secured. All rights reserved. Reprinted by permission.)

40. Rafael Benedito, "En Lara, *El amor brujo*, hablando con Manuel de Falla," *La Patria*, 15 April 1915, cited in Gallego, *Conciertos de inauguración*, 131–32.

41. Gallego, *Conciertos de inauguración*, 132.

42. Blas Vega, "Falla y el flamenco," 11–14.

43. Mitchell, *Passional Culture*, 36. See also Emma Díaz Martín, "Las echadoras de cartas en la provincia de Cádiz: Una actividad femenina marginal," in *Antropología cultural de Andalucía*, edited by S. Rodríguez Becerra (Seville: Consejería de Cultura de la Junta de Andalucía, 1984), 324.

without leave from God."⁴⁴ A supple, stepwise melody in the oboe on V of C (re-hearsal 2) offers a brief ray of light. This transitory hope, however, abruptly yields to despair via the 5–♭6 motion in the bass that introduces Candelas's first solo, the savage "Canción del amor dolido" (Song of a Broken Heart).

In this, the score's first strong point of harmonic arrival, Candelas declares that she doesn't know "what [she feels], nor what is happening to [her]" since "that damned gypsy" abandoned her. As she discharges her emotions, her spirits plum-met, for María's stage directions indicate that each stanza be sung with a specific emotion (pain, dread, anger, anguish, bitterness, delirium), culminating in mad-ness (*locura*). Unlike Lucia ("di Lammermoor"), who loses her mind at the conclu-sion of Donizetti's opera, the threat of mental deterioration assaults Candelas from the outset, reinforced by the obstinate pedals, the circling of the oboe around C, and intermittent hemiolas (as in mm. 3–4).⁴⁵ As her final, desperate "¡Ay!" fades, the clock strikes midnight via a D-major chord colored with C♯ and G♯. Throwing incense on the fire's dying embers, the women pray to the Virgin Mary as Candelas prepares to dance the "Danza del fin del día" (Dance for the End of the Day), later known as the "Danza ritual del fuego" (Ritual Fire Dance).⁴⁶ Appealing to the di-vine power of incense, she cries, "Holy incense! . . . Cast out the evil and bring in the good!"⁴⁷ But what "good" does Candelas seek? The Virgin's indifference to sexual desire? Courage to stand up to her wayward lover? Driving *pizzicati* in the violas suggest that Candelas is mesmerized by her own uncertainty.

The same *pizzicati* prod her into the "Ritual Fire Dance." This earliest incarna-tion of what would become Falla's most popular work accompanies Candelas's ini-tial attempt at exorcism. An introductory twenty-four-bar pedal on E, embellished with upper-neighbor motion and enhanced with an E♮/E♭ false relation in the piano at mm. 16–17, recalls the E-based *fuego fatuo* motive of the introduction. Spat out here in a rapid trill, it punctuates the three sections of the dance (introduction, A, and B), suggesting that Candelas has yet to liberate herself from love's stranglehold. Finally, a twenty-nine-bar coda vigorously asserts E major, marshaling repeated E-major scalar flourishes now stripped of Phrygian inflection, 2–5–1 motion in the bass (mm. 236–37), followed by relentlessly reiterated E-major chords (see musical example 11). Throughout, Candelas dances wildly to banish all thought of her demon lover. But in the final two measures, E major, pounded out so mercilessly and for

---

44. Translations are taken from Antonio Gallego, ed., *Manuel de Falla, El amor brujo, 1915 Version* (London: Chester Music, n.d.); see also Gallego, *Conciertos de inauguración,* 144–62.

45. See Catherine Clément, *Opera, or the Undoing of Women,* translated by Betsy Wing (Minneapolis: University of Minnesota Press, 1988). *Lucia di Lammermoor* is interpreted on pages 88–91.

46. Gallego, *El amor brujo,* 120.

47. "¡Incienso santo! ¡Incienso nuevo! ¡Sarga la malo y entre lo bueno!" Gallego, *El amor brujo,* 189. Spelling irregularities convey nonstandard Spanish.

Musical Example 11. (above and overleaf) Falla, *El amor brujo*, "Ritual Fire Dance," mm. 249–261. (Chester Music Ltd. International copyright secured. All rights reserved. Reprinted by permission.)

so many bars, unexpectedly reveals itself not as a tonic but as a dominant. Its resolution to an A-minor root position chord, never previously established as a tonal center, thus conveys little more than limp exhaustion.

Other highlights include "El romance del pescador" (The Tale of the Fisherman), in which Candelas narrates the story of a traveler mourning unrequited love. The river, from which the fisherman is "pluck[ing] little fishes," counsels the forlorn wanderer to visit a witch's cave, where magical solutions lie. Unlike the flashy "Ritual

Fire Dance," this understated number relies on utter simplicity of texture, melodic ideas, form, harmony, and phrase structure. In addition, it ends with a delicate but definite authentic cadence (V7–I in F), in contrast to the unconvincing conclusion of the "Ritual Fire Dance." In this discreet way, Candelas commences her inner transformation, and the rest of the drama is the inevitable consequence of this quiet resolve. No longer willing to be her man's victim (though not yet fully independent), Candelas repairs to the witch's mountain cave. It is empty but for the will-o'-the-wisp, who doggedly pursues her, accompanied by *tremolo* and *glissandi* in the piano (part 2, Introduction). A bitonal sonority (E minor/F♯ major, mm. 8–10) yields to the repeated-note cornet theme (m. 12–18), which in turn blossoms into the "Danza del fuego fatuo" (Dance of the Will-o'-the-Wisp), the weight and substance of which balance the earlier "Ritual Fire Dance." This leads to Candelas's second vocal solo, the "Canción del fuego fatuo" (Song of the Will-o'-the-Wisp), which compares the ironies of love to the elusive creature now taunting her in the darkened cave: love is "just like the will-o'-the-wisp. . . . You flee from it and it pursues you, you call it and it runs away." The rigid verse structure involves three repetitions of an *aaba* verse, each separated by a ritornello and containing the familiar *seis con décima* (see musical example 12). This unflinching musical structure projects stoicism and distancing even in the sultry second verse, which describes the stirrings of love ("born in August nights when the heat bears down"). As the will-o'-the-wisp abruptly vanishes, Candelas exults "the cave is mine!" and in a throaty recitative declares, "By Satan! By Barrabas! I want the man who forgot me to come for me!" to introduce the "Conjuro para reconquistar el amor perdido" (Spell to Recapture Lost Love). The piano descends to a low rumble via a whole-tone scale, and Candelas's lover, known in the scenario only as "the Gypsy," emerges from the shadows.

Faced with his physical presence and accompanied by a gently swaying 7/8 *guajira* (that Cuban dance normally involves alteration of 3/4 and 6/8), Candelas begins to "dance around [her lover] to seduce him."[48] Not only does he fail to recognize her in the half-light, but her come-on turns out to be a ruse, for the *guajira*, itself evocative of dance-salon music, leads to the "Danza y juego de la bruja fingida" (Dance and Game of the Make-Believe Witch), Candelas's denunciation and the climax of the entire score. *Pizzicato* strings and a *tremolo* in the piano begin. Then the newly liberated woman holds forth:

> You are the evil gypsy that a girl once loved.
> You didn't deserve the love that she gave you!

In short, Candelas assumes the power of the absent witch from whom she sought help in the cave's dark recesses. Of course, the implements of magic and the means to use them had always been within her. Now a tower of strength, she intones:

> Don't come close, don't touch me, for I'm an out-and-out witch!
> And whoever tries to touch my arm will be burned!

Only when the young man hears Candelas laugh—at his discomfiture—does he recognize her. Dazzled by her magnificence, he asks her pardon, but she only gazes into the breaking day. In the finale, "Las campanas de amanecer"(The Bells of Dawn), repeated open fourths and fifths suggest the unreserved pealing of bells; mesmerizing pedal tones follow. Candelas proclaims the dawn and the advent of her "glory,"

---

48. The *guajira* theme was originally part of a projected fourth movement of *Noches en los jardines de España* (*Nocturnos*), a tangolike movement called "Cádiz" (Gallego, *El amor brujo*, 30).

Musical Example 12. Falla, *El amor brujo*, "Canción del fuego fatuo,"
mm. 51–53. (Chester Music Ltd. International copyright secured.
All rights reserved. Reprinted by permission.)

rounding off her final phrase with a telling reworking of the *guajira* music: if moments earlier its metrical sinuousness bespoke her powers of seduction, in the finale it heralds her newfound resolve in an unwavering 4/4 meter. This decidedly nonexotic conclusion to an *andalucista* work confirms that Candelas, like all of María's female characters, has both feet firmly on the ground.

A score that combined impressionistic harmonies, symphonic string writing, dance music, motives of reminiscence, and flamenco riffs proved too much for many of Madrid's critics, however.[49] Most problematic was the proximity of "low" and "high" art. Although some admired Falla's efforts to raise flamenco to the level of art music, others found nothing but incompatibility in *El amor brujo*'s diverse elements, believing that Pastora was out of her depth.[50] Others attacked its stylistic eclecticism as insufficiently "Spanish," a deficiency attributable to Falla's "obsession" with the modern Russian and French schools. At least that was the explanation given by "Tristan" of *El Imparcial,* who priggishly observed that "one cannot compose Spanish music while thinking of Debussy and Ravel."[51] No one seemed to notice the following inconsistency: critics found *La vida breve,* with its obvious debts to Leoncavallo and Wagner, appropriately Spanish, whereas *El amor brujo,* in which Falla confronted the flamenco idiom in a far more thoroughgoing way, was attacked as "foreign." The reasonably healthy run of twenty-eight performances confirms that *El amor brujo* enjoyed some popular success, however.

Taking some of these reactions to heart, over the next ten years Falla adjusted *El amor brujo*'s structure, pacing, and plot. Before finally completing the definitive ballet version (discussed in chapter 6), he composed two concert versions, one for full orchestra (1915–16) and one for chamber orchestra (1917).[52] He also arranged the "Intermedio" and "Ritual Fire Dance" for sextet (strings and piano); the latter also appeared in an arrangement for organ (1921) by Richard Ellsasser and for cello and piano (1938) by Grigor Piatigorsky. There were also solo piano versions of the same by Falla himself and arrangements for piano four hands and two pianos.[53]

That the "Ritual Fire Dance" became a pianistic tour de force is due principally to Artur Rubinstein. The Polish pianist played frequently in Spain during World War I and was so popular there that Alfonso XIII's personal secretary gave him a Spanish passport and safe conduct.[54] In his memoir *My Young Years,* Rubinstein describes his introduction to the "Ritual Fire Dance" one evening in Madrid (the year is not given). He recalls going with Falla to see Pastora Imperio in *El amor brujo:* "It was given late at night in a theater after the regular play. . . . The music was performed by five or

49. See Mitchell on the "artificiality of orchestrated allegedly gypsy superstitions" (*Flamenco Deep Song,* 164). The small ensemble for the 1915 version, which consisted of flute doubling on piccolo, oboe, French horn, B♭ cornet, tubular bells, strings, and piano, was less "symphonic" than the definitive version of 1925, with its expanded orchestra.

50. The mixed reception to *El amor brujo* is discussed in Hess, *Manuel de Falla and Modernism in Spain,* 57–59.

51. The lawyer Santiago Arimón wrote for the Madrid daily *El Imparcial* under the pseudonym Tristan. See Ángel Sagardía, "A torno a Manuel de Falla y al crítico Santiago Arimón, Tristan," *Radio Nacional,* September 1934, AMF press file.

52. On 28 March 1916, the concert version was performed by the Sociedad Nacional de Música at the Hotel Ritz, Madrid, with the Orquesta Filarmónica under the direction of Enrique Fernández Arbós. Additional versions are described in Gallego, *El amor brujo,* 141.

53. Gallego, *Catálogo,* 217–21.

54. Julián Cortes-Cavanillas, *Alfonso XIII y la guerra del 14* (Madrid: Alce, 1976), 190–92.

six players, the usual ensemble one hears at nightclubs; the pianist played on an upright piano."[55] Despite his claims of an "elephant's memory," Rubinstein's account leaves several questions unanswered. He could not be describing the initial run of *El amor brujo*, since he was not in Spain between 15 April and 5 May, when the first performances took place.[56] Nor is the ensemble of "five or six players" consistent with the orchestration of the 1915 version. (If Rubinstein were referring to the concert performance of 28 March 1916 at Madrid's Hotel Ritz—he could have heard it, since he played Saint-Saëns's Piano Concerto in G Minor with Madrid's Orquesta Sinfónica on the twenty-seventh—his description of the nightclub setting is inconsistent.)[57] Perhaps he is referring to the sextet version, which may have figured in Pastora's informal performances in her various Madrid haunts.[58] Another layer of mystery is added by the fact that Pastora Imperio is not listed in the Madrid press's *cartelera* (entertainment schedule) during April 1916.

Whatever his introduction to the "Ritual Fire Dance," Rubinstein was soon programming it to wild acclaim. His first recording was a piano roll, which he made in March 1922.[59] As for 78 rpm discs, he initially resisted that technology, maintaining that the piano always sounded "like a banjo." In January 1929, however, he spent a day at the Gramophone Company of London, where he recorded several pieces twice each, once on a Steinway and once on a Blüthner. Among them was the "Ritual Fire Dance," which he recorded only on the Steinway.[60] On 24 January 1929, he wrote Falla of his wish to record the "Ritual Fire Dance" and the "Dance of Terror" at that firm's London studio—even though he had just done precisely that, as Harvey Sachs observes. Rubinstein assured Falla that his rights would be honored.[61] He made three more recordings, each with its own integrity.[62] There is the sultry shaping of the melodic line in the 1922 version, for example, the driving intensity in 1947, and Olympian grandeur in 1961; in all, Rubinstein judiciously adds small amounts of "filler" and occasional octave doublings, enhancing Falla's rather spartan arrange-

55. Artur Rubinstein, *My Young Years* (New York: Knopf, 1973), 472.

56. Rubinstein first played in Spain in August 1915, when he performed Brahms's Concerto no. 1 in D Minor in San Sebastián under Enrique Fernández Arbós. See *Rubinstein y España: Exposición homenaje a Arturo Rubinstein* (Madrid: Turner, 1988), 164.

57. Nor could he have attended a performance of the concert version of *El amor brujo* on 29 April 1917 at the Teatro Real, since he was in Barcelona at that time. *Rubinstein y España*, 165.

58. Gallego, *Catálogo*, 122.

59. It was rereleased on *The Young Artur Rubinstein, 1919–1924*, Klavier KCD–11101.

60. Harvey Sachs, *Rubinstein: A Life* (New York: Grove, 1995), 226.

61. Letter, Rubinstein to Falla, 24 January 1929, AMF correspondence file 7543; see also Sachs, *Rubinstein*, 170.

62. Volumes 2, 18, and 70 of the *Rubinstein Collection*. RCA Red Seal, 09026–630002–2, and 09026–63018–2, and 09026–63070–2.

ment.[63] Besides these sound recordings, Rubinstein performed the "Ritual Fire Dance" in the 1947 movie *Carnegie Hall*, discussed in chapter 9.

Eventually, however, Rubinstein began to consider the "Ritual Fire Dance" a liability. In an interview conducted around 1960, he explained:

> I still now have to live to a great extent on the "Fire Dance" of Falla, which I made into a piano piece on one unfortunate night in Spain. . . . You know, if I hadn't repeated it [in Madrid] for the third time I might have been killed. The audience wouldn't let me go. They shrieked and yelled. I was unwilling to play three times the same piece, but they wouldn't let me off. Then I discovered that that was a piece which absolutely fascinated all the audiences of the world, including Chinese, Japanese, wherever you can imagine. I think when the moon will be open for concerts I will play right away the "Fire Dance" and I might get away with it.[64]

The "Ritual Fire Dance" syndrome, if it can be so described, thus resembles the craze for Paderewski's Minuet in G Major, a work he reportedly came to loathe, or Rachmaninoff's Prelude in C♯ Minor op. 3 no. 2, of which its creator so wearied that he once refused to play it to a reverently expectant audience of "Flatbush 'flappers.'"[65] As we shall see, the "Ritual Fire Dance" syndrome continued well after Falla's death, and its trajectory often challenged the ephemeral divide between "high" and "low" art, just as the 1915 Madrid premiere of *El amor brujo* had done.

ECLECTICISM AND THE "PROGRESS OF SOCIETY"

The mixed reaction to *El amor brujo* aside, Falla's fortunes in his native country were improving. So was artistic life in Spain: as the Great War was devastating Central Europe, Madrid enjoyed a revitalized international profile as the capital of a neutral state. It also became a haven for war-weary artists and musicians.[66] Some, like Rubinstein, had difficulty booking engagements in greater Europe. Others, like Stravinsky, who visited Madrid and Seville in spring 1916, came out of curiosity and to promote their works. There were also Florent Schmitt, Vincent d'Indy, the French pianist Blanche Selva, and others, such as Diaghilev and his Ballets Russes, who so dazzled the Spanish public in 1916 and 1917.

63. Rubinstein's claim that he asked Falla if he could arrange the "Ritual Fire Dance" for piano solo is also misleading, since his recordings stray relatively little from Falla's arrangement, which, as noted, appeared in 1915 and was reissued in 1920.

64. Unidentified transcript found in the Rubinstein family archives, probably by a journalist for the Canadian Broadcasting Company (CBC), cited in Sachs, *Rubinstein*, 157.

65. Harold C. Schonberg, *The Great Pianists* (New York: Simon and Schuster, 1963), 370; on Rachmaninoff, James Huneker is cited on 374.

66. See Hess, *Manuel de Falla and Modernism in Spain*, 45–59.

One meeting ground for Spaniards and international visitors was Madrid's Residencia de Estudiantes (Students' Residence), founded in 1910. Modeled after the residential colleges of Oxford and Cambridge (and tastefully restored in recent years), the "Resi" attracted some of the best minds in pre–Civil War Spain.[67] Student boarders, including Salvador Dalí, Luis Buñuel, and Federico García Lorca, enjoyed a fine library with generous browsing and lending privileges, an unprecedented situation in Spanish libraries, where librarians were likelier to equate a simple request to peruse the catalog with a desire to see "the Mystery of the Stigmata or . . . a demonstration of the Seven Deadly Sins."[68] At least, that had been the experience of the British Hispanist John B. Trend, who lectured at the Resi and published the first substantive English-language biography of Falla.[69] Other foreign visitors included Henri Bergson, H. G. Wells, Albert Einstein, G. K. Chesterton, Marie Curie, Paul Valéry, Le Corbusier, Walter Gropius, Paul Claudel, and John Maynard Keynes. Music was also important at the Resi, from Lorca's spontaneous performances at the piano (he often accompanied himself while singing his folk song arrangements) to formal recitals by Landowska, Milhaud, Stravinsky, Poulenc, Ravel, and Segovia. Spanish composers Ernesto and Rodolfo Halffter, Oscar Esplá, Gustavo Pittaluga, Jesús Bal y Gay, and of course Falla all tested new works, and music critics such as Olin Downes of the *New York Times* and Adolfo Salazar of *El Sol* lectured on the latest trends.[70]

Salazar's journalistic stature reminds us how much the press had expanded during Falla's absence. *El Sol* was established in 1917 by Ortega y Gasset; that he was able to found not only that daily but several other publications, including the prestigious *Revista de Occidente*, was due both to family connections and to the fact that from around 1910 the Restoration government began easing its censorship laws.[71] Within a few years, an impressive number of daily newspapers, in which political persuasions and aesthetic sensibilities sometimes merged, was available to a variety

67. Gibson, *Federico García Lorca*, 78–83. A memoir by Alberto Jiménez-Fraud, founder of the Residencia, is in "The 'Residencia de Estudiantes,'" *Texas Quarterly* 4 (1961): 48–54. See also Manuel Fernández-Montesinos, *Federico García Lorca en la Residencia de Estudiantes* (Madrid: Fundación Federico García Lorca, Amigos de la Residencia de los Estudiantes, 1991).

68. John Brande Trend, *A Picture of Modern Spain* (London: Constable, 1921), 38.

69. Trend, *Manuel de Falla and Spanish Music*. Trend discusses the Residencia in *A Picture of Modern Spain*, 33–44.

70. Alfredo Valverde, "Música en la Residencia de Estudiantes: Federico García Lorca," *Tutti música* 3, no. 7 (1998): 11–13; Gilbert Chase, *The Music of Spain*, 2d rev. ed. (New York: Dover, 1959), 198–207; Jesús Bal y Gay, "La música en la Residencia," *Residencia* (Mexico City), December 1963, 77–80.

71. Gray, *Imperative of Modernity*, 107–8.

of readerships.[72] Music criticism also took on new life, with Julio Gómez of *El Liberal*, Víctor Espinós of *La Época*, and Matilde Muñoz of *El Imparcial* (apparently the only female music critic in pre–Civil War Spain) holding forth on performances, personalities, and occasionally musical politics.[73]

Still, Falla sometimes felt compelled to get away from Madrid. For years, he had been frustrated by its musical intrigues, and now he was beginning to crave silence and a gentler pace. On 28 June 1915, he traveled to Sitges, the Mediterranean fishing village south of Barcelona that for decades had doubled as an artists' colony. Between 1892 and 1899, for example, Sitges hosted the Festes modernistes (Modernist Festivals), a series of exhibitions and musical performances.[74] It was also the base of operations for Santiago Rusiñol, who welcomed fellow artists to his house, the Cau Ferrat (Den of Iron), a fantastic jumble of ironwork, tile, and art treasures.

Overlooking the sea at the Cau Ferrat's upright piano, Falla orchestrated *Noches en los jardines de España*, which Rusiñol's own paintings had inspired six years earlier. By now, of course, Falla had also been stimulated by his visit to the Alhambra; in fact, the first of *Noches*'s three movements refers directly to the Alhambra's sister palace, the Generalife ("En el Generalife"). With their impressionistic titles, the movements correspond only loosely to traditional concerto form, although some traces of time-honored procedures remain. Listeners will probably hear the theme at rehearsal 10 (movement 1) as a "second group," for example, and rehearsal 20 as akin to a recapitulation. (Demarquez favors categorizing the latter as "a re-exposition, if such pedantry were in keeping with such enchantment.")[75] The second movement, "Danza lejana" (Distant Dance), is a *fête galante*, with fleeting snatches of melodies and continual play of light and shadow, while the third, "En los jardines de la Sierra de Córdoba" (In the Gardens of the Sierra de Córdoba), which recalls the coexistence of Christian and Moorish cultures in that province, alludes to rondo form. Both movements, though less weighty than "En el Generalife," equal it in coloristic range and sensual beauty.

Noches is anything but a solo concerto. The piano part, although prominent, is often cast as one more orchestral voice, as an additional thread in Falla's tapestry of arresting colors. Although the piano rarely announces themes not stated elsewhere

72. By the 1930s, there were over 2,000 newspapers in Spain. John A. Crow, *Spain: The Root and the Flower*, 3d ed. (Berkeley: University of California Press, 1985), 409. See also Henry F. Schulte, *The Spanish Press, 1470–1966* (Urbana, Chicago, and London: University of Illinois Press, 1968).

73. A detailed and comprehensive overview of the Spanish musical press is Jacinto Torres Mulas, *Las publicaciones periódicas musicales en España (1812–1990): Estudio crítico/ bibliográfico, repertorio general* (Madrid: Instituto de Bibliografía Musical, 1991).

74. J. F. Ràfols, *Modernisme i modernistes* (Barcelona: Edicions Destino, 1982), 52–68. An overview of the *Festes modernistes* is given in Hess, *Enrique Granados*, 181–82.

75. Demarquez, *Manuel de Falla*, 88.

in the orchestra, it offers what other instruments cannot, such as crystalline textures reminiscent of Ravel's *Jeux d'eaux* (movement 1, rehearsals 3 and 17) or an imitation of *punteado* guitar (movement I, rehearsal 20). The piano aptly imitates the vocal freedom of *cante jondo* style, as in the *fioritura* writing (e.g., in movement 3, rehearsal 28), which pianists variously interpret as mellifluous (Clara Haskill) or "punchy" (Robert Cassedesus).

Insofar as *Noches* mirrors the play of water, light, and shade in the "gardens of Spain" it also pays tribute to the French music Falla so admired. Often his coloristic palette simply celebrates beauty for its own sake: the muted trumpets in movement 1 (before rehearsal 19) or the violas' dark swirls that open movement 2 are two spots that leap to mind. Elsewhere, color changes enhance the formal design, as in the canonic dialogue between the piano and other part-time soloists (violin 1, viola, and cello after rehearsal 17) or the *attacca* into movement 3. In that superbly balanced transition, the listener is assaulted with a rush of sensations, from the finely traced harmonies in the celesta, flute, and piccolo (movement 2, rehearsal 21) to the answer by the English horn and muted trumpet, against tremolo strings and a spooky cymbal roll over a persistent B♭. The moment of transition occurs when, having traversed several registers, the B♭ slides abruptly to A♮, a relationship immediately taken up by the piano. The rocking half step A♮–B♭, the quintessential flamenco interval, then explodes into the furious "En los jardines de la Sierra de Córdoba" (see musical example 13).

This seamless quality, especially noteworthy in the first movement, is attributable to the close relationships among many of the principal themes. Melodies tend to be narrow in range, often no more than a third. Several examples are given in musical examples 14a, 14b, 14c. As a result, trying to determine what is derived and what is new often proves fruitless. Can we consider the section at rehearsal 16 (movement 1) as "new," given its intervallic content? Surprisingly—and fleetingly—the discreet minor seconds of the principal theme ultimately explode into a blatant quotation of the theme from the prelude to *Tristan und Isolde* (two measures before rehearsal 24, movement 1). Instead of the "false sublimity [and] false profundity" of the "Tristan" chord (to extrapolate from Koechlin's review of *La vida breve*), Falla follows the motive with an impressionistic A♭ 9th chord, *fff*, marking the climax of movement 1. Falla's rich harmonic language also embraces quintal chords (in the misty opening of movement 1), whole-tone and nearly whole-tone chords (rehearsal 13, movement 1), and added-note chords, which enhance the great sigh between rehearsals 15 and 16, movement 1, in which G major slips to A♭ minor (with added sixth F) over dynamic swells. In short, *Noches* is Falla's most extended tribute to Debussy, Dukas, Ravel, and the other French colleagues toward whom he felt such empathy, especially in the difficult days of 1916.

In a third-person statement of the same year, Falla described *Noches* as sensory and pictorial ("impressionistic") rather than programmatic:

Musical Example 13. (above through page 96) Falla, *Noches en los jardines de España*, transition into movement 3, "En los jardines de la Sierra de Córdoba." (Reprinted by kind permission of Ediciones Manuel de Falla)

The author of these symphonic impressions for piano and orchestra thinks that . . . merely stating their titles should provide an adequate listening guide. Although in this work—as should occur in all those that legitimately aspire to be musical—the composer has followed a predetermined plan from a tonal, rhythmic, and thematic point of view, a detailed analysis of its purely musical structure could perhaps digress from the purpose for which it was written, which is none other than to evoke places, sensations, and sentiments.[76]

76. "Piensa el autor de estas impresiones sinfónicas para piano y orquesta que . . . la sola enunciación de sus títulos debería constituir una guía suficiente para la audición. Aunque en esta obra—como debe ocurrir con todas las que legítimamente aspiren a ser musicales—el autor haya seguido un plan determinado desde el punto de vista tonal, rítmico y temático, un análisis detallado de su estructura puramente musical podría quizás desviar del fin para que fue escrita, fin que no es otro que el de evocar lugares, sensaciones y sentimientos" (program notes for the premiere of *Noches*, 9 April 1916, believed to be by Falla, cited in Nommick, *Jardines de España*, 17).

Yet *Noches* is retrospective and anticipatory at the same time. Certainly its debt to impressionism, then on the verge of losing ground in Europe, is unmistakable—and not just because the composer called attention to "sensations." But Falla's casting of the piano as one more element in the ensemble also looks forward to the 1920s, when, eschewing waves of impressionistic color, he would explore a drier, more astringent sound world in the work for harpsichord and five instruments he called "Concerto," however much he intended its modestly nonvirtuosic keyboard part as one more voice in the ensemble.[77]

On 22 July, Falla left Sitges for Barcelona, staying first at the Palace Hotel and then with the Martínez Sierras, who were in the Catalan capital and with whom he

77. This is elaborated upon in Yvan Nommick, "Un ejemplo de ambigüedad formal: El *Allegro* del *Concierto* de Manuel de Falla," *Revista de Musicología* 21, no. 1 (1998): 2n3.

would remain until the end of the year.[78] As a houseguest, Falla was rather a handful. María recalls his childlike ways:

> In the mornings, we would act out on a daily basis a bit of tragicomedy. I, who have always interpreted my role as housewife with playful gratification, have consistently taken pains to insure that our table be as well appointed as our means have permitted. . . . I would go shopping, therefore, rather early, not as one fulfilling an obligation, but seeking a pleasure that also provided me with some healthful exercise. And upon opening the door to go out into the

78. Nommick, *Jardines de España*, 10n11. He would occasionally return to Madrid, as he did, for example, on 28 August 1915, when he performed Pedrell's piano transcription of some of the *Cantigas de Santa María* with singer Elisa Ruiz Pujáls (Torres Clemente, "La presencia de Scarlatti," in Nommick, *Manuel de Falla e Italia*, 68).

III

En los jardines de la Sierra de Córdoba

Musical Example 14a. Falla, *Noches en los jardines de España*, movement 1, "En el Generalife," mm. 1–3. (Reprinted by kind permission of Ediciones Manuel de Falla)

Musical Example 14b. Falla, *Noches en los jardines de España*, movement 1, "En el Generalife," rehearsal 2. (Reprinted by kind permission of Ediciones Manuel de Falla)

Musical Example 14c. Falla, *Noches en los jardines de España*, movement 1, "En el Generalife," rehearsal 3. (Reprinted by kind permission of Ediciones Manuel de Falla)

street, I would invariably hear the voice of Don Manuel de Falla, who would yell from his room, "Wait! I shall accompany you!" Why did the great composer, continually lost in the labyrinth of his sonic mathematics, have to come along on a seemingly prosaic and materially motivated excursion—to buy vegetables and fish? Well, it was because he, super-nervous and a natural self-tormentor, had made my naturally healthy, earthbound, and solid person into the fantasma of a fragile being, incapable of defending herself against the dangers of street traffic, and had decided that if he didn't go through the streets by my side "to save my life" it was entirely likely that I would let myself be crushed by an automobile. Certainly I wouldn't wait for him—he was, in addition to being anything but a morning person, incredibly slow at dressing, at his toilette . . . at doing his weightlifting routine—. I'd run off to the market, make my purchases. He . . . would go out in search of me. Sometimes we would meet when I was already on the way home. Then he would berate me for my lack of prudence. I would poke fun at his fears. We would walk a moment together until he would enter the first church we encountered along the way to perform his devotions, and I would return home alone . . . and defenseless.[79]

That this amusingly dysfunctional "family" lived together almost six months is a tribute to the three artists' friendship and, quite likely, to María, the maternal figure who so ably and energetically cared for two men who depended on her for such diverse needs. By early 1916, the "natural self-tormentor" was back in Madrid putting the finishing touches on *Noches*, the April premiere of which was to be given by its dedicatee, Ricardo Viñes. But as late as mid-March, Viñes informed Falla that he would be unable to learn *Noches* in time, an admission that casts new light on the working habits of a pianist famous for his almost instantaneous musical memory.[80] Instead, the premiere took place in Madrid on 9 April 1916 with José Cubiles as soloist and Enrique Fernández Arbós conducting the Orquesta Sinfónica. Performed with Rimsky-Korsakov's *Antar* (Symphony no. 2), Beethoven's Symphony no. 7, and Dukas's *The Sorcerer's Apprentice*, *Noches* seems to have been the high point of the evening. One reviewer noted its sensuality, observing that "the sensibility of the composer has been touched by the majesty of the Andalusian night, when the stars twinkle in the sky, the flowers sigh in the earth, and distant murmurs bring us echoes of love."[81] Not surprisingly, the work became a favorite of Rubinstein's, even if his account of his first performance of *Noches* is pure fabrication. Claiming to have attended the premiere, Rubinstein later commented that because Cubiles "did not play [*Noches*] by heart . . . his performance lost much of its bite." He then remarks that he "fell in love with this work, and offered to play it at the last symphony concert of the season," capping that performance with the now popular "Ritual Fire Dance."[82] While Rubinstein certainly could have been in Madrid on 9 April (he played with the Sociedad Nacional de Música on the fourteenth), the last Orquesta Sinfónica

79. Martínez Sierra, *Gregorio y yo*, 130–31.

80. Viñes explained to Falla that nearsightedness kept him from learning it quickly from the manuscript. He did, however, play *Noches* in San Sebastián on 13 September 1916 (Nommick, *Jardines de España*, 30).

81. "La sensibilidad del músico ha sido sorprendida por la majestad de una noche andaluza, cuando las estrellas parpadean en el cielo, las flores suspiran en la tierra y rumores lejanos nos traen ecos de amores" ("Músicos y conciertos: Orquesta Sinfónica," *ABC*, 11 April 1916, 16).

82. Rubinstein, *My Young Years*, 477.

concert of the season was on 16 April, just before the orchestra left Madrid for a provincial tour, and the program included Mozart, Bach, Wagner, Strauss, and Manrique de Lara—not *Noches*.[83] Still, this additional lapse in Rubinstein's "elephant's memory" hardly diminishes the importance of his relationship to that work: not only did he introduce *Noches* to the Western Hemisphere (in Argentina) but he recorded it four times.[84] Recordings by Alicia de Larrocha, Aldo Ciccolini, Clara Haskil, Martha Argerich, Daniel Barenboim, and many others confirm the work's allure.

All the while, the war ground on. Falla, who later took such pains to distance himself from politics, publicly addressed some of the issues it raised. In 1915, he signed a manifesto condemning Spanish neutrality in light of Germany's "fermenting of egotism, of domination, and of shameless violence."[85] Published in the journal *España*, another of Ortega's ventures, this declaration was signed by numerous *aliadófilo* intellectuals: the endocrinologist and man of letters Gregorio Marañón, the historian Américo Castro, the law professor Fernando de los Ríos, and many others who would later involve themselves in the Second Republic. Falla also spoke out against German aggression in a memorial essay for Enrique Granados, who, along with his wife Amparo, perished in the English Channel in March 1916, when the English mail boat on which they were traveling was torpedoed by a German U-boat. The event caused shock waves throughout the Spanish musical community. Falla's piece appeared in April in the *Revista Musical Hispanoamericana*; in it, he mourned the loss of Granados's talent while laying the blame for his death squarely on the Germans, who had provoked a "barbarous and unjust war" and had "snatched away an artist of ours who so brilliantly represented Spain abroad."[86]

In other articles of 1916, Falla addressed the deleterious effects on European music of the "German tradition," starting with his prologue to Salazar's Spanish translation of Jean-Aubry's *La musique française d'aujourd'hui* (French Music of Today).[87]

---

83. *Rubinstein y España*, 165. The program for the 16 April concert is given in "Esta noche se verificará en el Teatro Real el quinto y último concierto de la Orquesta Sinfónica," *ABC*, 16 April, 1916, 15. A review appeared the next day. The provincial tour was announced in *ABC* on 19 April 1916 (14).

84. Sachs, *Rubinstein*, 157, 460–61.

85. "Manifiesto de adhesión a las naciones aliadas," *España* 1, no. 24 (July 1915): 282, cited in Hess, *Manuel de Falla and Modernism in Spain*, 61.

86. Manuel de Falla, "Enrique Granados: Evocación de su obra," *Revista Musical Hispanoamericana*, April 1916, 5, reprinted in Falla, *Escritos*, 25–26. On the magazine, which was transferred from Bilbao to Madrid in January 1914, see Jorge de Persia, "Falla, Ortega, y la renovación musical," *Revista de Occidente* 156 (1994): 102–16.

87. Manuel de Falla, "*La música francesa contemporánea*: Prólogo al libro de Jean-Aubry," *Revista Musical Hispanoamericana*, July 1916, 2–4, reprinted in Falla, *Escritos*, 43–50. On the 31 July 1916 issue, the cover reads *agosto* (August), but in the following issue the editors acknowledge this error.

Throughout that collection of articles and lectures, Jean-Aubry pursued the implications of the assertion he had made in 1914 apropos *La vida breve*, namely, that music
is the unique product of a race. In short, French composers had suffered undue
contamination by German influence, especially that of Wagner.[88] Jean-Aubry's view
is only one shade of the nationalistic sentiment then prevailing in French musical
circles. (He was not, for example, a member of the xenophobic National League for
the Defense of French Music, which tried to ban performances of then current
German music.)[89] Another point on the spectrum was represented by Fauré, who
in his prologue to the French edition of Jean-Aubry's book *encouraged* assimilating
foreign influences—including German ones—even as he lamented the war.[90] As one
who esteemed "the values that characterize the art created by a particular race," as
he proclaimed in the prologue to the Spanish translation, Falla was closer to Jean-
Aubry's "racialist" theories than to Fauré's openness to eclecticism. The same perspective emerges in another essay of 1916, "Introducción al estudio de la música
nueva" (Introduction to the Study of New Music), in which Falla attacked the op-
pressive German influence, this time targeting its "universal formulas," inimical to
"racial" expression. Perhaps with a Catholic viewpoint in mind, he also took aim at
eclecticism, that is, the weaving together of various doctrines in an informal unity.[91]
Falla found this objectionable in both artistic and social terms, writing: "What
progress could a society formed by eclectics make? And I'll go even further: I don't
believe in eclecticism. He who accepts and applauds the most opposite ideas and
opinions, either has none—in which case he can be useful for little or nothing—or,
if he has, is nothing but a timid or lazy person with the appearance of pleasant and
condescending urbanity."[92] To be sure, throughout these freewheeling diatribes Falla
acknowledged the validity of the "German tradition" insofar as it applied to German composers. But he insisted that its precepts not be arbitrarily applied to other
"races." And, in defending music written before the dubious effects of eclecticism
and romanticism had taken hold (he especially singled out Beethoven's affinity for
"Robespierrean ideas"), Falla took the bold and highly questionable step of blam-
ing "the Protestant tradition: that insidious tradition that has been the principal
cause, if not the only one, of the scorn that the music of the so-called classic period

88. See G. Jean-Aubry, *French Music of To-Day*, translated by Edwin Evans (1919; reprint, Plainview, N.Y.: Books for Libraries Press, 1976), 2–16.

89. On the league, whose presidents included Saint-Saëns, d'Indy, and Gustave
Charpentier, see Carlo Caballero, "Patriotism or Nationalism? Fauré and the Great
War," *Journal of the American Musicological Society* 52 (1999): 594.

90. This issue is explored in Caballero, "Patriotism or Nationalism?"

91. V. M. Martin, "Eclecticism," in *New Catholic Encyclopedia*, 5:40–41.

92. Manuel de Falla, "Introducción al estudio de la música nueva," *Revista Musical
Hispanoamericana*, December 1916: 2–5, reprinted under the title "Introducción a la música
nueva" in Falla, *Escritos*, 34.

evinced for music written before the seventeenth century."[93] In effect, the cranky "Introducción" anticipates Falla's later thinking. In 1916, his *aliadófilo* sentiments, which implicitly challenged the *germanofilismo* of the Spanish Church's hierarchy, qualified him as a liberal, despite his obvious hunger for unity and his distaste for "freethinking." In the 1930s, Falla's conception of a just but God-centered society would isolate him from many of his liberal colleagues, including some of the cosignatories of Ortega's manifesto. In his work, on the other hand, Falla would soon investigate music "prior to the seventeenth century" and with extraordinary results. Before this, however, came *The Three-Cornered Hat*. His collaborator on that project, Sergei Diaghilev, would tout the ballet as an exemplar of "Latin-Slav art" and a challenge to the Germanic hegemony against which Falla also rebeled.[94] *The Three-Cornered Hat* may have been all that and more. But it was also Falla's most commercially successful work to date, one that provided him, albeit temporarily, the material comfort that had long eluded him.

93. Falla, *Escritos*, 39–40. On musical anti-Protestantism in Spain, see Hess, *Manuel de Falla and Modernism in Spain*, 73–75.

94. See Arnold Haskell and Walter Nouvel, *Diaghileff: His Artistic and Private Life* (London: Gollancz, 1935), 280–81; and Nesta MacDonald, *Diaghilev Observed by Critics in England and the United States, 1911–1929* (New York: Dance Horizons, 1975), 225.

Chapter 5

International Acclaim: Modernist Folklore
and a Farewell to the Primitive

In February 1916, Falla, María, and Gregorio began work on the pantomime *El corregidor y la molinera* (The Magistrate and the Miller's Wife), inspired by Pedro Antonio de Alarcón's 1874 novel *El sombrero de tres picos* (The Three-Cornered Hat). Alarcón had based the novel on more than one version of a popular *romance* (oral ballad).[1] Other composers, most notably Hugo Wolf, also drew on this tale of eighteenth-century rural Spain.[2] It tells of the comely Frasquita, who is married to Lucas, the local miller and a hunchback (the *grotesco* was a stock figure in Spanish literature), whom she adores even when she is pursued by the senescent *corregidor*, who intrudes into their idyllic Andalusian village wearing the eponymous headgear. At least, this is the case with Alarcón's novel: in other versions, such as the ballad *El molinero de Arcos* (The Miller of Arcos), relations between Frasquita and the *corregidor* are consummated. The question of just how to end the traditional tale would

1. As late as 1977, this *romance* was still being sung in northern Spain. See John Hook, *Alarcón: El sombrero de tres picos*, Critical Guide to Spanish Texts, no. 41 (London: Grant and Cutler, 1984), 12.
2. Studies of Wolf's 1896 opera *Der Corregidor* (libretto by Rosa Mayreder) include Margarete Saary, *Persönlichkeit und musikdramatische Kreativität Hugo Wolfs* (Tutzing: Schneider, 1984). Other musical settings include Karel Korarovic's *Noc Simona a Judy* (Prague, 1892); Riccardo Zandonai's *La farsa amorosa* (Rome, 1933); and Julius Kalas's *Mlynarka z Granady* (Prague, 1954). For settings by Spanish composers, see Gallego, *Conciertos de inauguración*, 22–24.

prove critical for Falla in both the pantomime and its definitive version, the Diaghilev ballet.

In tracing the history of both works, we are reminded that for years the composer and María wrote one another light-hearted missives nearly daily. One of his first letters to her on *El corregidor*, dated 8 February 1916, reveals his direct involvement in the work's initial brainstorming stages: "I am spending much time with Gregorio. Yesterday we had a long session which should result in *quelque chose de bien* if I take advantage of it. I have begun occupying myself with the tunes for the pantomime, which we discussed in detail."[3] On 12 February, he wrote María of a recent meeting with Gregorio at which the composer played excerpts of the emerging pantomime score. Falla also commented, "I laughed a great deal over all the things you recounted in that special way of yours," and inquired whether she had received his two most recent letters (evidently he had written her twice between the eighth and the twelfth).[4] On the fifteenth, he wrote yet again, this time about the scene that would eventually become the "Dance of the Grapes." In this episode, modified slightly from Alarcón, Frasquita and Lucas tease the lascivious *corregidor* with the first fruits of their arbor so as to have the fun of watching him drool uncontrollably over Frasquita's charms and ultimately lose his balance.

It seems clear enough that Falla conferred with Gregorio over details of plot and production and promptly conveyed the substance of these discussions to María, who in turn sifted through the threesome's reactions to Alarcón's text (and to the popular ballad) and crafted them into the pantomime's final version.[5] As in *El amor brujo*, her "idealized female archetype" takes center stage. Frasquita, however, required little elaboration, for Alarcón's heroine is a capable and physically attractive young woman bent on defending her virtue against the *corregidor* while remaining true to her humpbacked husband. Her spunky fortitude is tested when the magistrate has his bodyguards (*alguaciles*) imprison Lucas, clearing the way for the *corregidor*'s nocturnal visit to the mill. Unintimidated, Frasquita pushes him into the millstream and runs away, whereupon the drenched *corregidor* removes his red cape and three-

3. Andrew Budwig, "The Evolution of Manuel de Falla's *The Three-Cornered Hat*, 1916–1920," *Journal of Musicological Research* 5 (1984): 194.

4. Letter, Falla to María Martínez Sierra, 12 February 1916, AMF correspondence file 7252.

5. Marginal notes in Falla's copy of the novel are in María's hand, and draft materials are typed with the sort of typewriter she used. Also the editorial markings on the typewritten copy correspond to her system of correction. See Gallego, *Conciertos de inauguración*, 72, 101; and Yvan Nommick, "*El sombrero de tres picos* de Manuel de Falla: Una visión a partir de los documentos de su Archivo," in *Teatro Real* (Madrid: Fundación del Teatro Lírico, Temporada, 1997–98), 45.

cornered hat and falls asleep in the couple's bed. Having escaped from jail, Lucas returns home to find hat and cape, symbols of authority, strewn in front of his house. Mad with suspicion and vengeful thoughts, he sets out to seduce the *corregidor*'s wife. After various contretemps and changes of clothing, the *corregidor* receives his comeuppance, largely through the calculations of the women, who acquit themselves far more sensibly than their excitable husbands. More than just a simple tale, however, the novel is complicated by the presence of a narrator, who tosses off the occasional barb or ambiguity while maintaining an ironic distance from the protagonists' foibles.

With her customarily light touch, María enhanced Alarcón's portrayal of female superiority. If Alarcón described his heroine as efficient and physically strong (a "colossal Niobe"), María contrasted Frasquita's skill and industry with Lucas's more easygoing nature so that she gracefully outshines her husband in the daily work of the mill.[6] Frasquita's responsiveness to the natural world also exceeds Lucas's, for it is she, not Lucas, who succeeds in teaching their pet blackbird to tell time.[7] Yet their two personalities meet in equilibrium, not competition; indeed, in transferring to the stage this marriage between equals María had only to draw directly on Alarcón's treatment of "directness, light-heartedness, gaiety, and trust" between the unlikely pair.[8] Like him, she set a wholesome tone, with the threat of seduction serving as little more than an excuse for slapstick. Program notes for the Madrid run of the pantomime, moreover, explicitly set forth this orientation, stating that "the authors of the mimed farce base it on the novel more than on the old and ignoble ballad," that is, the version in which Frasquita succumbs to the *corregidor*'s advances.[9] Yet in comparison with the novel María's ending is surprisingly ambiguous. In Alarcón's tidy final chapter, "Conclusion, Moral, and Epilogue," the *corregidor* apologizes to his wife and Frasquita and Lucas reaffirm their devotion. But in the pantomime the curtain falls on a helter-skelter four-way scuffle among the *corregidor* (disguised as Lucas), Lucas (disguised as the *corregidor*), Frasquita, and one of the *alguaciles*. With the question "did they or didn't they?" left wide open, "every spectator can resolve the drama as he or she sees fit," as María's program notes proposed.[10]

In May 1916, when Falla and María had been working on the pantomime intermittently for about three months, Diaghilev and his new choreographer, Leonid

6. Pedro Antonio de Alarcón, *The Three-Cornered Hat*, translated by Martin Armstrong (London: Gerald Howe, 1933), 9.

7. Chapter 6 of Alarcón's novel outlines similar accomplishments on Lucas's part, which María did not include.

8. Alarcón, *The Three-Cornered Hat*, 16.

9. "Los autores de esta farsa mímica han seguido más de cerca la versión de Alarcón que la del viejo y desenfadado romance" (program notes, "*El corregidor y la molinera*: Farsa mímica en dos cuadros," reprinted in Gallego, *Conciertos de inauguración*, 68).

10. "Los autores de esta farsa dejan que cada uno de los espectadores resuelva el caso en el sentido que mejor le agrade" (ibid., 72).

Massine, arrived in Spain with the rest of the company. The Ballets Russes's first visit had come about largely thanks to Alfonso XIII, who, having learned that Diaghilev was having difficulty finding bookings in war-torn Europe, wished to see himself as an artistic patron. (He even took to calling himself the "godfather to the ballet.")[11] Falla, who probably met Diaghilev at Cipa Godebski's Paris flat, now welcomed both him and Stravinsky, who was also on his first visit to Spain and with whom Falla attended the bullfight (see figures 6a, 6b).[12] Falla also provided advance publicity for Stravinsky in the form of a newspaper article, "El gran músico de nuestro tiempo: Igor Stravinsky" (The Great Musician of Our Time: Igor Stravinsky), in which he introduced the Russian composer to the Spanish public. While other Spanish critics took a self-congratulatory tone in discussing Stravinsky's first visit to Madrid, Falla condemned the Spanish capital's "polluted" musical atmosphere and bluntly doubted his compatriots' ability to appreciate the bold harmonies and novel orchestration of *Petrushka* and *Firebird*, both of which were conducted by Ernest Ansermet.[13] Such outspokenness could hardly have endeared him to the musical establishment.

Inspired by his surroundings and wanting to show appreciation to Alfonso XIII, Diaghilev decided to produce a ballet on a Spanish theme. He approached Falla, and together they considered "Andaluza," from *Cuatro piezas españolas*, and *Noches en los jardines de España*, which Falla vetoed, finding that work's fluid impressionism incompatible with the Ballets Russes's stylizations. Finally, they settled on the unfinished *El corregidor*, and Diaghilev even put Falla on his payroll, although the Russian impresario's haphazard business practices ultimately made this a mixed blessing. Yet Falla caused Diaghilev a few headaches as well. For example, a premiere in Rome was planned for December 1916, but the painstaking Falla finished the piano-vocal score only in early December. This left no time to complete the orchestration and unfortunately eliminated any possibility of an immediate performance.[14]

What sort of score did Falla finally compose? From *El corregidor*'s earliest stages, he emphasized mimetic devices, including birdcalls in the flute, depictions of the *corregidor*'s snoring through the labored repetition of a major seventh in the cello (part 2, rehearsal 74), and the locking of a door with "key, bar, and bolt" (con llave, tranca y cerrojo) with piccolo, E♭ clarinet, and string harmonics (see musical example 15). To provide folkloric ambiance, Falla borrowed a variety of popular melodies. Some reveal the characters' origins, such as the Murcian "paño moruno" theme,

11. Richard Buckle, *Diaghilev* (New York: Atheneum, 1984), 312. The invitation may well have originated with the Count of Cazal. See Rafael Domènech, "La Danza Pantomima Rusa," *ABC*, 2 June 1916, 3–4.

12. Stravinsky, *An Autobiography*, 62–64.

13. Manuel de Falla, "El gran músico de nuestro tiempo: Igor Stravinsky," *La Tribuna*, 5 June 1916, reprinted in Falla, *Escritos*, 27–30. Stravinsky's Spanish tour of 1916 is discussed in Hess, *Manuel de Falla and Modernism in Spain*, 98–104.

14. Budwig, "Evolution," 195.

Figures 6a, 6b. Line drawings of (*a, top*) Falla and (*b, bottom*) Stravinsky by Picasso. (Estate of Pablo Picasso/Artists Rights Society [ARS])

Musical Example 15. Falla. *El corregidor y la molinera*, part 2, rehearsal 74. (Chester Music Ltd. International copyright secured. All rights reserved. Reprinted by permission.)

the same as that used in the first of the *Siete canciones populares españolas* and scored here in the low strings to introduce the ungainly Lucas.[15] For Frasquita's theme, Falla used what may be a variant of an Extremaduran *jota*, despite the character's Navarrese origins. Presented in teasing fragments, the theme also surfaces in the brief and open-ended finale. Indeed, if the listener knows the witty and colorful final "Jota" from *The Three-Cornered Hat*, which capitalizes more fully on the same material, it is difficult not to hear the finale of *El corregidor* as only a pale harbinger of things to come.

While a premiere by the Ballets Russes was in limbo, the pantomime went forward. On 7 April 1917, *El corregidor y la molinera* opened with Diaghilev's authorization at Madrid's Eslava Theater.[16] There Gregorio had recently launched the Teatro de Arte, an experimental company intended to revitalize Spanish theater. Along with George Bernard Shaw's *Pygmalion* and Henrik Ibsen's *A Doll's House*, Gregorio presented up and coming Spanish playwrights such as Lorca, whose first play, *El maleficio de la mariposa* (The Butterfly's Evil Spell), premiered in March of 1920 to resoundingly negative reviews.[17] For the premiere of *El corregidor*, Turina conducted a chamber orchestra of seventeen players from Madrid's Orquesta Filarmónica. The actors—Luisita Puchol as Frasquita, Ricardo de la Vega as the *corregidor*, and Pedro

15. García Matos, "Folklore en Falla," 47–67. See also Miguel Manzano Alonso, "Fuentes populares en la música de *El sombrero de tres picos* de Manuel de Falla," *Nasarre* 9, no. 1 (1993): 119–44.

16. There are at least two published references to Diaghilev's collaboration: Tomás Borrás, "Eslava: *El corregidor y la molinera*," *La Tribuna*, 8 April 1917, 7–8; and Miguel Salvador, "La Semana teatral: Eslava, *El corregidor y la molinera*," *España, Semanario de la Vida Nacional* 3/116 (1917): 12. See also Budwig, "Evolution," 196n14.

17. Checa Puerta, "Los Teatros de Gregorio Martínez Sierra," 124. See also Rodrigo, *María Lejárraga*, 177–78; and Gibson, *Federico García Lorca*, 89–98.

Sepúlveda as Lucas, the hideous but affectionate hunchback—drew warm applause. So did the set, which, modeled on the *costumbrista* (folkloric) school of painting, was replete with Talavera porcelain, tools, pitchers, and other rustic accoutrements. Practically all the critics praised its authenticity, a notable exception being Falla's ally, Salazar, who detected links to the conventionalized nationalism of *zarzuela* and related genres and briefly mused over how the set might have been realized "in the hands of a Benois."[18]

Salazar, however, raved about the score, as did all the other critics. If existing tensions between Gregorio Martínez Sierra and certain members of the Madrid press provoked isolated attacks on the production (M. Y. of *El Mundo* summed up *El corregidor y la molinera* as "a mess of the kind Mr. Martínez Sierra perpetrates with consummate ease," and Tristan condemned the production as "one more blow to Alarcón's great novel"), Falla was exempt from their brickbats.[19] M. Y. even urged readers "to save Falla from this lamentable shipwreck," while Tristan, who had attacked with such gusto the composer's "obsession" with the modern French school in *El amor brujo*, now deemed the score of *El corregidor* a marvel, "[with] much color: there are surprising effects of timbre and of orchestration, mostly always precisely coordinated with the action, and which provoke[d], in accordance with the author's intentions, the public's laughter."[20] Others heaped praise on the score as well, with one critic attributing "all the descriptive force, the comic element, the grotesque touches, the caricatures of the dramatis personae—everything, absolutely everything" to the music.[21]

More significantly, critics applauded *El corregidor y la molinera* for its "authentically Spanish" (as one put it, "legitimately" Spanish) atmosphere. Several even saw it as a vindication, with Miguel Salvador most voluble on this point. Perhaps with Tristan in mind, he derided those who "present Falla as equally influenced by *ravelismo*, *debussismo*, and *strawinskismo*, without specifying what these different '-ismos' consist of, what their substance might be. There is nothing more arbitrary than such a

18. "¡Qué lástima que la escena aparezca digna de un entremés de los hermanos Quintero!" ("*El corregidor y la molinera* [*El sombrero de tres picos*]," *Revista Musical Hispano-Americana* 9 no. 4 [April 1917]: 8–12, reprinted in Gallego, *Conciertos de inauguración*, 41–65).

19. "En suma: la farsa . . . es un estropicio de los que con tanto desparpajo perpetra el Sr. Martínez Sierra" (M. Y., "Eslava: *El corregidor y la molinera*," *El Mundo*, 8 April 1917, 2). See also Tristan, "*El corregidor y la molinera*: Teatro Eslava," *El Liberal*, 8 April 1917, 2.

20. "En *El corregidor y la molinera* hay color muchas veces, casi siempre: hay efectos sorprendentes de timbre y de orquestación, las más de las veces ajustadísimos al asunto y que promueven, como el autor pretende, la risa del auditorio" (Tristan, "*El corregidor y la molinera*," 2).

21. "La fuerza descriptiva, el elemento cómico, los trazos grotescos, la caricatura de los caracteres—todo, absolutamente todo—está confiado a la música" (Geiger, "En Eslava: *El corregidor y la molinera*," *La Nación*, 8 April 1917, 10).

condemnation, for, indeed, it is as virulent condemnations that such remarks have been intended."[22]

The only negative review of substance appeared in the Catholic daily *El Debate*. Although critic J. M. O. praised Falla's score, he warned the public against the moral implications of the ambiguous ending. Given the three collaborators' wholesome intent, these high-flown remarks must have come as a surprise:

> *El sombrero de tres picos*, by the illustrious Don Pedro Antonio de Alarcón, served Martínez Sierra and Falla for the creation of the pantomime that opened yesterday evening at the Eslava to the public's approbation. . . . The authors [leave the ending open] so that "each spectator may resolve the matter however he or she sees fit." To our understanding, this is one of the defects of the farce . . . better that such tales were not brought to the stage, since theatricalization allows the eyes to receive thoughts and intentions that are not, in truth, the most appropriate lesson for those who esteem . . . matters so delicate as . . . the sacredness of the home.[23]

This put Falla in a tricky position. Rather than exempting him from the production's "defects," as other reviewers had done, the critic for *El Debate* saw him as coperpetrator (Alarcón's novel had "served Martínez Sierra and Falla for the creation of the pantomime"). While we can be fairly certain that Falla saw the notice, we cannot be sure of his reaction. Did he find in it echoes of Fedriani's endless scolding? Did it strike him as little more than knee-jerk moralizing? If it gave him any pause at all, he made no changes whatsoever to *El corregidor*, and the pantomime received over sixty performances in Madrid before playing in Barcelona and San Sebastián. Only later would Falla reevaluate the moral impact of his dramatic works and be guided by his latent prudishness.

Diaghilev, who arrived in Madrid in late May 1917 for the Ballets Russes's second Spanish season, also wanted the open-ended conclusion changed, though not

22. "A Falla se le presenta igualmente como influido de *ravelismo, debussismo* y *strawinskismo*, sin decir en qué consisten estos *ismos* y cuál sea su substancia; nada más arbitraria que semejante *tacha*, pues por tacha y despectivamente se la aplica" (Salvador, "La semana teatral," 11). A similar defense was mounted by R. White in "*El corregidor y la molinera*," *El Universo*, 8 April 1917, AMF press file.

23. "*El sombrero de tres picos*, del ilustre D. Pedro de Alarcón, es el que ha servido a los Sres. Martínez Sierra y Falla para la creación de la pantomima estrenada ayer tarde en la Eslava, con aplauso del público. . . . Los autores [dejan el final irresuelto] para que 'cada uno de los espectadores resuelva el caso como mejor le agrade.' A nuestro entender, es ésta uno de los defectos de la farsa . . . mejor fuera que cuentos de esta naturaleza no fuesen llevados a la escena, ya que la manera teatral hace entrar por los ojos pensamientos e intenciones que no son, la verdad, la más propicia lección para quienes estimen . . . materias tan vidriosas como . . . la intangibilidad del sagrado del hogar" (J. M. O., "*El corregidor y la molinera* en Eslava," *El Debate*, 8 April 1917, 3). J. M. O. does not appear in Rogers and Lapuente, *Diccionario de seudónimos literarios españoles*.

for moral reasons. Rather, he and Massine urged Falla to expand the ending into a "fuller, more powerful finale" so as to riotously accompany the mockery of the *corregidor* by a crowd of townspeople.[24] Falla reported all this to María, addressing her as "chère madame et amie":

> Never have I seen the Real as it is now. There's not *a single empty seat*. Another thing, as I've already told you I had feared would happen, is that I'll have to make significant modifications in the second act of *El Corregidor* so that it will be more *choreographic*. This seems absolutely right to me, so much so that it doesn't bother me to get back to work on it again. So there will be two versions: the original (which will stay as it is, for acting companies) and the choreographic version, which will be for the Russians. The modifications haven't yet been determined. The only thing that is certain at this point is that I'll have to come up with a long finale.[25]

Even in Spanish-speaking countries, the version "for acting companies" has had much less staying power than the ballet. On the latter, Diaghilev and Massine continued to advise Falla, urging him, for example, to eliminate many of the pantomime's mimetic devices. Falla did not exactly greet this suggestion with enthusiasm. He complained to María that "the musical dialogue—over which I worked so hard and which really constitutes the novelty of this little work—does not interest [Diaghilev and Massine] in the least, because, as Massine has told me, if I do everything myself, what is left for him?"[26] Yet after eliminating much of the slapstick and mimesis Falla expanded several thematic fragments into full-blown numbers, which afforded more generous choreographic treatment.[27] A case in point resulted from Massine's framing of the ballet's second half with crowd scenes. The spotty, mechanical repetition of the central theme that opens part 2 of the pantomime developed into the graceful Neighbors' Dance ("Seguidillas"), and of course the exuberant Final Dance ("Jota") replaced the original inconclusive ending. These independent numbers also became Falla's most popular symphonic works and figure in the repertory of the world's greatest orchestras.

In late June, Falla traveled to Barcelona for that city's premiere of *El corregidor* on 1 July 1917 at the Teatro de Novedades. Since the Ballets Russes was then performing in Barcelona, Falla's lawyer friend Leopoldo Matos accompanied him to

24. Leonid Massine, *My Life in Ballet*, edited by Phyllis Hartnoll and Robert Rubens (London: Macmillan, 1968), 115.

25. Letter, Falla to María, 8 June 1917, cited in de Persia, *Poesía*, 119.

26. Letter, Falla to María, 22 June 1917, cited in Gallego, *Conciertos de inauguración*, 28–29.

27. More detailed comparisons between the ballet and pantomime scores are found in Budwig, "Evolution," 198–203; and Gallego, *Conciertos de inauguración*, 33–37. For a comparison of musical, visual, and choreographic elements, see Hess, *Manuel de Falla and Modernism in Spain*, 111–29.

smooth out contractual arrangements with Diaghilev, who was only just starting to pay the composer. (At one point, poor Falla, who eventually dedicated the ballet to Matos, confided to María that he was "worn out from this economic battle with the Muscovite Theater.")[28] By early July, the "Muscovites" had sailed for South America, leaving Diaghilev and Massine behind. Massine now began working with a gypsy dancer, Félix Fernández García, whom he had met in Madrid.[29] So inspired was Massine that he organized an impromptu tour of Spain, presumably so that the unlikely foursome—himself, Diaghilev, Fernández García, and Falla—could observe regional dances firsthand. In his memoirs, Massine engagingly describes their nocturnal visits to the best flamenco bars in Seville, Córdoba, and Granada, as well as other activities (see figure 7).[30]

That heady mood quickly dissipated when it became clear that the company was once more in dire financial straits. Falla's next meeting with Diaghilev probably took place that fall in Madrid, when the impresario was trying to arrange a Spanish tour. By spring 1918, the world famous Ballets Russes was performing in such outposts as Logroño and Alcoy, as well as in larger cities; the tour yielded little, however, and by its end Falla had no reason to imagine that *The Three-Cornered Hat* would ever see the light of day.[31] He began working on other projects, including an opera on a libretto by María. In late June, however, Diaghilev managed to secure an engagement in London, whereupon Alfonso XIII, the "godfather to the ballet," issued a safe conduct that allowed the company to transport its extravagant sets and costumes through war-torn France. By the time the Armistice was signed in mid-November, Diaghilev was established in London. He declared to the British press that "the war [had been] nothing but a struggle between two cultures" and that the Ballets Russes would "introduce into [its] programmes . . . samples of German classicism only to serve as a contrast to the brilliance and life of Latino-Slav art," thus provoking a rather fruitless debate with critic and Wagner scholar Ernest Newman.[32]

In spring 1919, Diaghilev was finally able to inform Falla that the world premiere of *The Three-Cornered Hat* would take place in July at the Alhambra Theater. At that time, the composer was mourning the passing of his father, José María, who had died on 12 February at the age of seventy. His death may well have caused the

28. Letter, Falla to María, 19 June 1917, cited and translated in Budwig, "Evolution," 196.

29. Lynn Garafola, "The Choreography of *Le Tricorne*," in *Los Ballets Russes de Diaghilev en España*, edited by Yvan Nommick and Antonio Álvarez Cañibano (Madrid: Instituto Nacional de las Artes Escénicas y la Música, 2000), 89–95.

30. Massine, *My Life*, 116–18. On Fernández García's tenure with the company and his dashed hopes of dancing the role of the Miller due to mental instability, see Parmenia Migel, *Pablo Picasso: Designs for "The Three-Cornered Hat"* (New York: Dover, 1978), v–vii.

31. Pahissa, *Vida y obra*, 106. According to Pahissa, Falla consulted Matos on Diaghilev's behalf, whereupon Matos "regularized [Diaghilev's] situation" by finding him "an excellent situation with an impresario." This is not borne out by other accounts, however.

32. MacDonald, *Diaghilev Observed*, 225.

Figure 7. Falla with Leonid Massine in the Patio of the Lions in the Alhambra, June 1916. (Reprinted by kind permission of the Archivo Manuel de Falla)

forty-two-year-old Falla to remember his father's business failures, which, having occurred when José María was roughly the same age as Falla, had placed such a burden on his firstborn. In a letter of 17 April to the painter Ignacio de Zuloaga, Falla simply referred to his father's death as "a great misfortune," a laconic statement that is one of few references to the elder Falla in all of the composer's voluminous correspondence.[33]

Falla hoped to attend rehearsals and the premiere of *The Three-Cornered Hat* but was keenly aware of financial constraints. In discussing this with Diaghilev, he delicately alluded to the impresario's "wise foresight," which might enable Falla to maintain his household while in London.[34] In other words, Falla, on the verge of international fame, still depended on income from private teaching and tours (principally with the dynamic Polish singer Aga Lahowska, with whom he collaborated fairly regularly), income he would forfeit while away. On 10 May, Diaghilev made several last-minute requests: (1) that Falla perform the piano solo in *Noches en los jardines de España* as a "symphonic interlude" at the premiere, (2) that he hunt down Arbós's

33. Letter, Falla to Zuloaga, 17 April 1919, cited in Federico Sopeña, ed., *Correspondencia entre Falla y Zuloaga, 1915–1942* (Granada: Ayuntamiento de Granada, 1982), n.p.

34. Letter, Falla to Diaghilev, 30 April 1919, cited in de Persia, *Poesía*, 124.

orchestration of Albéniz's *Iberia* to be used for the same purpose, and (3) that he bring along thirty pairs of castanets—fifteen of high quality and fifteen average. As if this were not enough, Diaghilev also asked Falla to compose a short introduction "in a tonality that corresponds to the rest of the work." It would accompany the viewing of the enormous drop curtain by Picasso, who, having already collaborated with Diaghilev in the notorious "cubist" ballet *Parade*, was now in London working on the sets and costumes for *The Three-Cornered Hat*.[35] Diaghilev also conveyed Picasso's suggestion that Falla add voices, not only in the still unwritten introduction but throughout the ballet, explaining that Picasso "thinks this would be very Spanish."[36]

In mid-June, Falla arrived in London. Tamara Karsavina, who danced the role of the Miller's Wife, later recalled his modesty, noting that the "great musician, gentle and unassuming," even served as rehearsal pianist.[37] When not thus engaged, Falla observed firsthand the transformations his modest pantomime had undergone. He was not disappointed. Instead of the realistic, almost photographic, orientation of the pantomime's decor, Picasso's fanciful costumes and set, with its cubist orientation, now graced the stage, leaving *costumbrismo* far behind (see figures 8a, 8b). Also modernist in orientation was Massine's stylized choreography, which departed significantly from classical Spanish dance. Extravagant gestures emerged, for example, in his vision of the Miller. (As in *Parade*, characters were identified by roles rather than names.) Transformed from a hunchback into a virile young man, now the Miller would perform a virtuosic second-act *Farruca*, which Massine himself danced, adding many "twisted and broken gestures."[38] For the "fuller, more powerful finale" he and Diaghilev had envisioned two years earlier, Massine inserted "hilarious groups of peasants as well as some grotesque, deformed creatures."[39] Trooping onto the stage in Picasso's garish costumes, the horde of riotous bumpkins would toss an effigy of the *corregidor* in a *pelele* (straw dummy), after Goya's famous painting. It was a decidedly *un*idealized ending to this telling of the traditional Spanish tale.

Again, Falla rose to the occasion. To accompany this Rabelaisian parting shot, he took fragments of the pantomime's ending and wove them, along with new motives, into the colossal "Jota." This traditional Spanish dance in brisk triple time (associated mainly with Aragon Province) often contains a prominent castanet part and has been widely imitated by non-Spanish composers. Falla introduces his "Jota" with a nine-bar whole-tone passage, *fortissimo* and harmonically static (see musical example 16). Noisy, brash, and evoking the earnestness of a town band, the "Jota"

35. On Picasso's curtain and costumes, see Douglas Cooper, *Picasso Théâtre* (Paris: Éditions Cercle d'Art, 1967), 37–42. See also Philippe Durey and Brigitte Léal, eds., *Picasso: El sombrero de tres picos* (Paris: Spadem, 1993).

36. Letter, Diaghilev to Falla, 10 May 1919, cited in de Persia, *Poesía*, 124.

37. Tamara Karsavina, *Theatre Street: The Reminiscences of Tamara Karsavina* (London: Dance Books, 1981), 300–301.

38. Massine, *My Life*, 141.

39. Massine, *My Life*, 142.

Figures 8a, 8b. Stage designs for (*a, top*) *El Corregidor y la molinera* (reprinted by kind permission of the Archivo Manuel de Falla) and (*b, bottom*) *The Three-Cornered Hat*, designed by Picasso (Estate of Pablo Picasso/Artists Rights Society [ARS]).

Musical Example 16. (above, opposite, and overleaf) Falla, *The Three-Cornered Hat*, "Jota,"
introduction. (Chester Music Ltd. International copyright secured. All rights reserved.
Reprinted by permission.)

FINAL DANCE (JOTA)

incorporates blatant horn calls, a delayed entry in the castanets, and the bombastic simplicity of a steadfast tonic-dominant alternation. It can only mean caricature. But this hardly undermines the music's raw excitement; indeed, to attach to the "Jota" greater depth or seriousness of purpose is to overlook the composer's sensitivity to folklore's potential for irony, to the nod of self-recognition. In fact, the new finale comes full circle, back to Alarcón's novel, recalling the waggish narrator, who having playfully mocked authority and social mores throughout *El sombrero de tres picos*, notes tongue in cheek in the final sentence the passing of "the good old times symbolized by the three-cornered hat."

Hours before the premiere, Falla learned that his mother, María Jesús, was gravely ill. He decided to return home immediately and was accompanied to the train station by several dancers in their opening night costumes. (However much Falla appreciated their solicitousness, he had Pahissa suppress this episode in the first edition of the latter's biography, presumably wishing to avoid the image of himself going about in public with a bevy of scantily clad dancers.)[40] The journey was long and anxious. Once in Spain, Falla had the shock of reading in the Madrid newspaper *ABC* that the gentle woman who had given him his first piano lessons had already passed away. When he arrived home, his grief poured forth, profound and unabashed. As his sister María del Carmen later recalled: "He could not bring himself to enter [his home], and remained in the vestibule, completely disheartened . . . [and] without uttering a single word, he burst into tears like a child. Never had I seen him cry, so I was incredulous, thinking him too strong for tears."[41] Sustained by both a strong emotional bond and musical memories, the relationship between Falla and his mother was clearly one of the most important of his life. Surely, he found solace in the company of his siblings, especially the sympathetic María del Carmen. Ironically, María Jesús's passing occurred on 22 July, the day of the premiere of *The Three-Cornered Hat*; as Falla mourned, the London critics waxed exuberant. They applauded the ballet as the perfect expression of Spanish "spirit, character, and temperament," with Falla's score "as national in form and character as anything well could be."[42] Leigh Henry congratulated the absent composer for having created "for the first time in Spanish music, an [essentially Spanish] sense of humor" and Edward Dent commended Falla's incorporation of both "a Spanish outlook on [folklore] and a Spanish outlook on music in general."[43] Diaghilev was so pleased that he telegraphed Alfonso XIII's secretary to report on the brilliant premiere, a bittersweet triumph for the composer, given his recent loss.

40. Pahissa, *Vida y obra*, 213–14.

41. María del Carmen to Viniegra, in *Vida íntima*, 102, translated in Budwig and Chase, *Manuel de Falla*, 23.

42. *Daily Telegraph*, 23 July 1919, AMF press file.

43. Leigh Henry, "The Russian Ballet: M. de Falla's Ovation," New York Public Library, Dance Division, clippings file; Edward Dent, "Music: A Spanish Ballet," *Athenaeum*, 1 August 1919, 691 AMF press file.

A similar reaction greeted *The Three-Cornered Hat* in Paris, where the ballet played on 23 January 1920 and which the composer attended. Critics such as Adolphe Boschot and Gustave Samazeuilh commended its "quintessentially Spanish" qualities, and Roland-Manuel, one of Falla's staunchest supporters, could find no higher praise than to exclaim, "Behold—at last!—a composer who creates Hispanism the way Monsieur Jourdain spoke prose."[44] In Paris, now so different from the anxious city he had left in August 1914, Falla encountered two compatriots, the theater director Cipriano Rivas-Cherif and the playwright, novelist, and future president of the Second Republic, Manuel Azaña, both ardent *aliadófilos* during the war, like Falla. In the vestibule of the Opéra, the two young men embraced their internationally famous compatriot (Falla had taken the time to secure tickets for them). Azaña was so moved by *The Three-Cornered Hat* that he wrote a long, glowing essay for the Madrid daily *El Imparcial*, in which he praised both the ballet's stylization of Spanish tradition and the truth inherent in its unsentimental depiction of Spanish life, which he found full of "misery and vice" and "cruel" humor.[45]

Whatever the ballet's international acclaim, its slapstick and unmitigated irony, so different from *zarzuela*'s rosy outlook, met with resistance in Madrid the following year. Although some forward-looking critics applauded its potentially liberating influence on Spanish art, others found the ballet to be a travesty of the national image and attacked Massine's "frenetic" choreography, Picasso's "cubist" sets, and Falla's "disrespectful" score.[46] It is worth noting that the ballet's most virulent detractors were employed by right-wing dailies. One, writing in the Granada-based *La Alhambra*, who signed his review V., was almost certainly that paper's editor, Francisco de Paula Valladar.[47] He complained that Spanish character was constantly being ridiculed through artistic extremism and mourned the Madrid public's apathy in the face of a caricature like *The Three-Cornered Hat*. When he insisted, moreover, that, as in the case of the ballet, "we ought to protest against those Spanish in origin and name who would nevertheless turn into an *españolada* one of the most admirable works of nineteenth-century Spanish literature," he could only have had Falla and Picasso in mind. (An *españolada* is a work that depicts Spain through clichés—passionate gypsies, virile bullfighters, doleful guitarists.) Another critic excoriated the ballet as "an ostentation of modernism and dislocation"; he wrote for the right-wing daily *La Acción*, a *germanófilo* paper during the war. Then there

44. "Voici—enfin!—un compositeur qui fait de l'hispanisme, comme M. Jourdain faisait de la prose" (A. Roland-Manuel, "*Le Tricorne* à l'Opéra," *L'Eclair*, 26 January 1920, AMF press file).

45. Manuel Azaña, "Nota sobre un baile español," *El Imparcial*, 20 February, 1920, reprinted in Manuel Azaña, *Obras completas* (Mexico City: Ediciones Oasis, 1966), 1:216–18.

46. The reaction to the ballet in Spain is discussed in Hess, *Manuel de Falla and Modernism in Spain*, 130–60.

47. Jorge de Persia, *I concurso de cante jondo, 1922–1992* (Granada: Archivo Manuel de Falla, 1992), 28–29.

was the irascible Víctor Espinós, who wrote for the Catholic daily *La Época* and later held important positions in Franco's government. So exercised was Espinós by the image of Spain the ballet would project abroad (foreign critics' approbation of its "Spanish temperament" notwithstanding) that he roundly condemned *The Three-Cornered Hat* as unworthy even of "a chapter out of the Black Legend," that centuries-old propaganda campaign engineered to undermine Hispanics that Franco would later evoke to attack enemies of his regime.[48] Once again, Falla's national sympathies had failed to pass muster, at least among the political right.

NEW UNDERTAKINGS

After the triumphant London premiere of *The Three-Cornered Hat*, Falla began several new projects. In October 1919, he set two "Moorish melodies" for the fourth act of *El corazón ciego* (The Blind Heart), a Martínez Sierra production about social pressure to marry.[49] More substantive was the *Homenaje a Debussy* for solo guitar, completed in August 1920. It first appeared in a musical supplement of *La Revue Musicale* dedicated to the memory of Falla's revered colleague, who had died in March 1918. Also honoring Debussy were Dukas, Ravel, Roussel, Satie, Schmitt, Bartók, Malipiero, and Stravinsky. This collective effort recalls the sixteenth-century *tombeau* (an instrumental lament on some individual's death), which, like its counterpart the literary *tombeau*, often involved multiple authors. *La Revue Musicale* also published several commemorative essays, including Falla's "Claude Debussy and Spain." In it, Falla praised Debussy's ability to create Spanish music by osmosis, as it were: despite limited knowledge of Spain, Debussy had convincingly evoked that country in works such as "Ibéria," the piano prelude "La Puerta del Vino," and "Soirée dans Grenade" from the solo piano suite *Estampes*; even works without explicitly Spanish intentions (he mentions *Danse profane*, *Fantoches*, and *Masques*) were filled with the "modes, cadences, harmonic progressions, rhythms" of what Falla called "natural" Spanish music (folk or popular). On these grounds, he described the second movement of Debussy's string quartet as "one of the most beautiful Andalusian dances ever written."[50] So compelling did Falla find these works—all

48. See Philip Powell, *Tree of Hate* (New York and London: Basic Books, 1971); and William S. Maltby, *The Black Legend in England: The Development of Anti-Spanish Sentiment, 1558–1660* (Durham, N.C.: Duke University Press, 1971).

49. O'Connor, *Gregorio and María Martínez Sierra*, 126. *El corazón ciego* premiered on 16 October 1919 at Madrid's Teatro Eslava, although the date is often given as November 1919 in San Sebastián. There were two restagings after the initial Madrid production (which received fifty-six performances), one on 1 December 1920 and another on 13 May 1925. I wish to thank Professor Dru Dougherty of the University of California, Berkeley, for this information.

50. Manuel de Falla, "Claude Debussy et l'Espagne," *La Revue Musicale* 1, no. 2 (1 December 1920): 207–8, reprinted and translated in Falla, *Escritos*, 72–78.

composed without recourse to literal quotation—that he applauded them as manifestations of "truth without authenticity," high praise indeed from one who so painstakingly searched for "truth" in all aspects of life. Falla himself indulged in literal
quotation, however, in the final bars of his *Homenaje,* in which he saluted "Latinité"
by conspicuously inserting a motive from "Soirée dans Grenade." Hints of Debussy's
atmospheric piano piece, such as insistent minor seconds and a hypnotic *habanera*
rhythm, permeate the rest of the work.

A bigger project was the *Fantasía bética,* the virtuosic work for solo piano completed in 1919. With the moniker *bética* ("baetica" being the Roman name for
Andalusia) and an aggressively *andalucista* style, Falla paid "homage to [the] Latin-
Andalusian race."[51] The work came about thanks to Rubinstein, who, mindful of
Falla's and Stravinsky's financial difficulties during the war, requested a solo piano
work from each.[52] Yet neither the *Fantasía* nor Stravinsky's *Piano Rag Music* satisfied Rubinstein. He was so put off by *Piano Rag Music*'s blatant percussiveness that
he never played it, and he performed the equally percussive but less parodic *Fantasía*
only a few times, first in New York on 8 February 1920 and then on a handful of
other occasions before letting it slip from his repertory.[53] It also seems to have slipped
his mind, for in the early 1920s he asked Falla to write him a piano piece. After Falla
politely observed that he had already done precisely that, the suave Polish pianist
lamely muttered something about the *Fantasía*'s undue length.[54]

The relentlessly "primitive" *Fantasía* is peppered with fourth- and second-based
harmonies, often pounded out in ostinato fashion. Accompaniment figures evoke
the open strings of the guitar; in fact, several passages could be transferred to that
instrument (see musical example 17) and abundant dissonances simulating guitar
"crushes" fall on strong beats, as Bryan R. Simms has observed.[55] Short, abrupt
motives of narrow melodic range, such as the ungainly seconds thumped out by
the pianist's left thumb (mm. 16–21), are surrounded by swirling figurations. Yet

51. Letter, Falla to José María Gálvez (1926), cited in Gallego, *Catálogo,* 170.

52. The terms of Stravinsky's contract for the *Piano Rag Music* were executed between
March and May 1918, and he completed the work on 28 June 1919. See Taruskin, *Stravinsky
and the Russian Traditions,* 2:1477. See also a letter concerning payment, Falla to Stravinsky, 1
May 1918, Robert Craft, ed., *Stravinsky: Selected Correspondence* (New York: Knopf, 1984), 2:162.

53. Rubinstein played the *Fantasía* in London (1922); Madrid, Málaga, and Barcelona
(1923); Buenos Aires (1924); Paris (1925); and Cádiz (1926). See Sachs, *Rubinstein,* 169; and
Enrique Franco, "El rey Arturo en la Corte de Madrid," in *Rubinstein y España,* 21. The
date of the premiere of the *Fantasía,* which is often given as 20 February 1920 in New York,
was in fact 8 February (i.e., in competition with a Carnegie Hall recital by Josef Hofmann)
at the Ritz-Carlton Hotel for the Society of the Friends of Music. Critic F. G. lists "two
numbers from manuscript of Manuel de Falla, 'Dance' from *El amor brujo* and a Spanish
fantasie," in "Rubinstein in New Music," *Musical America* 31 (14 February 1920): 51.

54. Pahissa, *Vida y obra,* 115.

55. Bryan R. Simms, *Music of the Twentieth Century: Style and Structure* (New York:
Schirmer, 1986), 256–57.

Musical Example 17. Falla, *Fantasía bética*, mm. 332–37. (Chester Music Ltd. International copyright secured. All rights reserved. Reprinted by permission.)

the *Fantasía* is strongly rooted in classic form. Its ternary structure embraces an A section that unfolds in three clearly defined theme-groups, including opening material based on the A Phrygian scale, a contrasting section centered on B (m. 36), and a closing group, also on B (Molto Lento, m. 121ff.). The closing group, embellished by grace notes of sevenths and ninths (m. 135), recalls the microtones common in flamenco singing. A central slow section, an Intermezzo in G♯ minor (mm. 205–70), contains Phrygian coloring and overlapping, hemiola-punctuated scalar themes, only one of which contains a melodic leap beyond the range of a third. A brash recapitulation of the opening material (A Phrygian) affirms E as tonal center, for both second and third "themes" return in that key area (mm. 306 and 338, respectively); likewise, E is the tonal center of the pounding coda (beginning at m. 370). In short, the *Fantasía*'s large-scale formal structure rests on the principle of tonal organization by fifth-related key areas dispersed in thematically coherent groups, as does many a traditional form.

All told, the piece deserves a second look. Rubinstein's complaint about its length is untenable, for the *Fantasía* takes only about twelve minutes to perform. Its rather unimpressive career may be due to the fact that amateurs are daunted by its technical difficulties while professional pianists doubt its "effectiveness."[56] Yet it is worth noting that while the *Fantasía* has enjoyed less popularity than *Noches* the New York audience greeted its premiere warmly, even if one critic applauded it as "reveal[ing] the musical self-possession of the disciple of d'Indy [!]."[57] Also, the Czech-American

56. Gilbert Chase, "Falla's Music for Piano Solo," *Chesterian* 21 (1940): 46. See also Linton E. Powell, *A History of Spanish Piano Music* (Bloomington: Indiana University Press, 1980), 95–96.

57. F. G., "Rubinstein in New Music."

pianist Rudolph Firkusny was sufficiently interested in the *Fantasía* to play it privately for Falla in April 1945; mainly, however, it has been associated with Alicia de Larrocha, thanks to widely circulated rereleases of her 1958 performance on the old Hispavox label.[58] As for the *Fantasía*'s significance in terms of Falla's evolution as a composer, do we not experience the work on a new level if we remember that, whatever Falla's aversion to hegemonic "universal formulas" of the "German tradition," in the *Fantasía* he placed his knowledge of Andalusian music in the service of time-honored formal parameters? In this valedictory to the flamenco style with which he had defined himself, the spontaneous folklorist was gradually being drawn to an abstract realm in which "purity" and once-maligned "universalism" would hold sway.

Other efforts from this period fared worse than the *Fantasía*. The light opera in three acts, *Fuego fatuo* (Will-o'-the-Wisp), begun with María in 1918 and based on melodies of Chopin, must be counted among Falla's more unfortunate decisions.[59] First, it was one of the main reasons that he turned down Diaghilev's offer of *Pulcinella*, that curious work based on manuscripts then thought to be by Pergolesi (the majority are by Domenico Gallo) with which Stravinsky made such a splash. Since there is no extant correspondence between Falla and Diaghilev on *Pulcinella*, it is unclear exactly when and under what terms the offer was made. It may have been during the summer of 1918 when Diaghilev was in Madrid, in which case Falla probably at least considered the idea (Stravinsky received his commission in the fall of 1919).[60] In any case, Falla wasted most of the summer of 1918 working in the blistering Madrid heat on *Fuego fatuo*, which ultimately enabled Stravinsky to proclaim *Pulcinella* his "discovery of the past, the epiphany through which the whole of [his] late work became possible," all part of his strident campaign against folklorism.[61]

Second, the opera caused considerable friction between Falla and the Martínez Sierras. According to María:

> The Chopinesque work had to have three acts. [When] two of these were done
> . . . the famous scruples arose in the conscience of the composer. The dramatic

58. Letter, Falla to Bernardo Iriberri, 16 August 1945, AMF correspondence file 7124. See, for example, de Larrocha's recording on EMI Classics (7–64527–2).

59. A full account of Falla's borrowings from Chopin, along with extant sketch materials, is in the facsimile edition by Yvan Nommick, ed., *Manuel de Falla: Fuego fatuo— Edición facsímil de los manuscritos 9017–1, LII, A2, A4, A6, A9, A10 del Archivo Manuel de Falla* (Granada: Publicaciones del Archivo Manuel de Falla, 1999).

60. A letter from Ansermet to Stravinsky of 10 June 1919 indicates that the project was by then at least in the conceptual stage. See Taruskin, *Stravinsky and the Russian Traditions*, 2:1462–65.

61. Igor Stravinsky and Robert Craft, *Expositions and Developments* (Garden City, N.Y.: Doubleday, 1962), 128–29. The political dimension of Stravinsky's campaign for "pure" music is discussed in Richard Taruskin, "Russian Folk Melodies in *The Rite of Spring*," *Journal of the American Musicological Society* 33 (1980): 501–43.

conflict . . . concerned two women who sighed for the love of one man. . . . Falla's modesty became worked up, his natural gentlemanliness could not consent even for an instant to cheapen the concept of the "eternal feminine" with dubious motives. Although I nearly killed myself trying to explain to him that between two angels in a state of grace there could be no conflict, and that if both sopranos were saints the good public would die of boredom, there was no means of convincing him. Thus we left the opera, incomplete, having lost several months of work along the way.[62]

María penned her account decades after the fact, by which time Falla's proximity to sainthood had been trumpeted in several quarters. In fact, there is no evidence that the composer considered the plot morally objectionable. On the contrary, he personally approached theater directors in Madrid, Barcelona, and Paris but found none interested in *Fuego fatuo*. Albert Carré of the Opéra-Comique even expressed surprise that Falla's score relied almost solely on Chopin, saying, "You should write original music!"[63] (Given that Stravinsky would soon reap the benefits of working with other than "original" music in *Pulcinella*, there is a disconcerting irony in Carré's critique.) Significantly, the aborted opera responds to the intensifying conflict between Falla's evolving modernist sensibility and his attachment to the familiar diction of popular idioms. For while he was laboring over *Fuego fatuo* he was also starting the puppet play *El retablo de Maese Pedro* (Master Peter's Puppet Show). This was thanks to a commission from that important patron of the arts, the princesse de Polignac, née Winnaretta Singer of the North American sewing machine family. In 1901, recently widowed (Ian Gibson describes her as "discreetly lesbian"), she built an enormous Greek Revival mansion in Paris's upscale sixteenth *arrondissement*. Many of her more important commissions were presented in its theater, including Stravinsky's *Renard*, Milhaud's *Les Malheurs d'Orphée*, and Tailleferre's Piano Concerto, all sophisticated companions to the *Retablo*, which premiered there in 1923, when, after much prodding by Polignac, Falla finally completed it.[64] The paradox is that in toiling over *Fuego fatuo*, Falla, poised on the brink of a modernist, cosmopolitan style, was still bent on churning out a crowd-pleaser in a commercial genre he had effectively outgrown.

The final blow to Falla's friendship with Gregorio and María occurred during their next collaboration, the tragicomedy *Don Juan de España* (Don Juan of Spain). For months, Falla procrastinated over the incidental music. (Since no sketches have

62. Martínez Sierra, *Gregorio y yo*, 146.

63. As Gregorio was then on leave from the Eslava, the theater was temporarily being managed by the composer Manuel Penella, who rejected *Fuego fatuo*. See Pahissa, *Vida y obra*, 119–20.

64. Gibson, *Federico García Lorca*, 93. Jeanice Brooks, "Nadia Boulanger and the Salon of the princesse de Polignac," *Journal of the American Musicological Society* 46, no. 3 (1993): 415–68.

been discovered, it is impossible to know what work, if any, he did on *Don Juan* beyond the customary three-way brainstorming with the Martínez Sierras.) As in her account of *Fuego fatuo*, María attributed Falla's stalling to his strict moral code; again, while this *may* have been the reason, there is no evidence for María's proposition.[65] Frustrated with Falla's slowness—what Fedriani might well have called his "self-love"—Gregorio and María finally engaged Conrado del Campo, and on 18 November 1921 *Don Juan de España* opened at the Eslava with del Campo's music. Falla took swift action. Describing his "shock" at seeing press notices of the production, he demanded that Gregorio state in writing that "the *essential* idea of the last two . . . acts belong[ed]" to Falla, reminding Gregorio that the Don Juan theme was one on which he had "thought with such optimism . . . ever since [living] in Paris."[66] Surely this was an unlikely reaction for anyone scandalized by the use of Don Juan's licentiousness as subject matter.

Gregorio, expert in manipulating the vagaries of intellectual property rights, was equally quick to respond. His letter to Falla is a small masterpiece of diplomacy and wit:

> My dear Falla: I don't know whether to be mortally offended or to take as a bit of a joke the certified letter I've just received from you. I'll choose the second, since I think that over the course of our friendship I have given you too much evidence of solidarity, loyalty, and affection to admit the possibility of premeditated offense on your part. . . . I hope that this *masterpiece* [the Don Juan legend] . . . will contain enough motives and musical inspirations for composers around the world to squabble over, but of course I will reserve for you the music for the last act, "Tragic Shadow," if you wish, because . . . I believe that no one could create better than you the immoral, demonic, and tragic music that is required. And now . . . so that you are not "shocked" again, and so that I won't go out of my way not to feel offended, I will thank you to send me by certified mail a list of all the musical "situations" that you may have entrusted to me so that I can erase them from my memory and not fall into the temptation of taking advantage of another's creativity. . . . Yours, with as much affection as ever, although as hurt as you can imagine.[67]

"Essential ideas" and "another's creativity"—the delicate bonds that had joined the threesome in a fruitful working relationship had unraveled. Surely Falla was not amused by Gregorio's dig at the composer's alleged affinity for "immoral" music. But Gregorio's closing may have given him pause, as would the thought of ending his friendship with María, once so gratifying. Did he ever stop to examine his own

65. Martínez Sierra, *Gregorio y yo*, 147.

66. Letter, Falla to Martínez Sierra, 25 November 1921, archive of the Lejárraga family, Madrid, cited in Rodrigo, *María Lejárraga*, 195, draft in AMF correspondence file 7251/3.

67. Letter, Gregorio to Falla, 26 November 1921, cited in Rodrigo, *María Lejárraga*, 196.

role in the conflict? Did it cross his mind that perhaps his fussiness and delays infuriated others? Probably not, and the friendship effectively ended because of Falla's heightened sense of betrayal. Not until two decades had elapsed, when he fell on hard times in Argentina, would he attempt reconciliation with his old friend.

THE HALCYON YEARS BEGIN: AT HOME IN GRANADA

In the fall of 1919, Falla began thinking seriously of moving to Granada, whose aching beauty had so impressed him on his trip there with María in 1915. He was tired of the noise and congestion of the capital, and in the aftermath of his parents' deaths he was perhaps also seeking a change of environment. His sister, María del Carmen, approaching her fortieth birthday and from all appearances a confirmed spinster— as that society certainly would have tagged her—was willing to accompany her brother Manolo. They left Madrid in September, staying at the Pensión Carmona in the Calle Real de la Alhambra, as arranged by the guitarist Ángel Barrios.[68] During this exploratory visit, Falla met Lorca, who one night after a concert recited an ode to the city of Granada.[69] Suitably inspired, Falla and María del Carmen returned in 1920, this time to make Granada their home. The first house they rented (Falla preferred not to own property) was also in the Calle Real de la Alhambra but at no. 40. By early 1922, they were residing at the edge of the Alhambra, in a *carmen* at Calle de Antequeruela Alta no. 11. Of Arabic origins, the word *carmen* does not have an exact English translation. But it generally refers to a hillside house, often tall and narrow and with a walled garden symbolizing the Islamic ideal of the inner paradise, a "reflection of heaven."[70] This was the ideal setting for the spiritual and artistic tranquility Falla craved.

One of his first activities in Granada was helping to organize a competition for singers of *cante jondo*, or flamenco deep song.[71] The contest, which was probably an inspiration of Lorca's friend Miguel Cerón Rubio, would be held in June 1922 during Corpus Christi.[72] In honor of spontaneous and "natural" performance, professional *cantaores* (singers) would be ineligible. What did such an undertaking

68. Letter, Falla to Ángel Barrios, 4 August, cited and translated in Budwig, *Manuel de Falla*, 7.

69. Also present was John Trend. See his *Picture of Modern Spain*, 237–38, 243–44.

70. Ian Gibson, *The Death of Lorca* (Chicago: Philip O'Hare, 1973), 8.

71. As Timothy Mitchell points out, the term *flamenco* not only refers to a dance style but is "first and foremost a folk song style" in which both singers and dancers deal with often troubling emotions, such as rage, jealousy, or death. Out of this turmoil arose the term *cante jondo*, the Andalusian variant of *cante hondo* or "deep song" (Mitchell, *Flamenco Deep Song*, 1). Mitchell discusses the contest on pages 165–77.

72. Gibson, *Federico García Lorca*, 109. A still valuable overview of the contest is in Eduardo Molina Fajardo, *Manuel de Falla y el "cante jondo"* (Granada: Editorial Universidad de Granada, 1962).

mean? Flamenco's social status, which, as noted, proved a liability for some critics of *El amor brujo*, ensured that a bourgeois public would not necessarily appreciate a genre whose original practitioners hailed from the lowest rungs of society, including criminals and prostitutes. Flamenco's lineage resembled that of the Argentine tango, which originated in Buenos Aires' houses of prostitution, or jazz, which is associated with the African American underclass (the spirit of which Lorca compared to *cante jondo* and enshrined in his poetry).[73] As flamenco came to enjoy a degree of popularization, however, its intellectual protectors feared that mass culture and commercialization were undermining its "authenticity." Significant here was the primitivist movement: just as Picasso elevated African masks to "high art" and Ravel celebrated precolonial innocence in the *Chansons madécasses*, Falla and his colleagues cherished an idealized view of flamenco as a vehicle for the "purity" and "sobriety" of racial utterance.[74] Of course, the idea of exalting some utopian purity through musical performance is fundamentally naive; further, as Timothy Mitchell has argued, at least some flamenco genres are the result not of purity but of "ethnic chaos."[75] Tellingly, the same author also notes the primitivist tendency to make "a god out of the ungovernable parts of the self," an idea that might well apply to Falla, with his studied outward behavior.[76]

Support for the contest among *granadinos* was by no means unanimous. The critic Francisco de Paula Valladar attacked it for the same reasons he had savaged *The Three-Cornered Hat*: flamenco was "one more *españolada*" in that it promoted the stereotype of "an Andalusia disheartened and sad, decadent and ruined, in which misery and ignorance reign," that is, it perpetuated the romantic caricatures of Spain crafted by Washington Irving, Théophile Gautier, and Gustave Doré.[77] Less ideologically minded citizens felt that the municipal government should spend its funds on more pressing needs, while others feared that too much ink spilled in analyzing a spontaneous folk genre would result in pedantry.[78] For months prior to the contest, a heated polemic enlivened Granada's newspapers, including *El Defensor de Granada*, *El Noticiero Granadino*, *La Voz de Granada*, and Valladar's own *La Alhambra*. As in Madrid five years earlier, when addressing French and German

73. See, for example, "El rey de Harlem" (The King of Harlem) from the collection Federico García Lorca, *Poeta en Nueva York* (Poet in New York) edited by Piero Menarini (Madrid: Espasa Calpe, 2002), which was written during Lorca's stay at Columbia University during most of academic year 1929–30.

74. Glenn Watkins summarizes Falla's perception of flamenco as a "vanishing rarity" in *Pyramids at the Louvre: Music, Culture, and Collage from Stravinsky to the Postmodernists* (Cambridge: Harvard University Press, 1994), 72–73.

75. Mitchell, *Flamenco Deep Song*, 168.

76. Mitchell, *Flamenco Deep Song*, 161.

77. Francisco de Paula Valladar, "La Andalucía, sus leyendas pintorescas y la Alhambra," *La Alhambra*, 15 January 1922, cited in de Persia, *I concurso de cante jondo*, 29.

78. De Persia, *I concurso de cante jondo*, 33.

musical traits, Falla did not shun controversy. Vigorously defending the contest's ideals, Falla's essay "La proposición del cante jondo" (The Aim of Cante Jondo) appeared in the liberal *El Defensor de Granada* on 21 March 1922. Taking the position that authentic *cante jondo* had "degenerated into ridiculous[ness]," Falla identified the musical stages of this decay: "The limits of the restricted melodic range in which the songs unfold have been awkwardly enlarged; the poverty of tonality has replaced the modal richness of its ancient scales, which causes the steady use of the only two modern scales, those that monopolized European music for more than two centuries; the phrase, in short, grossly metrified, loses by the day that rhythmic flexibility that used to constitute one of its greatest beauties."[79] Falla's critique of tonality and its attendant "poverty" corresponds exactly to his earlier remarks on music prior to the seventeenth century, whose modal language he had defended from the "scorn" heaped on it since "the so-called classic period." (At least in his polemic on flamenco, Falla refrained from dragging Protestantism into the matter, as he had done in 1916.) Significantly, Falla's preservationist goals also reflect the contest's "neoclassical" orientation.

Lorca, a native of Granada, was a central participant in the contest's organization. Innately musical, he had a fine ear, played some flamenco guitar, and was a gifted pianist and arranger of folk melodies. It has even been suggested that had Falla come to Granada a few years earlier, when Lorca was making fundamental career decisions, the impulsive and highly emotional young man might have opted for music.[80] In any case, his poetry exudes musicality in imagery, rhythm, and subject matter; the fact that he "supplies constant cues for music in his writing," as critic Alex Ross points out, is certainly part of Lorca's appeal to composers.[81] Supporting the contest from Madrid was Salazar, who became one of Lorca's closest associates. Older than him by eight years, Salazar seemed more at ease with his homosexuality than Lorca was with his, and their friendship, along with Salazar's championing of the young poet's works, helped sustain Lorca through various emotional crises.[82]

79. "Los límites del reducido ámbito melódico en que se desarrollan los cantos han sido torpemente ampliados; a la riqueza modal de sus gamas antiqísimas, ha sustituido la pobreza tonal que causa el uso preponderante de las dos únicas escuelas modernas, de aquellas que monopolizaron la música europea durante más de dos siglos; la frase, en fin, groseramente metrificada, va perdiendo por día aquella flexibilidad rítimica que constituía una de sus más grandes bellezas" (Manuel de Falla, "La proposición del cante jondo," *El Defensor de Granada*, 21 March 22, cited in Christoforidis, "Un acercamiento," 11).

80. José Mora Guarnido, *Federico García Lorca y su mundo* (Buenos Aires: Losada, 1958), 159. An account of Lorca's early musical training is given on pages 70–78.

81. Alex Ross, "Deep Song: Lorca Inspires an Opera by Osvaldo Golijov," *New Yorker*, 1 September 2003, 128–29.

82. Gibson, *Federico García Lorca*, 104. Paul Binding treats the relationship between Lorca's homosexuality and his work in *Lorca: The Gay Imagination* (London: GMP Publishers, 1985), especially the *Sonetos del amor oscuro* (Sonnets of Dark Love) on pages 205–12.

In January 1922, a few months before the contest, Lorca wrote Salazar about a series of short poems that would eventually become the "Poema del cante jondo" (Poem of Flamenco Deep Song): "The poem is full of gypsies. . . . It's the first expression of a *new orientation of mine* and I don't yet know what to say to you about it . . . but it certainly breaks new ground! The only person who knows about it is Falla, and he's really enthusiastic!"[83] Falla had good reason for enthusiasm. In the "Poema del cante jondo," Lorca drew on the time-honored musical forms of flamenco—*siguiriya, soleá, saeta,* and *petenera*—as vehicles for powerful images of death, timelessness, nature, and imperturbability, all propelled by hypnotic rhythms.[84] Shortly thereafter, Falla likely guided Lorca in preparing a lecture on *cante jondo*.[85] In that famous talk, presented in Granada on 19 February 1922, Lorca mentioned flamenco's "pure" oriental heritage, lamenting that its transcendence was blemished by "immoral things, the tavern, the late-night orgy, the dance floors of flamenco cafés, ridiculous whining" and was stained with "the dark wine of the professional pimp," an assessment entirely congenial to Falla.[86] To inaugurate the contest, on 7 June 1922 Lorca recited portions of the "Poema del cante jondo" at the intimate, Moorish-style theater of the Hotel Alhambra Palace, a stone's throw from Falla's *carmen*. The same gathering featured a rare performance of flamenco by guitarist Andrés Segovia, also brought up in Granada, who was then launching an international career. An anonymous essay, one intimately related to Falla's views on flamenco, was read by the politician and intellectual Antonio Gallego y Burín.[87] The contest also attracted several foreign visitors, including John Trend; the German-born composer, conductor, and ethnomusicologist Kurt Schindler and his wife Ursula Grenville; and the British critic Leigh Henry (see figure 9).[88] Among the prize winners was an eleven-year-old, Manuel Ortega, known as El Caracol, who later would become one of the

83. Letter, Lorca to Salazar, 1 January 1922, translated in Gibson, *Federico García Lorca,* 109.

84. Gibson, *Federico García Lorca,* 110. Lorca was inspired by musical procedures in other works, such as the "Suite" from late 1920, which he thought of calling *El libro de diferencias* (102). There is also the well-known *Romancero gitano* (Gypsy Ballads) from 1924–25.

85. Gibson, *Federico García Lorca,* 112–13.

86. Federico García Lorca, "Deep Song," in *In Search of Duende,* translated from the Spanish by Christopher Maurer (New York: New Directions, 1998), 1–2.

87. *El "cante jondo" (cante primitivo andaluz): Sus orígenes, sus valores musicales, su influencia en el arte musical europeo* (1922; reprint Granada: Archivo Manuel de Falla, 1997), 16. See also de Persia, *I concurso de cante jondo,* 88.

88. See also the photograph in de Persia, *Poesía,* 160. Falla wanted to invite Stravinsky and Ravel, but the municipal government refused to provide funds (Gibson, *Federico García Lorca,* 114).

Figure 9. The *cante jondo* contest, line drawing by Antonio López Sáncho. (Reprinted by kind permission of the Ayuntamiento de Granada)

great *cantaores* of the century.[89] Another winner, the seventy-two-year-old Diego Bermúdez, known as El Tenazas, ultimately disappointed.[90]

Exhausted by the administrative work of the contest and embittered by the indifference of so many *granadinos* to their native art, Falla ultimately found the *cante jondo* contest discouraging. But he was glad to have worked so closely with Lorca, whose childlike enthusiasms complemented the older man's more tempered—but no less childlike—outlook. They were soon collaborating again, this time on the "Teatro Cachiporra Andaluz" (Andalusian Punch and Judy Theater). As with the *cante jondo* contest, their interest stemmed from preservationist impulses, this time to revive the Andalusian puppet tradition. Their one and only performance took place on 6 January 1923 (Epiphany) at the Lorca home; tellingly, it trained a singularly modernist lens on folk puppetry. On the program were Lorca's adaptation of an old Andalusian story, *La niña que riega la albahaca y el príncipe preguntón* (The Girl Who Waters the Basil and the Inquisitive Prince); *Los dos habladores* (The Two Talkers), then attributed to Cervantes;[91] and, in keeping with the Feast of Epiphany, the thirteenth-century *Misterio de los reyes magos* (Mystery of the Three Wise Men). For incidental music, Falla blended modern, traditional, and popular elements, inserting into *Los dos habladores* the "Devil's Dance" and "Waltz" from *L'Histoire du soldat* and into *La niña que riega* Debussy's "Doll's Serenade" (from the *Children's Corner Suite*), Ravel's *Berceuse*, and his own arrangement of a seventeenth-century

89. Gibson, *Federico García Lorca*, 115. See also the recording *I Concurso de cante jondo,* CD Sonifolk 20106 M–17273–1997.

90. Mitchell, *Flamenco Deep Song*, 170–71.

91. Gibson, *Federico García Lorca*, 119.

dance, the "Españoleta y paso y medio," which he found in volume 3 of Pedrell's magisterial *Cancionero musical popular español*.[92] As for instrumentation, Falla used the unlikely—and decidedly parodic—combination of *laúd* (a steel-strung instrument that resembles a large, flatback mandolin), violin, and clarinet. He and Lorca also playfully stuffed wads of newspaper into the strings of the family piano. Although the intention was to simulate a harpsichord, the result must have been closer to the prepared piano of the 1940s.[93] Ten years later Lorca remembered the care Falla lavished on the production:

> Three days before our theater opened I went to Falla's house and heard him playing the piano. I knocked on the door. He didn't hear me. I knocked more loudly. Finally I entered. The maestro was seated at the instrument with a score . . . in front of him.
> "What are you doing, maestro?"
> "I'm getting ready for the concert in your theater."
> That's Falla: in order to amuse some mere children he was going to the trouble of getting everything just right. Because that's Falla's way: the awareness of and search for perfection.[94]

Did Falla's ongoing "search for perfection" reflect agonizing "self-love" or sensitivity to God's innocents? How easily the porous boundaries between these extremes— and others' perception of them—could shift! As noted, it was at around this time that Falla's path to perfection began to narrow, taking him farther into himself. To be sure, he continued to enjoy excursions, sometimes with high-spirited children (see figure 10). Also, his fondness for intellectual company and ideas sometimes took him to the Café Alameda, the meeting ground for Granada's intellectuals (the group was known as "El Rinconcillo," the "little corner"), where he held honorary status. Habitués, many of whom were younger than Falla, included Lorca, Barrios, Segovia, the journalist José Mora Guarnido, and the artist Hermenegildo Lanz; foreign visitors to Granada, such as Rudyard Kipling, H. G. Wells, Rubinstein, and Landowska, were also welcomed into the "Rinconcillo" and were even taken on "privileged tours of secret Granada."[95] Through his various magazine subscriptions, as well as his correspondence with Casella, Poulenc, Jean-Aubry, Ravel, Roland-Manuel, and many others, Falla stayed abreast of musical developments in greater Europe. He and María del Carmen also entertained visitors at the little *carmen*. Still, he was increasingly drawn to silence and things of the spirit, needs he could usually satisfy in Granada. In the coming years, such needs would intensify.

92. Felipe Pedrell, *Cancionero musical popular español*, 4 vols. (Valls: E. Castells, 1917–21).

93. Pahissa, *Vida y obra*, 127.

94. Pablo Suero, "Hablando de 'La Barraca' con el poeta García Lorca," *Noticias Gráficas*, 15 October 1933, cited in Gibson, *Federico García Lorca*, 119.

95. Gibson, *Federico García Lorca*, 60.

Figure 10. Antonio Luna, Falla,
Federico García Lorca, José
Segura, and children on an
excursion in Granada Province,
1923. (Reprinted by kind
permission of the Archivo
Manuel de Falla)

Whatever their enthusiasm for modernist puppetry, Falla and Lorca's plans to take the Teatro Cachiporra Andaluz to Europe and South America came to nothing. The brevity of this venture was due in part to Lorca's law studies, which, after considerable procrastination, he finally completed in late January 1923 (he was never seen to open a law book again). Between 1922 and 1924, he and Falla worked intermittently on a comic opera, *Lola la comedianta* (Lola, the Actress), about a woman who makes sport of men's feelings, which they possibly envisioned as part of their puppet repertory.[96] As Gibson has suggested, Falla, fresh from his break with María and Gregorio, may well have seen Lorca as his new librettist.[97] But such a relationship was not to be. Although Falla approved Lorca's synopsis and even made a few general musical decisions, as with *Don Juan de España*, he seems never to have written a note of the score. Did he ultimately find *Lola* so frivolous as to be unworthy of his attention? Or was he simply too involved with other projects to devote his full attention to what would surely have been a brilliant collaboration? Whatever the reason, nothing came of the project.

96. The most complete discussion of the projected collaboration is in Federico García Lorca, *Lola la comedianta*, edited by Piero Menarini (Madrid: Alianza, 1981), 53–90.

97. Gibson, *Federico García Lorca*, 124–25.

Another work from the early Granada years originated from Falla's sense of charity. In 1921, he read *Mi viaje a la Rusia Sovietista* (My Journey to Soviet Russia) by Fernando de los Ríos. A socialist and member of the University of Granada law faculty (he was one of Lorca's professors), de los Ríos, like Falla, had signed Ortega's manifesto in 1915.[98] As one who also occasionally visited the Café Alameda, he may have gotten to know Falla in the congenial atmosphere of the "Rinconcillo"; de los Ríos was also a music lover (his ten-year-old daughter Laura sang in the Epiphany puppet play at the Lorca home). Falla, who probably attended de los Ríos's lecture of 4 April, praised the book as "notablísimo," surely on account of its plea that spiritual values play a role in social change.[99] His own atheism notwithstanding, de los Ríos believed socialism to be a "moral imperative"; in 1926, he would describe it as a way to "refresh and spiritualize souls . . . to open wide the floodgates of the sentiment, buried these days, of the religiosity of life."[100] He also addressed the refugee situation in the Soviet Union, that is, the plight of more than two million Russians who had been imprisoned on the Eastern Front during World War I and were now dispersed throughout the country and going hungry. The League of Nations was attempting to deal with this problem, as an acquaintance of Falla's, the diplomat Ricardo Baeza, informed him.[101] When Baeza asked Falla to compose a score whose proceeds would help the refugees, the result was his arrangement of the well-known "Song of the Volga Boatmen," which Falla completed in March 1922.[102] This brief, austere statement consists of two alternating themes, one of which is recycled five times in three pages of music with increasingly compelling harmonies. In the third statement of this theme, for example, Falla takes up the quartal sonority E–A–D–G introduced in m. 3 (third beat), rebalances it on G (rather than A, as in m. 3, where it nonetheless obscures its potential dominant function), and opens up a new range of color with chords from the flat direction, all punctuated by the piano's extreme register (see musical example 18).

98. A charming account of de los Ríos's imaginative and flexible classroom style is in Mora Guarnida, *Federico García Lorca y su mundo*, 148–65.

99. Letter, Falla to Zuloaga, 15 December 1921, cited in Sopeña, *Correspondencia entre Falla y Zuloaga*, n.p.

100. Fernando de los Ríos, *Mi viaje a la Rusia Sovietista, Obras completas*, edited by Teresa Rodríguez de Lecca (Madrid: Fundación Caja de Madrid, Anthropos Editorial [Barcelona], 1997), 2:8. The 1926 quote is from de los Ríos's *El sentido humanista del socialismo*, cited in Piero Menarini, Introduction to Lorca, *Poeta en Nueva York*, 24. De los Ríos accompanied Lorca to the United States in 1929.

101. F. S. Northedge, *The League of Nations: Its Life and Times, 1920–1946* (New York: Holmes and Meier, 1986), 77. Baeza's letter is cited in Gallego, *Catálogo*, 190.

102. Stravinsky arranged the same melody shortly after the abdication of Nicholas II in April 1917 to replace Alexis Feodorovich Lvov's "God Save the Tsar." See Taruskin, *Stravinsky and the Russian Traditions*, 2:1183. See also Eric Walter White, *Stravinsky: The Composer and His Works*, 2d ed. (Berkeley: University of California Press, 1979), 546.

Musical Example 18. Falla, *Canto de los remeros del Volga* (Song of the Volga Boatmen), mm. 17–22. (Reprinted by kind permission of Ediciones Manuel de Falla)

Falla's affinity with Russia had long been stimulated by his regard for Stravinsky and Glinka, whom he, Diaghilev, and others included in a loose "Latino-Slav" (read anti-German) fraternity, which, as we have seen, was also linked to the concept of "Latinité." But this affinity carried with it political implications. When Russia became the Soviet Union, Spanish leftists became increasingly taken with this model of government; after labor upheavals in Spain during the summer of 1917, Spain was even known to some as the "Russia of the West."[103] Falla's liberalism during World War I, coupled with his socialist leanings in the early 1920s, thus made his anxieties of the 1930s all the more acute, as he despaired of ever reconciling Christian principles of social justice with the accelerating anticlericalism of so many Spanish communists and socialists during that violent decade.

But such conflicts would have seemed unimaginable to Falla during his early years at Calle de Antequeruela Alta no. 11. Moving to Granada was a new beginning. To be sure, he had lost both his parents, but he and María del Carmen could count on one another for a sense of family. A cheerful person of fairly simple needs, María del Carmen took on the running of the household, correctly believing this to be an important contribution to her brother's creativity. (She had at least one servant.) Falla's previously uncertain finances had been substantially boosted by the success of *The Three-Cornered Hat*, and he could now select students with care. Although he had not completely distanced himself from Madrid's musical politics (reading the sniping remarks on the premiere of *The Three-Cornered Hat* could hardly have been gratifying), he was no longer involved with the intrigues of the

103. Meaker, "A Civil War of Words," in Schmitt, *Neutral Europe*, 2.

capital's theater scene. Most significant of all was his abandonment of the musical language with which he had defined himself in *La vida breve*, the *Cuatro piezas españolas*, the *Siete canciones populares españolas*, *Noches en los jardines de España*, *El amor brujo*, *The Three-Cornered Hat*, and the *Fantasía bética*. A new stylistic agenda, the cosmopolitan and "universalist" idiom of neoclassicism, now claimed his attention.

Chapter 6

The European Neoclassicist: Finding His Voice

In praising the "masterpieces of Falla's maturity," *El retablo de Maese Pedro* (1923) and the Harpsichord Concerto (1926), Robert P. Morgan has noted "great economy and concision . . . [a] stark, hard-edged style reflecting not only current neo-classical tendencies but, more specifically, Falla's growing interest in earlier Spanish art music."[1] As we have seen, values such as balance, brevity, economy, and wit had taken hold in France before the outbreak of the Great War. In its aftermath, many composers continued to revive baroque and classical procedures: counterpoint, sonata form, reduced performing forces, and the use of generic rather than poetic or "impressionistic" titles. By clothing these time-honored formal abstractions in bold new harmonies and arresting timbres, moreover, composers could be "modern" and traditionalist at the same time. Essentially anti-Teutonic in origin, neo-classicism, as the movement increasingly came to be known, also eschewed overt programmatic references (such as those found in Richard Strauss's symphonic poems), as well as nationalist or populist allusions.[2] All of this was undertaken on

---

1. Robert P. Morgan, *Twentieth-Century Music* (New York and London: Norton, 1991), 267.

2. The use of the label *néoclassicisme* (and *nouveau classicisme*) is traced in Messing, *Neoclassicism in Music*, 1–59. The Spanish *neoclasicismo* appears relatively infrequently in musical discourse, although, as argued below, many musical and literary values in Spain during the 1920s and early 1930s corresponded to the tenets of European neoclassicism.

the premise of creating "pure," "objective," or "universal" music, a point on which Stravinsky was particularly vociferous.

DEFINING MOMENTS: *EL RETABLO DE MAESE PEDRO*
AND THE HARPSICHORD CONCERTO

In *El retablo de Maese Pedro* and the Harpsichord Concerto, Falla, like his contemporaries, created spare textures and astringent harmonies. But instead of turning to eighteenth-century models he dug even deeper into the past, exploring the thirteenth-century Cantigas de Alfonso X, "El Sabio" (The Wise), the seventeenth-century guitar treatises of Gaspar Sanz, and other examples of Spain's rich medieval and Renaissance heritage. Of course, this repertory abounded in the very "modal richness" that Falla had praised in *cante jondo*, a populist genre if there ever were one. Thus, his use of modality marked a suggestive new path for neoclassicism while subtly asserting Spanish identity, even in this presumably "universalist" context. Here Falla was aided by the prevailing mood in Spanish literary circles. Whether resuscitating Golden Age poetic forms or the Andalusian dialect of the Punch and Judy show, dramatists and poets, like composers, were engaged in a fascinating dialogue between past and present, elite and popular, all within the quest for national identity with a modernist hue.[3]

In neoclassicism, Falla found his true voice. But, although he had been drawn to "early music" for years, it was not until late April of 1919 that he began to feel confident of its relevance to his own music, specifically, in *El retablo de Maese Pedro*, which he was then negotiating with the princesse de Polignac. At that time (ironically, he was in the midst of the *andalucista Fantasía bética*) he reported to Diaghilev that the *Retablo* was "very advanced," a statement that turned out to be overly optimistic.[4] This profoundly non-*andalucista* work is based on the episode from Cervantes's *Don Quijote* (part 2, chapter 26) in which the protagonist and his squire, Sancho Panza, wander into Maese Pedro's puppet theater. There a performance of the medieval tale "The Liberation of Melisendra" is narrated by Maese Pedro's assistant, a young boy known as the *trujamán*. Don Quijote, of course, is intimately familiar with chivalric literature; in fact, his immersion in it has shaped his singular worldview. He notices several errors of fact in the boy's account and twice corrects him from the audience, once with a paean to the virtues of "unadulterated truth" (*una verdad limpia*). A third error, however, is too much for the Knight of the Sad

3. For a summary of Jorge Guillén, Pedro Salinas, and Rafael Alberti, who revived Golden Age poetic forms, see Ángel del Río, *Historia de la literatura española*, rev. ed. (New York: Holt, Reinhardt, and Winston, 1963), 2:237–39.
4. Letter, Falla to Diaghilev, 30 April 1919, cited in de Persia, *Poesía*, 124. At one time, Falla discussed publicly the possibility of producing *El retablo de Maese Pedro* under the auspices of the Ballets Russes. See G. Jean-Aubry, "De Falla Talks of His New Work Based on a Don Quijote Theme," *Christian Science Monitor*, 1 September 1923, 17, AMF press file.

Countenance. Although Maese Pedro reminds him that "thousands of plays [are] presented almost daily that are full of improprieties and discrepancies," Don Quijote cannot separate fiction from life. With frenzied strokes of his sword, he demolishes puppets and stage, believing he is defending civilization against the infidel.

Unlike his previous theatrical efforts, Falla adapted Cervantes's story himself.[5] What were the elements in it that most appealed to him? Especially provocative are the questions of narrative authority and the separation of truth from falsehood, for Don Quijote, whom criticism has variously regarded as either an idealist or a buffoon, sees the world in his own way.[6] This, of course, awakens his unquenchable desire to "right the unrightable wrong," as a more recent retelling of the novel would have it. These themes, leavened with a conspicuous dose of wit, attracted Falla and prompted him to experiment musically and dramatically. For one thing, he solidified his ideas on writing for the harpsichord in the *Retablo*. Here Wanda Landowska inspired him. In November 1922, she gave two concerts at Granada's Hotel Alhambra Palace; during her visit, she and Falla talked animatedly of harpsichord writing. Landowska later recalled how Falla wrote her the very next day, saying that "reading the *Retablo* and all [Landowska's] precious indications on the use of the harpsichord awakened . . . a multitude of ideas and of projects to realize."[7] Landowska's visit was also a pleasant social experience for Falla and María del Carmen if the broad smiles in a group shot taken at this time are any indication (see figure 11). Besides venturing into harpsichord writing, the use of puppets attracted Falla and brought out his more winsome qualities. It was also a point on which he had rather strong ideas, at least as far as the *Retablo* was concerned. He specified puppets for *all* the characters: small ones to enact "The Liberation of Melisendra" and life-sized marionettes for the nonpuppet roles (Maese Pedro, the *trujamán*, Don Quijote, Sancho Panza, and the spectators). This complicated arrangement would later be modified (see figure 12), but it was one Falla discussed at length with his various collaborators—Manuel Ángeles Ortiz, Hermenegildo Lanz, and, in 1926 for the Amsterdam production, Luis Buñuel. All this, in addition to actually composing the music, caused him to miss the princesse de Polignac's initial deadline of July 1919 by some four years, much to her annoyance.[8]

---

5. An interpolation, the "Ode to Dulcinea" (rehearsal 86), is extracted from book 1, chapters 2, 3, 6, 8, 46, and 52. See Gerlinde Ernst, "Manuel de Falla (1876–1946): *El Retablo de Maese Pedro (Meister Pedros Puppenspiel)*," Ph.D. diss., University of Erlangen, 1994. A more detailed discussion of the *Retablo* in relation to Cervantes's novel is in Hess, *Manuel de Falla and Modernism in Spain*, 199–208.

6. Hess, *Manuel de Falla and Modernism in Spain*, 207, 217–26.

7. Denise Restout, comp., ed., and trans., with Robert Hawkins, *Landowska on Music* (New York: Stein and Day, 1964), 346.

8. Their correspondence is found in Christoforidis, "Aspects of the Creative Process," 174–80.

Figure 11. Falla with (left to right) Francisco García Lorca, Antonio Luna, María del Carmen, Federico García Lorca, Wanda Landowska, and José Segura in Granada, 1922. (Reprinted by kind permission of the Archivo Manuel de Falla)

Two months prior to its official premiere at the Hôtel Singer-Polignac, the *Retablo* was presented in Seville in concert format, that is, without puppets. Participants included members of what would soon be known as the Orquesta Bética de Cámara (Chamber Orchestra of Andalusia). It seems that the administrative headaches of *cante jondo* were not so debilitating to Falla after all, for he now undertook the civic project of founding the orchestra along with the cellist Segismundo Romero and the *maestro de capilla* (chapel master) of the Seville cathedral Eduardo Torres. (Its first conductor would be Falla's student Ernesto Halffter.) Following the precepts of neoclassicism, the Bética's goal was to promote both new and "ancient" music; a second goal was to raise the level of orchestral playing in Spain.[9] Foreign visitors attending the premiere of the *Retablo* included Trend, Jean-Aubry, and Schindler,

9. Harper, *Manuel de Falla*, 31–32. On its inaugural concert of 11 June 1924 in Seville's Teatro Llorens, see Yolanda Acker, "Ernesto Halffter: A Study of the Years 1905–46," *Revista de Musicología* 17 (1994): 114. The term *bética* is most commonly translated as "Andalusian." Salazar, however, refers to it as the "poetic name" of Seville's principal river, the Guadalquivir ("Bética, vient de Bétis, nom poétique du Guadalquivir, fleuve de Séville") (Adolfo Salazar, "Espagne: L'Orquesta Betica de Camara," *La Revue Musicale* 7, no. 1 [1 November 1925]: 79n1).

Figure 12. Falla with the Don
Quijote marionette for the Venice
production of *El retablo de Maese
Pedro*, 1932. (Reprinted by kind
permission of the Archivo
Manuel de Falla)

and the work met with near unanimous approval.[10] Much of this was due to the
interest Falla's remarkable change of style provoked. Gone are the waves of impressionistic color of *Noches*, the impassioned *andalucismo* of *El amor brujo*, and the
"colorful" orchestration of *The Three-Cornered Hat*. Rather, Falla concentrates
on differentiating the timbres of a small, heterogeneous chamber ensemble, writing
against the romantic concept of "blended" sound, with two "ancient" instruments,
the harpsichord and harp-lute, especially prominent. Falla also put his personal stamp
on these backward-looking gestures, as, for example, in the harpsichord's support of
the *trujamán*'s narrative. Here, instead of adhering to the norms of eighteenth-century
recitative, the composer evokes the shrill, singsong quality of the *pregonero* (town
crier) shouting the latest news from the village square. In the performance instructions to the Chester edition, Falla specified a voice "which is nasal and rather
forced—the voice of a boy shouting in the street, rough in expression and exempt
from all lyrical feeling," making explicit his intention to combine a drawing room
instrument with adolescent yelling. Another conspicuous reference to the past, also
reinterpreted by Falla, is the opening *Sinfonía*. Modeled on the baroque concerto
grosso, the *Sinfonía* is spiced up with the witty "wrong note" style common in European neoclassicism (see musical example 19). Similarly pungent are the other fan-

10. Hess, *Manuel de Falla and Modernism in Spain*, 225–31.

Musical Example 19. Falla, *El retablo de Maese Pedro*, recapitulation of *Sinfonía*. (Chester Music Ltd. International copyright secured. All rights reserved. Reprinted by permission.)

fares, especially that accompanying Maese Pedro's call (rehearsal 9), which outlines an A-major triad against an E♭-major chord and marks the words "I begin!" With the addition of the horns (and excluding the passing F♮ in the trumpet), an octatonic scale, C–C♯–E♭–E–F♯–G–A–B♭, emerges, the pitch collection so favored by Stravinsky that now marked Falla's new "beginning."

In his preliminary work on the *Retablo*, Falla "saturated himself" in the music of Cervantes's period, as he told Jean-Aubry in an interview.[11] His sources include guitar works by Gaspar Sanz and Antonio de Cabezón's *Diferencias sobre el canto del caballero* and *Pavana milanesa*; sources not confined to Cervantes's period were folklorist Dámaso Ledesma's *Cancionero salmantino* and Pedrell's *Cancionero musical popular español*.[12] Falla's numerous but subtle borrowings, moreover, correspond to a central feature of Cervantes's novel, namely, the ambiguity between *its* sources and narrative authority. In the *Retablo* scene, for example, Cervantes draws on a Carolingian ballad (*romance*) and the conventions of chivalric literature.[13] Falla eventually decided on a *gallarda* by Sanz ("Entrance of Charlemagne," rehearsal 19), a *tonada* from Francisco de Salinas's treatise *De musica libri septem* of 1577 ("Melisendra," rehearsal 30) and another melody probably derived from Salinas (vocal line, rehearsal 59), fragments of the madrigal "Prado verde y florido" by Francisco Guerrero ("Ode to Dulcinea," rehearsal 86), the Spanish "Royal March" (rehearsal 96), and a fragment from the Catalan Christmas carol "El dessembre congelat" (rehearsal 78).[14] Especially significant is Falla's witty self-quotation. As Melisendra and her husband, Don Gayferos, are escaping their Moorish pursuers, the composer introduces the main melody of the "Canción del fuego fatuo" from *El amor brujo* (rehearsal 75), the theme of which is pursuit and retreat. Stated by the xylophone and the horns and punctuated by timpani and tenor drum, the insistent theme cuts through the clangorous orchestral texture and is an ironic but assertive farewell to *andalucismo* (see musical example 20).

While in Seville for the performance Falla received an invitation from Schindler to compose a viola and piano suite or sonata for the Berkshire Festival, which Eliza-

---

11. Jean-Aubry, "De Falla Talks of His New Work," 17. Christoforidis details Falla's preliminary work in "Aspects of the Creative Process," 102–12.

12. Dámaso Ledesma, *Cancionero Salmantino* (Madrid: Imprenta Alemana, 1907); on the *Cancionero musical popular español* see above, 132.

13. George Haley, "The Narrator in *Don Quijote*: Maese Pedro's Puppet Show," *Modern Language Notes* 80 (1965): 145–64. See also Hess, *Manuel de Falla and Modernism in Spain*, 204–8.

14. Falla took the Sanz *gallarda* from a transcription of that composer's *Instrucción de música sobre la guitarra española* of 1674, the Salinas excerpts from volume 1 of Pedrell's *Cancionero*, and the Guerrero madrigal from Esteban Daza's 1576 intabulation, *El parnaso*. On the Guerrero madrigal, see Antonio Gallego, "Dulcinea en el prado (verde y florido)," *Revista de Musicología* 10 (1987): 685–99. My discussion of Falla's sources is indebted to Christoforidis, "Aspects of the Creative Process."

Musical Example 20. (above and opposite) Falla, *El retablo de Maese Pedro*, rehearsal 75. (Chester Music Ltd. International copyright secured. All rights reserved. Reprinted by permission.)

beth Sprague Coolidge had established in mid-1918.[15] Unfortunately for the viola repertory, Falla turned Schindler's offer down, since he felt he could not meet the deadline of early August; also he was off to his beloved Paris to prepare for the full premiere of the *Retablo*. Still, he accepted Coolidge's invitation to attend two chamber music concerts in Rome, leaving Paris on 1 May. Despite the possibility of labor protests (Mussolini had prohibited all celebrations of this workers' holiday), the journey itself was largely uneventful.[16] Besides attending both concerts, which featured works by Gian Francesco Malipiero, Ernest Bloch, and Rebecca Clarke, Falla visited museums and played the piano into the wee hours of the morning with Vittorio Rietti, Casella, and Malipiero.[17] The only misadventure of the trip occurred on a visit to the Vatican one morning. There Falla became so enraptured with the "primitives," that he and Schindler lost track of the time and arrived late to a lunch Coolidge had scheduled. As one who "did things the North American way, everything down to the minute," she did not conceal her displeasure, as Falla remembered years later.[18] From Rome, Falla traveled north to Florence, where he visited Mario Castelnuovo-Tedesco. After Padua and Venice, he went on to Stresa, where he met his former collaborator Aga Lahowska. In one of her letters, she had sighed that it would be "truly horrible" not to see Falla in Italy and later teased him when his whereabouts were finally "un tout petit peu plus precisées!"[19] All told, the Italian sojourn seems to have been entirely carefree and spontaneous, a relaxing preparation for the *Retablo*'s Paris premiere.

It may well have been the event of the season. Wladimir Golschmann conducted, and Landowska, whose conversations on harpsichord playing had awakened in Falla "a multitude of ideas," played in the chamber ensemble. The sets and two ranks of fanciful puppets were designed by Falla's compatriots Manuel Ángeles Ortiz and Hermenegildo Lanz. Among those who applauded the premiere were Picasso, Paul Valéry, the artist Henri de Regnier, José María Sert (Falla's friend and future collaborator), Stravinsky, and Poulenc; the latter was so fascinated by Landowska's playing that he set about writing the *Concert Champêtre* for harpsichord and or-

---

15. Bergadà, "La relación de Falla con Italia," in Nommick, *Manuel de Falla e Italia*, 29. See also Cyrilla Barr, "A Style of Her Own: The Patronage of Elizabeth Sprague Coolidge," in *Cultivating Music in America: Women Patrons and Activists since 1860*, edited by Ralph Locke and Cyrilla Barr (Berkeley: University of California Press, 1997), 191; Barr, *Elizabeth Sprague Coolidge: American Patron of Music* (New York: Schirmer, 1998), 150–51; and Alfredo Casella, *Music in My Time*, translated and edited by Spencer Norton (Norman: University of Oklahoma Press, 1955), 162.

16. Pahissa, *Vida y obra*, 128–29.

17. Bergadà, "La relación de Falla con Italia," in Nommick, *Manuel de Falla e Italia*, 29.

18. Pahissa, *Vida y obra*, 129. Still, Coolidge recalled Falla with admiration. See Barr, *Elizabeth Sprague Coolidge*, 151.

19. Letter, Lahowska to Falla, 14 May 1923, cited in Bergadà, "La relación de Falla con Italia," in Nommick, *Manuel de Falla e Italia*, 30n40.

chestra. Also present was Ricardo Viñes, whose manual dexterity earned him the privilege of operating one of the marionettes. The performance was a triumph, with critics applauding both the score's delights and Falla's finesse in balancing many diverse elements. (One headline proclaimed him "Maese Falla.")[20] As a result, the *Retablo* attracted the notice of several prestigious organizations and subsequently appeared on Jean Wiéner's concert series (Paris, November 1923) and at the International Society of Contemporary Music (Zurich 1926, Venice 1932).

There was also a performance with the fledgling League of Composers, which was based in New York. This important entity was established in 1923 when several board members of the International Composers' Guild (founded in 1921 by Edgard Varèse and Carlos Salzedo) split off from the guild for reasons ranging from organizational skirmishes to suspicions of anti-Semitism (as it happened, the League was predominantly Jewish).[21] Additional friction between the League and the Guild ensued when Leopold Stokowski, who had conducted the American premiere of *El amor brujo* with the Philadelphia Orchestra the previous year, tried to talk Claire Reis, now the League's executive director, into relinquishing the performance rights she had obtained for the *Retablo* so that he could conduct it for the Guild.[22] The energetic Reis, a pianist, writer, and patron of the arts, held her ground. Motivated by a strong social conscience, she believed that an audience for new music could develop more naturally from "the man on the street" rather than from a musical elite with fixed ideas. The *Retablo*, with its artful mix of the erudite and the popular, corresponded perfectly to her ideal.[23]

But how would the work go over with a public in which Cervantes's *Don Quijote* figured less than prominently in the collective consciousness? The first New York *Retablo* was part of an all-Falla concert held on 29 December 1925 at Town Hall.[24]

20. Corpus Barga, "El Retablo de Maese Falla," *El Sol*, 20 June 1923, 1.

21. Carol J. Oja, *Making Music Modern: New York in the 1920s* (New York: Oxford University Press, 2000), 217–18.

22. Oliver Daniel, *Stokowski: A Counterpoint of View* (New York: Dodd, Mead, 1982), 246–47. The premiere of *El amor brujo*, with Stokowski and the Philadelphia Orchestra, took place 15 April 1922. See Preben Opperby, *Leopold Stokowski* (New York: Hippocrene, 1982), 275.

23. Carol J. Oja, "Women Patrons and Crusaders for Modernist Music: New York in the 1920s," in Locke and Barr, *Cultivating Music in America*, 248. See also David Metzer, "The League of Composers: The Initial Years," *American Music* 15 (1997): 56–57.

24. Some of Falla's music had already been performed under the League's auspices, including four of the *Siete canciones populares españolas* (11 November 1923, Klaw Theater) and the "Seguidilla murciana" and "Jota" from the same set (25 November 1923, Anderson Galleries), both with soprano Raymonde Delaunois and pianist LeRoy Shield (on 25 November only). See Oja, *Making Music Modern*, 378.

Among other enticements, it competed with Percy Grainger's choral and orchestral concert at Aeolian Hall and a performance by Paul Whiteman's orchestra at Carnegie Hall, for which crowds waited two hours. The League-sponsored concert included some of Falla's most *andalucista* works: excerpts from *El amor brujo,* Salud's aria from *La vida breve,* and "Nana" and "Polo" from the *Siete canciones populares españolas.* There was also Eva Gauthier's performance of "Les colombes" and "Séguidille," from the *Trois mélodies. New York Times* critic Olin Downes dismissed these as "spurious modern French and cheap Spanish, respectively" (he obviously missed the potential for caricature in "Séguidille"), and he was hardly more sympathetic to the vocal chamber work, *Psyché,* which he called "a wandering affair."[25] But for the *Retablo,* in which Willem Mengelberg conducted members of the New York Philharmonic, Landowska, and singers Raymonde Delaunois, William Simmons, and Rafaelo Díaz, Downes had nothing but praise. Especially spectacular were the two ranks of marionettes, cleverly designed by Remo Bufano. The Don Quijote puppet alone was six feet tall. Another novel element was the presence of black-robed figures that manipulated both sets of puppets, as in Bunraku puppetry. Perhaps with these dark beings, visible to the audience, Bufano intended a discreet allusion to the dim recesses of Don Quijote's mind, misunderstood by a prosaic world that so readily sees "unadulterated truth" in crude either/or and black/white terms.[26] Downes himself noted Falla's deft balancing of disparate elements, writing that

> the character of the work was felt and appreciated. . . . *El Retablo* furnishes a score which De Falla has wrought with extraordinary fineness of touch and deftness of hand. He has combined with rare success the contrasting elements that his subject provides. There is the blend of the human and the mechanically theatrical, of the popular and the archaic. The music is Spanish, racial, without being a mere retailing of popular idioms. Simple as it often sounds, it is actually a tour de force, and this in an appropriately small frame.[27]

Thus Falla's new, non-*andalucista* style gave delight in New York. Even more enthusiastic was Oscar Thompson, who insisted that the League had never introduced a work "so felicitous, so novel, so delectable."[28]

Not surprisingly, the League programmed the *Retablo* again, this time alongside Stravinsky's *L'Histoire du soldat* at that work's American premiere on 25 March 1928 at the Jolson Theater. And a happy pair it was: Downes declared that "nothing could

25. Olin Downes, "Music: De Falla's Marionette Opera," *New York Times,* 30 December 1925, 10.

26. Interpretations of the *Retablo* scene are discussed in Hess, *Manuel de Falla and Modernism in Spain,* 217–24.

27. Downes, "Music," 10.

28. Oscar Thompson, "*El Retablo* Delights at American Premiere," *Musical America* 47 (9 January 1926): 7.

have been a better prelude for the beautiful and inspired music of de Falla than the bitter, bare music of Stravinsky."[29] Pierre Monteux conducted players from the New York Philharmonic and singers from the Metropolitan Opera: George Raseley (Maese Pedro), Carl Schlegel (Don Quijote), and Ruth Rodgers (the *trujamán*).[30] Although Irving Weill wished that the *Retablo* had been sung in English, he nonetheless proclaimed the event an antidote to the "Brahms-sodden" ambiance of New York's musical life.[31]

In Spain, critics greeted jubilantly the news of the *Retablo*'s North American triumph, insisting that it had put Spanish music on the map once and for all and would dispel the image of Spain as a country of primitive gypsy music lacking in "composers."[32] "So much for our insignificance!" Salazar gloated.[33] Well might the distinguished critic exult: Spanish arts and letters were enjoying an impressive renaissance throughout the world, as Lorca, Dalí, Miró, and others were creating some of their greatest works at the height of the Silver Age. At the same time, however, civil liberties were being curtailed. In September 1923, a military uprising (*pronunciamiento*) had ushered in the dictatorship of General Miguel Primo de Rivera. A backslapping type on good terms with Alfonso XIII, Primo was more or less tolerated by many Spaniards, even if some intellectuals felt the sting of censorship (Unamuno, for example, was exiled to the Canary Islands).[34] Falla continued his work, largely unaffected (see figure 13). But by the end of the decade Primo's failure to legitimize his rule would lay the groundwork for military revolt, and after a series of short-lived governments the stage would be set for the establishment of the Second Republic in 1931 and the forced abdication of Alfonso XIII.

If prior to the early 1920s Falla had been attacked for his susceptibility to foreign influences, now the Spanish musical press compared him favorably with foreign composers, especially Stravinsky. This is apparent in the reviews of the Madrid premiere of the *Retablo* in March 1924, which coincided with the first performance of *Pulcinella* there.[35] Falla went to Madrid for the concert and to greet Stravinsky, who

29. Olin Downes, "Stravinsky Poem Wins at Premiere," *New York Times*, 27 March 1928, 27.

30. "Music Here and Afield," *New York Times*, 25 March 1928, 9.

31. Irving Weill, "'Soldier' Given with Pantomimic Rite," *Musical America* 47 (31 March 1928): 1, 7.

32. See, for example, Camille Mauclair, *Histoire de la musique européene, 1850–1914* (Paris: Librairie Fischbacher, 1914), 283–84.

33. Adolfo Salazar, "La vida musical: *El Retablo de Maese Pedro* en Nueva York," *El Sol*, 28 January 1926, AMF press file.

34. An overview of the dictatorship and its opponents, which included intellectuals, politicians, regionalists, and elements of the military, is found in Shlomo Ben-Ami, *The Origins of the Second Republic in Spain* (Oxford: Oxford University Press, 1978), 1–25.

35. See especially Adolfo Salazar, "Polichinela y Maese Pedro," *Revista de Occidente* 4 (1924): 229–37, translated as "*Pulcinella* and *Maese Pedro*," *Chesterian* 6 (1926): 119–25.

Figure 13. Falla at his desk at home in Granada, 1924, photographed by Rogelio Robles Pozo. (Reprinted by kind permission of the Archivo Manuel de Falla)

would conduct on this "joyful occasion," as Falla put it to the Russian composer in one of the several letters they exchanged on the subject.[36] One afternoon in Madrid, Stravinsky gave a private performance for Falla, Salazar, Miguel Salvador, and Ernesto Halffter of the Concerto for Piano and Wind Instruments.[37] Later, at the Palace Hotel, the Russian composer gave an interview to the Spanish press, vigorously promoting "objective" music while attacking the "artificial" folklorism of his former mentor Rimsky-Korsakov, a stance he would come to relate directly to Falla's new style.[38]

During the early 1920s, Falla finished the second of the two orchestral suites from part 2 of *The Three-Cornered Hat* (Three Dances) and orchestrated a prelude by Salazar. In addition, he tinkered with passages of Pedrell's unstaged opera of 1902, *La Celestina*, as at least one sketch indicates.[39] He also continued working with the Orquesta Bética, with Salazar sometimes articulating Falla's values on behalf of the ensemble. In an article for *La Revue Musicale*, for example, Salazar explained how Falla's concept of orchestral balance was being realized, namely, that "after strict and detailed study, [Falla] assigned nearly mathematical limits" to the various in-

36. Letter, Falla to Stravinsky, 1 March 1924, in Craft, *Stravinsky: Selected Correspondence*, 2:165.

37. Adolfo Salazar recalls the event in "La vida musical: Una nueva visita de Strawinsky," *El Sol*, 23 November 1933, 4.

38. Hess, *Manuel de Falla and Modernism in Spain*, 187–92.

39. There is some discussion about the exact date of the late-fifteenth-century Spanish literary classic by Fernando de Rojas on which Pedrell (and later Joaquín Nin-Culmell) based operas. See Stephen Gilman's introduction to Fernando de Rojas, *La Celestina: Tragicomedia de Calisto y Melibea* (Madrid: Alianza Editorial, 1969), 8.

strument families of the Orquesta Bética.[40] With its two horns and two trumpets (but no trombones), paired woodwinds, four first violins, three seconds, two violas, two cellos, one bass, percussion, harp, and piano or harpsichord, as the music demanded, the new ensemble would fulfill its goal of exuding "classic and modern beauty at the same time."[41] This calculated aesthetic explained Falla's arrangement of Debussy's *Prélude à l'après-midi d'un faune*, in which he eliminated two of the four horns, inserting trumpets at rehearsal 3 to compensate for the missing horns. Despite Ernesto Halffter's contention that Falla's reorchestration sounded better than the original, the differences are negligible.[42]

Even as his own style approached Stravinskian neoclassicism, Falla continued to admire Debussy. This was not necessarily a fashionable position, for in the 1920s many critics and composers, including Stravinsky himself, were sneering at "the mists of Impressionism."[43] That Falla did not blindly follow trends set by others is evident in *Psyché*, that gossamer chamber work for voice, flute, harp, and string trio on a text by Jean-Aubry. Like the *Retablo*, *Psyché* had a long gestation period: although Jean-Aubry gave him the text in 1917, Falla did not finish the work until September 1924. With its delicately balanced added-note chords, often unresolved, its long pedals, and chantlike melodic lines, *Psyché* displays Falla's versatility as a colorist. The predominance of flute and harp, along with the presence of the viola, recall both Debussy's late Sonata for Flute, Viola, and Harp and Falla's hopeful conversations with his mentor of more than a decade earlier on the harp and its coloristic possibilities. Tellingly, alongside washes of color and impressionistic sonorities, Falla juxtaposes textures of linear clarity, as in the second vocal statement, with its voice exchange between voice and cello, mm. 38, 40 (see musical example 21).

Since his stint as the Martínez Sierras' eccentric house guest, Falla had always enjoyed Barcelona, which, like Cádiz, senses strongly its proximity to the sea. He also had several friends and professional contacts there. So in February 1925, he attended the premiere of *Psyché* at Barcelona's Palau de la Música Catalana, that brick, mosaic, and stained-glass fantasy designed by Lluís Domènech i Montaner and considered emblematic of Catalonian musical culture. Members of the Orquesta Bética performed *Psyché*; for whatever reason, Falla felt he had to conduct the intimate chamber work. It ended up being overshadowed by the other music on the program, which included some imposing Russian scores, and critics barely acknowledged it.

40. Salazar, "Espagne," 79.

41. Salazar, "Espagne," 79–80.

42. Letter, Ernesto Halffter to Falla, 19 November 1924, AMF correspondence file 7096. The Debussy arrangement does not appear in Gallego's catalog because Falla's notes for it were donated to the AMF (by Luis Izquierdo) after the catalog was published. It was performed on 10 December 1924 at Seville's Teatro de San Fernando. Falla reorchestrated the Overture to Rossini's *Barber of Seville* for similar reasons.

43. See Paul Landormy, "Le déclin de l'Impressionisme," *La Revue Musicale* 2, no. 4 (1921): 97–113.

Musical Example 21. Falla, *Psyché*, mm. 34–47. (Chester Music Ltd. International copyright secured. All rights reserved. Reprinted by permission.)

In recent decades, however, the work has been rehabilitated through recordings by several important artists, including Victoria de los Ángeles and the adventuresome American soprano Dawn Upshaw, even if first-time listeners continue to insist that "it doesn't sound at all like Falla." To sum up this *homenaje a Debussy*, we might return to Falla's own description of Debussy's "Spanish" works, those manifestations of "truth without authenticity" he so aptly praised in his memorial essay of 1920. The "truth" of *Psyché* has as its basis Falla's admiration, unswayed by critical opinion, for his admired friend and colleague, and its musical language revels in the spirit of impressionism rather than the letter.

Falla persisted in conducting his own music, despite his less than imposing podium presence. A few months after his visit to Barcelona, we find him in Paris at the Trianon Lyrique, on 22 May 1925, conducting the "definitive" *El amor brujo*. As noted, since the Madrid premiere of ten years earlier he had been experimenting with different possibilities for his homage to gypsy song. A major incentive had come in December 1919, when he signed a contract with Chester of London, at which point he, María, and Gregorio began the final adjustments (fortunately all undertaken before the falling-out over *Don Juan de España*). As with the transformation of *El corregidor y la molinera*, the changes are significant. The spoken passages, typical of popular theater in most Western countries, were eliminated and some musical numbers reshuffled. Falla also reworked aspects of the instrumentation in accordance with some of the post-1915 arrangements.[44] Furthermore, now that *El amor brujo* was a ballet Candelas would no longer sing; rather, the vocal solos, in some respects the focal point of the work, would be sung by an anonymous voice backstage, offering an omniscient perspective on Candelas's despair and eventual triumph. Textual adjustments in the songs included the elimination of the verse in "Canción del fuego fatuo" that describes the origins of love ("born in August nights when the heat bears down"), which Falla may have decided was overly explicit.[45] There were also changes to the scenario. In the 1915 version, the male lover is so dimly sketched that we are hard-pressed to understand Candelas's obsession. In the later version, dramatic conflict is heightened through two new characters: Carmelo, a "nice" young man who courts Candelas even as she remains bewitched by the specter of her former lover; and Lucia (a minor character in the 1915 version), who agrees to flirt with the specter so that he no longer stands between Candelas and Carmelo. Lucia ultimately succeeds, Candelas and Carmelo exchange the perfect kiss, "life triumphs over death and over the past," and the specter perishes, "conquered by love."[46]

One could quibble that this plot is also unconvincing. But it was *El amor brujo*'s color and dash that most interested the international musical public. Like other reviewers of the Paris premiere, Jean Gaudrey-Réty emphasized the brilliance of the choreography. Indeed, Falla could not have asked for more gifted dancers: Antonia Mercé (known in the world of Spanish dance as "la Argentina") and Vicente Escudero created the principal roles. Much the same as his compatriots had done in 1914 with *La vida breve*, Gaudrey-Réty praised *El amor brujo*'s innate—rather than merely decorative—Spanishness. Curiously, he verges on describing Falla as a romantic, comparing *El amor brujo* with Stravinsky's *L'Histoire du soldat*, which was also on the program: "The proximity of this work to *L'Histoire du soldat* forms a very curious contrast. All the dynamism of the music of Stravinsky, arising from the void, turns into an inert mass before this ardent energy, this nostalgia, completely captivating and enveloping, which emerges from the cadences of M de Falla."[47] This emphasis on "ardent energy" and "nostalgia" in a work begun a decade earlier only

44. Gallego, *El amor brujo*, 118–42, 140–41, esp.

45. Gallego also expresses relief that the "vulgar" strophe was suppressed. Gallego, *El amor brujo*, 138.

46. Synopsis, from piano-vocal score of 1921, reproduced in Gallego, *El amor brujo*, 206.

47. Jean Guadrey-Réty, "*L'amour sorcier*," *Comoedia*, 27 May 1925, cited and translated in Gallego, *El amor brujo*, 274.

highlights Falla's stylistic departure from these very qualities. In the United States, the backward-looking *El amor brujo* was not as favorably received. The Boston Symphony Orchestra's performance of the concert version under its recently appointed conductor, Serge Koussevitzky, disappointed critic Henry Taylor Parker. He normally signed his reviews H. T. P., which won him the moniker "hard to please,"[48] and his reaction to *El amor brujo* confirms this reputation. Worse than the absence of dramatic orientation was the fact that "the intrinsic and veritable Spanish quality in de Falla's music is to most of us a sealed book. His own countrymen extol it. Various commentators harp upon it. Fine-tempered Spaniards undoubtedly thrill to it."[49] He allowed that, although "Falla will not ply the surface-tricks nor accept the traditional matter of Spanish music conventionalized," the "gypsy-tang often sounded Oriental." In other passages, Parker found the composer's procedure to be "plainly Parisian." In other words, the hybrid qualities that had sabotaged the 1915 *El amor brujo* were similarly problematic to some critics of its metamorphosis of ten years later.

Although Parker may have been exceptionally hard to please, it cannot be denied that Falla's *andalucista* music made only uncertain inroads in "serious" music circles in the United States, especially in comparison with the dazzling New York *Retablo*. On 13 March 1926, Koussevitsky and the Boston Symphony Orchestra performed the Three Dances from *The Three-Cornered Hat* at Carnegie Hall, sharing the program with Germaine Tailleferre, Paul Hindemith, and other contemporaries. Olin Downes wrote: "Much modern music was heard yesterday. Much of it was of dubious quality." Yet in discussing the Three Dances, Downes criticized the *lack* of Falla's "modernist" tendencies, considering the piece little more than "patches of melody and rhythm strung together with orchestration intended to be effective in the Spanish manner . . . anything but convincing." In an obvious reference to the *Retablo*, moreover, the hard-hitting Downes observed that "what is good in the music is principally its instrumentation, while the bite, the atmosphere, the personality of scores of de Falla which came later than this one are conspicuous by [their] absence."[50] Twice more that week Falla's music was played in Carnegie Hall, although neither performance was reviewed. On 18 March, Paul Kochanski offered the Franck sonata, *Pulcinella*, and "a group of small pieces by Mozart, Rameau, de Falla, Boulanger, and Brahms." On the twentieth, Fritz Kreisler, like Kochanski, juxtaposed the formidable Franck sonata with various *morceaux*: "an album leaf entitled 'Marguerite'" by Rachmaninoff; a Hartmann transcription of Debussy's "Girl with the Flaxen Hair"; and three Kreisler transcrip-

48. Beth Levy, "'The White Hope of American Music'; or, How Roy Harris Became Western," *American Music* 19, no. 2 (2001): 149.

49. H. T. P. [Henry Taylor Parker], "Baffling Moderns, Stirring Classics, also Koussevitzky," *Boston Evening Transcript*, 18 October 1926, 8. See also in the same newspaper a more favorable piece by C. S. S., "Love the Sorcerer," 16 October 1924, 4.

50. Olin Downes, "Boston Symphony Orchestra," *New York Times*, 14 March 1926, 11.

tions, including "a Spanish dance of de Falla."[51] Thus, for the U.S. audience of the mid-1920s, Falla had something of a split personality, in which the tempered modernism of the *Retablo* stood in unconvincing conflict with conventionalized Spanishness, which sometimes presented itself in the form of an ephemeral "album leaf."

In March 1926, the Metropolitan Opera House produced *La vida breve*. Falla took pains to ensure the credibility of the Spanish popular idiom, as his instructions to general manager Giulio Gatti-Casazza on the *cantaor*'s music, so critical in that regard, make clear. He stipulated that the "voice of the *cantaor* should imitate the popular style without ever using the *lyrical theatrical* style. The voice somewhat nasal: the *ornaments almost glissando, tossing them off* after accenting the initial note. The guitar (one or three at most) very rhythmic and marking the accents".[52] On a double bill with Stravinsky's *Le rossignol*, *La vida breve* opened on 6 March 1926. Lucrezia Bori sang the role of Salud. This versatile soprano's repertory ranged from opera to popular Spanish-language hits such as Sebastián de Yradier's "La paloma" and Quinito Valverde's "Clavelitos." In concert, she had recently performed "Life for the Laughter-Loving," as the title of Salud's first-act aria "Vivan los que ríen" was awkwardly translated.[53] Not surprisingly, critics considered Bori's performance in *La vida breve* an asset, with P. V. of *The World* hailing it as one of "such rare loveliness and such pathos that she was given an ovation."[54] Oscar Thompson called attention to the singularity of the event, observing that "only in the case of Granados's *Goyescas* had [Spanish] been used previously for opera at the Metropolitan"; indeed, "groups of Spanish-Americans . . . gave warmth to . . . a Spanish singer in that rarest of Metropolitan mediums, a genuine Spanish opera."[55]

Novelty aside, Thompson found *La vida breve*'s dramatic limitations all too apparent. Acknowledging that the opera had "been referred to as the Spanish *Cavalleria Rusticana*," he found the resemblance "a very superficial one," arguing that "*La vida breve* narrowly misses being no opera at all, so much of it is pantomime and tableau."

51. "Kreisler Has Big Audience," *New York Times*, 21 March 1926, 26.

52. "La voz del *cantaor* debe imitar el estilo popular sin emplear jamás el estilo *lírico teatral*. Voz algo nasal: los *ornamentos quasi glissando, lanzándolos* después de acentuar la nota inicial. La guitarra (una o tres como máximum) muy rítmica y marcando los acentos" (letter, Falla to Gatti-Casazza, 19 February 1926, cited in Nommick, *Jardines de España*, 29).

53. Oscar Thompson, "Spanish Novelty Introduced with Stravinsky Opera," *Musical America* 43, no. 21 (13 March 1926): 4.

54. P. V., *The World*, 20 March 1926, 13 (untitled article).

55. The situation for Spanish-language opera at the Met has not improved. After five performances of *Goyescas* in 1916 and the same number for *La vida breve* ten years later, *El amor brujo* was performed once in 1962 (see chapter 9). Information on performances may be found on *Annals of the Metropolitan Opera, 1883–2000: The Complete Chronicle of Performances and Artists* (CD-ROM, Metropolitan Opera Guild, 2001). I wish to thank John Koegel for providing this information.

Furthermore, Salud's "actual death is attributable to an operatic variety of syncope
. . . neither very tragic nor very pathetic. . . . The climax suffers for want of preparation. It is difficult to make a death episode . . . without having previously brought
the characters into more prosilient relief than those of the Shaw–de Falla opera.
Theatrically, the work is one of continuous ineptitude."[56] Still, Thompson felt that
the music reflected "admirable workmanship" and an "abundance of atmosphere"
and that it was "at all times fluent and direct." To him, Falla seemed less a dramatic
composer than "a minor symphonist astray in alien grounds."[57] Similarly, Olin
Downes considered *La vida breve* to be "hardly theater at all," although he found it
"interesting in spite of inequalities of inspiration and workmanship."[58] A reviewer of
the performance of 25 March concurred, describing *La vida breve* as "less an opera
than a symphonic poem with mimetic and vocal adjuncts."[59]

By the time these lukewarm comments appeared, however, Falla had several other
projects on his mind, all of which called forth his new style. One was the "Soneto a
Córdoba" (Sonnet to Córdoba) for solo voice and harp-lute (or piano) on a text by
the Spanish Golden Age poet Luis de Góngora (1561–1627). The work came about
thanks to Lorca, who, along with his colleagues, admired Góngora's works for their
self-imposed restraint and "objective beauty, beauty pure and useless, free of personal confessions and sentimentality." In this vein Lorca called for "clarity, measure and order" in contemporary poetry, an almost Stravinskian viewpoint.[60] With
several other poets, Lorca organized a tercentenary festival in Góngora's honor,
featuring readings, discussions, and drama. Since Falla was a respected senior member and spiritual guide of the "Rinconcillo," Lorca presented him with the text of
Góngora's "Soneto a Córdoba" in the hope that he would set it.[61] Though initially
lukewarm, Falla was soon won over by the poem's lofty sentiments and perhaps by
his young friend's exuberance. The "Soneto" premiere took place not at the festival
but in Paris in May 1927 (the same month as the festival); fragments of it also appeared in the Málaga-based periodical *Litoral* that spring.[62] Reminiscent of early

56. Thompson, "Spanish Novelty Introduced," 4.

57. Thompson, "Spanish Novelty Introduced," 4.

58. Olin Downes, "American Premiere of Two Operas," *New York Times*, 8 March 1926, 9.

59. B. L. D. "Two Novelties Repeated," *Musical America* 43, no. 23 (27 March 1926): 9.
The fifth and final Metropolitan Opera performance of *La vida breve* was on 5 April, also
paired with *Le Rossignol*.

60. Federico García Lorca, "The Poetic Image in Don Luis de Góngora," cited and
translated in Gibson, *Lorca*, 158; for the original, see Federico García Lorca, *Obras
completas*, 5th ed. (Madrid: Aguilar, 1963), 62–85. See also C. B. Morris, *A Generation of
Spanish Poets, 1920–1936* (Cambridge: Cambridge University Press, 1969), 23–24.

61. Falla's status is summarized in Nigel Dennis, ed., *El epistolario (1924–1935): José
Bergamín–Manuel de Falla* (Valencia: Pre-Textos, 1995), 15. See also Pahissa, *Vida y obra*, 155.

62. The "Soneto" was published in its entirety in 1930 by Oxford University Press with
a translation by John Trend.

baroque monody, the "Soneto" reflects the composer's increasing attraction to stark-
ness, economy, and "pure music," that is, "objective" music "free of personal confessions and sentimentality," to borrow Lorca's description.[63]

The Generation of '27, as some of these poets came to be known, was passionately interested in Golden Age theater, especially that of Calderón de la Barca and
Lope de Vega. As a result, three-hundred-year-old genres were now given new life.
Falla found one of them, the *auto sacramental*, especially congenial. Dating from
the Middle Ages and associated with the feast of Corpus Christi, the *auto sacramental*
(or *auto*, as it is sometimes known) invariably involves an enactment of the Last Supper. Traditionally its performance setting was the public square, to which celebrants
would carry the consecrated host and where the play itself might be interspersed
with ample amounts of music, dance, and shorter dramatic works (*entremeses*).[64]
Falla wrote incidental music for three *autos*: Calderón de la Barca's *El gran teatro
del mundo* (The Great Theater of the World), Lope de Vega's *La vuelta de Egipto*
(The Flight from Egypt), and *La moza del cántaro* (The Maid with the Water Jug).[65]
El gran teatro del mundo, which premiered on 27 June 1927 at the University of
Granada, has received the most critical attention, due mainly to its wide range of
musical borrowings. These include a fanfare by Gaspar Sanz, one of the Cantigas de
Alfonso X, "Alaben al Señor" (Praise the Lord), three selections from Pedrell's
Cancionero, "Ama al otro como a tí" (Love Your Neighbor as Yourself), "Rey de
este caduco imperio" (King of this Exhausted Empire), and "Toda la hermosura
humana" (All Human Beauty). Perhaps most significant is the so-called Dresden
Amen, which Mendelssohn, Karl Loewe, and Ludwig Spohr all used to emblema-
tize Catholic church music.[66] Falla's experience of it, however, came from Wagner's
Parsifal, a work he admired for its religious message.[67] Given the abundance of these
quotations, it is perhaps not surprising that someone as modest as Falla refused to
publish the score of *El gran teatro del mundo*, reasoning that it did not contain enough
original music. Still, the work is a complex and illuminating statement of the

63. Pahissa, for example, refers to the "austere character" of the "Soneto" (*Vida y obra*,
156–57). See also Hess, *Manuel de Falla and Modernism in Spain*, 266.

64. Antonio Rey Hazas and Florencio Sevilla Arroyo, eds., *Pedro Calderón de la Barca:
El gran teatro del mundo* (Barcelona: Planeta, 1991), 22.

65. Falla's incidental music for the two Lope de Vega works remains unpublished. The
composer also began to write adaptations of Calderón's *Circe* and *Los encantos de la culpa*
(Christoforidis, "Falla, Manuel de," in *Diccionario de la música española e hispano-
americana*, 4:902).

66. Larry Todd, "Mendelssohn," in *The Nineteenth-Century Symphony*, edited by
D. Kern Holoman (New York: Schirmer, 1997), 86.

67. Theodore Beardsley, "Manuel de Falla's Sources for Calderón's *Gran teatro del
mundo*: The Autograph Manuscripts," *Kentucky Romance Quarterly* 16 (1969): 63–74. See
also Elena Torres Clemente, *Manuel de Falla y las Cantigas de Alfonso X El Sabio* (Granada:
Universidad de Granada, 2002).

composer's belief system, both aesthetic and religious: redolent of Spanish Catholic identity, *El gran teatro del mundo* conjoined the exquisitely simple flavor of Golden Age music with a redemptive gesture from late German romanticism—all in the halcyon days of the Silver Age.

Yet not all was complete harmony with Falla and the Generation of '27. In December 1928, the *Revista de Occidente* published the first two parts of the highly unorthodox "Oda al Santísimo Sacramento del Altar" (Ode to the Most Holy Sacrament of the Altar), a poem by Lorca dedicated to Falla. That fall, tormented by emotional and sexual conflicts, Lorca returned to the faith in which he had been raised, or at least to his selective understanding of Catholicism's more comforting imagery. For some reason, he let the ode go to press without consulting Falla, suggesting, as Gibson has proposed, that he sincerely believed the poem was *not* blasphemous.[68] Yet Lorca could hardly have imagined that Falla would find gratifying the description of God as "alive in the Sacrament, vibrant, naked" or of the consecrated host as a "small flour tambourine." Neither would Falla consider Lorca's situating the host "above the turning world of wheel and phallus" as anything but an assault on Catholic doctrine. Having learned of the poem through his friend Pepe Segura, Falla read it and sent Lorca a candid objection: "To you, who knows me so well, I don't need to say what are the differences that separate us regarding the theme of your Ode. If I were treating it, I would do so with my spirit *on its knees*, and fervently hoping that all of humanity would sanctify itself through the virtue of the Sacrament."[69] Falla nonetheless took pains to avoid hurting Lorca, noting the "honor" done him by the dedication and appealing to their friendship: "You understand me, Federico, and forgive me if I bother you in any way. How I would regret this! What's clear is that, as always happens in your works, in this one there are indisputable beauties and dexterities of expression; but since it concerns you, I can't hide from you—as I would with someone else—my true impression. That would be contrary to the friendship and loyalty I owe you."[70] Still bending over backward to spare Lorca's feelings, Falla acknowledged that the poem was incomplete. Therefore, he would "put his hope in the definitive version and in the remainder of the poem."[71] But the final section, "Flesh," completed in 1929, would have been even less pleasing to the composer:

> It's your vanquished flesh, broken, trampled
> that defeats and dazzles our own flesh. . . .
> Oh, Body of Christ! Oh, Body of absolute silence,
> where the swan burns and the leper shines!

68. Gibson, *Federico García Lorca*, 223–24.

69. Letter, Falla to Lorca, 9 February 1929, cited in Francisco García Lorca, *Federico y su mundo* (Madrid: Alianza Tres, 1981), 155.

70. Lorca, *Federico y su mundo*, 155.

71. Lorca, *Federico y su mundo*, 155.

Oh blank, sleepless Form!
Angels and dogs barking against the whisper of veins.[72]

However we may view Falla's unrelenting obedience to Church teachings, the episode shows him in an entirely positive light. Although he felt duty bound to speak his mind—as gently as possible—he was charitable enough to forgive the youthful indiscretion. Lorca, on the other hand, seems to have been embarrassed by the matter and perhaps visited the composer's *carmen* less frequently as a result.[73] (No written reply from Lorca has survived, although his brother Francisco is certain that he responded to Falla.)[74] Evidently, the poet's admiration for Falla was so great that the mere though of causing him any discomfort was more than he could bear.

In musical circles, Falla's rigorous Catholicism was being increasingly associated with his new style. Mainly, this was due to the Harpsichord Concerto of 1926, which he began in October 1923 at Landowska's request.[75] Although the work caused her to tremble "with joy and happiness," it also brought about the undoing of their friendship.[76] One problem was performance rights, an issue complicated by the absence of a formal commission: Landowska wanted to both premiere the concerto and obtain from Falla "exclusive rights to perform the work on harpsichord, as opposed to performances on piano." After prolonged deliberations, Falla allowed her to give the premiere and granted the exclusive performance rights she had requested, albeit for one year only.[77] Another problem was Falla's slowness in completing the score. Of course, Landowska understood at least in principle his plodding creative process, for she explained to the New York critic Lawrence Gilman that the concerto's intrinsic depth justified Falla's letting it "come to life little by little."[78] But eventually his delays were too much for her, for she had initially hoped to perform the concerto during the 1923–24 season. When it became clear that this would be impossible, she and Stokowski discussed a Philadelphia premiere for the following year; again this hope was dashed.[79] Landowska was especially peeved when she

72. Translated by Greg Simon and Steven F. White in Federico García Lorca, *Federico García Lorca: Collected Poems, a Bilingual Edition*, edited by Christopher Maurer (New York: Farrar, Straus, Giroux, 2001), 598–609.

73. Gibson, *Federico García Lorca*, 225.

74. Lorca, *Federico y su mundo*, 156.

75. Christoforidis, "Aspects of the Creative Process," 176.

76. Letter, Landowska to Falla, 21 September 1926, cited and translated (from French to Spanish) in de Persia, *Poesía*, 183.

77. Falla stipulated that this arrangement would be subject to exceptions, such as when Landowska was unavailable for an important performance (letter, Falla to Landowska, 3 February 1926, cited in Christoforidis, "Aspects of the Creative Process," 177n14).

78. Letter, Landowska to Gilman, 24 December 1926, cited in Christoforidis, "Aspects of the Creative Process," appendix 4.1, 1.

79. Christoforidis, "Aspects of the Creative Process," 176.

learned that Falla had discussed details of the concerto ("our concerto," as she put it) with Arthur Honegger, and she concluded from this that "everyone" knew it but her.[80] In short, even a great artist such as Landowska was unprepared for Falla's unforgiving and time-consuming struggle over every note, a condition that was becoming more acute with each passing year.

But Landowska never disparaged the piece itself and with good reason. In the concerto, Falla takes as a point of departure principles introduced in the *Retablo*—clarity of texture, use of preexisting materials and procedures, and heterogeneous timbres—and refines them to new levels of distillation. In addition to the harpsichord, the concerto calls for violin, flute, oboe, clarinet, and cello; as mentioned above, Falla conceived the harpsichord as one more element of the chamber ensemble, cadenzalike passages notwithstanding. The first movement is based almost entirely on a sixteenth-century song, "De los álamos vengo madre," by the Extremaduran composer Juan Vásquez, the intervallic structure of which Falla altered only minimally (see musical example 22a). By way of the same theme, he alludes to traditional form: the Vásquez tune's most complete presentation occurs in the section that would roughly correspond to the second-theme group of a sonata-form movement (rehearsal 3). Yet, despite suggestive aural signposts (second-theme group, strong recapitulation), the brief movement fits only imperfectly into sonata-form design, mainly because it lacks a true development section, with the customarily dramatic juxtaposition of tonalities.[81] Yet the motivic economy is striking: the Vásquez tune's terminating figure (motive x) is clearly related to the rising and falling seconds of the first-group theme, which Falla slightly altered (see musical example 22b).[82] The similarity of the cello theme at rehearsal 4 likewise confirms Falla's ability to wring almost an entire movement out of these spare musical materials.

In the second movement, Falla continues to exploit stepwise motion by quoting plainchant. The theme of the preludelike opening explicitly refers to the traditions of Spanish Catholicism, for it has been linked to the *Pange lingua moro hispano*, a chant some have labeled Mozarabic.[83] Many Spanish composers, including Juan Urreda, Antonio de Cabezón, Sebastián Aguilera de Heredia, Juan Bautista Cabanilles, Tomás Luis de Victoria, Nicolás Ledesma, and Hilarion Eslava, drew on the *Pange lingua*, which is associated with the feast of Corpus Christi, the same

80. Letter, Landowska to Falla, 28 June 1926, cited in Christoforidis, "Aspects of the Creative Process," 178n19.

81. As Nommick argues, a more convincing parallel is with the baroque concerto grosso ("Un ejemplo de ambigüedad formal," 28).

82. Additional transformations of the theme are given in Nommick, "Un ejemplo de ambigüedad formal," 22.

83. It is impossible to so describe the *Pange lingua* on the basis of existing knowledge of Mozarabic chant, an insight for which I would like to thank Grayson Wagstaff.

Musical Example 22a. Falla, Harpsichord Concerto, Vásquez tune, motive x.

Musical Example 22b. Falla, Harpsichord Concerto, motive x (movement 1, mm. 1–3, transposed).

feast that dominates *El gran teatro del mundo*.[84] In fact, Falla's manuscript is dated "A. Dom. MCMXXVI—In festo Corporis Christi," although the composer told Trend that finishing the movement on that day was "a matter of pure chance."[85] Another motive, intervallically related to the *Pange lingua* and consisting of four notes, replicates the pitches of the psalm intonation used by Haydn, Fux, Mozart ("Jupiter" symphony, movement 4), and Mendelssohn, for whom the motive explicitly symbolized Catholic Church music in the slow introduction of his "Reformation" Symphony.[86] Twice Falla gives it canonic treatment at the octave. Then, after four measures of "white" sound on a sustained quartal harmony (rehearsal 7), he casts the motive in F major, now against grinding A-major chords in the harpsichord, rolled for maximum sonority. Gradually thinning in texture, the theme drags its way to another eruption of scales in the woodwinds, "ribbons of scales," to borrow Stravinsky's description of the similarly careening Variation A of his Octet (see musical example 23). In the witty third movement, Falla evokes the spirit of Domenico Scarlatti through rhythmic play (3/4, 6/8 alteration), brilliant keyboard figurations such as interlocking thirds (two measures before rehearsal 2), and baroque-style ornamentation such as the solitary mordent on the dominant a measure before rehearsal 6. Unlike the first movement, the sonata-form layout here is fairly straightforward, joining "a pre-classic monothematicism with the . . . notion of 'theme-group,'" as Nommick has observed.[87] In sum, the Harpsichord Concerto takes the "fineness of touch" that critics applauded in the *Retablo* to an abstemiousness of musical

84. See Gianfranco Vinay, "Scarlatti e Stravinsky nel *Concerto* per clavicembalo," in *Manuel de Falla tra la Spagna e l'Europa*, edited by Paolo Pinamonti (Florence: Olschki, 1989), 185–87.

85. Trend, *Manuel de Falla and Spanish Music*, 157.

86. Todd, "Mendelssohn," 86–87.

87. Nommick, "Un ejemplo de ambigüedad formal," 18.

Musical Example 23. (above and opposite) Falla, Harpsichord Concerto, movement 2, mm. 35–45. (Reprinted by kind permission of Ediciones Manuel de Falla)

materials the composer could barely have imagined just a few years earlier when he was immersed in the guitar-based sonorities and affective drama of *andalucismo*.

Unfortunately, the concerto got off to a rocky start. Landowska received the final pages of the third movement only a few days before the premiere, which took place on 5 November 1926 at Barcelona's Palau de la Música Catalana.[88] She also had to contend with rumors that Falla would play the work and Ernesto Halffter would conduct, a violation of the "exclusive harpsichord rights" granted her in February 1926. Falla had to soothe her indignation by assuring her that Ernesto was not involved with the premiere; he was, however, upset that Halffter had misrepresented him.[89] Falla himself would conduct, as he had done, for better or for worse, with *Psyché*. But rehearsal time was limited, and the players, members of the Orquestra Pau Casals, read from hastily prepared handwritten parts. Some critics were kind enough to allow for these difficult conditions, but others deemed the concerto an aberration, a "spontaneous arrest of [Falla's] artistic personality" in which the composer seemed "inferior to himself."[90] An even more damning reaction greeted the U.S. premiere (6 January 1927, Carnegie Hall), with Landowska and five members

88. Christoforidis, "Aspects of the Creative Process," 180.

89. Letter, Falla to Landowska, 23 October 1926, cited and translated in Budwig, "Manuel de Falla's *Atlántida*," 255–56.

90. "[El concierto] . . . puede considerarse como un espontáneo arresto de su genio artístico" (B., "Música de Cámara: Festival Manuel de Falla," *Correo Catalan*, 9 November 1926, 6); "Se muestra muy inferior a sí mismo" (Z., "De Música: Festival Manuel de Falla," *El Liberal*, 6 November 1926, 3).

of the Boston Symphony Orchestra. Gilman tactlessly commented that the concerto, with its limited personnel, "must be a singularly welcome addition to any orchestra's repertoire—for it permits the band as a whole to spend a sybaritic half hour in the smoking room or at some nearby cinema."[91] Richard L. Stokes, complaining of Falla's "incompetency," commented that "one may be pardoned for regarding as barbarous a work in which are mingled Spanish dance airs, medieval modes and eighteenth-century dances—and all of them deranged by an admixture of modernistic dissonance."[92] Only Downes was remotely sympathetic. Acknowledging the hall's unsuitability for a six-player chamber work, he observed the concerto's "freedom in tonal relations and harmonic effects," all of which "ill conceal[ed] the cloven hoof of Stravinsky."[93] Interestingly, the *Retablo* insinuated itself into many of the reviews: several critics unfavorably compared the concerto with the earlier work, which Gilman recalled as an "authentic masterpiece . . . in which pathos and fantasy and beauty are summoned with so delicate and sure a touch."[94]

This bleak scenario changed, however, with the concerto's Paris premiere in May 1927. Falla himself played it, first on the harpsichord and then on the piano. French critics seized on the work's "mystical" qualities, which they linked to Spain's long tradition of mystical literature (St. Theresa of Ávila and St. John of the Cross), painting (Francisco de Zurbarán and José Ribera), and music (Tomás Luis de Victoria).[95] Marcel Delannoy, for example, observed "gravity . . . mystical purity, images of extraordinary spiritual evolution," while Émile Vuillermoz maintained that the work would "definitively orient our contemporaries' research toward a series of mysteries, of sound and of color."[96] Vuillermoz even linked the concerto with the composer's persona, observing that "over the years Manuel de Falla becomes more spiritual, more emaciated. . . . It seems that all guilty sensuality has died in him. He has conquered the voluptuousness of the ear with the victories of an ascetic and

91. Lawrence Gilman, "Music: Landowska Plays a Modern Concerto for Harpsichord," *New York Herald Tribune*, 7 January 1927, 18. See also "Landowska a Feature with Boston Band," *New York Evening Journal*, 7 January 1927, 38.

92. Richard L. Stokes, "Realm of Music," *Evening World*, 7 January 1927, AMF press file. Similar reservations are expressed, albeit in a kindlier tone, in W. J. Henderson, "The Boston Symphony Concert," *New York Sun*, 7 January 1927, AMF press file.

93. Olin Downes, "Music," *New York Times*, 7 January 1927, 14.

94. Gilman, "Landowska Plays a Modern Concerto," 18.

95. The notion of musical mysticism was well entrenched in French constructions of Spanish music. See Emilio Ros Fábregas, "Historiografía de la música en las catedrales españolas: Nacionalismo y positivismo en la investigación musicológica," *Codex XXI* (1998): 74–77.

96. "On voit . . . cette gravité, cette pureté mystiques, images d'une extraordinaire évolution spirituelle" (Marcel Delannoy, *Chantecler*, 24 March 1928, n.p., AMF press file); "Le *Concerto* de Manuel de Falla orientera définitivement les recherches de nos contemporains vers une série de mystères du son et de la couleur" (Émile Vuillermoz, "La Musique: Le 'Concerto' de Manuel de Falla," *Excelsior*, 12 June 1927, AMF press file).

monk."[97] Critics of the concerto's Madrid premiere (5 November 1927) followed suit, emphasizing purity and renunciation of effect and waxing euphoric over Falla's rigorous path to musical perfection. Víctor Espinós, who in 1921 had trashed *The Three-Cornered Hat*, now praised the concerto's "cathedral-like *Lento*," while another critic likened the work to the spiritual exercises of St. Ignatius Loyola.[98] Since then, the concerto has enjoyed a certain success in "serious music" circles: Falla not only recorded it (see figure 14), but he performed it at the 1928 International Society for Contemporary Music (ISCM) festival in Sienna.[99] In 1947, Stravinsky conducted it at Dumbarton Oaks. The U.S. composer Samuel Adler has written a work for the same combination of instruments, *Acrostics: Four Games for Six Players* (1985). It has had far less impact on the broader musical public, however, and Landowska never definitively incorporated it into her repertory. But it was a revelation for anyone following developments in Spanish music. As the composer Joaquín Nin-Culmell has said, "Falla's Concerto proved that it was possible to write Spanish music without sounding like Valverde."[100]

These happy and productive years were marred only by the occasional spasm of ill health, which included dizzy spells and vision problems during the mid-1920s. (Falla felt well enough to ignore his doctors' advice that he stop smoking, although he would sometimes mischievously cut cigarettes in half to convince himself that he was smoking less.) Along with the sociable María del Carmen, he continued to receive guests. Ravel came in October 1928, Casella (to whom Falla described the little *carmen* as a "casa para muchachos") in January 1929, and Milhaud in April 1929.[101] Ever apologetic about his piano playing, Falla nonetheless gave an all-Scarlatti recital at the Granada Athenaeum on 11 December 1927, an appropriate choice given that composer's ubiquitous presence in the final movement of the Harpsichord Concerto.[102] Throughout the late 1920s, Falla received several honors, some of which commemorated his fiftieth birthday in 1926. Besides various "Falla festivals"

97. "D'année en année Manuel de Falla se spiritualise et s'émacie. . . . Il semble qu'en lui soit morte toute sensualité coupable. Il a remporté sur la volupté de l'oreille des victoires d'ascète et d'anachorète" (Vuillermoz, "La Musique").

98. A detailed account of the concerto's reception is in Hess, *Manuel de Falla and Modernism in Spain*, 245–61.

99. The concerto, however, was selected by the international committee of the ISCM, not by the Spanish section, as neither Madrid nor Barcelona was willing to pay Falla's travel expenses to Sienna. On 7 June 1928, Edward Dent wrote Falla, saying that some of the composer's "English friends" would foot the bill. See Bergadà, "La relación de Falla con Italia," in Nommick, *Manuel de Falla e Italia*, 39–40.

100. Personal interview with the author, January 2000.

101. On these visits, see de Persia, *Poesía*, 150 (Ravel); Bergadà, "La relación de Falla con Italia," 47 (Casella); and Budwig, "Manuel de Falla's *Atlántida*," 125 (Milhaud).

102. Torres Clemente, "La presencia de Scarlatti en la trayectoria musical de Manuel de Falla," in Nommick, *Manuel de Falla e Italia*, 88–89.

Figure 14. Falla in Paris rehearsing for a recording of the Harpsichord Concerto, 14 May 1927, with Marcel Moyse (flute), Émile Giodeau (clarinet), Georges Bonneau (oboe), Marcel Darrieux (violin), and Auguste Gruque (cello). (Reprinted by kind permission of the Archivo Manuel de Falla)

(8–9 February 1927, Granada; 17 March 1927, Barcelona; and 5 November 1927, Madrid), the municipalities of Seville and Cádiz honored him (1926), as did Gaudix in Granada Province (1927).[103] International tributes included being named Chevalier de l'Ordre National de la Légion d'Honneur in March 1928 and a member of the Royal Swedish Academy of Music in Stockholm the same year.[104] On 13 May 1929, Falla was elected to the Real Academia de Bellas Artes de San Fernando, although, due to his long-standing frustration with that entity, he never read his acceptance speech. Perhaps it was Stravinsky who best summed up the musical intelligentsia's reaction to Falla's new style. On 22 June 1927, the Russian composer attended London's Falla Festival, which featured the *Retablo* and the Harpsichord Concerto. He later observed that "these two works [gave] proof of incontestable progress in the development of [Falla's] great talent. He has, in them, deliberately emancipated himself from the folkloristic influence under which he was in danger of stultifying himself."[105] Although Stravinsky's praise of Falla was clearly an endorsement of his own nonfolkloric agenda, it was also genuine and representative of critical opinion.

Falla himself sometimes enhanced his growing reputation as an ascetic. In May 1925, he declared to the French newspaper *Excelsior* that "every year, I take a cure of

103. Chinchilla, "Cronología," in Nommick, *Manuel de Falla en Granada*, 164–65.
104. Chinchilla, "Cronología," in Nommick, *Manuel de Falla en Granada*, 166.
105. Stravinsky, *Autobiography*, 133.

solitude in a little village in Andalusia, not speaking to anyone for ten or twelve days. There I prepare to work."[106] These "cures," as much for the body as for the soul, sometimes coincided with Granada's Corpus Christi celebration, which Falla found increasingly noisy and commercialized and was always eager to escape. A telling episode (described by Nin-Culmell as "vintage Falla") reveals the extent to which religious nature and musical style were increasingly seen as one in Falla. Following the Paris premiere of the Harpsichord Concerto, pianist Marie André, a former pupil of Planté, gave a reception at her home in the Quai Voltaire. The guests, of whom Nin-Culmell was one, eagerly awaited Falla's arrival. When he finally showed up, Mme André exclaimed, "Le maître est arrivé!"and dropped to her knees to show reverence for the purity of his music. A collective gasp went up from the guests, who sensed that Falla would hardly appreciate such an extravagant gesture. Yet, rather than scolding Mme André, Falla, too, knelt down, promptly embracing his hostess. That playful gesture, with its offbeat mix of wit and humility, effectively said, "Look, we're all God's creatures—none of us is on any pedestal."[107] Moments later, Falla and Mme André got up off the floor and the party could begin.

THE ALLURE OF THE LOST CONTINENT

In 1926, Falla discovered the epic Catalan-language poem "L'Atlàntida" by the poet-priest Jacint Verdaguer (1845–1902).[108] During the late-nineteenth-century flowering of Catalan language and culture known as the Renaixença (Renaissance), Verdaguer led a literary circle in Vic, a cathedral city some fifty kilometers north of Barcelona. In 1877, he won the Jocs Florals (Floral Games), a poetry contest loosely based on the Germanic Sängerkrieg, with "L'Atlàntida."[109]

A creation myth, the epic links the destruction of the lost continent of Atlantis to the rise of Spain and subsequent Christianization of the Americas, which Verdaguer, and later Falla, unreservedly applauded. Along with several mythological figures, the poem features Falla's boyhood hero, Christopher Columbus, who, as the "bearer of Christ," is the object of a long meditation by Queen Isabella (the "Catholic"). "L'Atlàntida" awakens the ancestral Iberian memory with copious references to the Pyrenees, the Strait of Gibraltar, and three regions especially dear to

106. "Chaque année, je fais une cure de solitude dans une petite ville de l'Andalousie ne parlant à personne pendant dix ou douze jours. C'est là que je me prépare à travailler" ("Manuel de Falla par lui-même," reproduced in *La Revue Musicale*, 6, no. 9 [1 July 1925]: 94).

107. Personal interview with Joaquín Nin-Culmell, January 2000.

108. The title of Verdaguer's poem is normally given in Catalan ("L'Atlàntida") and Falla's composition in Castilian (*Atlántida*).

109. Philip Ward, *The Oxford Companion to Spanish Literature* (Oxford: Clarendon, 1978), 604. See also Arthur Terry, *A Literary History of Spain: Catalan Literature* (London: E. Benn; New York: Barnes and Noble, 1972), 73–77.

Falla: Cádiz, Granada, and Barcelona. Throughout, allusions and symbols abound, with an occasionally exhortatory tone reminding us of Carl Jung's description of symbols' power to reveal "collective transformation."[110] From the opening of the first canto, "Veus eixa mar" (Behold This Sea), the reader learns that the fertile land in which "sheep grazed" and "birdsong and maidens' canticles resounded" is now under water. This return to formlessness confirms the dark and punishing nature of the continent's submersion ("O Atlantis! Where have you gone? The Almighty struck a heavy blow with his left arm and with a mortal surge the sea engulfed you"). From a world "without form and void," immersed elements can be newly "recombined in cosmic patterns," however.[111] What eventually arose from this watery unconsciousness was the hopeful message of Christianity, the element of "L'Atlàntida" most compelling to Falla.

The poem's first canto depicts the burning of the Pyrenees. According to mythology, this occurred in the time of Alcides (the original name for Heracles/Hercules), who rescues Pyrene from the conflagration.[112] As daughter of Tubal and queen of Spain, Pyrene informs Alcides that she was deposed by Geryon, the three-headed monster who set fire to the mountains. As Pyrene dies, Alcides promises to found a city (Barcelona) on her burial site. Again the theme of rejuvenation is significant, now through the Heraclitean view of fire as an "agent of transmutation."[113] Fascination with fire, moreover, is well entrenched in Iberian folk tradition and is still evident in the ritual bonfires of St. John's Eve in Catalonia and of St. Joseph's Day in Valencia.

Fire may purify the forces of evil but so can heroic deeds. Alcides now travels south to Cádiz, where he seeks to kill Geryon. After waging battle, presumably against the darker elements of the unconscious, Alcides makes his way to the Garden of the Hesperides, an enclosed, Eden-like setting in which nature has been tamed and the seven Pleiades frolic about a magic orange tree. The tree, in turn, can be said to straddle the underworld (roots), the middle world or earth (trunk), and heaven (uplifted branches).[114] Yet even Paradise harbors enemies, for Alcides must now kill the dragon guarding the tree. Again rebirth follows destruction: as the Pleiades mourn the demise of Atlantis, Alcides removes several branches and plants the shoots. As he does so, a divine voice warns of the wages of sin.

---

110. C. G. Jung, *Memories, Dreams, Reflections*, recorded and edited by Aniela Jaffé, translated from the German by Richard Winston and Clara Winston (New York: Random House, 1965), 209.

111. J. E. Cirlot, *A Dictionary of Symbols*, translated from the Spanish by Jack Sage, 2d ed. (London: Routledge and Kegan Paul, 1971), 365.

112. Alcides is the patronym formed from the name Alceus, Alcide's grandfather. See Pierre Grimal, *The Dictionary of Classical Mythology*, translated by A. R. Maxwell-Hyslop (Oxford and New York: Blackwell, 1986), 193.

113. Cirlot, *Dictionary of Symbols*, 105.

114. Cirlot, *Dictionary of Symbols*, 347.

The final portion of "L'Atlàntida" abruptly shifts from mythological time to the historical past. Like the rest of the poem, it contains suggestive imagery. The setting is the Alhambra, where Queen Isabella recounts to her husband, King Ferdinand, a dream in which a dove plucked her engagement ring off her finger and dropped it in the sea. That this symbol of wholeness and continuity fell into the void was part of a larger design, however, for Isabella sees "islands in flower" emerging from the watery depths. Convinced that the dove was the Holy Spirit showing her the location of the Indies, Isabella decides to offer her jewels to Columbus so that he can evangelize this uncharted territory. As the queen declares in the poem's final line, only then will she be able to die in peace.

Verdaguer's imaginative account of the initial impetus for the evangelization of the New World offers a striking parallel with the narrative of Christianity. As the religion scholar Mircea Eliade has pointed out, the Christian tradition "valorizes historical time," since the Gospels took place in a specific historical era, that is, when Pontius Pilate governed Judea. For the Christian, therefore, Christ's birth and passion occurred in history, not merely "in the beginning." Accordingly, the very concept of "history" takes on a new meaning, for it presents itself as "a new dimension of the presence of God in the world."[115] Christians reading Verdaguer's final scene are likely to be left with a similar impression: that mythological time and its trappings—burning mountains, three-headed monsters, magic trees—have been swept aside in favor of a landmark event that occurred in a real historical moment, however embellished by the poetic voice.

Falla now proposed to set this unabashedly Iberian account of Christian evangelism. Numerous composers, from Cardinal Pietro Ottoboni (*Il Colombo*, 1691) to Philip Glass (*The Voyager*, 1992), have interpreted Columbus's journey.[116] Some treatments, such as the North American S. G. Pratt's cantata *The Triumph of Columbus* (1892), take it as an occasion for "universal joy and feeling of exultation" while others downplay bombast and heroism.[117] The best-known example of Columbus-inspired music is probably Milhaud's monumental opera *Cristophe Colomb*, on a libretto by Paul Claudel. With its huge chorus, film images, and multiple orchestras, the work has been criticized for grandiosity and lack of coherence, and after its premiere at the Berlin Staatsoper (5 May 1930) Milhaud set about revising it. Relevant here are (1) Milhaud's dedication of *Christophe Colomb* to Falla, and (2) the fact that the opera was linked to *Atlántida*'s initial stages. In October 1927, José María Sert asked Falla to compose a score for a pantomime scenario on

115. Mircea Eliade, *The Sacred and the Profane*, translated from the French by William Trask (New York: Harcourt, Brace and World, 1959), 111–13.

116. Robert M. Stevenson, "Musical Remembrances of Columbus's Voyages," *Inter-American Music Review* 15, no. 2 (1996): 1–71.

117. See the preface, by S. G. Pratt, cited in Stevenson, "Musical Remembrances of Columbus's Voyages," 38.

the life of Christopher Columbus he and Claudel had begun earlier that year.[118] Claudel, unconvinced by what little he knew of Falla's music, developed the scenario and eventually decided to work with Milhaud, his collaborator in the 1923 ballet *La création du monde*.[119] Sert and Falla, on the other hand, persevered with *Atlántida*, which was initially conceived as a pantomime for the Exposición Iberoamericana, which opened in Seville in 1929. Of course, Falla never completed *Atlántida*, and his failure to do so cast a pall over the remainder of his creative life.

In the beginning, however, Falla attacked his new project with gusto. First, he set about learning Catalan, a language distinct from Spanish. Next he selected those passages in Verdaguer's ten-canto epic best suited to musical realization and, much as he had done with *Don Quijote*, adjusted the original. That is, he interpolated passages from an earlier Verdaguer poem, "Colom" (Columbus), scriptural verses, and other sources, including several lines of his own. In some instances, Falla's adjustments enhance Columbus's role. For both "Colomb amb sos companys" (Columbus and his Companions) and "Les caravelles" (The Caravels), he used passages from "Colom"; in the latter, he portrayed Columbus's crew as "filled with faith, strength and courage, joined in brotherly agreement" on the three great ships manned by the "children of Iberia . . . the Castilian, the son of Catalonia, the Galician, the Andalusian and the Cantabrian."[120] For "La nit suprema" (The Supreme Night), which depicts Columbus keeping watch on the *Santa María* while his crew sleeps through "the august silence of this sacred night," Falla combined the text of "Colom" with lines from the book of Psalms (Vulgate) and the Alleluia verse for the Easter mass.[121] For the crew's singing of the luminous "La salve en el mar" (The Salve on the High Seas), he experimented with several textual possibilities, finally stitching together excerpts from the Vespers hymn "Ave maris stella," the Litanies of the Virgin, and a poem, "Los milagros de nuestra Señora" (The Miracles of Our Lady), by the medieval Spanish author Gonzalo de Berceo.[122]

During summer 1928, Falla wrote Sert that he was thinking about composing *Atlántida* as an oratorio and "leaving the mis-en-scène for a later date."[123] But by 10

118. Budwig, "Manuel de Falla's *Atlántida*," 120–21.

119. Letter, Claudel to Milhaud, 4 November 1927, in Jacques Petit, annotator, *Correspondence Paul Claudel–Darius Milhaud, 1912–1953*, Cahiers Paul Claudel, no. 3 (Paris: Gallimard, 1961), 83.

120. Translation by Angela Buxton in *Manuel de Falla, Ernesto Halffter: Atlántida*, liner notes (Auvidis Valois, AD 4685, 1993). For an overview of Falla's interpolations, see Budwig's concordance libretto, "Manuel de Falla's *Atlántida*," 362–436.

121. The line "Dies sanctificatus illuxit super terra" is Falla's modification of the "Dies sanctificatus illuxit nobis: venite gentes, et adorate Dominus: quia hodie descendit lux magna super terram," from the Alleluia verse. Another Latin passage in "La nit suprema," "factus est [Dominus] firmamentum meum," is from Psalm 17:19. I am grateful to Vincent Corrigan for this clarification.

122. Budwig, "Manuel de Falla's *Atlántida*," 108–10.

123. Letter, Falla to Sert, 5 July 1928, cited in Budwig, "Manuel de Falla's *Atlántida*," 124.

November of that year, he had completed both a scenario and a libretto, which he mailed Sert. As Andrew Budwig has observed in his exhaustive study of the extant autograph materials for *Atlántida*, this document is our principal source for Falla's earliest conception of the work, although the composer himself confessed to Sert that he was communicating these ideas to him "with many reservations" (muy reservadamente).[124] Consisting of a Prologue and two parts, the scenario-libretto is full of exuberant visual suggestions: walls, arches, towers of the submerged Atlantis, and "monstrous, glowing fish." Falla also suggested that Sert conceive of these images as if he were looking at them through the stained-glass windows "of old cathedrals."

With scenario and libretto in place, Falla could begin composing, and on 9 December 1928 he began the Prologue. With its two pianos and two harps, the Prologue's widely spaced harmonies suggest the vastness of the submerged landmass, with its hollow glories, now buried.[125] Perhaps to his surprise, Falla—the consummate miniaturist—soon realized that *Atlántida* was expanding well beyond his initial conception. But he remained enthusiastic, reporting to Matos on "the proportions the work [was] assuming" and predicting that it would "comprise three extensive parts";[126] in March 1929, he declared his intention "to burn the Pyrenees," a reference to the "L'incendi dels Pirineus" movement. Even sleeplessness contributed to *Atlántida*'s progress, as Falla informed Matos: "Taking advantage even of my hours of insomnia, Atlas, Hercules, Pyrene and Columbus accompany me on a daily basis, and, thank God, rare is the session devoted to them that is not fruitful. . . . Now the work will have three parts, plus the Prologue, and will therefore take up a whole program."[127] Thus *Atlántida* continued to grow, its projected dimensions outstripping any of Falla's previous works. Still, a performance venue was by no means assured. True to form, the composer failed to meet deadlines for both the Exposición Iberoamericana and the Exposición Internacional in Barcelona, which ran from 1929 to 1930 and featured the Orfeó Català, the former workers' chorus so emblematic of Catalan identity.[128] Yet enough rumors about *Atlántida* were floated that the musical world became curious. On 10 April 1931, Stokowski wrote Falla with the following idea:

---

124. Letter, 10 November 1928, cited in Budwig, "Manuel de Falla's *Atlántida*," 450.

125. Folio B1 is marked "comienzo 9/XII/28." See Budwig, "Manuel de Falla's *Atlántida*," 130n2.

126. Letter, Falla to Matos, 18 September 1929; see also a letter from Falla to Sert of 1 March 1929, cited in Budwig, "Manuel de Falla's *Atlántida*," 139 and 132–33, respectively.

127. "Y aprovechando hasta las horas de insomnia, Atlas, Hércules, Pírine y Colón me acompañan diariamente, y gracias a Dios, raro es el rato que les dedico que no resulta fructífero. . . . Ahora tendrá la obra tres partes, más el Prólogo, y ocupará por lo tanto un programa completo" (letter, Falla to Matos, 31 December 1929, AMF correspondence file 7264–027).

128. Budwig, "Manuel de Falla's *Atlántida*," 121, 136.

I often think how wonderful could be a modern drama based on one of the Greek dramas of Sophocles or Euripides which would be brief and simple . . . having a chorus and orchestra back of the stage so that they would be invisible, and having on the visible part of the stage either pantomimists or very large sized marionettes about six meters high. . . . The music produced by the invisible orchestra, chorus, and perhaps solo singers not to be continuous, but only to sound at the great moments of the drama. If it would appeal to you to write such a work, it would be a great artistic pleasure to me to produce it in America, and perhaps also in Europe.[129]

True, Stokowski does not specifically mention *Atlántida*. But the fact that he targets its essential qualities (mythology, the presence of chorus and orchestra, and pantomime), suggests that he had some inkling of what Falla was about. Both Stokowski's description and Falla's initial conception, moreover, neatly correspond to current musical-dramatic trends, apparent, for example, in Stravinsky's *Oedipus Rex*, which, with its restrained stage action and "universal" theme, had premiered four years earlier. In proposing giant marionettes, Stokowski may even have had in mind his thwarted desire to introduce the *Retablo* in the United States. With his genius for marketing classical music, Stokowski would have been ideally positioned to premiere *Atlántida*: a self-described "egocentric" ("I always want to be first," he later declared), it was only natural that he try to get his hands on the score before anyone else.[130]

How different *Atlántida*'s fate might have been had Falla been ready to accept Stokowski's invitation! But the composer's delicate health had already begun to wage war on the cantata. Having earlier suffered occasional vision problems, in late spring 1928 Falla had his first serious bout with iritis, an inflammation of the iris that is often accompanied by severe pain. (It was then that he began typing his letters, always apologizing for the impersonal tone he believed this set.) Then a hemorrhage incapacitated him for nearly three months. It occurred in late January 1930, when Alfonso XIII dismissed Gen. Primo de Rivera. Noting the end of Primo's seven-year regime, Falla commented wryly to Salazar that "the end of the dictatorship has coincided with the beginning of another, to which my doctor wishes me to submit."[131]

Even had he enjoyed the best of health, Falla was probably intimidated by *Atlántida*. Whatever his initial optimism, eventually he found it difficult to confront its increasingly sprawling proportions, and the grandeur of Verdaguer's poem was similarly daunting. Then there was his old enemy, scrupulosity, which returned with a vengeance. Never having composed any liturgical music, Falla was suddenly afraid

---

129. Letter, Stokowski to Falla, 10 April 1931, AMF correspondence file 7664. Stokowski wrote Falla in English.

130. Telecast, 13 September 1977, cited in Abram Chasins, *Leopold Stokowski: A Profile* (New York: Hawthorn, 1979), ix.

131. Letter, 31 January 1930, cited in Budwig, "Manuel de Falla's *Atlántida*," 143n2.

of giving offense to God in his settings of religious texts. By any standard, his manipulation of such texts was completely innocuous. For example, he wished to introduce "La veu divina" (The Divine Voice) with the acclamation "Sanctus, Sanctus, Sanctus! Dominus dixit." He would follow this with Verdaguer's fourth canto, a plaint on the sinful nature of man that culminates with a query uttered by the divine voice: "What harm have I done you, daughter of Eve, that you offend me so?" Falla, however, seems to have believed that the divine voice was addressing him directly. What of his own imperfect nature? What entitled *him* to comment on the wages of sin? Only ecclesiastical approval could assuage his worries on this point, and he wrote at least twice to Gaspar Pintado, the rector of a Jesuit college for advice on what pitfalls to avoid when "singing the [Creator's] infinite glories."[132] Once his fears had been dismissed by Church authority, he went forward with the sacred text. But such agonized precautions took their toll in time, energy, and concentration.

Still, there were long stretches when Falla could devote himself wholeheartedly to *Atlántida*. In June 1930, he entrusted his correspondence to María del Carmen, who effectively became her brother's personal secretary while she continued to run the household. Thanks in no small part to her solicitousness, Falla was able to work more or less regularly on *Atlántida* for two years. He had every reason to hope that one day the international musical community would applaud it as a work of art and be inspired by its profession of faith.

FIGUREHEAD FOR YOUTH: FALLA AS TEACHER

If Falla won the respect and affection of the poets of the Generation of '27, his standing among young Spanish composers was even more assured. Mainly, they were captivated by his neoclassical works, as Nin-Culmell's reaction to the Harpsichord Concerto attests. Much as Stravinsky considered the *Retablo* and the concerto "proof of incontestable progress in the development of [Falla's] great talent," the new generation of Spanish composers looked to these scores "for guidance and inspiration," as Gilbert Chase has observed.[133]

Due in part to Falla's guidance and inspiration—not to mention his international success—Spanish music had been transformed. Like Falla, many younger composers discarded the guitar-based sonorities and folkloric gestures of *andalucismo* to try their hands at *universalismo*. Abandoning nationalistic descriptive titles, such as *Zambra granadina* (Fiesta in Granada) or *Serenata andaluza*, they now applied "classicizing" labels, baptizing their works with such generic titles as sonatina, fugue, or

132. Letter, Falla to Pintado, 22 October 1928; see also letter of 4 December 1929. Both are cited and translated in Budwig, "Manuel de Falla's *Atlántida*," 142–43.

133. Chase, *Music of Spain*, 311. A similar evaluation is in Jorge de Persia, *Los últimos años de Manuel de Falla* (Madrid: Sociedad General de Autores de España, 1989), 21–23.

the names of various baroque dances.[134] For the blended sound of the symphony orchestra they substituted heterogeneous timbres in small, distinctive ensembles, which they enlivened with witty or pungent harmonies. They were also rabid anti-romantics. Especially outspoken was Gustavo Pittaluga, a member of the Grupo de los Ocho (Group of Eight), an entity loosely modeled on the French Les Six, which met at Madrid's Residencia de Estudiantes to perform new works and discuss aesthetics. At one such meeting, Pittaluga famously defended "objective" music, declaring: "no romanticism, no chromaticism, no divagations—and no chords of the diminished seventh!"[135]

Falla noted some practical dimensions of this paradigm shift in a 1929 article he wrote for the Madrid-based journal *La Gaceta Literaria*.[136] He observed, for example, that *zarzuela* no longer dictated a Spanish composer's success: although the genre still attracted a wide popular audience, "serious" composers could now make their careers without it. Nor did they have to study abroad, as the career of Ernesto Halffter confirmed. Not only did Halffter complete his studies in Spain, but his Sinfonietta in D Major of 1925 enjoyed its first success in Madrid, Barcelona, and Seville rather than Paris or London. That work, which derives from the standard symphonic formal arrangement (Pastorella, Adagio, Minuet, and Allegro giocoso), represented the new spirit, as did Halffter's ballet, *Sonatina*, which contains a rigaudon, sarabande, and gigue.[137] There were also a Prelude and Fugue, orchestral suite, gigue for guitar, sonata for cello and piano, and three sonatas for solo piano composed by Ernesto's brother, Rodolfo. Others, such as Pittaluga, Salvador Bacarisse, and Julián Bautista, followed suit.

As for Falla's stand on romanticism, a survey conducted by the Polish journal *Muzyka* is revealing. (Also polled were Frederick Delius, Dukas, Edward Elgar, Honegger, Erich Wolfgang Korngold, Ernst Krenek, Sergei Prokofiev, and Ravel.) In his brief remarks, Falla acknowledged the "achievements" of romantic masters but warned against the "serious impediments in the romantic trend."[138] He

134. Messing, *Neoclassicism in Music*, 38, 45.

135. Gustavo Pittaluga, *Musicalia* (Havana), nos. 15–16 (January-April 1931), cited and translated in Chase, *Music of Spain*, 203. On the Grupo de los Ocho and the Generation of '27, see Emilio Casares, "Música y músicos de la generación del 27," in *La música en la generación del 27: Homenaje a Lorca, 1915–1939*, edited by Emilio Casares (Madrid: Ministerio de Cultura, 1986), 20–37.

136. Manuel de Falla "¿Cómo ven la nueva juventud española?" *La Gaceta Literaria* 3, no. 51 (1 February 1929): 1, reprinted in Falla, *Escritos*, 122–23, 127–30. On *La Gaceta Literaria*, see Douglas W. Foard, *The Revolt of the Aesthetes: Ernesto Giménez Caballero and the Origins of Spanish Fascism*, American University Studies, ser. 9, no. 70 (New York: Peter Lang, 1989).

137. See Acker, "Ernesto Halffter," 110–22.

138. "Romantyzm w Muzyce," *Muzyka* (1928): 140, translated from the Polish by Alan Lem and cited in Michael Christoforidis, "Manuel de Falla and Romanticism: Insights into an Uncited Text," *Context* 6 (summer 1993–94): 26.

also took pains to distance himself from its influence. Allowing that "in *Noches en los jardines de España* and some theatrical works [of his] . . . one could find certain resonances of romanticism," Falla insisted that his more recent works, such as the Harpsichord Concerto, were "totally free of such influences; they rather approach the preclassical style." In other words, Falla was reiterating his stance of 1916, when he had so warmly praised "music written before the seventeenth century." Yet as Christoforidis has observed, Falla's sketches for the *Muzyka* statement show the composer's increasing preoccupation with the relationship between artistic utterance and societal trends. In an early draft, Falla equated romanticism with "freethinking," maintaining that once this loosely defined concept was translated into musical terms, it could "only lead to chaos insofar as its equilibrium, proportions, frenetic expression, and rhythmic/tonal structure are concerned."[139] This less than watertight parallel between freethinking and musical chaos was subsequently toned down. But it is essentially the same idea Falla had advanced in 1916, when he attacked the vagueness of eclecticism and Beethoven's suscepti-bility to "Robespierrean ideas."

Yet in April 1927 Falla presented an all-Beethoven concert at Granada's Athe-naeum. It consisted of the Sonata in C Minor op. 13 (the "Pathétique") and the Sep-tet in E♭ Major op. 20, which he conducted. The homage, which commemorated the centenary of Beethoven's death, may seem inconsistent with the Germanophobia of some composers, most notably Stravinsky, in the aftermath of the Great War, including Falla's own dim view of Beethoven's "Robespierrean" tendencies. Despite some reservations, however, there were aspects of Beethoven that Falla admired. In addition to the Lydian slow movement of the String Quartet in A Minor op. 132, which he had commended for its "preclassical" virtues, Falla also found praisewor-thy the "nobility and lack of self-interest with which [Beethoven] served music, convinced of its elevated social mission."[140] Evidently in Falla's system of values, the ill effects of freethinking could be trumped by the promise of social conscience, personal integrity, and the occasional return to a style that pre-dated "the insidious Protestant tradition."

Falla dissociated himself from romanticism on other occasions as well. In Oc-tober 1929, the Madrid daily *La Libertad* ran a lengthy article on him, which pro-claimed, "Falla es un romántico" (Falla is a romantic). Its author, journalist Darío Pérez, had reached this conclusion largely on the basis of Falla's fondness for soli-tude in his "ivory tower" in Granada and his antipathy toward the commercial-ization of art.[141] As we have seen from Falla's anxieties about setting sacred texts,

---

139. Christoforidis, "Manuel de Falla and Romanticism," 27.

140. See Christoforidis, "Manuel de Falla and Romanticism," 29. He also discusses Falla's article on Beethoven, which was published in the German newspaper *Vossiche Zeitung* and appeared in the Barcelona daily *La Noche* on 26 March 1927, AMF press file.

141. Darío Pérez, "Figuras de España: Manuel de Falla," *La Libertad,* 2 October 1929, 3.

his fear of misrepresentation sometimes verged on the maniacal. But his reaction to Darío Pérez's half-truths and outright fabrications seems justified, and the composer felt compelled to write an open letter to *La Libertad* clarifying the matter. In correcting Darío Pérez, a droll sense of humor was Falla's chief weapon.

He begins by expressing his "heartfelt thanks" for Darío Pérez's efforts, acknowledging the "goodwill of all" involved. Then, Falla cuts to the chase:

> Let's begin with "romanticism." In effect: those of us born in the past century have to a greater or lesser degree paid it tribute. Such is shown, insofar as my music is concerned, in *Vida breve* and *Noches*; but as for what romanticism has of excess, of formulas of deceptive profundity, of egotism, of dramatic exasperation . . . nothing is more contrary to my sympathies. By contrast, when romanticism reveals evocative force and lyric expansion (as long as this has been expressed simply and naturally and without mixing in proud intentions) it inspires the greatest sympathy in me, and the reflection of this same sympathy is what can be found in the works already cited. On the other hand, I don't think there's anything more opposed to romantic ideology than my latest works, starting from the *Retablo*.[142]

So far, Falla has done little more than assert the artistic image he had been cultivating for years. But there are also assertions about his person to be rectified:

> And now let's move on to my character. If one day I should have the great pleasure of receiving you in Granada, you'll see that such an "ivory tower" doesn't exist. . . . I live in a *carmen* (of which you have generously made me owner) without surrounding myself with "trophies" of any kind and seeking only in this Alhambra of my long-standing predilection that silence so necessary for those of my occupation and so difficult to find in a large, modern city. . . . But this letter is becoming interminable, and I don't want to abuse your kindness any longer by rectifying other details of less import. . . . Sincerest

---

142. "Empezaremos por el 'romanticismo.' Efectivamente: cuantos nacimos dentro del pasado siglo le hemos pagado en menor o mayor grado nuestro tributo. Así lo acusan, en lo que a mi música se refiere, la *Vida breve* y las *Noches*; pero en cuanto el romanticismo tiene de ilimitación, de fórmulas de engañosa profundidad, de egoísmo, de exasperación dramática . . . nada más contrario a mis simpatías. En cambio, cuanto el romanticismo revela de fuerza evocadora y de lírica expansión (siempre que haya sido expresado de modo simple y natural, y sin mezcla de orgullosas intenciones) me inspira altísima simpatía, y el reflejo de esta misma simpatía es el que puede encontrarse en los trabajos antes citados. Por el contrario, nada creo más opuesto a la ideología romántica que mis producciones últimas a partir del *Retablo*" (*La Libertad*, 9 October 1929, reprinted in Falla, *Escritos*, 131).

and repeated thanks, and very cordially extending to you my hand, I beg you to consider me your affectionate servant.[143]

So, while reveling in an avalanche of tongue-in-cheek honorifics, Falla managed to link romanticism with character defects. In addition to their negative impact on the human psyche, "egotism" and "proud intentions" yielded dubious artistic results. So, for that matter, did "vanity," another of Falla's pet peeves. On this point, Brahms especially set him off. In a letter of February 1928 to Salazar, he thundered:

SOUND THE ALARM. Your recent enthusiasm for Brahms has left me stupefied. "Retour" à Brahms! Why, that's all we need! Music full of vanity, like its author, and with a long beard, also like its author. Certainly music with a long beard inculcates great respect. This is the case with the Third Symphony of Saint-Saëns. The Second is much superior . . . but it lacks a beard, or if it has one, it's short. For this reason the Third is always played and never the Second. But to continue with Brahms: undoubtedly we're dealing with an artist of indisputable probity . . . but how much harm has he done without compensation of the slightest benefit! Imagine, the music *that counts* would be exactly the same if he had never existed; on the other hand, much *that doesn't count* might "count" if "Herr Brahms" (as the Wagner family called him) had limited himself to writing Hungarian dances. Certainly I'm perfectly well aware of the origin of Arbós's devotion, of Rubinstein's, of Casals's, for that music. It's very natural, and the same thing would have happened to me had I been in their place; it's the music that evokes childhood or first youth and that they constantly heard people going crazy over when they were studying in Germany; but "music" in all this plays nothing but a secondary role. I repeat that, far from criticizing that devotion, I find it entirely justified, and that, as far as artistic honor and noble intention, only an idiot could deny their presence in that music. In addition, there are moments in which one "breathes" with satisfaction while hearing it, but unfortunately, all of a sudden something will surface (tonal digression, melodic "artifice," "profound" formulas, etc., etc.) that not only cuts off the "breathing" that has begun, but (and this is the worst

143. "Y ahora pasaremos a mi carácter. Si algún día tengo el mucho gusto de verle por Granada, verá usted que no existe tal 'torre de marfil.' . . . Vivo en un carmen (del que generosamente me hace usted propietario) sin rodearme de 'trofeos' de ninguna clase y buscando tan sólo en esta Alhambra de mi vieja predilección ese silencio tan necesario a todos los de mi oficio y tan difícil de hallar en una gran ciudad moderna. . . . Pero esta carta se va haciendo interminable, y no quiero abusar más de la bondad de usted rectificando otros pormenores de menos monta. . . . Gracias sincerísimas repetidas, y estrechando muy cordialmente [la] mano, le ruego me crea su afectísimo servidor" (Falla, *Escritos*, 132).

thing) makes one totally lose track of what one is hearing. Well. Don't think, dear Adolfo, that I'm trying to impose my way of hearing and thinking in this or any other matter—God save me!—, the only thing I desire is that we don't throw away all that we're achieving in Spain, and with such hard work. It's a grave responsibility for you, for me, and for everyone, and only, only for this reason have I decided to SOUND THE ALARM.[144]

With this curious mixture of indignation and downright silliness, Falla was once again arguing that only humility could lead from vanity to purification, the narrow path toward which involved renunciation of all romantic excess. Spain, moreover, had to follow that very path if it was ever to be taken seriously in the world of music. Fortunately, in addressing Spain's young composers en masse, Falla sounded less preachy than in his private communication with "dear Adolfo." In Salazar's 1929 study, *Sinfonía y ballet*, for example, Falla exclaimed warmly: "Oh, young composers! I have years enough to exhort you to speak freely, according to what your own heart dictates. This liberty is the most difficult thing to achieve, but it's also the only thing worth achieving."[145] Of course, urging a young person to "follow your own heart" can be construed as pure romanticism. But Falla believed that the ultimate liberty— freedom to act upon the dictates of the conscience—came only from total obedience to God. It may well be that his inveighing against proud intentions and vanity echo Fedriani's warnings about "self-love" of a quarter-century earlier, with Falla now in the position of authority. But benign self-interest surely motivated him as well. For as he confronted *Atlántida* and the mysteries it portended he undoubtedly felt the need to buck up his own spirits as he embarked on a life of greater asceticism and silence.

Accompanying Falla's growing spirituality were the writings of the French Catholic philosopher and man of letters Jacques Maritain. Since his Paris years, Falla had associated with various Catholic intellectuals and artists, including Poulenc, Milhaud, Claudel, and the critic J. P. Altermann. Others were converts, such as Roland-Manuel (Alexis Levy). Born a Jew, Roland-Manuel eventually developed a religious fervor exceeding that of many Catholics, a spirit that, as noted, informed his 1930 biography of Falla. The imagery and mystery of Catholicism also attracted non-Catholic intellectuals, including André Gide, a Protestant, and Simone Weil, a middle-class Jew who worked in factories out of solidarity with the masses despite

---

144. Letter, Falla to Salazar, 5 February 1928, AMF correspondence file 7573, cited in Falla, *Escritos*, 125–26, with slight variations. It is not clear whether Falla knew Brahms's *Four Serious Songs*, op. 121, the first of which incorporates Ecclesiastes 3:19 ("for all is vanity"). Uninfluenced by Falla's diatribe, Salazar later addressed Brahms in *El siglo romántico* (Madrid: J. M. Yagües, 1936), 372.

145. Adolfo Salazar, *Sinfonía y ballet* (Madrid: Editorial Mundo Latino, 1929), 235–36. Falla's remarks first appeared in "To the Young Composer: Señor Manuel de Falla and German Formalism," *Daily Mail*, 19 July 1919, AMF press file.

a tortured body and soul. Reflecting such sympathies was Maritain's *L'Art et scholastique* (Art and Scholasticism), a copy of which Falla received from the author in 1928. The composer was especially impressed by Maritain's unabashed nostalgia for the Middle Ages, when "the artist had only the rank of artisan" and "man created more beautiful things . . . and adored himself less."[146] As for artistic expression in relation to society, Falla longed for the day when individualism could be restrained via a "natural social discipline," as Maritain put it. Waxing enthusiastic to his French colleague, Falla told Maritain that "certain confluences in our aspirations make me appreciate your work in a very special way."[147] As we have seen, Falla sought to realize these spiritual confluences, such as the absence of vanity and proud intentions, into musical utterances while censuring music that seemed to ignore these principles.

As the guiding force for Spanish music—a status he consistently disparaged—Falla gave his private students the full benefit of his generous and attentive spirit. If earlier he had taught out of necessity, now he could select his students carefully. One for whom both he and María del Carmen cherished a special affection was Rosa García Ascot, who worked with him during his second Madrid period. Besides playing works in progress for "Rosita," Falla encouraged her to play several of his compositions, such as a two-piano arrangement of *Noches en los jardines de España*, which they performed for the Société Musicale Indépendante in Paris in June 1920.[148] In 1934, she performed the Harpsichord Concerto at the Residencia de Estudiantes on a program that included Schoenberg's first Chamber Symphony and Stravinsky's Octet.[149] As with his other students, he encouraged her to analyze Scarlatti's sonatas, which he preferred to Beethoven's.[150] From 1938 to 1939, García Ascot studied with Nadia Boulanger but remained in contact with Falla until she and her husband, the composer Jesús Bal y Gay, emigrated to Mexico after the Spanish Civil War (see figure 15). Practically all of her works, which are neoclassical in orientation, remain unpublished.[151]

146. Jacques Maritain, *Art and Scholasticism and the Frontiers of Poetry*, translated by Joseph W. Evans (New York: Charles Scribner's Sons, 1962), 22.

147. "Certains coincidences d'aspirations me font aimer votre oeuvre d'une façon toute special" (letter, Falla to Maritain, 26 May 1928, cited in Christoforidis, "Aspects of the Creative Process," 26n14).

148. De Persia, *Poesía*, 82.

149. Jesús Bal y Gay and Rosita García-Ascot, *Nuestros trabajos y nuestros días* (Madrid: Fundación Banco Exterior, 1990), 209; see also Maestro Jacopetti, "La música y los músicos,"*Ahora*, 24 June 1934, AMF, press file.

150. Torres Clemente, "La presencia de Scarlatti," in Nommick, *Manuel de Falla e Italia*, 98n114.

151. García Ascot's recollections of Boulanger are in Bal y Gay and Garcia Ascot, *Nuestros trabajos y nuestros días*, 45–50. See also Xoan M. Carreira, "García Ascot, Rosa," in Casares, *Diccionario de la música española*, 5:426.

Figure 15. Jesús Bal y Gay, his wife
Rosa García Ascot, and Manuel de
Falla in a composition lesson,
September 1935. (Reprinted by kind
permission of the Archivo Manuel
de Falla)

Ernesto and Rodolfo Halffter, Salazar, and Bal y Gay were also among Falla's students. Our clearest understanding of his methods, however, comes from Joaquín Nin-Culmell. Falla had met the young man in Paris, unaware that his old friend Joaquín Nin had a musical son.[152] Intrigued by the Harpsichord Concerto and convinced that Falla was unique among human beings, in the summer of 1930 the twenty-two-year-old Nin-Culmell checked into a pension in Granada. From there, he could hear the fountains of the Alhambra and walk to Falla's *carmen* for lessons. The young composer had already digested Debussy's style, as is clear from his *Trois impressions* for piano, which he brought to his first lesson with Don Manuel. (As Nin-Culmell quickly learned, Falla objected to the title "maestro," insisting that "there is only one maestro.") The first of these "impressions," "Habanera," confirms the power of compositional models. Dedicated to Falla, it mirrors many of the strategies Debussy had used in "Soirée dans Grenade" and to which Falla himself had alluded in his *Homenaje a Debussy* for guitar. For example, Nin-Culmell's "impression" maintains an insistent *habanera* rhythm by means of the repeated dotted-eighth-sixteenth rhythm in the melodic line and incorporates abrupt changes of dynamics, including a final diminuendo. At that first lesson, he and Falla also

152. Of the three Nin children, Joaquín was the youngest (see viii). Anaïs died in 1977 and Thorvald in 1991. Their mother, Rosa Culmell, divorced Joaquín senior in 1924. See Deirdre Blair, *Anaïs Nin: A Biography* (New York: Putnam, 1995), 71.

discussed the other *Impressions*. One, "Las mozas del Cántaro" ("The Girls with Water Jug," after the painting by Goya), became a favorite of the Spanish pianist Ataulfo Argento before he abandoned the piano for conducting. The other, "Un jardín de Toledo" (A Garden in Toledo), contains added-note chords and virtuosic flourishes. (In fact, the piece was inspired not by Toledo but by the garden at the Benedictine monastery, Santo Domingo de Silos in Burgos Province, but the young composer felt that the title "A Garden in Burgos" would be unenticing.) Falla praised Nin-Culmell's efforts but warned him against falling into the "composer-pianist" syndrome, in which the fingers dictate musical ideas.

At that same lesson, Falla exhorted the young man to "confront the great musical forms," which, of course, he himself had been doing for the past decade. This advice fell on receptive ears: under Falla's guidance, Nin-Culmell put aside impressionistic character pieces and over three summers in Granada (1930, 1932, and 1934) completed the *Sonata breve* (1932) and the Piano Quintet (1934–36). He also began the classically oriented Piano Concerto with Falla, but completed it only in 1946. Nin-Culmell's recollections of their work on the *Sonata breve* are especially telling. Falla always prepared for the lesson by studying in advance the student's manuscript in progress. Upon returning to Nin-Culmell the draft of the *Sonata breve*, Falla explained that he had penciled in his comments very lightly so that they could later be more easily erased! Falla's tendency toward self-effacement—literally—did not convince Nin-Culmell, who kept the annotated draft of the *Sonata breve* among his personal papers for over seventy years, along with his copy of Lucas's *L'acoustique nouvelle*, which is also sprinkled with Falla's delicate marginalia.

Many of Falla's comments on the *Sonata breve*, both written and verbal, addressed texture and form. In lieu of block chords in the first movement, for example, he suggested independent contrapuntal lines to confer integrity on the bass. This was consistent with Falla's distaste for "beautiful chords," as he wryly called them, which he believed impeded the independent bass movement essential to musical growth. He also proposed altering the second theme of the first movement by inserting a perfect fourth (F♯–B, m. 35) for a more angular melodic profile. Instead of static chords to introduce the theme, Falla proposed adding motivically related sequences at mm. 21–22 and 25–26. He also advised extending the coda for formal balance.

The second movement underwent similar alterations. Initially it contained parallel chords in three to five voices, but Falla stripped these down to single lines, often in bare octaves. Remarking that one always had to look for a theme's contrapuntal implications, he suggested introducing canons; perhaps not surprisingly, the resulting contrapuntal texture based on Nin-Culmell's terse theme recalls the second movement of the Harpsichord Concerto (see musical example 24). Falla also believed that the principal theme of Nin-Culmell's third movement could stand on its own. By eliminating a superfluous left-hand line in the opening measures, Falla paved the way for a fugato; again, in the interest of large-scale equilibrium, Falla suggested extending the third movement's development to compensate for the brevity

Musical Example 24. Joaquín Nin-Culmell, *Sonata breve*, movement 2, Andante, mm. 1–24. (Copyright in U.S.A. and all countries, 1934, by Oxford University Press. Copyright assigned, 1955, to Rongwen Music, Inc. Reproduced by permission of Broude Brothers Limited, sole selling agent.)

of the corresponding section in the first movement. As a final balancing gesture, he proposed reintroducing the second theme of the first movement into the *Sonata breve*'s final measures. So successful were these modifications that the *Sonata breve*, which was published in 1934, served as Nin-Culmell's calling card when he applied to study composition with Dukas at the Paris Conservatory—and was accepted.[153]

Nin-Culmell was much taken with the way art and life overlapped in Falla's very existence. For example, when Falla asserted that "counterpoint is much more important than fugue, since fugue is a crystallized form, and counterpoint, on the contrary, is more *principle* than *form*," it was understood that Don Manuel was in-

---

153. Nin-Culmell's compositions are listed in Hess, "Nin-Culmell, Joaquín," in Sadie and Tyrell, *Revised New Grove Dictionary*, 17:926–27.

directly evoking the notion of God as the first and absolutely necessary principle over "that which is seen" (form).[154] Falla also placed a high priority on individual integrity, always within the framework of a divine plan. He was adamant that each student must find his or her own way, maintaining that *his* solutions, *his* style, and *his* way of confronting the mysteries of art were no blueprint for anyone else. The very idea that he might influence others to compose in his way was repugnant to him, for he did not want to be so much a *teacher* of composition as a guide. As Nin-Culmell and others have confirmed, this attitude rested on faith. That is, Falla was convinced that once a student's musical gifts, intellectual conviction, and personal integrity were awakened, once they met in accordance with higher principles, the student's inner voice would show the way.

Falla was always concerned for his students' personal welfare. In Nin-Culmell's case, this meant regular invitations to dinner, since the young man's financial circumstances were precarious in the early 1930s. (To be sure, these invitations had their drawbacks. Dinner with Falla and María del Carmen was extremely late, even by Andalusian standards, and Nin-Culmell was often ravenous by midnight, when it was finally served. On other occasions, Falla would inquire if Nin-Culmell had received ecclesiastical permission to eat meat on Fridays, to which the hungry young composer would respond lamely in the affirmative.) While teaching Rosa García Ascot in Madrid, and under considerable financial strain himself, Falla gave her large quantities of extra time. On Ernesto Halffter's behalf, Falla sought professional opportunities and offered musical suggestions galore, as the four-hundred-plus pieces of correspondence between them attest. With other composers, he had less direct contact, but he went out of his way to offer encouragement. One of these was Bàrbara Giuranna, whom he met in Sienna in 1928; in 1936 she would become the first Italian woman composer represented at the Venice Biennale. Giuranna was grateful to have met Falla, whom she thanked with "great admiration" for his interest.[155]

Falla's students had ample opportunity to observe their teacher's habits, which ranged from his strange hours to his obsession with germs and hygiene and his fervent attention at mass. Once, Nin-Culmell entered Falla's house to find his teacher on his hands and knees on the kitchen floor, which was covered with cockroaches. Wielding a bedroom slipper, Don Manuel was putting them to death one by one. To ameliorate their sad fate and assuage his tender conscience, however, he personally declared to each insect, "My dear, you are a creature of God with as much right to live as I. But this is impossible!"[156] Following hard on each individual benediction was the final death blow.

154. Joaquín Nin-Culmell, "Manuel de Falla, pedagogo," *Revista de Occidente*, no. 188 (1996): 41. See also W. A. Wallace, "Form," in *New Catholic Encyclopedia*, 5:1013.

155. Bergadà, "La relación de Falla con Italia," in Nommick, *Manuel de Falla e Italia*, 44, 59–60. See also Harvey Sachs, *Music in Fascist Italy* (London: Weidenfeld and Nicolson, 1987), 97.

156. Larry Weinstein, dir., *Fuego y agua: Vida y música de Manuel de Falla* (video) (Madrid: Rhombus RTVE, 1991).

The best summary of these "halcyon days" in Granada comes from one who lived it. Nin-Culmell has written:

> How quickly the hours and the days passed! The cigarettes cut in half to please his doctor, walks in the Paseo de los Mártires . . . jokes instigated by María del Carmen . . . calls from friends in Granada . . . visiting Federico García Lorca's house, where we heard him sing and play his versions of popular songs in which he released all of his *duende*, poet-musician and the last of the troubadours. A whole world that has passed so quickly that we still haven't realized it's passed.[157]

For Falla, that world's "passing" began with the establishment of the Second Republic in 1931. Initially, he supported its program of agrarian reform, labor rights, and educational equality, all to benefit Spain's underclass. But his skepticism about "free-thinking"—individual liberty over obedience to God, as he defined it—ultimately caused him to break ranks. Falla's vision of a narrow path to purification had inspired his greatest musical creations, but it would prove small consolation during the conflicts that lay ahead.

157. Nin-Culmell, "Manuel de Falla, pedagogo," 45–46. *Duende*, often associated with flamenco, can connote a "Dionysian inspiration always related to anguish, mystery and death" (Gibson, *Federico García Lorca*, 113–14). Lorca explained *duende* by recalling gypsy singer Manuel Torre's observation on *Noches en los jardines de España*: "Whatever has black sounds has *duende*" (Federico García Lorca, "Play and Theory of Duende," in *In Search of Duende*, 49).

Chapter 7

"Far above the Workings of Politics"

On 12 April 1931, municipal elections were held throughout Spain. The result was a resounding vote of no confidence for the monarchy, and by the fourteenth Alfonso XIII had sailed for France and forced exile. Jubilant Spaniards took to the streets. In Madrid, the imposing statue of the goddess Cibeles was hung with the Republican tricolor, and as citizens celebrated the peaceful transfer of power the Republican anthem resounded along with the "Marseillaise," a symbol of liberty.[1] It went unremarked, however, that conservative parties still dominated rural parts of central Spain, Galicia, Andalusia, and Extremadura and that Republicans and Socialists had won by only slightly more than half the vote. Also lurking in the background was resentment from more liberal sectors toward the Spanish Church and its long-entrenched power over education and social mores.

FALLA AND THE REPUBLIC

How did Falla greet this momentous news? Having taken a liberal stance during the Great War, in 1931 he found himself of the same mind as most of the cosignatories

---

1. Gabriel Jackson, *The Spanish Republic and the Civil War, 1931–1939* (Princeton: Princeton University Press, 1965), 25. The tricolor and the Republican anthem (the "Himno de Riego") were officially adopted at the end of April. See also Paul Preston, *A Concise History of the Spanish Civil War* (London: Fontana, 1996), 24–26.

of Ortega's manifesto, that is, strongly pro-Republican. Like many of them, Falla took a dim view of the monarchy and what he considered its inherent artificialities.[2] He also applauded the Republic's goal of social justice: having paid homage to Spain's underclass and raised funds for Russian refugees through his music, Falla gave regularly to the poor and felt genuine respect toward those from the lower rungs of society. Also his view of the artist as a humble craftsman, as articulated by Maritain, resonated with the Republican view of the common laborer's inherent dignity, suggested in the opening line of the new constitution: "Spain is a democratic Republic of workers."[3] In short, Falla both supported the advent of the Republic and was amazed at how smoothly it had all transpired, writing Trend in early May that "the manner in which this revolution has been carried out is miraculous." Optimistically, the composer placed his faith in God that the Republic would "continue to pursue a peaceful course."[4]

Yet the government's first major test presented itself in the form of a challenge to the very faith that Falla—and many others—professed. Weeks after the election, a riot involving monarchists and Republicans broke out in Madrid. Several churches were burned, and a spate of antireligious vandalism followed in Andalusia. Uneasily, Spaniards observed the official reaction. Besides radical elements, the new government included practicing Catholics, such as President Niceto Alcalá Zamora. There were also left-leaning moderates who considered religion a matter of individual conscience, such as Manuel Azaña, who had addressed so compellingly the complexities of Spain in his review of *The Three-Cornered Hat*. Having long blamed the Church for Spain's backwardness, Azaña, now minister of war, initially refused to call the Civil Guard to squelch the riots and offered the ungraceful explanation that the burning of all the convents in Spain was not worth the life of a single Republican.[5]

Along with many Spaniards, Falla disapproved of the government's inaction. On 14 May, he and several likeminded *granadinos* telegraphed Alcalá Zamora, complaining that "small groups have been committing all manner of sacrileges for two days" and noting the authorities' slow response.[6] In fact, Falla and his colleagues were two days late: on 12 May, the government had reversed its noninterventionist policy and the Civil Guard was called in. Historian Gabriel Jackson has speculated on the rea-

2. Personal interview with Joaquín Nin-Culmell, January 2000.

3. Frank Sedwick, *The Tragedy of Manuel Azaña and the Fate of the Spanish Republic* (Columbus: Ohio State University Press, 1963), 85.

4. Letter, Falla to Trend, 4 May 1931, cited and translated in Budwig and Chase, *Manuel de Falla*, 28.

5. See Vicente R. Pilapil, "Azaña y Díaz, Manuel," in *Historical Dictionary of the Spanish Civil War, 1936–1939*, edited by James W. Cortada (Westport, Conn.: Greenwood, 1982), 63.

6. "Grupos no numerosos han estado dos días cometiendo en la ciudad toda clase de sacrilegios" (draft [in a hand other than Falla's] of a telegram to Niceto Alcalá Zamora from Falla, Eusebio Borrajo, José Segura, and Hermenegildo Lanz, among others, AMF, correspondence file 6788).

sons for the delay. Since most politicians probably did not share Azaña's virulent attitude toward the Church, it may have been that the government was reluctant to shoot (rather than persuade) so early in its existence. There was also the equivocal attitude of many Spaniards toward the Catholic hierarchy: attendance at mass was low, and anticlerical feeling was hardly new in Spain.[7] Yet Spaniards continued to baptize their children, marry, and receive final rites within the Church, and the bourgeoisie sent its offspring to reputable Catholic schools. Furthermore, as Francis Lannon points out, piety "has never been expressed only through attending church on Sundays and receiving the sacraments," adding that pictures of the Virgin Mary were hung over the beds in some Spanish brothels.[8] Why, then, did large crowds stand by as religious monuments were savaged? Evidently, those who felt that the Church had sinned against the Spanish people were prepared to tolerate momentary violence against it.[9]

Not Falla, however. As he told Fernando de los Ríos (his acquaintance from the Café Alameda was now minister of justice), he agonized "every time the Spanish state officially confirms its rationalism or its anti-religious concept."[10] But had the government "officially confirmed" an antireligious stance? In mid-April, it announced its intention to secularize schools, cemeteries, and hospitals; permit divorce; and reduce the number of religious orders. On 6 May, just before the church burnings occurred, it decreed that religious instruction, previously obligatory, would now be offered only upon parental request, and on 22 May it prohibited the display of saints' images and religious objects in the schools. Giving added clout to these proposals was the Republic's massive education and literacy programs for workers and *campesinos*, which included creating almost ten thousand classrooms between 1931 and 1933 alone.[11] These policies, along with a proclamation of complete religious liberty, antagonized members of the Church hierarchy and pained many practicing Catholics. Most bishops interpreted the reforms as violations of the Concordat of 1851, which stipulated that "the Apostolic Roman Catholic religion . . . continues to be the only one of the Spanish nation."[12] A far smaller contingent of priests be-

7. See Joan Connelly Ullman, *The Tragic Week: A Study of Anticlericalism in Spain, 1875–1912* (Cambridge: Harvard University Press, 1968).

8. Lannon, *Privilege, Persecution, and Prophecy*, 22.

9. Jackson, *Spanish Republic*, 34–35; see also Mitchell, *Betrayal of the Innocents*, 76–85.

10. Letter (draft), Falla to de los Ríos, 19 June 1931, AMF correspondence file 7492; see also de Persia, *Poesía*, 220.

11. See Douglas W. Foard, "A Chronology of the Spanish Civil War: 1930–1939," in Cortada, *Historical Dictionary of the Spanish Civil War*, 483–84. On the Republic's expansion of education, see Carolyn P. Boyd, *Historia Patria: Politics, History, and National Identity in Spain, 1875–1975* (Princeton: Princeton University Press, 1997), 199.

12. Hughey, *Religious Freedom in Spain*, 23. Hughey discusses the conflict between supporters of the Concordat and the constitution of 1876 on pages 74–75; see also 117–37.

lieved that the anticlerical legislation was a momentary overreaction that would be ameliorated over time.

Surely, Falla followed the intense debate in early October over Article 26 of the new constitution. Article 3, which separated church and state (a principle many Catholics favored), had already passed by a vote of 278 to 41. Article 26, on the other hand, caused a furor, for it sought to restrict in practical terms the power of the religious orders. Not only would their role in teaching be sharply curtailed, but they would now have to register property and income. A testy, anticlerical tone informed parliamentary debate: when de los Ríos attempted to mediate by citing the Church's charitable and medical work, Azaña promptly attacked the proselytizing function of many of these activities, arguing that in a true democracy decisions over birth, marriage, burial, and education depended on one's individual conscience. Then, in a speech of 13 October 1931, he uttered the infamous phrase "Spain has ceased to be a Catholic country," a pronouncement that was technically correct but unnecessarily strident to many Catholics.[13] Yet Azaña's fateful words appeared in banner headlines throughout Spain, fueling the perception that the Republic was bent on destroying the Church.

Given the inflammatory official discourse and distortion by the media, it is difficult to know Falla's understanding of the religious legislation. It was hardly his habit to unthinkingly defend the Church, as his challenge to *germanofilismo* during the Great War attests. He also complained more than once that some of its current practices were contrary to "the example of Christ." Yet, while he lamented the violence against religious objects and the animalistic frenzy with which it was often perpetrated, he expressed hope that the Spanish Church would emerge from this dark period "strong and cleansed of the impurity and ignorance that had regrettably weakened it," as he told poet Gerardo Diego.[14] To Cardinal Vidal i Barraquer, a member of the liberal wing of the Church hierarchy (he was criticized for his fondness for jazz), Falla poured out his heart in a lengthy screed. He lamented everything from irregularities in the mass, the deficient attitude (*nada edificante*) of many priests and altarboys, and, significantly, the indifference of the Spanish Catholic press to the Church's intellectual wing. (Falla was so distraught that he even complained to the cardinal about the tacky altar decorations provided by "young ladies whose good intentions do not correspond to the loftiness of their mission.") Even in the midst of this jeremiad, Falla optimistically proposed that the Spanish Church could rise above the present crisis—if only it would follow its own teachings.[15]

13. José María Marco, *Manuel Azaña: Una biografía* (Barcelona: Planeta, 1998), 182–83.

14. Letter, Falla to Diego, 6 March 1932, in Sopeña, *Correspondencia Gerardo Diego–Manuel de Falla*, 175.

15. Letter (draft), Falla to Vidal i Barraquer, 1932, month unknown, AMF correspondence file 7744.

Thus, whatever his initial sympathy for the Republic, Falla parted company with it on a point that many in a pluralistic world take for granted: the secular state. For him, Spain without "the gospel" was "a deep wound . . . in the soul."[16] Falla not only spoke of this to his friends, but he thought it his duty to communicate his anguish to those in positions of authority. Mainly, he placed his hope in de los Ríos, with whom he had a personal relationship and who could be counted on for moderation. Falla's letters to him often appeal to their friendship and sometimes take a highly emotional tone, as when the composer describes the "horrible moments of despair" he suffered in the wake of the May church burnings, which he "counted among the most horrible of [his] life."[17] On other occasions, however, he prodded de los Ríos on policy. Regarding civil ceremonies devoid of religious content, Falla complained that the "sacred name of God . . . [was being] implacably suppressed . . . from all manifestations of an official nature, while the most filthy blasphemies proliferate in public."[18] On the secularization of education, Falla worried that "there are schools in which the teachers tear out pages of Sacred History (surely those from the New Testament) to the point of not using . . . those telling the history of Spain, the reign of the Catholic monarchs, the Reconquest, the discovery of America, and the unity of Spain, that is to say, the only definitively glorious thing we've ever done."[19] Elsewhere, Falla wondered how religious values could be instilled if the crucifix were "pulled from the schools"; on a proposed institute for Arab Studies, the composer queried sarcastically: "Maybe in the School of Arab studies that they plan to establish in Spain the study of the Koran will be prohibited?"[20] In short, Falla articulated a perception many Spaniards shared. "Why," he demanded, "confuse an anticlerical position with an anti-Christian offensive?"[21] De los Ríos, who probably sighed every time he received a letter from Falla, assured the composer of his balanced approach to these matters and, when his busy schedule permitted, detailed some of the frustrations such moderation entailed.[22] This was hardly comforting to Falla.

16. Letter, Falla to Diego, 6 March 1932, in Sopeña, *Correspondencia Gerardo Diego–Manuel de Falla,* 174–75.

17. Letter (draft), Falla to de los Ríos, 19 June 1931, AMF correspondence file 7492; see also de Persia, *Poesía,* 220.

18. Letter, Falla to de los Ríos, 23 January 1932, AMF correspondence file 7492.

19. "Hay escuelas en las que los maestros arrancan páginas de la Historia Sagrada (sin duda las del Nuevo Testamento) y hasta inutilizan . . . las de la Historia de España que narran el reinado de los Reyes Católicos, con la Reconquista, el descubrimiento de América y la Unidad de España: es decir, lo único definitivamente glorioso que hemos hecho" (letter, Falla to de los Ríos, 10 June 1932, AMF correspondence file 7492).

20. "¿O es que en la Escuela de Estudios Árabes que se proyecta establecer en España se va a prohibir el estudio del Corán?" (letter, Falla to de los Ríos, 23 January 1932, AMF correspondence file 7492).

21. "¿Por qué confundir una posición anticlerical con una ofensiva anticristiana?" (letter, Falla to de los Ríos, 23 January 1932, AMF correspondence file 7492).

22. Letter, de los Ríos to Falla, 19 April 1932, AMF correspondence file 7492.

Eventually, Falla's position on the religion question attracted public scrutiny. In March 1932, a councilman from Seville, Alberto Fernández Ballesteros, proposed that City Hall honor the composer for having founded the Orquesta Bética de Cámara, which was based in Seville. In the daily *El Liberal*, Ballesteros acknowledged that Falla had already been named an "adopted son" of Seville under "a past municipal government," with its "so-called holidays, suffused with official coldness, ritual speeches, culminating in the superannuated laurel wreath and the inevitable certificate" (Ballesteros is referring to the 20 March 1926 ceremony during Primo de Rivera's dictatorship when Falla was named *hijo adoptivo* or "adopted son").[23] In lieu of empty ceremony, the present government, which Ballesteros hailed as "republican, democratic, and modern," would now honor Falla and the orchestra members with a full performance of the *Retablo*. Touched by Ballesteros's kind words, Falla was all in favor of recognizing the players, describing them as "young men who, with such heroic disinterest, have known how to preserve 'the sacred fire.'"[24] But an entity that described itself as "republican, democratic, and modern" surely aroused his suspicions, and on 23 March, he tried to explain himself to Ballesteros, writing: "I've always been opposed to anything signifying an homage for myself." In the same letter, however, he acknowledged "the noble ends to which . . . the earnings from the [projected] concert are directed."[25]

Ballesteros evidently misunderstood this less than definitive response, and by mid-April, the Republican press was announcing the *homenaje*.[26] Falla wanted no part of it, and shortly thereafter unofficial word of his refusal to accept the honor leaked to the conservative press. Right-wing journalists made hay with the news: the Seville-based *La Unión*, for example, reported that the composer "cannot accept an homage from those who are apologists for laicization and have banished the crucifix from the schools."[27] Ever fearful of misrepresentation, or "deformation," as he called it, Falla attempted to clarify his position. In an open letter to *La Unión*, he argued that he had never referred to "'apologists of laicization,' as *La Unión* state[d]." He also offered a portion of a letter he had written to Segismundo Romero

23. "Llamadas fiestas, caladas de frío oficial, de discursos rituarios, culminantes en la vetusta corona de laurel y el inevitable pergamino" (A. Fernández Ballesteros, *El Liberal*, 12 March 1932, AMF press file).

24. "Esos muchachos que con tan heróico desinterés han sabido conservar 'el fuego sagrado'" (letter, Falla to Ballesteros, 23 March 1932, AMF correspondence file 6969).

25. "Siempre he sido contrario a cuanto para mí tenga la significación de homenaje. . . . Los nobles fines a que . . . se destinarán los ingresos de los conciertos" (letter, Falla to Ballesteros, 23 March 1932, AMF correspondence file 6969).

26. See "Ernesto Halffter y el homenaje a Falla," *El Sol*, 24 March 1932, 1; and "Sobre el homenaje a Falla," *El Liberal* (Seville), 17 April 1932, both in AMF press file.

27. "[Falla] no puede aceptar un homenaje, de quienes hacen la apología del laicismo y han desterrado el Crucifijo de las escuelas" ("Cock-tail sevillano: Ahí va eso," *La Unión* [Seville], 31 May 1932, typewritten transcript, AMF carpeta 6418/71).

on the matter, which Romero gave him permission to reprint. In every paragraph, Falla's horror of politicization emerges. "I would regret that, as usually occurs now," he wrote, "someone . . . could confer on this an erroneous *political* significance, when, as you know, this only obeys my deepest convictions, now aroused by the circumstances. . . . If God is now *officially* denied all recognition, how could I, His poor creature, accept it?"[28] Thus, although he was not necessarily attacking "apologists for laicization" per se, nor venturing an opinion on the question of religious freedom and individual conscience, Falla saw *himself* as incapable of "accepting anything resembling an homage, *whatever its origins may be*, when God, who is above everything, is officially denied all homage."[29] He did, however, plead on behalf of the faithful. "We Christians of Spain," he lamented, "are undergoing moments of profound bitterness and mourning, but I understand that we must never use religion as a political weapon, nor use personal attack, nor anything similar to defend it, which would contradict the true spirit of Christianity."[30]

Immediately Falla became a hero to the political Right. His photo appeared on the cover of the magazine *La Hormiga de Oro: Ilustración Católica* (see figure 16), and throughout Spain, Catholic and right-wing newspapers reprinted his letter or portions thereof. Nearly all gave pride of place to its most quotable line: "If God is denied 'official' recognition, how could I, His poor creature, accept it?" In Cádiz, a letter of support for the composer circulated, and for several days the *Diario de Cádiz* published lists of signatories, 580 in all.[31] In early July, that paper also printed a response from Falla in which he thanked his supporters for their recognition of his "strong convictions and deep religious feelings." Yet, as ever, he explicitly cautioned against "a possible political interpretation [of the incident], which I always try to carefully avoid."[32] Of course, the signatories' sincerity and their familiarity with the details of the case remain unknown.

28. The letter to Romero is in two installments, 3 and 11 April 1932. The portion cited is from 3 April and appears in Manuel de Falla, *Cartas a Segismundo Romero*, transcribed and edited by Pascual Pascual Recuero (Granada: Ayuntamiento de Granada, Patronato "Casa-Museo Manuel de Falla," 1976), 278.

29. "[No puedo] aceptar nada que tenga carácter de homenaje *sea cuál fuere su procedencia*, cuando a Dios, que está sobre todas las cosas, se le niega oficialmente todo homenaje" (Manuel de Falla, "Una carta de Don Manuel de Falla," 8 June 1932, *La Unión*, AMF press file).

30. "Y los cristianos de España atravesamos momentos de amargura y duelo profundos; pero yo entiendo que no debemos jamás servirnos ni de la Religión como arma política, ni tampoco emplear el ataque personal, ni nada parecido para defenderla, contraviniendo con ello el verdadero espíritu del cristianismo" ("Una carta de don Manuel de Falla").

31. The figure is given in "Carta al ilustre maestro gaditano Manuel de Falla," *Diario de Cádiz*, 26 June 1932; see also the same newspaper on 21 and 22 June, both in AMF press file.

32. "Carta del ilustre gaditano Don Manuel de Falla," *Diario de Cádiz*, 3 July 1932, AMF press file.

Figure 16. Cover, *La Hormiga de Oro: Ilustración Católica*, 23 June 1932. (Reprinted by kind permission of the Archivo Manuel de Falla)

A month later, the event was still attracting notice. In his usual feisty style, the right-wing music critic Víctor Espinós speculated on the long-term effects of Falla's actions in *El Defensor de Córdoba*. For one thing, the composer was now "in the suspects' quarantine," as Espinós put it, and he would be forever associated with other right-wing artists and intellectuals.[33] Espinós also noted the deafening silence in the Republican press over the matter, observing that "it's barely made a dent in one sector of the press . . . it's as if [Falla] didn't exist."[34] This was certainly true, for most Republican papers, including *El Heraldo de Madrid*, *La Vanguardia*, *La Voz*, *La Libertad*, and *El Sol*, did not touch the issue. An exception was *El Socialista*, which offered an editorial on Falla's letter entitled "Incongruencia católica" (Catholic Incongruence). Unfortunately, it falls far short of the objective inquiry that might have offered a counterweight to the Right's grandstanding. Noting Falla's "bizarre solidarity with God," the author explored the complexities of "official" versus personal religious observance:

> Certainly the State does not render homage to God, for this is impossible: the
> State doesn't attend mass, doesn't confess, doesn't make an act of contrition,

33. Víctor Espinós, "El 'Te Deum' de Falla," *El Defensor de Córdoba*, 7 July 1932, AMF press file.

34. "Apenas ha tenido eco en una parte de la prensa . . . [es] como si [Falla] no existiera" (Espinós, "El 'Te Deum' de Falla").

nor does it have a soul to save or to sell to the devil. . . . Homage is rendered to God by every man who wants to do so, in his conscience. And these two simple considerations should have sufficed for maestro Falla, so that he could have accepted without scruples the city of Alfonso the Wise [Seville] drinking a toast to him or erecting a street-sign that bears his name. The Supreme Creator would hardly have imagined itself supplanted nor felt jealousy over such a simple thing.[35]

The editorial also accused the Right of intensifying the impression that an ongoing, government-supported "religious persecution" was taking place. Lashing out at Catholic conservatives (among whose numbers Falla was now included), the writer demanded: "So what are they complaining about? Who is preventing them from 'tipping' concierges and obtaining balcony banners for the Sacred Heart for two or three pesetas? Let's reach an understanding and admit it: there is faith and there is liberty."[36]

Yet on other occasions, Falla was willing to associate himself with a "republican, democratic, and modern" perspective. Despite his refusal to accept honors from the secular state, Falla served in the first Republican government on the Junta Nacional de Música y Teatros (National Council of Music and Theaters). Junta members, who included Conrado del Campo, Amadeu Vives, Ernesto Halffter, and Salazar, were charged with developing arts subsidies, promoting Spanish music abroad, and formulating a national musical education plan.[37] It is worth pointing out that, although Falla began serving on the Junta in 1931, he officially accepted the appointment in November 1932, that is, *after* his disillusionment with Seville.[38] Because he lived in Granada, his involvement was minimal, however, and he relied on Salazar to represent his views at the Madrid meetings. For example, in August 1933 Falla voiced his support for incorporating the Seville Conservatory as a state institution. He not only considered Seville a viable challenge to Madrid's musical estab-

35. "Ciertamente, el Estado no rinde homenaje a Dios, porque le es imposible: el Estado no va a misa, ni confiesa, ni hace acto de contrición, ni tiene alma que salvar o que vender al diablo. . . . El homenaje a Dios se lo rinde, cada hombre que quiera hacerlo, en su conciencia. Y estas dos fáciles consideraciones debían haberle bastado al maestro Falla para haber aceptado sin escrúpulo un vino de honor o un letrero en una esquina que pudiera brindarle la ciudad de Alonso [*sic*] el Sabio. El Supremo Hacedor no se hubiera creído suplantado ni sentido celos en tan sencilla ocasión" ("Incongruencia católica," *El Socialista*, 14 June 1932, AMF press file).

36. "¿De qué se quejan, pues? ¿Quién les puso cortapisas para 'propinear' porteras y agenciar colgaduras a dos o tres pesetas para el sagrado corazón? Pongámos en un justo medio y convengamos: hay fe y hay libertad" ("Incongruencia católica").

37. Republican legislation regarding music is reproduced in Emilio Casares, ed., *La música en la generación del 27: Homenaje a Lorca, 1915–1939* (Madrid: Ministerio de Cultura, 1986), 256–64.

38. Letter, Falla to Ricardo Crueta, Director General de Bellas Artes, 15 November 1932, AMF correspondence file 7349.

lishment, but he cherished the hope of spending his twilight years there, surrounded by talented pupils.[39] Another project on behalf of the Republic that Falla at least considered was composing an anthem. Shortly after the electoral victory of April 1931 (and before the church burnings in May), Eduardo López Ramírez, president of the Asociación Juventud Republicana Independiente (Association of Independent Rebulican Youth), made this request. Falla scheduled a meeting with him, but López Ramírez failed to show up.[40]

Continuing outbreaks of church vandalism devastated Falla. In August 1932, he wrote de los Ríos, now minister of education: "Just last night, in spite of the precautions that have finally been taken, the St. Nicholas church continued burning to the ground, while someone brazenly rang the bells. What sorrow Spain causes, and how so many continue to destroy her!"[41] In the same letter, Falla referred to his personal ideals, which were "far above the workings of politics" (*tan por encima de cuanto a política trasciende*). Yet, as is clear from Falla's dealings with Seville, practically any action, public or private, could be invested with political significance in that volatile environment.

Falla's religious convictions also motivated him to become involved with the Catholic magazine *Cruz y Raya: Revista de Afirmación y Negación* (Plus and Minus: Journal of Affirmation and Negation), which was established in 1933 by an acquaintance, the writer José Bergamín. The deceptively simple title alludes to the Catholic view of error, which is either positive (a distortion of reality) or negative (an omission of reality).[42] Like Falla and other Catholic intellectuals, Bergamín feared for the Church's viability in the secular state. With *Cruz y Raya*, he aimed to offer a middle ground between the stridency of the extreme Right and the rabid anticlericalism of leftist (and even certain moderate) factions.[43] Projected contributors included Max Jacob, François Mauriac, Gide, Claudel, Maritain, and various Spanish intellectuals (according to Falla, those habitually overlooked by the Catholic press).

---

39. See Budwig, "Manuel de Falla's *Atlántida*," 118, 164. On the incorporation of the conservatory in conjunction with Ernesto Halffter's activities as its first director (from 1935), see Acker, "Ernesto Halffter," 139–47, 57.

40. Letters, Eduardo López Ramirez to Falla, 25 April 1931; and Falla to López Ramírez, 27 April 1931, both in AMF correspondence file 7385. As noted, the "Himno de Riego" was adopted as an official anthem in late April.

41. "Anoche mismo, a pesar de las precauciones por fin adoptadas, la iglesia de San Nicolás seguía ardiendo hasta su destrucción, mientras alguien volteaba desvergonzadamente las campanas . . . ¡Qué pena da España, y como entre los unos y los otros la siguen destruyendo!" (letter, Falla to de los Ríos, 13 August 1932, AMF correspondence file 7492).

42. J. B. Nugent, "Error," in *New Catholic Encyclopedia*, 5:521.

43. Dennis, *El epistolario*, 26.

To the composer's eventual sorrow, the hope that *Cruz y Raya* could remain "above the workings of politics" would prove futile.[44]

At first, as with the Republic itself, Falla reacted enthusiastically to *Cruz y Raya*. He was quick to praise Bergamín's inaugural statement, which set forth the magazine's intent to "clarify things well," to "refine our thought to its ultimate, definitive essence . . . [which] has a name: Christ."[45] Expressing to Bergamín his "great faith" in these editorial principles, Falla was confident that the new publication would "represent something completely different" while remaining within "those boundaries of [Catholic] thought . . . we have promised to uphold."[46] He also volunteered to distribute subscription information to his friends and accepted Bergamín's invitation to serve on the editorial board. But even at this early stage Falla permitted himself some gentle remonstrances. Fearing that those who "only skim the surface" would misconstrue Bergamín's sometimes provocative style, the composer wondered if this might put the magazine's "Christian prestige" at risk. But, whether out of politeness or ambivalence, Falla did not elaborate, and, as in his dealings with Ballesteros, he was less than transparent in his objections. Even the literary scholar Nigel Dennis has found that identifying the passages Falla found troublesome is a matter of pure conjecture.[47]

Falla's own contribution to *Cruz y Raya* was an article commemorating the fiftieth anniversary of Wagner's death. Between low spirits, unsteady health, and discouragingly low creative productivity—not to mention his innate scrupulosity—Falla seems to have tortured himself over the short piece. He also inflicted numerous delays and missed deadlines on Bergamín, who more than once was obliged to scramble for last-minute substitutes.[48] Bergamín's behavior during this editorial nightmare is a tribute to his genuine respect for Falla: more than once he politely yearned to leave the asphyxiating summer heat of Madrid for a few days of relaxation, which, as he pointed out to the composer, he could do only if the next issue were in place.[49] At least Falla realized what an inconvenience his tardiness had caused, and when the article finally arrived in Madrid in September 1933 Bergamín had to convince the composer to accept payment.

In the article itself, Falla argues that Wagner, a fine composer who chanced to be born into that "enormous carnival known as the nineteenth century," was unduly

---

44. Bergamín himself admitted as much after the war. See José Bergamín's prologue to *Cruz y Raya, Antología* (Madrid: Turner, 1974), 9, cited in Dennis, *El epistolario*, 32.

45. Dennis, *El epistolario*, 66–67.

46. Letter, Falla to Bergamín, 18 May 1933, cited in Dennis, *El epistolario*, 74–75.

47. Letter, Falla to Bergamín, 18 May 1933, cited in Dennis, *El epistolario*, 75 (see esp. n. 44).

48. Letter, Bergamín to Falla, 21 June 1933, cited in Dennis, *El epistolario*, 82–83.

49. Letter, Bergamín to Falla, 29 July 1933, cited in Dennis, *El epistolario*, 90.

susceptible to "error." His more significant errors included "abused chromaticism," "infinite melody," and, like his compatriot but aesthetic opposite Brahms, "vanity." Although Falla harped on this point (the word *error* or its synonym *yerro* appears eleven times in an article of under three thousand words), he excepted *Parsifal*, which he considered "a clear testament of faith—of redemptive Christian faith—that Wagner, in the confines of his life and yielding to a latent and pure impulse of his disorderly conscience, tried to oppose to lamentable ostentations of the past."[50] Having paid homage to *Parsifal* in *El gran teatro del mundo*, Falla now hailed Wagner's final utterance as nothing less than redemptive. Not only a work of art, but also a personal victory over error, *Parsifal* embodied a crucial aspect of Catholic theology, one, moreover, alluded to in *Cruz y Raya*'s very title. Obviously, the question of error—both positive and negative—was very much on Falla's mind.

Yet as far as the composer was concerned, *Cruz y Raya* gradually transgressed the "boundaries of Catholic thought." To him, one of the more disturbing examples of this tendency was Bergamín's interpretation of Velázquez's famous *Crucifix*. In it, Bergamín expounds on the nature of the devil. Born anew each day, Lucifer might appear as an angel of light, possibly in the form of sexuality or "demons of the body," which, Bergamín held, was also the "common denominator" of Freudian pscychoanalysis.[51] Bergamín then takes the bold position that the Velázquez *Crucifix* itself could be interpreted as "a vivid portrait of the devil" (un vivo retrato del Demonio), that is, of the devil "behind the cross."[52] This suggestion of interchangeability between Christ and the devil, coupled with references to sexuality, was hardly to Falla's liking. Still, as politely as he had protested to Lorca over the "Oda al Santísimo Sacramento del Altar," he couched his misgivings to Bergamín in terms of friendship and the common good of Christians:

> As always when I read something of yours, I discover admirable things with which I absolutely agree; but there are others of which I cannot say the same, as, for example, in your reference to the Velázquez crucifix. How could what you say be true when contemplating it has elevated our souls to God so many times? And this is a test that admits no deception. I think, moreover, that given the things we Christians of Spain, regrettably, are suffering, it's not the moment to "diminish" (in whatever way) what the crucifix may signify. Surely you see that I'm speaking to you "with my hand on my heart," as merits your friendship, which I so much esteem and which I reciprocate with all my heart as well.[53]

50. Manuel de Falla, "Notas sobre Ricardo Wagner en el cincuentenario de su muerte," reprinted in Falla, *Escritos*, 137–46. This is discussed in Hess, *Manuel de Falla and Modernism in Spain*, 280–84.

51. José Bergamín, "La importancia del Demonio," *Cruz y Raya*, 15 August 1933, 9–51, quoted at 24.

52. Bergamín, "La importancia del Demonio," 46.

53. Letter, Falla to Bergamín, 4 November 1933, cited in Dennis, *El epistolario*, 107–8.

Whatever Falla's flexibility toward his friends' lack of religious orthodoxy, the printed word was an altogether different matter. Now that *Cruz y Raya* had flunked "the test that admits no deception" Falla tried to resign from the editorial board, for besides his reservations over the magazine's tone was his ongoing fear of "misrepresentation" of his role in the publication. As he explained to Bergamín, living in Granada made it impossible for him to share the work equally with the other editors and therefore his name ought not appear with theirs. But just as the extreme Right found in Falla a compelling figurehead so did moderate Catholic intellectuals. When Bergamín pointed out that his name would enhance *Cruz y Raya*'s reputation, a middle ground was arrived at: as of January 1934, the magazine's front matter would begin listing Falla as a founder rather than an editor.[54]

But Falla's relationship with the publication deteriorated further when *Cruz y Raya* butted heads with politics. This came about after the elections of November 1933, in which Falla voted for the first time. When the right-wing coalition he favored won, he expressed cautious optimism to Matos: "Be it God's will that these elections bring us better times! But I don't want to get my hopes up, thinking of all that still remains to be 'righted' in Spain. And clearly in saying this, I'm only thinking of divine justice."[55] The winning party, the CEDA, promoted the social philosophy of Pope Leo XIII, whose encyclical *Rerum novarum* of 1891 emphasized the dignity of the worker and the need of the state to protect workers' rights.[56] To be sure, the Spanish Civil War historian Paul Preston has noted some "trappings of fascism" in the CEDA's workings.[57] Meanwhile, a stricter interpretation of fascism was emerging in a handful of other parties, including the blue-shirted Falange Española, which had been founded by the Andalusian lawyer José Antonio Primo de Rivera, the son of the dictator.[58]

Falla's hopes for the government for which he had voted were soon shattered. In October 1934, armed struggle in Asturias threatened public order when a confederation of leftist unions dominated by miners managed to defeat the Civil and Assault Guards and occupy several towns, presumably in preparation for a broader proletarian revolution. According to several accounts, the radicals had a sense of

54. See letters, Bergamín to Falla, 24 April 1933; and 23 May 1933, both cited in Dennis, *El epistolario*, 69, 77.

55. "¡Quiera Dios que estas elecciones nos traigan mejores tiempos! Pero no quiero hacerme ilusiones, pensando en lo mucho que aún queda por 'enderezar' en España. Y claro está que al decir esto pienso sólo en la divina justicia" (letter, Falla to Matos, 19 November 1933, AMF correspondence file 7264).

56. The CEDA (Confederación Española de Derechos Autónomos), was supported by landowners and Catholic labor unions. On *Rerum novarum*, see Paul E. Sigmund, *Liberation Theology at the Crossroads: Democracy or Revolution?* (New York and Oxford: Oxford University Press, 1990), 17–18.

57. The CEDA and fascism are discussed in Preston, *Coming of the Spanish Civil War*, 120–21.

58. Preston, *Concise History of the Spanish Civil War*, 29.

fairness: an investigating commission, which included Fernando de los Ríos, interviewed middle-class witnesses in Oviedo, who referred to the "nobility" of the miners and their respect for noncombatants during the conflict.[59] Still, looting took place, and there were several deaths, mainly of priests and members of the Civil Guard.[60] Since it was by no means clear that the regular Spanish army would fire on the miners, the government sent in the Foreign Legion, some of whose officers behaved honorably while others encouraged their troops to rape and torture.[61] All was confusedly reported in the media.

It was after being held prisoner by the miners that one of *Cruz y Raya*'s founders, Alfredo Mendizábal, concluded that Catholicism and communism were much closer than the official Church allowed. Anticipating the post–Second Vatican Council movement known as liberation theology, with its close (and controversial) links to Marxism, Mendizábal argued that communists might be "Christians without knowing it." As such, they could unite with Catholics against the "injustice and materialism" of capitalism, as long as they rejected violence in favor of "the revolution within."[62] In turn, Bergamín began to argue that Marxism was more effective than Catholicism in eliminating social ills, and proposed that the Church recognize its legitimacy. He expounded on these ideas—in his customarily "provocative" tone—in *Cruz y Raya*.[63]

This was too much for Falla. On 16 February 1935, he severed all ties with the magazine. Tellingly, his letter to Bergamín refers to "scruples" in relation to the law of God:

> I cannot continue sharing the responsibility for the magazine even in the extremely modest proportion that corresponds to those of us who boast the title "founder." And this I say thinking of and referring to the very *next number*. Given the sincerity of the friendship I profess to you, I write this with pain, thinking of the disappointment it may cause you, but my conscience urgently and definitely forces me to do this. It's not a question of scruples: it has to do

59. Jackson, *Spanish Republic and the Civil War*, 160.

60. Adrian Schubert, "The Asturian Revolution of October 1934," in *Revolution and War in Spain, 1931–1939*, edited by Paul Preston (London and New York: Methuen, 1984), 129–132.

61. Jackson, *Spanish Republic and the Civil War*, 157–58.

62. Mendizábal is quoted in Bergamín's "El estado fantasma y ¿en qué país vivimos?" *Cruz y Raya*, no. 20 (November 1934), cited in Dennis, *El epistolario*, 33–34. Bergamín also developed the idea of realizing Christian values without knowing it (hablar en cristiano sin saberlo) in his response to an address by Gide presented at the International Congress of Writers (Paris), 22 June 1935. See André Gide, *Defensa de la cultura*, translated by Julio Gómez de la Serna (Madrid: S. Aguirre, 1936), 35–52.

63. Bergamín also mentioned these thoughts in a letter to Arturo Serrano Plaja (a young Marxist writer), cited in Dennis, *El epistolario*, 36.

with nothing more than to fulfill with the Second Commandment the law of God in its most essential significance.[64]

Again, "principle over form" dictated Falla's behavior. Also, the elections of 1933 precipitated the end of his official service to the Republic. With the new government, the personnel of the Junta Nacional changed, and a coterie of Madrid-based *zarzuela* composers of his own generation, along with several librettists and impresarios, now dominated the committee.[65] Although Falla had voted for the more conservative agenda, his relationships with many of the Junta's new members were strained, since he had never made any secret of his distaste for Madrid's musical infrastructure. Disillusioned, he resigned from his brief service to the Republic.

Besides the mental turmoil that trying to remain "above the workings of politics" inflicted, Falla's physical health was precarious during this period. Now in his late fifties, he suffered from hemorrhages, dyspnea (labored breathing), and continued vision problems. Yet there were bright moments. He had his work, his students, his neighbors, his correspondence, and the constant ministrations of María del Carmen, who eased him through frequent fits of depression. One such low point occurred during the summer of 1934, when Joaquín Nin-Culmell was in Granada for lessons. He and María del Carmen contrived a practical joke to cheer Falla up: Nin-Culmell would disguise himself as the representative of a French cardinal and call at the *carmen* to discuss the latest edition of the French catechism. With María del Carmen's help, Nin-Culmell dusted his hair with talcum powder and, stuffing a pillow in his belt, donned the priest's cassock that María del Carmen had somehow managed to pinch from a nearby church. He also sported a pair of sunglasses. Upon entering the sitting room, Nin-Culmell greeted Falla in French (normally they used Spanish), and they proceeded to exchange pleasantries and discuss the finer points of the faith. As it happened, a few other callers were present. Not once did the trusting Falla imagine his visitor to be anything other than what he had claimed. Even María del Carmen's ill-concealed giggles—for which her brother gently reproved her—failed to arouse his suspicion. But the best part of all came when Nin-Culmell gradually began to unbutton his cassock. Falla's eyes widened in shock. What had come over the distinguished representative of the Church? María del Carmen's giggles were now past control, and she staggered helplessly from the room. Finally, Nin-Culmell removed the pillow and the dark glasses and all was revealed.

64. Letter, Falla to Bergamín, 16 February 1935, cited in Dennis, *El epistolario*, 37. Prior to the Second Vatican Council, the Second Commandment was "Thou shalt not take the name of the Lord thy God in vain." See, for example, *A Catechism of Christian Doctrine* (New York: Paulist Press, 1929), 62.

65. Michael Christoforidis, "Constructions of Manuel de Falla's Political Identity and Musical Nationalism in the 1930s," paper presented at the conference "Music in the 1930s: Nation, Myth, and Reality," Royal Holloway College, London, October 1998. I would like to thank Professor Christoforidis for making his work available to me.

Falla enjoyed several moments of hearty, therapeutic laughter. Even when racked with spiritual and physical pain, he could still enjoy a good joke—on himself. Alas, some of his more straitlaced guests were not amused.[66]

"SPES VITAE" (HOPE OF LIFE)

All the while, Falla struggled to keep composing. In the early days of the Republic completing *Atlántida* seemed perfectly realistic: in late 1931, he plunged back into "El incendi dels Pirineus" (The Burning of the Pyrenees), declaring to Arbós in January 1932, "I'm completely dedicated to *Atlántida* and want more than ever to finish it.[67] Stokowski continued to inquire about its progress to both Falla and Sert. On New Year's Day 1932, he wrote the composer: "I hope [*Atlántida*] will be completed soon as I should so much like to conduct it in the near future, if you are willing."[68] Falla immediately replied that "the progress of my work depends exclusively on what my health permits, but you can rest assured that I'll keep you up to date and will let you know when it is near completion."[69] Evidently thinking of a performance in America, Falla suggested to Sert that he design the set for the projected premiere at Barcelona's Liceu with Philadelphia's Academy of Music in mind.[70]

In 1932, Falla began what would be *Atlántida*'s most perfect moment, "La salve en el mar." As noted earlier, this section is not from Verdaguer's poem but rather is Falla's piecing together of excerpts from the Vespers hymn "Ave maris stella," the Litanies of the Virgin, and the poetry of Gonzalo de Berceo. Falla was inspired to include this episode on encountering Columbus's recollection of singing on the high seas "the Salve Regina and other texts and giving deepest thanks to our Lord" in *Cartas y Testamento de Cristóbal Colón* (The Letters and Will of Christopher Columbus). An inveterate annotator of his books, Falla underlined that passage in his 1921 edition.[71] One of the earlier versions of the "Salve" (there were seven in all) originally used compound meter; another involved three-part imitative counterpoint for male voices, each part representing the crews of the *Niña*, *Pinta*, and *Santa María*.[72] The sketches reveal a composer absorbed in experimentation, temporarily distracted from his cares.

66. Personal interview with Joaquín Nin-Culmell, January 2000.

67. "Estoy completamente dedicado a la *Atlántida*, con un deseo como nunca he sentido terminarla" (letter, Falla to Arbós, 4 January 1932, cited in Budwig, "Manuel de Falla's *Atlántida*, 154n1).

68. Letter, Stokowski to Falla, 1 January 1932, AMF correspondence file 7664.

69. "El avance de mi trabajo depende exclusivamente de lo que la salud me permita, pero puede usted estar seguro de que le tendré al corriente, previniéndole cuando se aproxime su terminación" (letter, Falla to Stokowski, 19 January 1932, AMF correspondence file 7664).

70. Budwig, "Manuel de Falla's *Atlántida*," 158.

71. *Cartas y Testamento de Cristóbal Colón* (Madrid: Perlado, Paez, 1921), cited in Budwig, "Manuel de Falla's *Atlántida*," 109.

72. Budwig, "Manuel de Falla's *Atlántida*," 186n1.

One side effect of seeking just the right formula for the "Salve" seems to have been a heightened striving for purity in nonmusical matters. In February 1932, Falla drafted his will, which contained the stipulation: "I . . . demand, in the most formal and definitive way, that in the execution and scenic interpretation of my works the purest Christian morals—without exception—be observed and that they always be accompanied by works of evident moral and artistic dignity."[73] This was fairly open-ended. But three years later, plagued by the idea that his dramatic works might be used "in the service of sin," Falla added a codicil prohibiting their performance unless his heirs needed the royalties as "an indispensable means of support."[74] If scrupulosity caused him to dismiss whatever pleasure the international public might take in *El amor brujo, The Three-Cornered Hat,* or *La vida breve,* at least it had not blinded him to his family's practical needs.

Falla also took comfort in the concentrated intensity of Golden Age polyphony. In much the same spirit as he essayed contrapuntal problems in "La Salve en el mar," he immersed himself in the music of Cristóbal de Morales and Tomás Luis de Victoria, especially the latter, who represented the spirit of the Counter-Reformation to many Spanish Catholics. Victoria was also the subject of a book by Falla's friend Henri Collet, the French musicologist and Hispanist. From Falla's annotations in his signed copy it is clear that Collet's descriptions of Victoria's "austere Catholicism" and "ardent mysticism" deeply impressed him.[75] Collet also held that Victoria "initiates us into the magnificent and tragic spectacle of sixteenth-century Spain," sentiments Falla surely related to the present "tragedy."[76] With Pedrell's *Complete Works* of Victoria at hand, Falla created what he called "expressive versions" of various compositions, adding discreet dynamic, articulation, and expression markings (he approached selected works of Morales, Guerrero, Escobar, and others similarly). Although he rarely departed from his sources in any substantive way, he occasionally altered a proportion sign.[77] Victoria's well-known "Ave Maria à 4" he transposed up a whole step.

These arrangements were not merely therapeutic diversions or private spiritual exercises. Falla also saw them as public utterances and for this reason considered conducting them, along with the *Retablo,* in a concert celebrating the inauguration of the museum at the monastery of San Telmo in San Sebastián on 3 September 1932. Paintings and frescoes by Falla's friends Zuloaga and Sert would be on display, and there would be a ceremony with remarks by various government officials, including de los Ríos. The presence of his old friend threw Falla into a fit of scrupulosity,

73. Budwig, "Manuel de Falla's *Atlántida,*" 460.
74. Both versions of Falla's will (February 1932 and August 1935) are translated in Budwig, "Manuel de Falla's *Atlántida,*" 458–59.
75. Henri Collet, *Victoria* (Paris: Librairie Félix Alcan, 1914).
76. Collet, *Victoria,* 9.
77. On Falla's altering of proportion signs (in "L'Amfiparnaso," a madrigal by Orazio Vecchi), see Gallego, *Catálogo,* 247.

however: while eager to pay homage to the two artists, he was unwilling to shake de los Ríos's hand in public, having by now decided that any meeting of the minds between them on the religion question was impossible. Falla spent days in agonized speculation over the "misrepresentation" such a handshake might imply.[78] Finally, he decided to participate, perhaps believing his "expressive versions" of Victoria would be an eloquent plea for Christian values. In fact, after the performance (on 3 September 1932) Sert told Falla, "today you made God come down to earth."[79] Still, the concert was blatantly politicized. The local Republican daily *Vasconia* noted that Falla's sense of "social mission" was superior to that of Albéniz, whose "excessively local" *Iberia* was a product of "the old regime." Falla, on the other hand, had taken his cue from Pedrell, who "advocated the art of the peasants" much as the Aragonese radical Joaquín Costa had ushered in a new epoch with his political writings.[80] Obviously musical utterances could be fitted to any number of viewpoints in pre–Civil War Spain.

From San Sebastián, the summer residence of the departed royal family, Falla and José ("Pepe") Segura, a professor from the University of Granada, traveled to Italy, where Falla would conduct the *Retablo* (as it turned out, in an equally politicized environment). In Geneva, they were joined by Segovia, who had volunteered to serve as one of Falla's "personal bodyguards" during the trip. Venice's Festival Internazionale, one of several established under Mussolini, maintained an international profile, programming works by Milhaud, Stravinsky, Turina, Honegger, Respighi, Walton, Bloch, and Hindemith.[81] According to Adriano Lualdi, a composer and the president of its commission, it also promoted an "unadulteratedly Italian and unadulterately fascist" outlook, mainly by avoiding "certain artistic poisons and drugs that have wreaked havoc beyond the Alps," clearly a reference to Schoenberg.[82] Not surprisingly, critics commended Falla for seeking inspiration

78. Personal interview with Joaquín Nin-Culmell, January 2000. Excerpts from de los Ríos's speech are reprinted in "El ministro de Instrucción Pública en San Sebastián," *El Sol*, 4 September 1932, 12. While Falla would have agreed with many points therein, such as the need to "integrate [knowledge and duty] with the integrity of our actions," he would hardly have found gratifying de los Ríos's warning against "a civilization of monks" (*anacoretas*).

79. Pahissa, *Vida y obra*, 136.

80. A. de Easo, "Artistas españoles: Manuel de Falla en San Sebastián," *Vasconia*, 1 September 1932, AMF press file.

81. The program is reproduced in Bergadà, "La relación de Manuel de Falla con Italia," in Nommick, *Manuel de Falla e Italia*, 53. See also letter, Segovia to Falla, 20 June 1932, cited on p. 51; and Sachs, *Music in Fascist Italy*, 89.

82. Fiamma Nicolodi, "Su alcuni aspetti dei festivales tra le due guerre," in *Musica italiana del primo novecento: La generazione dell'ottanta—Atti del convegno—Firenze 9–10–11 maggio 1980* (Florence: Olschki, 1981), 162, cited in Sachs, *Music in Fascist Italy*, 89.

from the "classics," whose "expressive sobriety" in the *Retablo* exuded "universalism" and the "essential Latin spirit."[83] These potent themes, so significant in the ideology of neoclassicism, proved sufficiently flexible to serve Mussolini in his campaign for a "universal fascism" based on classical ideals.[84] Thus, through no fault of his own Falla again failed to remain "above the workings of politics." But he was well satisfied with his experience in Venice and wrote María del Carmen that the concert was "truly unforgettable."[85]

Some recreation was now in order, however. Traveling by car with Segura and Segovia, Falla visited Padua, Mantua, Cremona, Milan, and Genoa. Unfortunately, on the way to Arles he developed a boil that caused sharp facial pains, and the otherwise carefree travelers had to stop in San Remo to find a doctor. With Segovia's wild hair uncombed and Falla's face grotesquely swollen (all three were covered with the dust of the open road) only Segura was presentable enough to address the doctor. Introducing "the great maestro Manuel de Falla" and the "great artist of the guitar, Andrés Segovia," he received a skeptical look. But the doctor gave such effective treatment that they were able to leave San Remo that afternoon. In Arles, where Segovia left them, Segura and Falla took the train to Barcelona. By now, the composer's face was bandaged, his beard was beginning to sprout, and his clothes were in a sorry state. In Barcelona, he refurbished his appearance so as to arrive in Granada a "new man."[86]

Refreshed, Falla took up *Atlántida* again. Probably around mid-1932, that is, before his trip, he had begun working with Verdaguer's ninth canto, which treats the destruction of Atlantis. This is indicated by a sketch labeled "La Torre dels Titans" (The Tower of the Titans). Had Falla completed this scene, which is modeled on the biblical story of the Tower of Babel, he would have depicted the blasphemous Atlanteans meeting their doom, a scene he could not have failed to connect to the situation in Spain.[87] Another sketch, dated 11 November 1932 and found in the same folio, shows the range of mood and meaning Falla confronted in *Atlántida*. In it, he follows a series of discordant four-part chords with a triadic Latin-texted setting of a fragment of the New Testament verse "Jesus said, 'Suffer the little children, and

83. Press reaction from *Gazettino di Venezia, Corriere della Sera, La Stampa, Il Lavoro fascista,* and *L'Illustrazione Italiana* is summarized in Bergadà, "La relación de Falla con Italia," in Nommick, *Manuel de Falla e Italia,* 55–56.

84. Emily Braun, "Political Rhetoric and Poetic Irony: The Uses of Classicism in the Art of Fascist Italy," in *On Classic Ground: Picasso, Léger, de Chirico, and the New Classicism, 1910–1930,* edited by Elizabeth Cowling and Jennifer Mundy (London: Tate Gallery, 1990), 345–58.

85. Letter, Falla to María del Carmen, 19 September 1932, cited in Bergadà, "La relación de Falla con Italia," in Nommick, *Manuel de Falla e Italia,* 54.

86. Pahissa, *Vida y obra,* 138–39.

87. Budwig, "Manuel de Falla's *Atlántida*," 164–65.

forbid them not, to come unto me'" (Matt. 19:14).[88] Did Falla intend this calming pronouncement as an antidote to the destruction music? As Budwig has speculated, the composer may have considered his fellow Spaniards wayward children, who after centuries of oppression and injustice could hardly be punished in the sight of God, even as many of them, poor and unenlightened, caused inestimable sadness with their destruction of holy places.[89] What might *Atlántida* have been had Falla pursued these tantalizing fragments! For he soon laid the destruction music aside, either in a spirit of resignation or because a bout of iritis that set in shortly after the Italian sojourn brought him rudely back to reality.

Falla's spirits were temporarily lifted when he attended another festival in his honor, this one on 13 December 1932 at Barcelona's Palau de la Música Catalana, organized by the Associació de Música "Da Camera." But at the beginning of 1933 he suffered a nervous collapse and was ordered by his doctors to stop working. Biographers have little to say about the nature of this attack of nerves; it seems that political tensions and a decline in his creative powers caused some form of emotional crisis rather than a full-blown nervous breakdown. He and María del Carmen decided to spend a few months in the gentle climate of Mallorca, then a quiet backwater undiscovered by the tourist industry. One therapeutic activity there was participating in the musical life of the local parish, over which Falla's friend, Padre Juan María Thomas, the organist at the Palma de Mallorca cathedral and conductor of the vocal ensemble Capella Clàssica, presided. Thomas was much taken with Falla's "expressive versions" of Spanish polyphony, although he was initially surprised by Falla's overriding of the rules that regulate the shift from binary to ternary in the "Sancta Maria" section of Victoria's "Ave Maria à 4." But one rehearsal convinced him. He later described how one day Falla was in the back of the sanctuary observing Thomas conducting the choir. Drawn to its excellent sound, the composer crept quietly toward the podium. Increasingly aware of Falla's presence, Padre Thomas relinquished his baton so that Falla could lead the choir all the way through to the last, whispered "Amen." During the moment of silence that followed, magic hung in the air. Then, simply and directly, Falla congratulated the choir for its spontaneity and went back to his pension! Much moved, Father Thomas attributed the drama of the longer note values to the composer's "admirable intuition and profound mystical sense."[90]

Father Thomas also volunteered, naively it seems, to assist Falla with his voluminous correspondence. Mainly this involved assuaging the composer's fear of

---

88. "Jesus ait: sinile parvulos, et nobite eos prohibere ad me venire" (Budwig, "Manuel de Falla's *Atlántida*," 166). The three-part setting for children's voices can be found in manuscript at the AMF.

89. Budwig, "Manuel de Falla's *Atlántida*," 166.

90. Juan María Thomas, *Manuel de Falla en la isla* (Palma de Mallorca: Ediciones Capella Clasica, 1946), 96–98.

misrepresentation or "deformation," as he was wont to call it. Thomas recalls: "Sometimes we would linger a long time in writing a simple telegram to a friend. How to end it? The word 'greetings' (*saludos*) isn't very expressive, Don Manuel would say. 'Let's put "fond greetings,"' I would suggest. 'I don't like the "fond."' 'Affectionate?' 'That's too much.' . . . It was more complicated with the kind of letter that could lend itself to false interpretations or deformations of his thought."[91] As Thomas tells it, Falla was skirting the fine line between scrupulosity and the normal care artists and writers take in expressing essence, nuance, allusion, or innuendo. What is significant in Falla's case is that he worried about it so. Decades earlier, Fedriani had lambasted his "suppositions, verifications, conjectures, quibbling, and other things of an equally ridiculous and foolish nature." Had his innate indecisiveness now reached the level of neurosis? If Falla anguished over a salutation, a handshake, or a misleading half-sentence in the newspaper, did this mean he was psychologically ill? Or was he simply following the painful path dictated by his conscience? His work on *Atlántida* over the next decade would reveal the extent to which these tendencies got the better of him.

During that initial stay on the island, Falla managed to embark on some new projects. One of these was a choral work, *Balada de Mallorca*. Taking a portion of canto X of *L'Atlàntida* (subtitled "Balada de Mallorca"), Falla fitted it to the Andantino section of Chopin's Ballade in F Major op. 38; thus, the piece recalls both his early love of Chopin and the thwarted opera *Fuego fatuo*. It also had the same advantage as his Victoria arrangements: by relying on the blueprints of preexisting material, Falla could be more or less certain that he would finish the piece. It is also safe to assume that his battered soul took comfort in concealing his personality throughout the work, in passing incognito, as it were. Indeed, the *Balada de Mallorca* contains much more Chopin than Falla. For four-part mixed choir, with occasional effusions of six- and even seven-part writing, Falla's *Balada* replicates Chopin's overall key scheme in that it ends in A minor, as does the op. 38 Ballade. To be sure, Falla adds an occasional Pulcinella-like passing tone to enhance the harmonic texture, as in mm. 11–13, where he not only alters the bass line but incorporates dissonances in the inner parts. Thomas, to whom the *Balada de Mallorca* is dedicated, premiered it on 21 May 1933 at the Third Chopin Festival at the Monasterio de Valldemossa, where Chopin and George Sand shivered through the winter of 1838–39. (Their stay, incidentally, was due to an earlier wave of anticlericalism in Spain: the eviction of the monks a few years earlier had enabled Chopin and Sand to rent a set of cells.) The following year, when Falla and María del Carmen returned to Mallorca, the Capella Clàssica performed the definitive version.

Also during that second stay in Mallorca he composed the *Fanfare sobre el nombre de Arbós* (Fanfare on the Name Arbós) for the seventieth birthday of Enrique Fernández Arbós, the champion of contemporary Spanish music who had conducted the pre-

91. Thomas, *Manuel de Falla en la isla*, 176–77.

miere of *Noches* almost twenty years earlier. The letters of the conductor's name (including Re/D for *R*, Do/C for *O*, and Sol/G for *S*) served Falla and fourteen other composers as basic compositional material; Falla, however, added E (Enrique) and F (Fernández), thus using all seven letters of the musical alphabet (see musical example 25). A brief thirty-eight measures for trumpets, horns, and drums, the piece is simple enough, consisting mainly of horn calls enhanced with major seconds, recalling the fanfares of the *Retablo*. The birthday celebration took place in Madrid on 28 March 1934, with Arbós himself conducting the Orquesta Sinfónica. He had little time to prepare, for as usual Falla sent the score at the last minute. Given the music's simplicity, it probably did not suffer too greatly, however.

Budwig aptly signals the composer's departure from Granada (bound for Mallorca) in February 1933 as the end of *Atlántida*'s "innocence," that is, the period during which Falla could realistically see his way to completing it. Now he could not help but realize that over five years had passed since he had written a major work.[92] If during his two stays on the island Falla devoted himself to other projects, it was surely because the cantata, as vast and unfathomable as the watery depths he sought to portray, seemed beyond him. Perhaps *Atlántida* even came to symbolize his own powerlessness: unable to find solace in its potentially consoling religious message, Falla seemed to struggle and flail, inexplicably deaf to its promise of regeneration, creative and otherwise.

Yet while agonizing over *Atlántida* he rejected other opportunities (presumably so as to concentrate on completing the cantata). In September 1934, Joan Gisbert of Barcelona informed him that the Fox Film Corporation (soon to be merged with Twentieth-Century Pictures under the now familiar rubric Twentieth-Century Fox) wanted to film *El retablo de Maese Pedro*. As Gisbert reported, they were "offering Don Manuel 50,000 pesetas for the permission to make it." "Even more [could] be gotten easily," he added optimistically.[93] Although the idea greatly appealed to Falla, he turned Fox down, explaining fatalistically that to interrupt his work on *Atlántida* now was to give up on it forever.[94] By the following year, he was considering, how-

92. Budwig, "Manuel de Falla's *Atlántida*," 169.

93. "La casa Fox editora de películas, . . . quiere filmar *El Retablo de Maese Pedro*, ofreciéndole a D. Manuel por el permiso de hacerla 50.000 pesetas, que facilmente aún se conseguirá más" (letter, Gisbert to María del Carmen, 29 September 1934, AMF correspondence file 7049–068).

94. Also involved with Fox's offer was Rafael Moragas, to whom Falla sent a telegram on 30 September (?) 1934 in response to Moragas's enthusiastic letter of the same date (AMF correspondence file 7303). Falla did attempt to film the *Retablo* on other occasions, once with "Chaliapin, in the United States" and then "with Hermann Scherchen, as director, in Europe," although no further details are known. See letter, Falla to Miguel Machinandiarena, Estudios San Miguel, Buenos Aires, 27 August 1945, AMF correspondence file 7226.

E F A R   B   O   S
E F A D(re) B♭ C(do) G(sol)

Musical Example 25. Falla, *Fanfare sobre el nombre de Arbós*, opening, trumpets only. (Reprinted by kind permission of Ricordi/BMG Publications)

ever unrealistically, various performance venues.[95] One possibility was the ISCM festival, scheduled for Barcelona in April 1936. How different Falla's legacy might have been had *Atlántida* been premiered on the same festival as the Berg Violin Concerto! Probably, he could have managed to prepare a fair copy for the Prologue, part 1, and most of part 3.[96] Yet, ever the perfectionist, the composer resisted the idea of a partial performance, undoubtedly fearing "deformation" of his total artistic vision. By the fall of 1935, when he realized he could not finish *Atlántida* by April, he resumed the "symphonic arrangement" of Pedrell's *La Celestina* he had begun a decade earlier. He failed to meet the deadline with that work as well, and the ISCM featured the "Three Dances" from *The Three-Cornered Hat*, hardly Falla's most "contemporary" utterance.[97]

In 1935, Falla briefly returned to the "halcyon days" with incidental music for *La vuelta de Egípto* (The Return from Egypt), an *auto sacramental* by Calderón de la Barca's great predecessor, Lope de Vega. As in *El gran teatro del mundo*, Falla borrowed from *Parsifal*, that "clear testament . . . of redemptive Christian faith," weaving into his score the so-called Faith motive prominent in the act 1 communion scene (see musical example 26). Falla also incorporated a fourteen-measure, unaccompanied, choral doxology for four voices, "Invocatio ad individuam trinitatem" (In-

95. Various letters of inquiry are cited in Budwig, "Manuel de Falla's *Atlántida*," 192.
96. Budwig, "Manuel de Falla's *Atlántida*," 193.
97. On *La Celestina*, see Gallego, *Catálogo*, 257; and Joan Llongueras, "Els programes del XIV Festival de la Societat Internacional per la Música Contemporánea," *Revista Musical Catalana* 33, no. 389 (1936): 183.

Musical Example 26. Sketch for *La vuelta de Egipto*, the "Faith" theme from *Parsifal*. (Reprinted by kind permission of the Archivo Manuel de Falla)

vocation to the Holy Trinity), onto which he tacked the "Amen" from Victoria's *Ave Maria à 4*.[98] *La vuelta de Egípto* was performed at the University of Granada on 9 June 1935 and the score remains unpublished. The manuscript copy is the only trace of Falla's final nod to Wagner.

Throughout much of 1935, Falla was so depressed that he sometimes felt incapable of envisioning any kind of meaningful life for himself. In February, he confessed, "I often have the feeling that life has virtually ended for me."[99] In May of that year, life did end for his former mentor, Paul Dukas. As he had done for Debussy some fifteen years earlier, Falla composed another haunting *hommage*, this one for piano and explicitly titled "*Tombeau*," and to which he would eventually add the subtitle *Spes vitae* (Hope of Life).[100] As in the *Balada de Mallorca*, *Atlántida* makes its presence felt, albeit more palpably. The widely spaced block harmonies, some with thick doublings and others with subtle dissonances, resemble its Prologue, and some of the motivic treatment reflects Falla's interest in counterpoint. The pianist's principal challenge is to find the most convincing way—out of seemingly infinite possibilities—to voice each chord while ensuring that each leads inexorably to one of the six main cadence points in this contained, hieratic work. These cadences, all on fifth-related key areas (an exception is the progression from B♭ major in m. 34 to D major in m. 36), generate the form of the *Tombeau*. So does the main melodic motive, D♭–C–C–A♭, which appears in various guises throughout: either truncated and transposed (A♭–G–G, m. 4), inverted and/or expanded (E♮–F–A♭–A♭, mm. 13–14; B♭–C♭–E♭♭–F, mm. 14–15), or otherwise modified (C–D♭–B♮–C, m. 22). Understated friction gradually accumulates through repeated melodic half steps and harmonic tension, never full-blown but always mysteriously stifled. All culminates in a haunting F-minor harmony, colored with a D♮, in the final, murmured bars.

Having availed himself of quotation in the *Homenaje a Debussy*, Falla quotes one of Dukas's works here, his Piano Sonata in E♭ Minor. In the coda (mm. 36–42) of *Pour le tombeau de Paul Dukas*, Falla takes a fragment from the third-movement trio, which Dukas used as a fugue subject (see musical examples 27a, 27b).[101] At the beginning of Dukas's fugue, which occupies the central position in this otherwise light, scherzolike movement, Dukas slowed the tempo to "plus lent" and indicated "mystérieusement." Surely this suggested to Falla the mystery of death and the "hope of [eternal] life," that is, the narrow path to salvation. This thought undoubtedly soothed him as he lamented his own frustrated existence.

The work appeared in a musical supplement of *La Revue Musicale*, which recalled, like the Debussy issue of December 1920, the collective authorship of sixteenth-

98. Eugene Casjen Cramer, *Tomás Luis de Victoria: A Guide to Research* (New York and London: Garland, 1998), 133.

99. Letter, Falla to Bergamín, 16 February 1935, cited in Dennis, *El epistolario*, 123.

100. As Gallego observes, the rubric *Spes vitae* also appears in the manuscript copy of the 1921 Chester edition of the *Homenaje a Debussy* (*Catálogo*, 252).

101. Crichton, *Manuel de Falla*, 72.

Musical Example 27a. Paul Dukas, Sonata in E-flat
Minor, movement 3, statement, fugue subject on
D#. (Reprinted by kind permission of Ricordi/
BMG Publications)

Musical Example 27b. Falla, *Pour le tombeau de Paul Dukas*,
mm. 36, from beat 4 to m. 38. (Reprinted by kind permission of Ricordi/BMG Publications)

century literary *tombeaux*. This time Falla's "coauthors" included Florent Schmitt,
Joaquín Rodrigo, Elsa Barraine, Tony Aubin, and a young Olivier Messiaen.[102] It
was only fitting that Joaquín Nin-Culmell should premiere the *Tombeau*, for by then
he was Dukas's student. This had come about on Falla's recommendation: with
characteristic ingenuousness, Falla had written a letter of recommendation for Nin-
Culmell, which he handed to the young composer in an unsealed envelope to personally deliver to Dukas. (Nin-Culmell fingered it curiously but did not open it.)
The atmosphere at the Conservatoire was very different from that of the little *carmen*
in Granada, with its practical jokes and family-style meals. Nin-Culmell recalls once
showing Dukas a new work, prompting him to inquire, "C'est une mélodie populaire?" "Pas encore!" (Not yet!) Nin-Culmell replied. In France in those days, one
did not speak so brazenly to one's instructors, and for several weeks the privilege of
accompanying *le maître* home in a taxi after lessons was denied Nin-Culmell. In premiering Falla's *Tombeau* (28 April 1936, Paris, Salle de l'École Normale), the young
composer paid homage to a respected mentor through a work by another mentor,
one respected *and* loved.

Meanwhile, tensions were rising in Spain. On 18 February 1936, the conservative
coalition for which Falla had voted in 1933 was supplanted by the Popular Front.
The victory of that leftist electoral alliance effectively signaled to the Right that it
would now have to destroy the government rather than work within it.[103] Random
violence surged again, and when another rash of church vandalism erupted Granada

102. Musical supplement, *La Revue Musicale* 14, no. 166 (1936).
103. Preston, *Concise History of the Spanish Civil War*, 60.

was especially affected. On 24 February, for instance, radicals "smashed the door of the convent of the Thomases and took many objects," and on 9 March they "set fire to the church of the Savior with its valuable images, among them a Christ of Mena, and the churches of St. Gregory and St. Christopher, throwing into a cistern an image of the Saint."[104] Nor were churches the only targets: on 10 March "the mobs assaulted the office of the newspaper *El Ideal,* destroyed the furniture and equipment, and set fire to the building."[105] All the while, the Falange was stepping up recruitment, especially among young Catholics and anti-Marxist workers. In increasing numbers, they drove through working-class neighborhoods firing at anyone they took for a *rojo* (red) as terror squads incited "mindless violence."[106]

A parliamentary crisis resulted in the dismissal of President Alcalá Zamora, whose Catholic ideals had given Falla hope in the Republic's early days but whom the leftist alliance now saw as too conservative.[107] In early May, Manuel Azaña became president. Falla took this opportunity to plead for religious values, a rather naive effort given Azaña's profound anti-Catholicism. Falla's letter to the new president of 23 May 1936 is striking for its personal tone and its appeals to Azaña's friendship; indeed, in places it is as if the two had just been exchanging pleasantries in the vestibule of the Paris Opéra. As in his dealings with the Seville City Hall, Falla spoke for Spanish Catholics. Here, however, instead of portraying himself as merely one more of "God's poor creatures," he took a much more emotional tack, referring grimly to the proximity of his own death:

> I want to express to you a strong desire, one many thousands of Spaniards share: that we see the end of this period of bitterness that Spanish Christians are suffering, because of the destruction of our temples, from the disgusting blasphemies, public and collective—begun with the most horrible insults to the Sacred Name of God, venerated until now in all centuries and by all cultured and uncultured peoples of the earth—and of the martyrdom of persons who have dedicated their lives to charity. For this reason, I appeal not only to the president of the Republic but to the person of such refined literary sensibility whom I have always considered a friend, that you help us in this critical moment, using your supreme authority.
>
> With this hope I direct this letter to you, the only one I have written in a long time because of a serious illness caused by all those sacrilegious events, which have put my life at risk. . . . And be absolutely certain that I speak to

104. "Sacrilegios, incendios y asaltos de iglesias," *Diario de Barcelona,* 18 April 1936, 13–14.

105. "Sacrilegios, incendios y asaltos de iglesias," 13–14. National statistics, which include the burning of 106 churches and eleven general strikes between 16 February and 16 April 1936, are given in Mitchell, *Betrayal of the Innocents,* 86.

106. Preston, *Concise History of the Spanish Civil War,* 64.

107. Preston, *Concise History of the Spanish Civil War,* 61.

you only as a Catholic, independent of any political interest (which I have never had) or from purely human interest, the mixing of which with religion has always struck me as reprehensible.[108]

With the outbreak of the war just weeks away, notions of "independence from any political interest" were more unrealistic than ever. On the eve of the conflict, Falla was exhausted. Having briefly served the Republic, he had at one time imagined that one could espouse religious sentiments and remain "above the workings of politics." In private and official correspondence, he had acted on the belief that the pen is mightier than the sword and had suffered the glare of publicity thanks to his insistence on spiritual values. Now, by his own account, he considered his very existence to be "at risk" and felt that his life had "virtually ended." To which side would a frail and weary man who saw God above all things declare loyalty once war broke out? In what would he seek solace, especially now that *Atlántida*'s "innocence" had passed? Given the sorry state of Spanish Catholicism, the cantata's emphasis on the Church triumphant may even have begun to strike Falla as hollow. Yet, either from obsession, fatalism, or superstition, he refused to give it up. Whatever the truth of Falla's doomed union with *Atlántida*, the musical paralysis it inflicted on him would now be exacerbated by three years of civil war.

108. Letter, Falla to Azaña, 23 May 1936, cited in Federico Sopeña, "La Espiritualidad de Manuel de Falla," in Pinamonti, *Manuel de Falla tra la Spagna e l'Europa*, 85.

Chapter 8

Falla and the Spanish Civil War

On 18 April 1936, the third congress of the recently reconstituted International Musicological Society took place in Barcelona, coinciding with the ISCM festival. Welcoming scholars to the inaugural meeting were Pablo (Pau) Casals and various Republican officials, including Ricardo de Ureta, the director general of fine arts. Casals thanked the Republic for "moral and material support," and Ureta, alluding to the political climate in Nazi Germany, observed that, since the world was "again becoming agitated," it was all the more important to work "for the triumph of music . . . under the sign of the Republic."[1] Ureta's remarks were not lost on Heinrich Besseler, the head of the German delegation, which had been diminished by the departure of several prominent musicologists from Germany. Feeling the sting of international isolation, Besseler complained of the Republic's anti-German stance.[2] Of course, in a matter of weeks Hitler, along with Mussolini, would be helping to shape the Republic's demise.

"Agitation" was also palpable throughout Spain, where many feared a military uprising. Parliamentary debate was dominated by belligerent speeches by José Calvo

---

1. Joan Salvat, "El III Congrés de la Societat Internacional de Musicologia a Barcelona," *Revista Musical Catalana* 33, no. 389 (1936): 187–88.

2. Pamela M. Potter, *Most German of the Arts: Musicology and Society from the Weimar Republic to the End of Hitler's Reich* (New Haven and London: Yale University Press, 1998), 84.

Sotelo, the leader of the right-wing monarchists, and vehement addresses by the communist Dolores Ibarruri, who was so fiery that she was known as "La Pasionaria."[3] By early May, the socialist politician Indalecio Prieto was warning an audience in Cuenca of the likelihood of a military coup, even identifying Gen. Francisco Franco as its possible leader.[4] Weeks later an ominous headline in *El Sol* read, "Spain . . . exudes an atmosphere of civil war."[5]

"THE BREATH OF GOD OVER OUR BAYONETS"

On 8 July, Falla articulated his views on the temper of the times. Earlier the poet Ramiro Maeztu had sought Falla's support in forming a Spanish version of Action Française, that anti-Semitic, anti-Republican, anti-Protestant, anti-Dreyfusard organization that served for decades as a mouthpiece for the French extreme Right.[6] Maeztu had also founded the far Right magazine *Acción Española*, which offered precisely the sort of stridency *Cruz y Raya* had tried to counterbalance.[7] Having resigned from *Cruz y Raya* because of that publication's excessive liberalism, Falla now rejected Maeztu's proposed "conservative counter-revolution." However tired he may have been of articulating his beliefs, he still had powerful words at his disposal, which he dictated to María del Carmen:

> The French Revolution was not fundamentally the work of writers and philosophers, but rather the result of the fact that Catholics had forgotten their principles of justice and love, which are essential to Christian belief. . . . The only solution for this is not a conservative counter-revolution . . . but rather another deeper and more noble revolution, guided by the love of God, above all things, and of our neighbor, as you would have him love you. Until this comes about, it is usesless to resort to tradition, a word which exercises an almost magical effect on some sectors of the Spanish population and with which they try to explain and justify everything. Every age demands new solutions and more generosity and love for our fellows. What does not conform

---

3. Preston, *Concise History of the Spanish Civil War*, 67. At one time, Calvo Sotelo also wrote musical criticism for the Catholic daily *El Debate* and reviewed important events, including the Madrid production of *Parsifal* on 1 January 1914 and several of Stravinsky's first performances in Spain. See Hess, *Manuel de Falla and Modernism in Spain*, 21, 98–100.

4. Jackson, *The Spanish Republic and the Civil War*, 205–6.

5. "España—dice 'Gaziel'—respira una atmósfera de guerra civil," *El Sol*, 16 May 1936, 3.

6. Edward R. Tannenbaum, *The Action Française: Die-Hard Reactionaries in Twentieth-Century France* (New York: Wiley, 1962), 228–51.

7. Mainer, *La edad de plata*, 329–30.

to this represents nationalist traditionalism which will finish, like any exaggerated nationalism, by opposing Christ's true teachings.[8]

Of course, Falla's desire to avoid a "conservative counterrevolution" was not to be realized. On 12 July, Falangists assassinated Lt. José Castillo, an officer in the Republican Assault Guards. In revenge, José Calvo Sotelo was kidnapped and murdered the next day. On the seventeenth, a series of military uprisings ensued in Spanish Morocco and spread throughout Andalusia. Gen. Franco assumed command of the Army of Africa, and in the space of a week Oviedo was seized, martial law prevailed in Pamplona, and most of Galicia had been taken. In Toledo, Colonel Moscardó holed up with a small band of fellow Nationalists, as Franco's side was known, in the imposing ancient fortress, the Alcázar, until that city fell ten weeks later. In late July, Hitler agreed to Franco's request for military aid; help from Mussolini was assured as well, as were volunteers and funds from the Comintern on behalf of the Republic.[9] Yet the Nationalists failed at several key points. In Madrid, for example, the uprising was put down by Republican (Loyalist) troops and people's militias, which were often hastily assembled from the members of labor unions. Untrained and poorly equipped, they defended Madrid from the Guadarrama Mountains. In Barcelona, where anticlerical mobs went so far as to display nuns' corpses outside a convent door, power also passed to the people in the streets.[10]

Falla's adopted city offered little resistance when the Nationalist rebellion began there on 20 July. The Left-leaning newspaper *El Defensor de Granada*, in which the composer had anonymously addressed *cante jondo*, was shut down, so only the Nationalist version of the news went into print, with conflicting radio broadcasts further confusing the population. Unlike Madrid and Barcelona, no arms were distributed among members of trade unions or leftist political organizations, despite their leaders' urgings. Without grenades, planes, or artillery, coordinating Republican sympathizers proved to be next to impossible, although clusters of workers, mostly unarmed, defended the Albaicín even after the Nationalists occupied City Hall.[11] A bombardment crushed these efforts, and days later Granada surrendered to the Nationalists.

What followed was utter hell. Fearing an attack from Republican territory, Nationalist death squads and militias killed thousands of *granadinos* suspected of

8. Letter, María del Carmen (on behalf of her brother) to Ramiro de Maeztu, 8 July 1936, cited and translated in Christoforidis, "Constructions of Manuel de Falla's Political Identity and Musical Nationalism in the 1930s," 7–8.

9. See Foard, "Chronology of the Spanish Civil War," 498–500.

10. Hugh Thomas, *The Spanish Civil War*, 3d ed. (New York: Simon and Schuster, 1986), 232–36. A grisly photo of the Barcelona convent is reproduced in Ann Wilson, ed., *The Spanish Civil War: A History in Pictures* (New York and London: Norton, 1986), 52.

11. Gibson, *Death of Lorca*, 60–63.

Republican sympathies. Those awaiting execution were deposited in trucks, which labored up the Cuesta de Gomérez to the "outside wall of the cemetery that faces the Cerro del Sol," that is, not far from Falla's house.[12] From there, he heard the gunshots emitted at dawn by the double-ranked firing squad. So intense was the rash of killings that bodies were buried in twos and threes, and the cemetery itself had to be enlarged. Among those executed were Constantino Ruiz Carnero, the editor of *El Defensor de Granada*; José García Fernández, a Protestant minister; five professors from the University of Granada, including Salvador Vila, the rector and a respected Arabist; and Rafael García Duarte, a professor of pediatrics who had long donated his services to the poor.[13]

Surely one of the most depressing moments in Falla's life came in mid-August when Lorca was taken. The poet had long antagonized the Right, for several of his plays were controversial. *Mariana Pineda* (1927) is set during a nineteenth-century uprising in Granada and concerns a young woman who dies rather than betray her liberal accomplices. The erotic *Amor de Don Perlimplín con Belisa en su jardín* (1933) was banned by Primo de Rivera, and *Yerma* (1934) was attacked by the Catholic press.[14] Lorca had also been active in the Republic's cultural programs, having established the traveling theater company La Barraca (the word means "cabin" or "hut"). Under its auspices, Lorca and his colleagues, many of them students, traveled throughout rural Spain presenting the works of Calderón, Lope de Vega, and others.[15] Although this idealistic project may have yielded few practical results, middle-class university students learned firsthand of the dire poverty to which so many Spaniards were condemned. Lorca's associations with Republican high officials even caused some Nationalists to reach the wild conclusion that he was a Soviet agent. Antigay sentiment also reared its ugly head: as some of the poet's assassins later told Gibson, "we [were] sick and tired of queers in Granada" and "we left [Lorca's body] in a ditch and I fired two bullets in his arse for being a queer."[16]

By early August, Lorca sensed that he was in danger. He found sanctuary with friends, the Rosales family; that two of their sons were among Granada's leading

12. Gibson, *Death of Lorca*, 75; Gibson cites *Death in the Morning* (London: Lovat Dickson, 1937), an account by the U.S. author Helen Nicholson, who was staying near the Alhambra at that time.

13. Gibson, *Death of Lorca*, 78–79.

14. On *Mariana Pineda*, see María Francisca Vilches de Frutos and Dru Dougherty, *Los estrenos teatrales de Federico García Lorca (1920–1945)* (Madrid: Tabapress and Fundación García Lorca, 1992), 42. Margarita Ucelay discussed the musical dimensions of *Amor de Don Perlimplín con Belisa en su jardín* in her edition of the same name (Madrid: Ediciones Cátedra, 1998), 205–12. *Yerma* and related issues are treated in Gibson, *Federico García Lorca*, 454–55.

15. Gibson, *Federico García Lorca*, 320–21.

16. This statement, attributed to Juan Luis Trescastros, who participated in Lorca's arrest, is cited and translated in Gibson, *Death of Lorca*, 128.

Falangists reflects the convoluted intertwining of political and personal loyalties that undergirded so much behavior during the Civil War. As Lorca's concealment was being planned, the idea of finding protection with Falla arose. Another son, Luis Rosales (also a poet), later explained:

> The possibility of getting Federico into the Republican zone was discussed. I could have done this fairly easily. . . . But Federico refused. He was terrified by the thought of being all alone in a no-man's-land between the two zones. Nor would he consider going to seek refuge in Manuel de Falla's *carmen*. Federico had had a bit of a literary row with Falla about his *Ode to the Holy Sacrament*, which he had dedicated to him. It's a pretty unorthodox poem and Falla, who was very Catholic, didn't like it. Anyway, Federico felt that to go there would be embarrassing and said that he would prefer to come to my house.[17]

We can only wonder how events might have unfolded had Lorca overcome his chagrin and gone to Falla's house, where he would have been welcomed with open arms. After all, Falla had limited regard for the laws of man, as we have seen in his advocacy of the "deeper and nobler revolution within." Especially telling is an episode related by the poet's brother Francisco. One day, when Federico was at Falla's house, news reached them that some prisoners had escaped from a nearby jail. One was approaching the *carmen*. When the maid began to lock the door, Falla shouted, "Open the door! They're being pursued by the law!" Falla's spontaneous and energetic reaction on behalf of some unknown unfortunate made a tremendous impression on Federico;[18] yet, ultimately, the composer's high ideals and moral dignity intimidated the poet in his hour of need.

On 16 August, after eight days with the Rosales family, the poet was apprehended.[19] Several people tried to act on his behalf, including Falla. According to the most reliable account, on 19 August he went to the civil government offices with two young Falangists he had met earlier that year.[20] During this grim errand, he would have overheard the effects of torture on the Nationalists' prisoners, whose screams rang through the streets. Yet Falla's efforts were in vain, for he learned through his escorts that Lorca, obsessed with death in life and work, had been shot

17. Interview between Ian Gibson and Luis Rosales, tape-recorded on 2 September 1966. Rosales's frequently repeated account has been much distorted by Spanish and foreign journalists. See Gibson, *Death of Lorca*, 88–89.

18. Lorca, *Federico y su mundo*, 153.

19. The visitor to Granada Province may wish to consult Gibson's guidebook of Lorca's Granada, including the route to Viznar, the site of the execution (outside the city limits). See Ian Gibson, *En Granada, su Granada . . .* (Granada: Diputación Provincial de Granada, 1997), esp. 155–61.

20. Lorca's friend José Mora Guarnido discussed the circumstances of the poet's death with Falla in Buenos Aires in the fall of 1939. See Lorca, *Federico y su mundo*, 196–201.

that morning. It had happened near Víznar, the Nationalists' place of execution northeast of Granada, not far from a natural spring the Arabs called the "fountain of tears."[21] Shortly thereafter, Falla attempted to intervene on behalf of one of the Lorca family's maids; again his efforts were to no avail.[22] Lorca's brother-in-law, Manuel Fernández-Montesinos, younger than the poet by two years and at one time mayor of Granada, was also killed. Later the Lorca family would recall with gratitude Falla's visits immediately after Federico's death.[23]

The vast numbers of executions in the face of such badly coordinated resistance led Gibson to call the repression of Granada "one of the outstanding crimes of the war."[24] Given the harrowing environment, it is safe to say that Falla risked his personal well-being when he intervened on Lorca's behalf. This, along with his subsequent visits to the poet's family, undoubtedly enhanced his reputation in right-wing circles as a *rojillo*, that is, as less than a full-fledged leftist but no friend of the Nationalists.[25]

Indeed, although probably consumed with fear, he questioned the Nationalists' practices. In September 1936, a month in which approximately 499 executions took place in Granada, Falla wrote an old friend from Cádiz, José María Pemán, a poet and playwright who was well connected with the Nationalists. Falla lamented the "satanic outrages perpetrated in Granada," insisting that their devastating effects were pushing him "to the brink of death."[26] He also confided:

> Now, new sorrows disturb my spirit: I mean to refer to the frequent application of the death penalty to persons whose crimes suggest, at least from all appearances, a notable disproportion. You without a doubt share these sentiments, for we all know of your elevated religious convictions and the nobility of your heart, and for this reason I make up my mind to write you, trusting that you, with all your prestige, could effectively influence . . . the matter in question.[27]

Probably Lorca's death was the main trigger for Falla's "new fear," and surely his remarks can be read as a criticism of the Nationalists. Yet even as he deplored acts

---

21. On the history of Ainadamar (the fountain of tears), see Gibson, *Federico García Lorca*, 466–67.

22. Personal interview with Joaquín Nin-Culmell, January 2000.

23. Lorca, *Federico y su mundo*, 153.

24. Gibson, *Death of Lorca*, 67.

25. Personal interview, Joaquin Nin-Culmell, January 2000.

26. Letter, Falla to Pemán, 18 September 1936, cited in Fernando Sánchez García, ed., *La correspondencia inédita entre Falla y Pemán* (Seville: Alfar, 1991), 62, 65. Statistics on the executions are in Gibson, *Death of Lorca*, 77.

27. Letter, Falla to Pemán, 18 September 1936, cited in Sánchez García, *La correspondencia inédita*, 65.

of unbridled Nationalist violence another portion of the same letter reveals a very different perspective:

> I well know that in these moments, given such numerous and horrendous crimes that determined the present movement for the salvation of Spain, serenity of judgment is incredibly difficult at times; but for this very reason I believe it a strict obligation for Christians that we convey our fears and our sorrows to those who, due to a host of grave responsibilities and preoccupations, sometimes find themselves fatally obliged to resort to expedient procedures that in normal times they would certainly not put into practice.[28]

Describing the uprising as the "movement for the salvation of Spain" hardly reveals the mindset of a *rojillo*. In fact, the phrase comes straight from Nationalist propaganda, as does Falla's description (in another letter to Pemán) of the Nationalists' taking of Málaga in early February 1937 as a "felicísima 'reconquista'" (a most fortunate reconquest).[29] The term *reconquest*, or "second conquest," as it was sometimes called, alludes to Christian Spain's routing of the Moorish "infidel" in the fifteenth century, a gratifying historical parallel for Nationalists, many of whom saw the Civil War as an equally holy crusade. Still, we cannot be sure to what extent this language actually reflects Falla's views. Was he ingenuous? Overcome by fear? Or was he trying out a bit of wartime bombast to solidify his bond with Pemán, whose friendship might prove advantageous in an uncertain future?

Another letter from this period, to Gen. Gonzalo Queipo de Llano, raises similar questions. The general had been actively involved in the repression of Granada. (He may even have given the order for Lorca's death, although Falla could not have known this).[30] After the outbreak of the war, Granada gave Queipo de Llano a commemorative album, but Falla had hesitated to participate in such an homage, fearing, as always, the appearance of political support. In October 1936, however, he wrote the general:

> Ever since I became aware of the homage Granada offered you for the splendid deed of July with which you initiated the movement for the salvation of Spain, I set the goal of affiliating myself with it, fulfilling an inescapable duty for all Spaniards worthy of the name; but being ill, I had to appeal to the kindness of some friends to inform me of the dedicatory text of the album . . . and this, along with the scruple that its redaction could be mingled with some . . .

28. Letter, Falla to Pemán, 18 September 1936, cited in Sánchez García, *La correspondencia inédita,* 65. Portions of the same letter are cited in de Persia, *Los últimos años de Manuel de Falla,* 24; and Budwig, "Manuel de Falla's *Atlántida*," 198, although the final clause is omitted in both.

29. Letter, Falla to Pemán, 12 February 1937, cited in Sánchez García, *La correspondencia inédita,* 66.

30. Gibson, *Death of Lorca,* 110.

possible political interpretation, in which case, given my lifelong withdrawal from the workings of politics, I would have registered my token of adhesion. Well, then: the effort with which my friends tried to placate me was useless, and thus the day arrived in which I learned with great disappointment that it was too late to . . . join the homage. For this reason, I now want to fulfill this desire, begging you, my general, that you accept the expression of the same that I direct to you with all my will placed in God and in Spain.[31]

Again Falla draws on Nationalist rhetoric to praise a leader of the rebellion. The slogan "For God and Spain" (Por Dios y España), which can still be seen on some monuments, was a rallying cry for Nationalist Catholics, as was "¡Viva Cristo Rey!" (Long Live Christ the King), which Falla incorporates into his very next sentence: "And I ask God that the sacred cry 'Long Live Christ the King!' that so many martyrs cry out upon death will have fruitful effect in the convictions and in the works of we Spanish Christians still living."[32]

What to make of this? Three months into the war and only two months after Lorca's death, Falla, always so fearful of "deformation" of thought, was describing the conflict as a necessary means of restoring spiritual values to Spain. To be sure, he did so privately, without the media commotion of the Seville episode. But can he really have been so naive as to imagine that his letter to Queipo de Llano would be interpreted as anything other than political support, however much he couched his remarks in religious terms and portrayed himself as an apologist for political neutrality? That he failed to publicly acknowledge the general but hastened to do so privately may even suggest a degree of sincerity in his "adhesion." But it may also suggest a fear of doing otherwise.

31. "Desde que me enteré del homenaje que le ofrecía Granada por la espléndida hazaña de Julio con que inició Vd. en España su movimiento salvador, hice el propósito de adherirme a él cumpliendo un deber ineludible para todo español que merezca serlo; pero hallándome enfermo, tuve que rogar a la bondad de algunos amigos que me informaran del texto dedicatoria del album . . . y ello ante el escrúpulo de que en su redacción pudiera mezclarse algún . . . posible interpretación política, en cuyo caso, dado el voluntario apartamiento en que, durante toda mi vida, me he hallado de cuanto a política trascienda, lo hubiera hecho constar como complemento de mi adhesión. Ahora bien: inútil fue el empeño con que procuraron complacerme aquellos buenos amigos, y de este modo llegó el día en que supe con gran disgusto mío, que era ya tarde para . . . adherirme al homenaje. Por eso quiero ahora cumplir aquel deseo, rogando a Vd. Sr. General, acepte la expresión del mismo, que le dirijo con toda mi voluntad puesta en Dios y en España" (letter, Falla to Queipo de Llano, 20 October 1936, AMF correspondence file 7459).

32. "Y a Dios le pido que el santo grito de 'Viva Cristo Rey' que tantos mártires lanzan al morir, tenga fecunda eficacia en el convencimiento y en las obras de los cristianos españoles que aún vivimos" (letter, Falla to Queipo de Llano, 20 October 1936, AMF correspondence file 7459).

That fall he followed the progress of Franco's army. In November 1936, he wrote César Pemán (the poet's brother), fervently wishing for the "desired and definitive" occupation of Madrid.[33] By then, the Republican government had fled to Valencia and a fierce Nationalist assault on the capital had begun. It was in the defense of Madrid that the mettle of the International Brigades was first tested. Volunteers from various European countries, the Soviet Union, and the United States (the latter were known as the Lincoln Brigade), defied the noninterventionist policy of the League of Nations and sought to counteract Axis aid to the Nationalists with equipment and manpower. (Hemingway evoked one such idealist with the character Robert Jordan in *For Whom the Bell Tolls.*) As a result, the "definitive" occupation of Madrid remained elusive.[34] Nationalist attacks around the capital during the winter of 1936–37, including the protracted Battle of Jarama, ended in stalemate, and Madrid fell only days before the end of the war.

However much he claimed to accept the "necessity" of the war, Falla was devastated by it. In late 1936, still feeling himself on "the brink of death," he suffered another nervous collapse. His doctors forbade him to work or write letters for several months. He also had the bad luck to swallow a metal dental hook, which painfully ulcerated his stomach.[35] As he confronted his own frailty and the confusion roiling around him, *Atlántida* lay fallow, and between July 1936 and July 1938 he barely touched it. Still, we find isolated references to the cantata in his correspondence from that period. For example, a letter from Sert of 19 October 1936 reminds us that *Atlántida* was still alive. Writing María del Carmen, who was again in charge of her brother's correspondence, Sert mentioned that Ansermet hoped to conduct the work in Geneva for the inauguration of the new Palace of Nations, which had been opening incrementally since spring 1936.[36] A performance there of *Atlántida*—a work that celebrates the glories of Spain—would have amounted to a bitter paradox, given the League's ineffectiveness in dealing with the Civil War, which involved dickering over the Nonintervention Agreement and looking the other way as German and Italian planes bombed the capital and Soviet tanks arrived at the Madrid front on behalf of the Republic.[37] In any case, *Atlántida* was nowhere near complete and Falla's health made travel impossible, even though Sert had offered to escort him and María del Carmen "from Cádiz or Burgos."[38]

33. "¡*Por cuantos motivos* estoy deseando leer sus anunciadas palabras en la anhelada y definitiva ocupación de Madrid!" (letter, Falla to César Péman, 17 November 1936, AMF correspondence file 7393).

34. See also Douglas Little, *Malevolent Neutrality: The United States, Great Britain, and the Origins of the Spanish Civil War* (Ithaca and London: Cornell University Press, 1985), esp. 221–65.

35. Budwig, "Manuel de Falla's *Atlántida,*" 195n2.

36. F. P. Walters, *A History of the League of Nations* (London: Oxford University Press, 1952), 699–700.

37. Walters, *History of the League of Nations,* 722–23.

38. Letter, Sert to María del Carmen, 19 October 1936, AMF correspondence file 7619/1.

On 28 December 1937, Falla lost his old friend Ravel. Roland-Manuel informed him that Ravel had requested a civil burial and had not received the sacraments. Yet both he and Falla took a charitable view of what was to them a significant lapse, sharing the hope that "the mercy of God and the merits of Our Lord must give . . . profound hope for the eternal well-being of [their] friend."[39] For the third time, Falla paid tribute to a deceased French colleague in *La Revue Musicale*.[40] In contrast to the "torture" of composing the Wagner essay, writing about Ravel seems to have afforded Falla a moment of quiet wonder. Marveling at Ravel's vivid and elegant orchestrations, Falla observed how subtly the Spanish idiom had insinuated itself into his music, which still remained entirely French. According to Falla, Ravel's mother, who had spent her youth in Madrid, had transmitted to her son memories of the *tertulias musicales* and *habaneras* fashionable in her day. In short, "Ravel's Spain was a Spain ideally sensed," a concept that must have held no small appeal for Falla in those bitter times.[41] Elsewhere in the essay, Falla gives pride of place to Ravel's "good and quiet soul." With his scant material circumstances ("an old piano, as modest as the household that surrounded it"), music drew Ravel into "an inner world that serve[d] as a refuge against . . . disturbing reality"; in addition, Falla detected a certain religious character, one with "pure and serene expression," in many of Ravel's works.[42] The early string quartet, for example, contained "echoes of the carillon of Assisi," and the second part and finale of the *Mother Goose Suite* exuded "a beautiful religious character" (85). In short, Falla's portrayal of Ravel as a quiet, modest man whose music reflected innate spirituality is not so very different from contemporaneous depictions of Falla himself.

"Pure and serene expression" could not have been further from the intensely politicized cultural scene in Spain.[43] On the Republican side, educational collectives, art exhibitions, dramatic presentations, poetry readings, and concerts were crafted to inspire political fervor in the mass audience; at the same time, the press denounced Hitler, Mussolini, "and his lackey, Franco" for their role in the "destruction of civilization."[44] Madrid's theater and concert seasons continued pretty much on

39. "Je me console en pensant que la Miséricorde de Dieu et les mérites de Notre Seigneur doivent . . . donner une profonde espérance quant au salud éternel de notre ami" (letter, Roland-Manuel to Falla, 3 January 1938, AMF correspondence file 7520).

40. Manuel de Falla, "Notes sur Ravel," translated by Roland-Manuel, *La Revue Musicale* 20, no. 189 (1939): 81–86. In September 1939, the essay was reprinted in Spanish translation in the journal *Isla*, which was based in Jerez de la Frontera.

41. "L'Espagne de Ravel était une Espagne idéalment pressentie" (Falla, "Notes sur Ravel," 83).

42. Falla, "Notes sur Ravel," 84–85.

43. This is discussed in Carol A. Hess, "Silvestre Revueltas in Republican Spain: Music as Political Utterance," *Latin American Music Review* 18, no. 2 (1997): 278–96. See also Mainer, *La edad de plata*, 333–39.

44. "La guerra de los fascismos contra la cultura," *Las Noticias*, 9 October 1937, 3.

schedule, and after a brief closure Barcelona's Liceu reopened in 1938, albeit with a defiant boycott of the Italian and German repertories. Politically active instrumental ensembles included the Orquestra Pau Casals, under the direction of the ardently anti-Fascist cellist. Perhaps the greatest display of the leftist-affiliated aesthetic sensibility was the Second International Writers' Congress, convened in July 1937 in Valencia and in which Falla's old friend and one-time ally José Bergamín participated.

The Nationalists initiated similar campaigns, especially after October 1936, when Franco established his first government in Burgos. Outside its headquarters flew the flags of its allies: Portugal, Italy, and Nazi Germany, with its bold swastika. Other alliances involved religious entities. On 1 July 1937, Spanish bishops endorsed the Burgos government in a collective letter, and on 28 August of the same year the Vatican formally recognized the regime. One cultural project originating in Burgos was the magazine *Radio Nacional*. Mindful of the alliance with Mussolini, this slim publication devoted an entire issue to Verdi, celebrating that composer's compatibility with "Spanish genius" and the "innately Italianate" quality of *zarzuela*.[45] Artists such as Carlos Saenz de Tejada painted scenes of church desecrations by the Republican enemies of Christ, and plays such as Pemán's blatantly racist *Almoneda* caused a great stir in Nationalist circles.[46] (Among those who congratulated Pemán on its successful premiere on 9 April 1937 was Falla, although it is not clear that he actually knew the work.[47]) Also in April of 1937, the impetus for a very different— and far more enduring—example of Civil War art came when Hitler's Condor Legion bombed Guernica, a Basque town utterly without defenses.[48] Picasso's *Guernica*, that powerful black, white, and gray canvas with its dismembered forms and twisted proportions, captures the agony of that day, which, incidentally, involved direct hits on several churches in that deeply religious region.

Another work by Pemán, the epic "Poema de la bestia y el ángel" (Poem of the Beast and the Angel), was, however, conspicuously linked to Falla's name. In it, Pemán took as a point of departure the Book of Revelation (with the Beast representing the "Reds") and incorporated events of the war such as the siege of the Toledo Alcázar. With its strident descriptions of crazed mobs and "Jewish gold," the result is downright embarrassing.[49] Nonetheless, Pemán considered the "Poema de la bestia y el ángel" "the definitive poem of this war." On 28 September 1937, he honored Falla with a reading of it at the home of Ramón Pérez de Roda, a neighbor of the composer's; the mayor of Granada, several university professors, and various

45. See "Notas y comentarios musicales," *Radio Nacional: Revista Semanal de Radio-difusión* 1, no. 11 (1938): 11.

46. A sample of Saenz de Tejada's work is in Wilson, *Spanish Civil War*, 126–27.

47. José María Pemán, *Obras completas* (Madrid: Escelicer, 1947), 4:455. Falla sent Pemán a congratulatory telegram shortly after the premiere. See Sánchez García, *La correspondencia inédita*, 25.

48. Preston, *Concise History of the Spanish Civil War*, 192–94.

49. Pemán, *Obras completas*, 1:140.

other citizens were also invited. The ample press coverage of the event included a report by the Seville-based (Nationalist) edition of *ABC* (a Republican edition was published in Madrid) indicating that Falla had set Pemán's poem to music "for the immortal glory of Nationalist Spain."[50]

Certainly Falla had done no such thing. He had, however, reluctantly agreed to compose a *Himno marcial* (Martial Hymn) using one of Pemán's texts, which was probably the cause of the confusion. The anthem came about thanks largely to Gen. Luis Orgaz, a monarchist who had been plotting against the Republic since its inception.[51] Shortly after the uprising, when the general was passing through Granada in a German Junkers, Falla received him. Later, in Burgos (only a few days after Lorca's assassination), Orgaz asked Falla to compose as quickly as possible "some marching songs to be sung by our soldiers, on words that I will ask the great Pemán to compose . . . so that the result may be what one can expect from the marriage of your two lofty minds."[52] Falla's refusal was polite (he recommended Ernesto Halffter or Turina) but firm.[53] But evidently he was not firm enough: unwilling to take no for an answer, Orgaz began hounding the composer, reiterating in a letter Falla received on 14 September his "invitation." Responding on the twenty-third, Falla lamented anew the state of his health and again mentioned Halffter and Turina, giving Orgaz every opportunity to relent. True to his tendency to send a mixed message, however, Falla also mentioned the possibility of arranging a "hymn by Pedrell" (the "Canto de los Almogávares" from *Los Pirineos*). The composer's speculative tone was too vague for Orgaz, who in a telegram on 13 October 1937 reiterated the need to accept "urgent responsibility" and badgered Falla "to make one more effort for our undefeated Spain."[54] Poor Falla responded a few days later, referring lamely to his "good intentions" and his desire to "glorify God and serve our homeland."[55] In this instance, his rhetoric had a decidedly tired ring.

Yet even in a project for which he evinced little enthusiasm, Falla's perfectionist streak prevailed. Scrupulosity may have prompted him, for example, to insist on

50. "El poema de la guerra: Letra de Pemán y música," *ABC* (Seville), 7 October 1937, AMF press file. When the war broke out, the Madrid office of *ABC*, formerly a monarchist paper, was taken over by a labor union, while the Nationalists published their own edition in Seville. *Ideal, Patria,* and the *Diario de Cádiz* also covered the event.

51. In June of 1932, he was arrested for his involvement in a monarchist conspiracy. See "El complot monárquico: El general Orgaz, deportado en Tenerife, fue detenido ayer en Las Palmas y quedó incomunicado," *El Sol,* 17 June 1932, 8. See also Thomas, *Spanish Civil War,* 59.

52. "Unas cuantas canciones de marcha para que fuesen cantadas por nuestros soldados, sobre letras que requeriré componga el gran Pemán . . . para que resultase lo que cabe esperar del maridaje de sus dos excelsos ingenios" (letter, Orgaz to Falla, 25 August 1937, AMF correspondence file 7350).

53. Letter, Falla to Orgaz, 3 September 1937, AMF correspondence file 7350.

54. Telegram, 13 October 1937, AMF correspondence file 7350.

55. Letter, Falla to Orgaz, 18 October 1937, AMF correspondence file 7350.

changes in Pemán's text, especially the line "el soplo de Dios sobre nuestras bayonetas" (the breath of God over our bayonets), which Falla feared might be interpreted as "an irreverence" given the implied union of "the name of God with an instrument of destruction."[56] News of a successful first rehearsal seems to have left the composer unmoved, although Orgaz waxed enthusiastic and Pemán exulted to Falla that "now, in the definitive version, [the *Himno*] will be distributed to all the military schools so that it will be learned and eventually used in the barracks."[57] In addition, a Captain Galisteo personally consulted Falla on a performance scheduled for the Academia de Alféreces (Academy of Lieutenants). Yet, as so often happened—even with works Falla cared deeply about—a "definitive version" eluded him. Days before the performance, he requested additional changes in the versification and gave last-minute instructions on the instrumentation (which he did not do himself). The following March, seven months after Orgaz's initial request, Falla assured Pemán that he was trying to "at last, finish the revision of the score of the *Himno* for band."[58] Not surprisingly, the project fell into oblivion well before the end of the war.

All the while, Falla sought justice on a personal scale, appealing to Pemán on behalf of friends and colleagues. Here, a command of Nationalist rhetoric certainly helped. For example, Falla wrote Pemán several times on behalf of a professor of law at the University of Granada, one Enrique Gómez de Arboleya, whose career seemed to be in jeopardy. Falla described him as "a fervent Catholic, endowed with rare moral and intellectual merits," who, "from the beginnings of the Nationalist Movement has generously sacrificed his own comfort and tranquility to patriotic duties, serving as a volunteer in a Nationalist militia and now has been elected in Granada by the Falange president of the Technical Council of Nationalist Education."[59] Other petitions to Pemán could be stated more neutrally, such as Falla's request that financing for the Orquesta Bética be maintained (which Pemán was able to procure).[60] Also claiming Falla's attention were irregularities at the Seville Conservatory, the state-administered institution established by the Republic in August 1933 but now in Nationalist hands. Having learned in July 1937 that payment of the instructors' salaries had been delayed, he telegraphed Pemán, who declared that he

56. Letter, Falla to Pemán, 6 October 1937, cited in Sánchez García, *La correspondencia inédita*, 36.

57. Letter, Pemán to Falla, 12 October 1937, cited in Sánchez García, *La correspondencia inédita*, 37.

58. Letter, Falla to Pemán, 17 March 1938, cited in Sánchez García, *La correspondencia inédita*, 40.

59. Letter, Falla to Pemán, 27 February 1937, cited in Sánchez García, *La correspondencia inédita*, 69. Falla's attempts to advocate on behalf of other individuals through Pemán are treated on pages 67–77.

60. Letter, Falla to Pemán, 18 February 1937, cited in Sánchez García, *La correspondencia inédita*, 57.

would devote his full energy to the situation. In a second telegram, Falla stressed the urgency of the situation, and weeks later Pemán assured him that all the instructors had been placed on the payroll and that he had taken up Conservatory-related matters with "the Generalísimo himself," that is, with Franco.[61]

When Falla could not praise a colleague's service to the Nationalist Movement, he appealed to friendship. Writing Capt. José Nestares on behalf of Hermenegildo Lanz, Falla's erstwhile collaborator in puppetry, who had been detained in the early days of the Granada repression and investigated by the Commission for the Purification of Personnel for Public Instruction (Comisión Depuradora del Personal de Instrucción Pública), the composer simply stated that "knowing that you, too, are his friend, I trust you share my sentiments and beg you to indicate to me what I could do, perhaps with your collaboration or in whatever form you believe most appropriate, to help our friend in this critical moment."[62] Additionally, he might praise artistic or musical talent. On 4 October 1938, he wrote the minister of education, Pedro Sainz Rodrigo, about obtaining a position for the composer Joaquín Rodrigo either "in radio, in a conservatory, etc.," that would permit him to remain in Spain. Describing Rodrigo (along with Ernesto Halffter, then in Lisbon after a less than gratifying two-year stint as director of the Seville Conservatory) as one of Spain's "few positive [musical] values," Falla also took pains to greet "His Excellency the Generalísimo."[63] His efforts paid off: Sainz Rodrigo found Rodrigo a position "with a salary of 5,000 pesetas" and promised to look into Halffter's situation.[64] Falla even prevailed upon General Orgaz, writing him to inquire if tax revenues could be raised in Granada for aviation to ward off air attacks so that monuments such as the Alhambra and the Generalife could be preserved. There is no record in the AMF of Orgaz's response to Falla's touching but naive request.

All Falla's letters to these Nationalist officials bear his peace symbol, the word *Pax* with a cross drawn through it (see figure 17). To Orgaz, who commented on it, he explained: "I have felt great satisfaction reading your words about the sign that presides over my letters, and I put, like you, all my hope in the possibility that Spain may soon enjoy the true peace of God after such heroic and admirable sacri-

61. Correspondence on the matter is in Sánchez García, *La correspondencia inédita*, 58–59.

62. Letter, Falla to Nestares, 3 September 1936, cited in Eduardo Quesada Dorador, "Imágenes de Manuel de Falla en Granada," in Nommick, *Manuel de Falla en Granada*, 149–50. For Falla's letter to Pemán on the matter (dated 27 February 1937), see Sánchez García, *La correspondencia inédita*, 72.

63. Letter, Falla to Sainz Rodrigo, 4 October 1938, AMF correspondence file 7562.

64. Letter, Sainz Rodrigo to Falla, 14 October 1938, AMF correspondence file 7562.

Figure 17. Falla's peace sign, which adorned his
correspondence during the Spanish Civil War.
(Reprinted by kind permission of the Archivo
Manuel de Falla)

fice . . . I'm sure that you, my dear General, like our undefeated Generalísimo, are
not far from thinking along these lines."[65]

"Hope" aside, Falla continued to suffer health problems. To some extent, he may
have adjusted to the shock of war, for he did not repeat the dire statements of August 1936, when he declared himself to be at the point of death. Yet in under a year
he underwent multiple surgeries, including an operation for a chest abscess (*fístula*)
in April 1937, which he described to Pemán as a "very delicate operation with a difficult stay in the clinic and quite a long convalescence."[66] Then, in August of that
year, he was operated on for an ulcer on his foot.[67] Side effects included high fevers
and flu. Not surprisingly, he confided to Pemán that his "health had taken a step
backward."[68]

We can only wonder, then, why Falla imagined that he could finish *Atlántida* by
the end of 1938. Yet this is what he told Zuloaga in a letter of 12 December 1937,[69] a
few days after Japan granted diplomatic recognition to Franco and Nationalist air-
craft bombed Barcelona, a prelude to the intense bombardments of that city in
March 1938. It may be that the possibility of a performance at La Scala during the

65. "Gratísima satisfacción he sentido a leer sus palabras sobre el signo que preside
mis cartas, y pongo como Vd. toda mi esperanza en que pronto pueda España gozar de la
verdadera Paz de Díos despues de tanto heróico y admirable sacrificio, . . . Seguro estoy
de que tanto Vd., mi querido General, como nuestro invicto Generalísimo no estén lejos
de pensar lo mismo que estoy diciendo" (letter, Falla to Orgaz, 18 October 1937, AMF correspondence file 7350).

66. Letter, Falla to Pemán, 25 August 1937, cited in Sánchez García, *La correspondencia
inédita*, 63.

67. Letter, Falla to Orgaz, 3 September 1937, AMF correspondence file 7350.

68. Letter, Falla to Pemán, 6 October 1937, cited in Sánchez-García, *La correspondencia
inédita*, 63. See also letter, Falla to Sert (draft), 19 July 1938, AMF correspondence file 7619/2.

69. Budwig, "Manuel de Falla's *Atlántida*," 204.

1938–39 season energized Falla, for he commented to Sert that the proposal, made by Jenner Mataloni, "pleased [him] greatly."[70] Another possible venue was the 1939 World's Fair. The young U.S. musicologist Gilbert Chase (a cousin of Joaquín Nin-Culmell) inquired about this in November 1938:

> I know you don't like to speak of your own affairs and of your work. Never-theless, I am enormously curious to know something about your *Atlántida*. I don't know if you are aware that here there were several friends of your music—myself among them—who wanted to premiere *Atlántida* on the oc-casion of the New York World's Fair next year (1939). Certainly all you need to do is choose the moment and the mode in which your work is to be given to the world. But as soon as you give the word, we're here—and this includes Olin Downes, the musical director of the New York World's Fair—to receive your work with rejoicing.[71]

Whatever *Atlántida*'s potential as a repository of hope, its creator's ill health and not unrealistic sense that the world was collapsing around him again caused the work to stall. From 1938 to early 1939, Falla accomplished little, and the sense of mystery that had enveloped *Atlántida* from its confident initial stages only deepened.

EVASION, ACQUIESCENCE, ENIGMA: FALLA'S DECLARATION

Throughout the war, the Burgos government tried to pressure Falla into publicly declaring solidarity. Sometimes this effort involved little more than routine press propaganda. In April 1938, for example, his music was conspicuously featured in a benefit concert for Auxilio Social, the Nationalist welfare organization. It took place in Santander, which had been in Nationalist hands since the previous August, thanks in large part to Mussolini. The program included the "Soneto a Córdoba" and two of the *Siete canciones populares*. At its by now routine conclusion, "hymns of the Nationalist movement were played by the band, with trumpets, and were listened to by the public with raised arms, . . . letting out with enthusiasm 'Vivas!' and shouts

---

70. Letter, Jenner Mataloni to Falla, 21 August 1937; and letter, Falla to Sert, 9 September 1937, both cited in Budwig, "Manuel de Falla's *Atlántida*," 203.

71. "Sé que no le gusta a Vd. hablar de sus propios asuntos y de sus trabajos. Sin embargo, tengo una curiosidad enorme para saber algo de su *Atlántida*. No sé si sabe Vd. que habían aqui varios amigos de su música—y yo entre ellos—que querían hacer estrenar su *Atlántida* en la ocasion del New York World's Fair el año que viene (1939). Claro que Vd. solo ha de escoger el momento y el modo en que se dará su obra al mundo. Pero en cuanto diga Vd. la palabra, estamos aqui—y esto incluye Olin Downes, director musical del World's Fair de New York—para recibir con regocijo su obra" (letter, Chase to Falla, 29 November 1938, AMF correspondence file 6883). See also letter, Sert to Falla, 14 June 1938, cited in Budwig, "Manuel de Falla's *Atlántida*," 205.

of the triumph of the New Spain."[72] Similarly, José Cubiles's performance in May 1938 of *Noches en los jardines de España* was billed as a demonstration of "patriotic enthusiasm and true love . . . toward the Movement, the soul and energy of Spain that leads Franco through the spiritual empire toward God."[73]

Sometimes critics for the *franquista* press would detect explicitly patriotic content in Falla's music. Among them was Luis Doreste Silva, whose "sentimental notes on a hearing of *Noches*" have to be one of the strangest readings in twentieth-century Spanish music criticism.[74] Inspired by a performance of 18 December 1937, the II Año Triunfal, or "Second Triumphal Year" (Nationalists marked time from July 1936, the beginning of the uprising), Doreste waxed effusive over the "priestly hands [that] have opened the missals of Manuel de Falla" in the creation of *Noches*. The work also evoked "a penitent whose soul is on its knees, in the light of Hispanic fervor, desirous of the immortal grace that descends at the instant of the pathetic and glorious communion, when the image of Calvary is driven in . . . [and] Christ, made rhythm . . . leads us by the hand."[75] In the same vein, Doreste likens the *cante jondo* element in *Noches* to "liturgical singing, the apotheosis of rhythms that expand the infinite flight of Hispanic throats," and the programmatic titles inspired by Granada (the last stronghold of the Moors) to the "triumph of Christian asceticism" over Islam. As a parting shot, the critic describes Falla himself "on the indestructible path, kneeling . . . before Pain and Joy, before Golgotha and the Resurrection of Spain, soaking his breast in the divine nectar of Eternity. . . . The lyrical missal has closed . . . [and] all the perfume of the intact and glorious Gardens of Spain, of her History and her unnumbered Victory, and without Death!"[76] So much for the oriental color, passion, sensuality, and echoes of love habitually detected in *Noches*!

---

72. "Por la banda de música y trompetas se tocaron los himnos del Movimiento y el Nacional, escuchados por todo el público brazo en alto, . . . dándose con entusiasmo los vivas y gritos de triunfo de la Nueva España" ("Concierto a beneficio de Auxilio Social," *El Diario Montañes*, 27 April 1938, AMF press file).

73. "Patriótico entusiasmo y verdadero amor . . . [al] Movimiento, alma y nervio de la España que conduce Franco por el Imperio espiritual hacia Dios" ("Pepe Cubiles con la Orquesta Bética en el 'Falla,'" *Diario de Cádiz*, 11 May 1938, AMF press file).

74. Luis Doreste Silva, "*Noches en los jardines de España*," unidentified press clipping from 23 December 1937, AMF press file.

75. "Un penitente con el alma de rodillas, en la luz de su fervor hispano, anhelante de la inmortal gracia que desciende, al instante de la comunión patética y gloriosa, cuando la imágen del Calvario está clavada . . . [y] Cristo, hecho ritmo . . . nos lleva de la mano" (Doreste Silva, "*Noches en los jardines de España*").

76. "[Falla] en el camino indestructible, arrodillado . . . ante el Dolor y la Alegría, el Gólgota y la Resurrección de España empapando su pecho del nectar Divino de la Eternidad. . . . El Misal lírico se ha cerrado . . . [y] todo el perfume de los Jardines intactos y gloriosos de España, ¡de su Historia y de su Victoria innumerable y sin Muerte!" (Doreste Silva, "*Noches en los jardines de España*").

One sort of propaganda dwelt solely on Falla's person. On 15 June 1937, the Granada-based *Patria* devoted a lengthy column to his accomplishments as an exemplary citizen of "Catholic and imperial Spain," noting: "We feel obliged to express to this exemplary man the testimony of our unsullied presence, of our admiration and respect . . . [and] with raised arms, we salute in Falla, the undying light that gloriously illuminates the new and old spirit, eternal and regenerated, of Catholic and imperial Spain."[77]

Other journalists took a rather less optimistic view of Falla on the "indestructible path," for at one point a rumor circulated that the composer was mentally ill. On 13 March 1937, Segismundo Romero published an open letter in which he repudiated the recent rumor of a "certain mental illness that our brilliant composer Don Manuel de Falla was suffering." Romero hastened to explain that "this news is absolutely false and without any foundation whatsoever, since the illness that Don Manuel de Falla really suffered this past year was gastrointestinal, caused by such intense and deep disappointments as he experienced upon learning of the burnings of churches and convents."[78]

Some journalists ventured to explicitly address Falla's political leanings. On 2 November 1937, a short but provocative column appeared in Granada's *El Ideal*, itself a response to an editorial in the Barcelona-based Republican daily *El Diluvio*, which had expressed surprise over "news" that Maestro Falla had declared himself for the Nationalists. (Of course, Falla had made no such official statement.) Scoffing at *El Diluvio*'s "surprise," *El Ideal* recalled Falla's reproof to Seville's City Hall of five years earlier while calling forth the specter of freemasonry, a favorite *franquista* target:

> We cannot explain *El Diluvio*'s amazement. We believe that Maestro Falla's patriotism has been well tested, so that one would be offended to think that, on this occasion, he could turn toward the Reds. He broke with them a long time ago. Doesn't *El Diluvio* remember his memorable words when he renounced the homage freemasonry was preparing for him, wanting to capture

77. "Nos sentimos obligados a manifestar a este hombre ejemplar el testimonio de nuestra asistencia acendrada, de nuestra admiración y acatamiento . . . [y] con el brazo en alto, saludamos en Falla, la luz imperecedera que ilumina gloriosamente el espíritu nuevo y viejo, perenne y renovado, de la España católica e imperial" ("Hombres de España," *Patria*, 15 June 1937, AMF press file).

78. "Esas noticias son absolutamente inexactas y sin fundamento alguno, puesto que la enfermedad que realmente padeció el pasado año don Manuel de Falla fue gastrointestinal, producida por los disgustos tan intensos y hondos que experimentó al conocer los incendios de iglesias y conventos" (Segismundo Romero, "El ilustre músico Don Manuel de Falla goza de buena salud," unidentified newspaper, 13 March 1937, AMF press file). The letter is addressed "to the director of the Falange Española," although it is not clear who circulated the rumor.

his support around 1932? "I can't accept homages when they are denied to God."[79]

The column concluded on a sharp note: "If *El Diluvio* knows Falla so little, it's the only entity in the Red Zone that doesn't know him."[80]

As ever, Falla took pains to avoid "deformation." Despite his unsteady health, he wrote an open letter to *El Ideal*, arguing, "It's absolutely true that, before as well as now, God is for me above all things, and that I did have to decline the [Seville] homage (in any case undeserved) . . . although neither the intention nor its origins were precisely those assigned it by *El Ideal*. But, I repeat it, the fact is correct and it will return to reinstate itself on any occasion that may require it."[81] In other words, loyalty to God—not to the political Right—had motivated Falla's rejection of the Seville *homenaje*. Once again, he managed to publicly affirm his religious convictions without committing himself to the Nationalists. His explanation, moreover, was one with which no Nationalist could possibly quarrel.

Still, it was not enough for Burgos. In early 1938, the government appointed Falla by governmental decree (and without his prior consent) to the presidency of the newly established Instituto de España.[82] This entity, which combined representatives of existing academies, had been formed to lend intellectual credibility to the regime, and presumably reinforced the expectation that the impending Nationalist triumph would rest not only on military strength but on intellectual and artistic stature, in contrast to "Bolshevik barbarism."[83] Corresponding members included Claudel, the historian Karl Burckhardt, and Stravinsky, all selected to enhance

79. "No nos explicamos el asombro de *El Diluvio*. Creemos que el maestro Falla tiene bien probado su patriotismo para que se le pudiera ofender pensando que, en esta ocasión, podría inclinarse del lado de los rojos. Hace mucho rompió con ellos. ¿No recuerda *El Diluvio* sus memorables palabras cuando renunció a un homenaje que le preparaba la masonería queriendo captar su voluntad, allá por el año 1932? 'Yo no puedo aceptar homenajes cuando se le niegan a Dios'" ("Falla con los 'facciosos,'" *Ideal*, 2 November 1937, AMF press file). The Franco government's fear of freemasonry is treated in Carr, *Spain*, 696–97.

80. "Si tan mal le conoce [a Falla] *El Diluvio*, es el único que no le conoce en la zona roja" ("Falla con los 'facciosos'").

81. "Es ciertísimo que, antes como ahora, Dios ha estado y está para mí sobre todas las cosas, y que hube de declinar el homenaje (de todos modos inmerecido) . . . aunque ni la intención ni la procedencia fueran precisamente las que se consignan en *Ideal*. Pero, lo repito, el hecho es exacto y volvería a producirse en toda ocasión que así lo exigiese" (Manuel de Falla, "Una carta de Falla," *El Ideal*, 4 November 1937, AMF press file).

82. Alicia Alted Vigil, *Política del Nuevo Estado sobre el patrimonio cultural y la educación durante la guerra civil española* (Madrid: Ministerio de Cultura, 1994), 239–48.

83. Gemma Pérez Zalduondo, "El nacionalismo como eje de la politica musical del primer gobierno regular de Franco (30 de enero de 1938–8 de agosto de 1939)," *Revista de Musicología* 18 (1995): 248–50; Alted, *Política del Nuevo Estado*, 239.

franquismo's prestige throughout the world, as the title of an article by Pemán, "Los mejores con nosotros" (The Best Are with Us), smugly suggested.[84] At the helm of this enterprise—or so Falla read in the newspapers—was "Presidente, don Manuel de Falla, de la Academia de Bellas Artes."[85]

With growing surprise, the composer followed reports of the inauguration ceremonies. On 6 January 1938, representatives of "Spanish intellectual life" and high-ranking Nationalists met at the University of Salamanca, Spain's most venerable institution of higher learning. For many, it was also a symbol of frustrated academic freedom: it was at Salamanca that the Inquisition apprehended Fray Luis de León in 1573 for subverting the faith, who, released after five years of torture and imprisonment, is said to have begun his next class by saying "Dicebamus hesterna die" (As we were saying the other day). Salamanca was also the site of the famous confrontation between Unamuno, the dean, and General Millán Astray, the founder of the Spanish Foreign Legion. Like Falla, Unamuno had initially supported the Republic but became disillusioned. At a university ceremony for the Día de la Raza (on 12 October) shortly after the outbreak of the war, Millán Astray began to perorate on the glories of Castile, while his followers began chanting the Foreign Legion slogan "Viva la Muerte" (Long Live Death) and the Nationalist chant "¡España!," after which three cries of "¡Una!," "¡Grande!," and "¡Libre!" resounded (Spain—one, great, free). This was more than Unamuno could stomach. But upon confronting the one-eyed, one-armed general (Millán Astray's battle injuries had earned him the moniker "el glorioso mutilado"), the dean was greeted with derisive screams, including "Death to intellectuals!" Unamuno then uttered his famously prophetic pronouncement, "Venceréis pero no convenceréis," which translates rather less euphoniously as "You will win, but you will not convince."[86] The next day Unamuno was removed from his postion as dean only to die in disillusionment a few months later.

Had Falla attended the Instituto ceremony, he would have been expected to answer in the affirmative to the question, "Do you swear by God and by your Guardian Angel to serve Spain perpetually and loyally, under the Empire and the standard of her living tradition, in her Catholicism, which the Pontiff of Rome incarnates; in her continuity, represented by the Caudillo, Savior of our people?"[87] Certainly he would have disapproved of any oath that linked Franco, the Caudillo, so closely to the Pope. But once aware of the nomination, neither did he insist on severing all connections with the Instituto, as is sometimes suggested.

True, Falla was irked by the manner in which the nomination had been publicized without his consent and he immediately sought Pemán's aid. In a telegram of

84. José María Pemán, "Los mejores con nosotros," *Orientación Española* (Buenos Aires), April 1938, cited in Alted, *Política del Nuevo Estado*, 241n10.

85. "En la histórica Universidad de Salamanca," *Patria*, 7 January 1938, 7. See also "Creation of the Spanish Institute," *Spain* 1, no. 19 (8 February 1938): 13.

86. Preston, *Concise History of the Spanish Civil War*, 156.

87. Alted, *Política del Nuevo Estado*, 240.

6 January, the composer explained that despite "complete respect for and loyalty to his Excellency the Generalísimo," health problems would prevent him from serving. Unable to assume such an "elevated and weighty responsibility," he asked that the Instituto find someone who could "effectively carry out the mission, as honorable as it is delicate, that in any case I judge to be too much for me."[88] A letter of 18 January reiterated these points.

Certainly Falla's argument was strong, and his lack of experience in governmental or administrative activities confirms just how much his name mattered to the Nationalists. If, as Paul Bowles once commented, Falla was known "to everyone in his country . . . from the porter who carries your trunk from the station, to the taxi-driver, to the grocer-woman," the Nationalists' targeting of him as the one who would lend the greatest luster to their profession of intellectuality was shrewd indeed.[89] Pemán hastened to assure Falla that unstable health was no obstacle, since the vice presidents and the rest of the Council would fulfill all his administrative responsibilities.[90] But, as he had done with *Cruz y Raya*, Falla opposed a nominal appointment on principle. Although he took pains to praise the Instituto's purpose and expressed gratitude for the invitation to serve Spain (adding that this was a duty every Spaniard "who deserves to be one must always be ready to perform"),[91] he consistently reiterated his unwillingness to assume responsibility for an entity he felt unqualified to lead. As for Pemán, after receiving three communications from Falla in the space of two weeks, each slightly more agitated than its predecessor, he finally gave up trying to persuade the composer. On 3 February, he reported to Falla that the nomination, a state matter, had been forwarded to Sainz Rodrigo, who in addition to being minister of education was a vice president of the Instituto. Falla expressed relief and gratitude.[92] But the wheels of bureaucracy turned with glacial speed, and throughout the spring of 1938 Falla continued to see himself described in the press as president of the Instituto de España.[93] Again he appealed to Pemán, and by late May he was using uncustomarily strong language, complaining to his usually loyal ally that "I fear that, as at other times, you will forget the matter again."[94]

88. Telegram, 6 January 1938, cited in Sánchez García, *La correspondencia inédita*, 48.

89. Letter, Paul Bowles to Bruce Morrissette, 7 November 1934, cited in Jeffrey Miller, ed., *In Touch: The Letters of Paul Bowles* (London: HarperCollins, 1994), 143.

90. Letter, Pemán to Falla, 11 January 1938, cited in Sánchez García, *La correspondencia inédita*, 49.

91. Letter, Falla to Pemán, 26 January 1938, cited in Sánchez García, *La correspondencia inédita*, 49–50.

92. Letter, Falla to Pemán, 12 February 1938, cited in Sánchez García, *La correspondencia inédita*, 50.

93. See, for example, "Instituto de España," *Unidad*, 21 April 1938, AMF press file.

94. Letter, Falla to Pemán, 20 May 1938, cited in Sánchez García, *La correspondencia inédita*, 52.

Finally, a decree of 18 June 1938 exempted the composer from "all executive functions related to the post of president of the Institute of Spain" for reasons of health.[95]

The key term here is *executive functions*, for at no point did Falla completely break
with the Instituto. In a letter to Sainz Rodrigo of 18 July 1938 (the second anniversary of the uprising), he asked: "I only have to request of you . . . that when it is
necessary that *my name appear linked to the position*, the status of 'elect' or 'without
function' be added to the title, or whatever form you find appropriate, since the
contrary would leave neither one of us in peace."[96] Was Falla's agitation over the
appointment grounded in his habitual fear of "deformation," that is, the deception
any nominal title implied? Did he accept the qualifications of "elect" or "without
function" because he was afraid not to or was there some sincerity in his halfway
position? Even if we allow for a degree of routine grandstanding another portion of
his letter to Sainz Rodrigo, coupled with his acceptance of the honorary position,
hardly reflects a desire to remain "above the workings of politics." He continued:
"In these days of anniversary, full of deep significance for all true Spaniards and also
because of the elevation—never more justified—of our undefeated Generalísimo
to the highest rank of the Army and of the Navy, receive and convey to His Excellency my repeated support, along with my most respectful and devoted greeting."[97]

By early 1938, Falla had changed. Whereas he had previously gone to great lengths
to explain his distance from politics, he was now willing to accept a degree of public affiliation, albeit a tenuous one, with the Nationalists. He also confided his sentiments to personal acquaintances, that is, to individuals with whom no ulterior
motive or desire for political expediency was imaginable. To Antonio Freixas in
Argentina, for example, he confided how much he suffered "with any war, however
just it may be, as in the present case" (de todo guerra por justa que sea, como en el
caso presente); tellingly, in addition to the peace symbol, "Pax," he also penciled
in the Nationalist slogan "¡Arriba España!" below his signature.[98] This was also a
decisive point in the war: in February, the counteroffensive on the Teruel front
(Aragón) ended with Franco's forces and Hitler's Condor Legion taking the city.
Despite the Republican troops' bravery, the Nationalists' material strength was

95. Alted, *Política del Nuevo Estado*, 247.
96. "Sólo he de rogarle . . . que cuando deba aparecer *mi nombre unido al cargo*, se
añada al título del mismo la cualidad de 'electo' o de 'sin ejercicio,' o cualquiera otra forma
que Vd. juzgue oportuna, pues de lo contrario no nos dejarán tranquilos ni a Vd. ni a
mí" [emphasis added] (letter [draft], Falla to Sainz Rodrigo, 18 July 1938, AMF correspondence file 7562).
97. "En estos días de aniversario, llenos de alta significación para todo verdadero
español y también con motivo de la exaltación, nunca más justificada, de nuestro invicto
Generalísimo a la más alta Jerarquía del Ejército y la Armada, reciba usted y transmita a
Su Excelencia mi adhesión reiterada, unida al más respetuoso y devoto saludo" (letter
[draft copy], Falla to Sainz Rodrigo, 18 July 1938, AMF correspondence file 7562).
98. Letter, Falla to Freixas (carbon copy), 25 May 1938, AMF correspondence file 6997.

bound to prevail, as defeats at Brunete and Belchite had already shown.[99] As for the Republic's decline in nonmilitary matters, in early March the Burgos government promulgated a law condemning as treason workers' strikes; shortly thereafter, the Republic's civil marriage law was repealed. There was a mounting sense that the Republic was doomed, as internal disputes intensified between those who sought immediate peace negotiations and those who would fight to the bitter end, even in the face of the Nationalist offensives then battering the Mediterranean region.[100]

During this period, Falla had the disconcerting experience of having his own death announced on the radio. In the early days of the war, Gen. Queipo de Llano had taken over the station in Seville to expedite the Nationalists' seizure of that city, and as the war progressed he became a radio personality–a loathsome one.[101] He delivered flamboyant, sometimes drunken, broadcasts in which he called the "Reds" all manner of names, bragged about the sexual prowess of his Moorish forces, and spared no detail of the conflict, however grisly.[102] If a press transcript of Queipo de Llano's announcement is to be believed, at some point in February 1938 the general observed that "when . . . the Glorious Nationalist Movement erupted, Maestro Falla joined up, with decisiveness, with energy, firmly, without fear of anything or anybody."[103] When we remember Falla's congratulatory letter to Queipo de Llano of October 1936, this interpretation of the composer's "loyalty" is not completely far-fetched, although the general's account of Falla's "fearlessness" is pure hyperbole: Falla "risked everything for the homeland, he risked his life, that of his family, his patrimony, everything, so that Spain might continue on the imperial paths that must lead her to finer destinies."[104] A few days later, however, the laconic headline "El maestro Falla no ha muerto" (Maestro Falla Has Not Died) appeared in the press. Evidently a typist had confused the name "Falla" with "Farias," a governor from Seville who had passed away the day before.[105] The reporter effusively praised Falla as the "glory of Nationalist Spain." We can imagine the composer shrugging his shoulders over the whole incident.

Finally, Falla gave the Nationalists what they wanted. His public statement of support, albeit a muted one, appeared in *Spain,* an English-language magazine

99. Preston, *Concise History of the Spanish Civil War,* 203.

100. Foard, "Chronology of the Spanish Civil War," 511.

101. A cartoon of Queipo de Llano behind the microphone (by a French artist) can be seen in Wilson, *Spanish Civil War,* 44.

102. Jackson, *Spanish Republic and the Civil War,* 298.

103. "Cuando . . . estalló el Glorioso Movimiento Nacional, el Maestro Falla se incorporó a él, con decisión, con energía, firmemente, sin temer a nada ni a nadie" ("Última charla del General Queipo de Llano," unidentified newspaper, February 1938, AMF press file).

104. "Lo arriesgó todo por su Patria, arriesgó su vida, la de su familia, su patrimonio, todo, para que España pudiera seguir por los caminos imperiales que habrán de llevarla a sus destinos mejores" ("Última charla del General Queipo de Llano").

105. Undated, unidentified press clipping, AMF correspondence file 7459.

published by the Spanish Press Services. That London-based entity was directed by Nationalist interests and promoted Franco's cause through leaflets, posters, and magazines.[106] *Spain* ran stories on "red mercenaries" and described the International Brigades as "the riff-raff of Europe . . . [who] stand for the negative principles of barbarism in this deadly assault . . . against Western civilization."[107] Obviously this editorial stance was by no means unanimously accepted throughout the British Isles: among the more notable supporters of the "riff-raff" were Samuel Beckett, C. Day Lewis, W. H. Auden, Stephen Spender, and George Orwell.[108]

Falla's declaration of solidarity appeared twice in *Spain*, first on 1 February 1938 under the title "My Hope" and then more prominently as a cover story with photo (and slight editorial changes) in the March issue. As always, he took pains to qualify his position and couch his views in Christian terms:

> History teaches, and experience proves, that nothing can be truly fruitful that is not animated by the spirit of God, in the absence of which Evil becomes the sole motive force. To pursue the deliberate aim of depriving man of the knowledge of Supreme Truth is, therefore, the most heinous crime that can be committed.
>
> For that reason, though I am not concerned with politics and every war causes me intense pain, I hail the National Rising in the hope that we shall no longer hear blasphemies shouted in our streets, see our churches and our cemeteries profaned and wrecked, our libraries looted, our treasures of art collected in the course of centuries rifled, and the ministers and servants of God subjected to martyrdom, all of which deeds have been committed with the satanic aim of eradicating from the conscience of man the eternal essence of his divine origin.
>
> This is what I feel and say in the Christian conviction that God is supreme, and in the firm hope that the day will come when Spain and all Nations may enjoy the blessings of True Peaces and the Justice, Equity and Mercy of Our Lord.[109]

Why this sudden public exposure? It may be that the appointment to the Instituto prompted Falla to seek a way of proving his loyalty to the Nationalists while still trying to distance himself from that organization. Yet we know that his statement was sincere. On 8 October 1938, he sent Roland-Manuel a copy of it (in Spanish), adding

106. The Burgos government also established a Tourism Department, which enticed visitors to "National Spain" through English-language brochures advertising tours of the "war routes" and urging the prospective tourist to "form [his or her] own judgment of the real situation in National Spain to-day." A sample brochure is reproduced in Wilson, *Spanish Civil War*, 138–39.

107. "The Ishmaels of Europe," *Spain* 1, no. 19 (8 February 1938): 8.

108. See Murray A. Sperber, ed., *And I Remember Spain: A Spanish Civil War Anthology* (New York: Collier, 1974).

109. See Manuel de Falla, "My Hope," *Spain* 1, no. 18 (1 February 1938): 3. On page 13 of the 8 February issue, Falla's photograph appears in a report on the founding of the Instituto de España, of which he is identified as president.

"maybe you already know of [it]."[110] He also explained himself to his young acquaintance from the United States, Gilbert Chase, with whom he had earlier discussed the possibility of performing *Atlántida* at the World's Fair. Unlike the vast majority of U.S. intellectuals, Chase supported the Nationalists, echoing Falla's own hope for "a united and Catholic Spain" and confiding in the composer his frustration that "hardly anyone" in the United States understood "the real truth about Spain."[111] Yet Falla's support is anything but unequivocal. He "hail[ed] the Nationalist uprising" not because of its political policies, institutions, or leaders but because it offered at least some "hope" that religion would be protected. For Falla, the Republic had utterly failed on this count, however impressive its agenda for the poor. Seeing no other possibility, he threw in his lot with what he considered the only viable alternative.

To be sure, Falla rested his support on faith and hope, which accounts for the open-ended title of his brief essay. He could have remained silent rather than confide his hope to an international audience. He may have felt, however, that with a few judiciously chosen words he could avoid further pressure from Burgos and still remain true to his principles.

What he failed to avoid was bitterness and bewilderment in Republican circles. Composer Enrique Casal Chapí, grandson of *zarzuela* composer Ruperto Chapí, reacted with an impassioned article on the grave implications for Spanish culture of Falla's declaration:

> A speech can reveal a man, but it can also ruin him. And Manuel de Falla has uttered one of the latter kind. An *official* speech, with all the aggravations implied by such a thing, taking place between traitors and enemies of the Spanish people. They require that the two or three artistic and intellectual figures in Spain who, by whatever means, find themselves on their side, serve them; even more when such are so scarce. And Manuel de Falla has fallen into the trap.[112]

110. Letter, Falla to Roland-Manuel, 8 October 1938, AMF correspondence file 7521.

111. "Creyendo en la España Católica y unida, soy partidario del movimiento Nacionalista . . . Pues encuentro aquí que casi nadie sabe la verdad acerca de España, ya persisten en creer que el Gobierno ateísta y anarquista es un gobierno lealmente democrático" (letter, Chase to Falla, 7 May 1938, AMF correspondence file 6883). It should also be noted that Falla's point about the "looting of libraries" and "rifling of art treasures" is misleading. Both sides took steps to protect art; in fact, the siege of Madrid is the only time Velázquez's *Las meninas* has left the Prado. See Emma Daly, "Defenders of Spain's Masterpieces: A Prado Show Honors Civil War Rescue Effort," *New York Times*, 17 July 2003, B1, 5.

112. "Un discurso puede revelar a un hombre, pero puede también hundirlo. Y Manuel de Falla ha pronunciado uno de estos últimos. Un discurso *oficial*, con todas las agravantes que tal cosa supone teniendo lugar entre los traidores y enemigos del pueblo español. Necesitan estos que los dos o tres valores artísticos e intelectuales de España que, sea por lo que sea, se encuentran en su zona, les sirvan; tanto más cuando tan escasos son. Y Manuel de Falla ha caído en el lazo" (Enrique Casal Chapí, "Música en la Guerra: Manuel de Falla," *Hora de España* 3, nos. 11–15 [1938]: 491).

Painting with a broad brush Falla's presidency of the Instituto as "a job with more shine than substance" (un puesto de relumbrón), Casal Chapí wondered about the composer's mental state, remarking, "For those of us who know something of Falla's life, this position of his seems to us the end result of his mental perturbation or the result of a fear that is perhaps subconscious."[113] Like Unamuno, with his nagging uncertainties, Falla was a "victim of mirages, of certain concepts that the enemies of the people and of liberty—which, when all is said and done, are the same thing—manipulate to their convenience."[114]

Falla's music, Casal Chapí held, "has its deepest roots in the people of Spain. And this people . . . is one that does not let itself be dominated, nor stepped on, nor reduced by petty tyrants from within, much less by tyrants from without. It is to this people . . . that Falla owes his magnificent oeuvre."[115] Obviously, for Casal Chapí, Falla's declaration was nothing short of a betrayal of this highly resilient community.

As for Falla's legacy, Casal Chapí ends on a note of resignation:

> We'll continue listening to the *Siete canciones populares españolas* and *El amor brujo* and the Concerto, because nowadays we can do without a car, or other material comforts, but what is indispensable to us is everything that has contributed and still contributes to our formation and spiritual life, and the music Falla has written is included in all that. But listening to it will no longer be anything to us but an aesthetic pleasure. In the perfection and in the character of that music there will always be the indication of the position, false at the very least, that the one who wrote it takes today, and this would also involve . . . yearning and sadness, yes, but at the same time an exaltation of our ideal, never a faltering in our struggle.[116]

113. "Para los que sabemos algo de la vida de Falla, esta posición suya nos puede aparecer como final de su perturbación mental o como resultado de un miedo tal vez subconsciente" (Casal Chapí, "Música en la Guerra," 491).

114. "[Falla es] víctima del espejismo de determinados conceptos que los enemigos del pueblo y de la libertad—que, en fin de cuentas, son la misma cosa—manejan a su conveniencia" (Casal Chapí, "Música en la Guerra," 492).

115. "Tiene sus más hondas raices en el pueblo de España. Y este pueblo es . . . el que no se deja dominar, ni pisar, ni reducir por los tiranuelos de dentro y, mucho menos, por los tiranos de fuera. A este pueblo . . . es al que Falla debe su magnífica obra" (Casal Chapí, "Música en la Guerra," 491).

116. "Seguiremos escuchando las *Siete canciones populares* y *El amor brujo* y el Concerto, porque nosotros hoy podemos prescindir de un automóvil como de otras tantas comodidades materiales, pero nos es imprescindible todo aquello que ha contribuido y contribuye a nuestra formación y vida espiritual; y la música que ha escrito Falla está ahí comprendida. Pero su audición no podrá ser ya para nosotros solamente un goce estético. En la perfección y en el carácter de esa música estará siempre el índice de la posición, falsa cuando menos, que hoy toma quien la escribió, y esto entrañaría también . . . añoranza y tristeza, sí, pero al propio tiempo una exaltación de nuestro ideal, nunca un desánimo en nuestra lucha" (Casal Chapí, "Música en la Guerra," 492).

Paradoxical here is the fact that both Casal Chapí and Falla believed that music could remain solely music: for Casal Chapí "an aesthetic pleasure" and for Falla "above the workings of politics." While Casal Chapí annihilated the very possibility of meaning in Falla's music, the Nationalists, as we have seen, invested it with quasi-religious hyperbole. Falla's response was the atrophy of his creative powers, a condition to which he was no stranger and which had already painfully slowed his progress on *Atlántida*.

By the time Casal Chapí's words were in print, Falla would have read of Hitler's annexation of Austria in March 1938, which was largely ignored by the Western democracies. He would have been aware of the Nationalists' continued attacks in Aragón and night raids by Italian bombers on Barcelona. Against this depressing backdrop, Falla was also preparing for another surgery. In early April, part of his lung was collapsed, a once common treatment for tuberculosis, with which he had recently been diagnosed. During his slow convalescence, Falla also dealt with various unrelated aggravations. He had reason to believe that his music had been used without his permission in the 1937 movie musical *One Hundred Men and a Girl*, a frothy film in which Stokowski, playing himself, conducts an orchestra of unemployed Depression-era musicians galvanized by the tirelessly perky Deanna Durbin.[117] Luckily this was a false alarm, as Chase verified by contacting Universal Pictures.[118] Another less-than-satisfying situation concerned Ernesto Halffter's orchestration of the *Siete canciones populares españolas*. Beginning in early 1939, he and Falla became embroiled in protracted discussions over Halffter's musical strategies, many of which Falla found questionable and on which he laboriously commented to Halffter in writing.[119]

As Falla's creative light continued to dim and his health pursued its slow decline, the Civil War ground to a close. By January 1939, the Nationalists were surging through Catalonia and on the twenty-sixth Barcelona fell with barely a struggle. The next day, mass was celebrated in the Plaça de Catalunya for the first time since the outbreak of the war. On 30 January, Falla congratulated Sainz Rodrigo on "the liberation of Barcelona" and instructed him to "once more do me the honor of conveying to the Generalísimo these cordial sentiments with . . . admiring gratitude"[120] In early February, Azaña and other government officials fled across the border into France, as did streams of refugees. Madrid, however, had still not fallen. But in March 1939, the same month in which Hitler obliterated what remained of Czechoslovakia, street fighting between the communists and other groups broke out in the now desperate Spanish capital. Finally, on 27 March, the Nationalists entered Madrid,

117. Letter, Falla to Chase, 12 December 1938, AMF correspondence file 6883.

118. Letter, Ruth Morrow, Publicity Department, Universal Pictures Company, Inc., to Chase, 8 February 1939, copy in AMF correspondence file 6883.

119. Acker, "Ernesto Halffter," 51–52.

120. "Una vez más me haga el honor de transmitir al Generalísimo estos cordiales sentimientos con . . . admirativa gratitud" (letter, Falla to Sainz Rodrigo, 30 January 1939, AMF correspondence file 7562).

and, as in Barcelona, hordes of refugees fled the city. On 1 April, Franco proclaimed victory.

Despite the rapidity with which Falla's enthusiasm for the Republic had plummeted on the eve of the Civil War, the Right had also failed to move him, as his repudiation of "tradition" and Maeztu's proposed "conservative counterrevolution" shows. Once war broke out, he was terrified by the repression in Granada. Yet he risked his personal safety to investigate Lorca's fate and afterward expressed his displeasure with the Nationalists' indiscriminate application of the death penalty. Only two months after Lorca's death, however, Falla was writing a double-edged letter to Queipo de Llano: while congratulating the general with apparent sincerity for his contributions to the Nationalist cause, he reiterated his "voluntary separation" from politics. Throughout the war, Falla relied on Nationalist rhetoric primarily when he was pleading on behalf of his friends, both Republicans and Nationalists. But he also drew on its high-flown diction when he had no apparent motive for doing so, such as when writing to his friends abroad. Other, more public gestures included composing the *Himno marcial*, the appointment to the Instituto de España, and the declaration in *Spain*. If the ill-fated *Himno* was largely prompted by Orgaz's importuning, Falla's failure to separate himself from the Instituto complicates his frequently stated resistance to political affiliation. As we have seen, by early 1938, and for reasons not completely clear, he decided to publicly state in *Spain* his hitherto private reactions to the political situation. Yet the declaration's subdued tone and emphasis on an unseen future cast a shadow on any partisan fervor the Nationalists attached to it.

We may never know exactly what Falla experienced between 1936 and early 1938. All evidence depicts a confused, sickly man who would alternately subject himself to public scrutiny or isolate himself, depressed, in his *carmen*. Consequently, he managed to confuse Republicans and Nationalists alike. For Casal Chapí, it was obvious that Falla had "fallen into the trap." For Sainz Rodrigo, however, whom Falla had congratulated in "these days of anniversary, full of deep significance for all true Spaniards," the matter was otherwise, as is evident in his own recollection:

> Manuel de Falla was well known throughout the world, but he was a Catholic ... well, a Catholic of the Left, who, moreover, didn't want to commit himself clearly to us. He ... accepted not too graciously [the presidency of the Instituto] and didn't stop until he had succeeded in weasling out of the responsibility under the pretext of delicate health. In fact, what interested us in Falla was his name, for we thought that in Europe people would say: "Well, they can't be such barbarians if they're appointing Falla to a directorial position of a cultural organization." Falla was a man with an equivocal attitude, and he never dared to take a stand.[121]

121. Interview, Alicia Alted and Pedro Sainz Rodríguez, February–March 1981, cited in Alted, *Política del Nuevo Estado*, 247n44.

In claiming that Falla "never dared to take a stand," of course, Sainz Rodrigo exaggerated. But in assessing Falla as "a man with an equivocal attitude" he was closer to the mark. However *un*equivocal his faith, Falla's day-to-day conduct was hesitant and tortured. Buffeted by the harshness of "circumstance," Falla's "equivocal attitude" was dictated by principles not of this world. Sainz Rodrigo could not have known that what looked like indecisiveness was in fact Falla's painstaking search, now exacerbated by the war, for the truth. But, although the composer's tendency to doubt, weigh, and seek divine guidance over the smallest of matters was, quite naturally, affected by the war, it was not brought on by it. Rather, "quibbling, conjecture, and vacillation," as Fedriani had tactlessly put it decades earlier, had always been a part of Falla's personality. Now it was being tested in terms of life and death. Falla's tepid Nationalist sympathies, linked solely to his faith, cannot be denied. Yet it is nonetheless ironic that the composer's consuming fear of "deformation," coupled with his habitual need to clarify and reclarify his position, even in an environment rife with distortion and lack of comprehension, ultimately obscured the view his compatriots—on both sides—held of him during the most cataclysmic period in twentieth-century Spain.

Chapter 9

Seeking the Lost Continent

With the war's end, the reconstruction of Spain began. Although officials sought to maintain an appearance of normalcy, many Spaniards suffered material deprivation, ranging from food shortages to lack of basic household supplies. Worse, the victors' desire for retribution was sweeping: the Law of Political Responsibilities made it a crime to oppose the Nationalist movement, and civil liberties were throttled.[1] Censorship, which remained in effect in various forms until Franco's death in 1975, was imposed not only in the media but in dress codes and public behavior. Most horrifying of all were executions in vast numbers of "enemies of the state," often without due process. Not for nothing has the postwar repression been described as "unquestionably the darkest phase of the Franco regime."[2]

ARGENTINA AND SELF-IMPOSED EXILE

Still, Falla could now turn his attention to other things, such as the invitation he had received in late January (in his capacity as "president" of the Instituto de España) from the Institución Cultural Española (ICE) of Buenos Aires. Would Falla be willing to conduct his works in a series of four concerts of Spanish music in that city's Teatro

---

1. Paul Preston, *The Politics of Revenge: Fascism and the Military in Twentieth-Century Spain* (London: Unwin Hyman, 1990), 41.
2. Mitchell, *Betrayal of the Innocents*, 99.

Colón later that fall? Rather than pleading ill health, as he had so often done in recent years, Falla decided to undertake the long trip. On 1 April, the same day Franco proclaimed the defeat of the "Red Army," the composer wrote Rafael Vehils, president of the ICE. While accepting the invitation, Falla commented that "in these moments of jubilation for our country, because of the peace achieved after so much pain and sacrifice, it's doubly gratifying for me to offer myself to you, Mr. President," a sentiment he may have penned with the censor in mind, given that much of Spain was anything but jubilant.[3] Without knowing it, Falla was beginning an entirely new chapter of his life.

For Buenos Aires, he decided to finish the four-movement suite, *Homenajes* (Tributes), which he had begun thinking about in 1938, and now resumed work on (see figure 18). This seemed feasible enough: for the first movement, he would simply use the *Fanfare sobre el nombre de E. F. Arbós* from 1934, while movements 2 and 3 would be orchestrations of the 1920 guitar piece *Homenaje a Debussy* (here entitled "A Claude Debussy: Elegía de la guitarra") and the 1935 piano piece *Pour le tombeau de Paul Dukas* (here entitled "A Paul Dukas: Spes Vitae"), respectively. The "Elegía" juxtaposes flashes of muted but arresting colors, as in the dusky initial statement of the principal theme in the violas, later punctuated by flourishes in the harp against *sul ponticello non saltando* interjections in the strings (rehearsal 8). "A Paul Dukas: Spes Vitae" works better in its original version, however, for, although Falla's orchestration illuminates some of its dense harmonies, the end result lacks the searing introspection of the piano piece. What *is* effective, however, is Falla's insertion of a brief reminiscence of the *Fanfare*, clear and direct, between the Debussy and Dukas tributes, perhaps as a subtle allusion to the proximity of light and shadow.

The fourth and final *homenaje*, "Pedrelliana," draws on themes from Pedrell's *La celestina*. As we have seen, Falla had admired his mentor's unperformed opera for decades. He was not alone: after the piano-vocal score appeared in 1903, the French critic Camille Bellaigue compared *La celestina* to *Tristan und Isolde* and tried (unsuccessfully) to arrange a performance of it at the Opéra-Comique.[4] Barcelona's Liceu rejected *La celestina* as well, an injustice Falla registered in his 1922 obituary essay for Pedrell, which is largely a philippic against the Spanish musical establishment. To be sure, Casals performed excerpts from *La celestina* in Barcelona in 1921, that is, during Pedrell's lifetime.[5] But, as Falla noted dryly in his essay, many in Casals's audience were unaware of Pedrell's existence and thought they were listen-

3. "En estos momentos de júbilo para nuestra Patria por la paz conseguida después de tanto dolor y sacrificio, me es doblemente grato ofrecerme a Vd. Sr. President" (letter, Falla to Vehils, 1 April 1939, AMF correspondence file 7738).

4. Remarks by Bellaigue, as well as Collet and Henri de Curzon, are in Goubault, *La critique musicale dans la presse française*, 471–72.

5. Manuel de Falla, "Felipe Pedrell," *La Revue Musicale* 4, no. 4 (February 1923): 1–11, reprinted in Falla, *Escritos*, 84–99.

Figure 18. Falla at the piano in his home in Granada just before leaving for Argentina, September 1939. (Reprinted by kind permission of the Archivo Manuel de Falla)

ing to a posthumous work by a seventeenth-century composer![6] Perhaps to redress his compatriots' sluggishness of two decades ago, in *Homenajes* Falla builds the rest of the suite to the last movement by making it the longest of the four. Rejecting *La celestina*'s Wagnerian sonorities, Falla instead emphasizes the opera's folkloric elements, drawing on its dancelike, tonal melodies, with their modal coloring and "open" harmonies (see, e.g., *Homenajes*, rehearsal 5). This selective glimpse of *La celestina* also incorporates recurring horn calls, which link "Pedrelliana" to both the opening "Fanfare" and the interlude between movements 2 and 3. Thus, the final movement of Falla's last completed work glances backward while it acknowledges the musical heritage of his native land and one of its principal promoters. But below the surface lurks Falla's frustration with Spain's musical infrastructure, which, as it turned out, would continue to affect him even in Argentina.

In his correspondence with Vehils, Falla requested that his activities be limited to conducting so as to avoid the fatigue of interviews and banquets.[7] While planning his travel, however, he felt fit enough to include Italy in his itinerary and wrote Goffredo Petrassi about stopping in Venice on his way to Buenos Aires.[8] Although this turned out to be impossible once the dates for Argentina were set, Falla told his Italian colleague of his hope to visit Venice the following summer, that is, once he was back in Spain.[9] Also related to Falla's projected return was newfound optimism over *Atlántida*. He now seemed reasonably confident of finishing it, writing Sert that "in September, God willing, we'll leave for Buenos Aires, where I must conduct some concerts; I wish you could come, too! In any case I very much want for us to see one another when I return, for I hope to be able to *push on* with our *Atlántida*, which has suffered so many long interruptions in these last years."[10] Clearly Falla had every intention of going back to Spain after a brief sojourn in America.

With the ever loyal María del Carmen, the composer sailed from Barcelona on 2 October 1939. Hitler's invasion of Poland a few weeks before had greatly discouraged Falla, who now expressed relief at leaving Europe for a time.[11] (As in 1914, Spain declared neutrality, Franco's unofficial support of Hitler notwithstanding.) In the press's coverage of Falla's departure, Espinós, now an ardent *franquista*, resurrected the *La Unión* incident one more time, remarking that Falla, "courted for a certain ceremony during the secular Republic, desisted, courteously and energetically, end-

6. Falla, "Felipe Pedrell," 98.

7. Letter, Falla to Vehils, 13 June 1939, AMF correspondence file 7738.

8. See letter, Falla to Petrassi, 8 April 1939, AMF correspondence file 7412.

9. Letter (draft), Falla to Petrassi, Granada, 24 June 1939, AMF correspondence file 7412.

10. "En Septiembre, Dios mediante, saldremos para Buenos Aires, donde debo dirigir unos conciertos, ojalá Vd. pudiera venir también! De todos modos deseo mucho que nos veamos al regreso, pues espero poder allí dar un *empujón* al trabajo a nuestro *Atlántida*, que tan largas interrupciones ha sufrido en estos últimos años" (letter [pencil draft, with emendations in ink], Falla to Sert, 12 July 1939, AMF correspondence file 7619/2).

11. Personal recollection, Sergio de Castro, public lecture, Granada, July 1992.

ing up by saying: where God and His Church are attacked and persecuted, there is nothing for me to do."[12] Now, Espinós went on, Falla was going to Latin America as "the ambassador prince of music," a bit of hyperbole that probably nettled the composer.

Their ship, the *Neptunia*, stopped in Rio de Janeiro, where passengers could briefly disembark. María del Carmen, whose worldview had been almost exclusively shaped by domestic routine and her brother's needs, was enchanted with this fleeting glimpse of Brazil. She confided to Germán and his family that "seeing those marvelous jungles, I was filled with admiration, to the point of thinking that the trip was worth it for this; I can count it as one of the best moments of my life."[13] As María del Carmen reveled in what seemed like paradise, Falla received a telegram from the Franco government (see figure 19). Much the same as he had been courted during the war, he now learned that a lifetime pension of 25,000 pesetas would be his when he returned to Spain. (Although Falla had every intention of going back, the government was taking no chances.) This was neither the moment to think of changing his immediate plans nor the time to involve himself in political machinations, however. On 18 October, he and his sister arrived in Buenos Aires.

Political and artistic ferment was palpable in Latin America's most European capital, with its Parisian-style boulevards, café life, and distinctive neighborhoods. Ousted in 1930 by a military coup, the Radical Party had won back control of Congress in 1937; even more powerful influences on Argentine politics were electoral fraud and collaboration with the military.[14] In non-Radical circles, pro-Axis sentiments had begun to take hold, along with an isolationist, ultranationalist mentality that helped set the stage for the ascent of Juan Perón, whom Franco would later protect.[15] As for the musical scene in 1939, Buenos Aires' two principal orchestras were the Orquesta Radio El Mundo and that of the Teatro Colón; three more would be founded in the coming decade. The Colón, which featured both opera and concert music, attracted a wide range of Argentine and international artists.[16] Composers

12. "Requerido para cierta actuación durante la República laica, la esquivó, cortés y enérgico, viniendo a decir: donde se ataca y persigue a Dios y a su Iglesia, yo no tengo nada que hacer" (Víctor Espinós, "Música: Falla va a América, el príncipe embajador," unidentified press clipping, 4 October 1939, AMF press file).

13. "Al ver aquellas maravillosas selvas me quedé admirada y hasta di por bien empleado el viaje; lo puedo contar como uno de los momentos mejores de mi vida" (letter, María del Carmen to Germán, his wife María Luisa López, and daughter Maribel, 15 November 1939, AMF correspondence file 7816).

14. Thomas E. Skidmore and Peter H. Smith, *Modern Latin America*, 5th ed. (New York and Oxford: Oxford University Press, 2001), 82–85.

15. David Rock, *Argentina, 1516–1987: From Spanish Colonization to Alfonsín*, rev. and exp. ed. (Berkeley: University of California Press, 1987), 358.

16. See Roberto Caamaño, *La historia del Teatro Colón, 1908–1968*, 3 vols. (Buenos Aires: Editorial Cinetea, 1979).

Figure 19. The Franco government offers Falla a lifetime pension in a telegram received aboard the *Neptunia*. (Reprinted by kind permission of the Archivo Manuel de Falla)

such as Juan Carlos Paz, Luis Gianneo, and Juan José Castro were experimenting with serialism, neoclassicism, nationalism, and jazz, and a twenty-three-year-old Alberto Ginastera, whose exuberant ballet suite, *Panambí*, had triumphed two years earlier at the Colón, had just completed his training at the National Conservatory.[17] Argentina's rich tradition of popular music attracted not only Ginastera and his colleagues but also the North American commercial music industry, as the ongoing popularity of the tango attests. Indeed, with Europe at war Latin American markets, including cultural markets, looked especially promising to the United States. Under the sway of the Good Neighbor Policy, music and film sought to build bridges between the two continents.[18] The results could be mixed, however, as happened with the 1940 movie *Down Argentine Way*, which provoked a furor in Buenos

17. Deborah Schwartz-Kates, "Ginastera, Alberto (Evarista)," in Sadie and Tyrell, *Revised New Grove Dictionary*, 9:875.

18. On Argentina's antagonism toward the Roosevelt administration's policy, see Rock, *Argentina*, 243–44.

Aires for its misleading and even patronizing viewpoint.[19] Other attempts by Hollywood to package the "Latin" temperament relied on similar objectification.[20]

Second only to the United States in its attractiveness to immigrants, Argentina had for decades beckoned workers and fortune seekers, mainly from Italy and Spain.[21] As a result of the Civil War, many Spanish intellectuals made Buenos Aires their home. Composers included Julián Bautista, who completed his second symphony there and taught several Argentine composers, including Alcides Lanza. Jaime Pahissa, who left Spain in 1937, explored expressionism and atonality through operas, symphonies, and symphonic poems. There were also Gregorio Martínez Sierra, who moved to Buenos Aires with Catalina Bárcena in 1936; the poet Rafael Alberti, who had been an active communist during the Republic; the historian Claudio Sánchez Albornoz; caricaturist Castelao (Alfonso Daniel Rodríguez Castelao); the actress Margarita Xirgu; and the former president of Spain, Alcalá Zamora, whose coffin was wrapped in a Republican flag when he died in Buenos Aires in 1949. There was also the high-spirited Spanish writer Ramón Gómez de la Serna (back in Spain he had appeared at a reception in blackface after a showing of the movie *The Jazz Singer*), who now mingled with the crowd at the journal *Sur*.[22] Thanks to its energetic and well-connected founder, Victoria Ocampo, that publication was a forum for some of the sharpest minds in Europe and the Americas. Contributors included Octavio Paz, Gabriela Mistral, and many native luminaries, including Jorge Luis Borges, who in addition to publishing original fiction and essays translated the poetry of Langston Hughes in its pages.[23] Also in Buenos Aires was the journalist José Mora Guarnido, an acquaintance of Falla's from "El Rinconcillo" days, on whom Falla called almost immediately to relate the harrowing experience of intervening on Lorca's behalf. (Mora Guarnido later commented on how shocked he was by Falla's diminished appearance in November 1939.) Ortega, who had fled to Paris on the outbreak of the Civil War, arrived in Buenos Aires weeks before Falla. In 1945, he returned to

19. See Walter Aaron Clark, "Doing the Samba on Sunset Boulevard: Carmen Miranda and the Hollywoodization of Latin American Music," in *From Tejano to Tango*, edited by Walter Aaron Clark (New York and London: Routledge, 2002), 267.

20. See Luis Reyes and Peter Rubie, *Hispanics in Hollywood: A Celebration of 100 Years in Film and Television* (Hollywood: Lone Eagle, 2000), esp. 18–22.

21. Skidmore and Smith, *Modern Latin America*, 71–75. Argentina is also home to 50 percent of Latin America's Jews, who began immigrating there as early as their expulsion from Spain in 1492. Cultural manifestations of immigration are summarized in Deborah Schwartz-Kates, "The *Gauchesco* Tradition as a Source of National Identity in Argentine Art Music (ca. 1890–1955)," Ph.D. diss., University of Texas, Austin, 1997, 73–82.

22. Román Gubern, *Proyector de luna: La generación del 27 y el cine* (Barcelona: Anagrama, 1999), 283–88.

23. John King, *Sur: A Study of the Argentine Literary Journal and Its Role in the Development of a Culture, 1931–1970* (Cambridge: Cambridge University Press, 1986).

Europe, and in his final, restless years turned down overtures from the Franco government before dying in Madrid in 1955.[24]

"I'll finish my latest work in your country," declared Falla on arriving in Buenos Aires. At least, this was the extravagant statement repeated in the press.[25] If accurately reported, it raises two questions: did Falla really think *Atlántida* was so far along as to be wrapped up in a single visit, or had he already decided to delay his return to Spain indefinitely, perhaps because the offer he received on the *Neptunia* had unnerved him? In any case, he immediately began preparing his concerts for the Teatro Colón, the biggest opera house in Latin America and one of the most acoustically refined in the world. With its seven tiers and French décor, the setting for the four programs of Spanish music (on 4, 11, 18, and 23 November) bordered on the magical: perhaps Falla, now an established international figure, even felt something akin to the thrill he had experienced thirty years earlier in Paris, when his good fortune in international musical circles had seemed so unreal. Conducting duties would be split with Juan José Castro (see figure 20), who helped Falla so assiduously with all the details of his stay in Buenos Aires that Falla joked with his Argentine colleague about having a "shadow" and repeatedly expressed gratitude for Castro's friendship. Works to be performed included Esplá's *Don Quijote velando las armas* (Don Quijote Keeping Watch over His Weapons), Turina's *La procesión del rocío* (The Procession of the Virgin of the Dew), Halffter's *Sinfonietta*, and selections by Granados, Pahissa, and others. Nearly all of Falla's mature output was represented, including *Noches en los jardines de España, El amor brujo*, selections from *The Three-Cornered Hat, Homenajes, Psyché*, "Soneto a Córdoba," the Harpsichord Concerto, and some "expressive versions" of the Golden Age repertory: a madrigal by Guerrero ("Prado verde y florido"), a *romance* and a *villancico* by Juan del Encina ("Qué es de tí, desconsolado" and "Tan buen ganadico"), and a *villancico* by Pedro de Escobar ("¡Ora, sus!"). For Morales's well-known motet "Emendemus in Melius," Falla used Kurt Schindler's edition of 1919, which is similar in spirit to his "expressive versions."[26] The last work of the final concert, held on 23 November (which, as journalists pointed out, was Falla's sixty-third birthday), was *El retablo de Maese Pedro*, conducted by the composer. According to an anonymous critic for *La Nación*, the public was ecstatic: "Falla, who from all appearances offered an impeccable interpretation, could appreciate anew, through the enthusiastic manifestations of applause, the admiration and sympathy that his presence has awakened in our public, to the point where it can be confirmed that in just a few

24   Gray, *The Imperative of Modernity*, 286.

25. See José María Fontova, "Terminaré mi última obra en vuestro país, nos ha dicho al llegar," *Noticias Gráficas*, 18 October 1939, cited in de Persia, *Los últimos años de Manuel de Falla*, 9.

26. Kurt Schindler, ed., *Spanish Sacred Motets* (Boston: Oliver Ditson, 1919). Falla explained this to the ICE in a letter of 28 August 1939, AMF correspondence file 7738.

Figure 20. Falla and Juan José Castro during a rehearsal at the Teatro Colón in Buenos Aires, November 1939. (Reprinted by kind permission of the Archivo Manuel de Falla)

days he has become one of the most popular figures in our artistic scene, acquiring all the respect and consideration to which his oeuvre entitles him."[27]

In addition to the warm reception at the Teatro Colón, Falla was honored by the Academia Nacional de Bellas Artes. At the ceremony, composer, conductor, and pianist Alberto Williams introduced Falla, who made brief remarks of gratitude. There was also an *homenaje* on 20 November by the local Asociación Wagneriana, one of several organizations that promoted new music.[28] Among other works, Concepción Badia performed the *Siete canciones populares españoles* with Francisco

27. "Falla, que ofreció una interpretación inobjetable bajo todo punto de vista, pudo apreciar nuevamente, a través de entusiastas manifestaciones de aplauso, la admiración y simpatía que su presencia ha despertado en nuestro público, hasta el punto de poderse afirmar que en contados dias se ha convertido en una de las figuras más populares de nuestro ambiente artístico, granjeándose todo el respeto y consideración a que por su obra se hace acreedor" ("Falla puso fin a su actuación," *La Nación*, 24 November 1939).

28. De Persia, *Los últimos años de Manuel de Falla*, 65.

Amicarelli at the piano.[29] When the audience clamored for an encore, she repeated four of the songs, two of which Falla himself played.[30] Whatever his misgivings about attending banquets and public ceremonies, Falla seems to have fully enjoyed his stay in Buenos Aires: his health was relatively stable, and he approached his work with something of his former enthusiasm. As Pahissa observed during a rehearsal, "his spirits [were] on top of the world" (una moral elevada hasta el cielo).[31]

Once the concerts were over, however, Falla did not follow his original plan of returning to Spain. Instead, he and María del Carmen traveled the approximately eight hundred kilometers northwest to the province of Córdoba, with its windswept mountain towns, pure air, and promise of rejuvenation, which Falla craved after the excitement of his triumph in Buenos Aires. They went first to the community of Villa Carlos Paz, whose hermitages bear witness to the region's strong Jesuit heritage.[32] Weeks turned into months, however, and eventually they set up house in Villa Carlos Paz. Since they had left most of their belongings in Granada, this meant starting over; by August 1940, however, they were ready to receive Rubinstein in their new home.[33] By the end of that year, they had moved to Villa del Lago, also in Córdoba Province. Soon, however, Falla became dissatisfied with his Villa del Lago house and friends began helping him look for another residence. A wealthy Spaniard, Francisco Cambó, found a chalet in the high-altitude resort of Alta Gracia, but the costly repairs it would require put the house out of Falla's reach. (Despite having been well paid for the Buenos Aires concerts he had generated little income from his compositions in recent years.) Unbeknownst to the composer, Cambó discreetly financed the repairs, and by early 1942 Falla was enjoying the newly refurbished chalet—his final abode—which he always considered a "divine gift."[34]

Unfortunately, Falla's health suffered over the course of these various moves. First, his tuberculosis flared up, and then in summer 1940 he underwent surgery for neck pains at the Spanish Hospital in Córdoba; follow-up treatments included daily injections and exposure to ultraviolet rays.[35] In September of that year, he suffered a se-

29. "La Asociación Wagneriana efectuará un homenaje al compositor Manuel de Falla," *La Nación*, 20 November 1939.

30. Juan Carlos Paz, "Música," *Reconquista*, 28 November 1939, cited in de Persia, *Los últimos años de Manuel de Falla*, 66.

31. Cited without attribution in de Persia, *Los últimos años de Manuel de Falla*, 64.

32. Since the arrival of the Jesuits in 1599, Córdoba Province has been a stronghold of the "conservative, if not reactionary" Argentine Roman Catholic Church. See Nicolas Shumway, *The Invention of Argentina* (Berkeley: University of California Press, 1991), 150.

33. See letter, Falla to Rubinstein, 10 July 1940, AMF correspondence file 7543.

34. Interview, Andrew Budwig and Mercedes Cambó (widow of Francisco), 6 April 1982, in Budwig, "Manuel de Falla's *Atlántida*," 222.

35. Letter, Falla to Padre Nemesio Otaño, 25 July 1940, AMF correspondence file 7366; see also Budwig, "Manuel de Falla's *Atlántida*," 217.

vere hemorrhage, which required several months of recuperation. Still, because his financial situation was so precarious, in December he forced himself to travel to Buenos Aires to conduct two concerts for Radio Mundo (see figure 21), even though he was not quite well. (The broadcast contains the only extant recording of Falla's voice.)[36] Especially onerous was finally giving up smoking, which his doctors had been urging for years. Now, however, he found it prudent to obey—more or less. But lack of nicotine often caused him to fall asleep while working, and he grumbled about the adverse effects of the "almost total prohibition on smoking" to Salazar, who, like many erstwhile Spanish Republicans, was living in Mexico.[37]

Even with these disruptions, Falla did not entirely stop composing. During 1941–42, he revised the orchestration of Pedrell's "Canción de la estrella," from *Los Pirineos*, giving its ungainly textures new elegance.[38] There was also *Atlántida*. Despite the composer's announcement in October 1939 that he would finish it in Argentina, progress had been minimal. In the spring of 1942, he resumed work on "La nit Suprema" and began to orchestrate the Prologue (he eventually made a fair copy of the latter in 1945).[39] Despite this slow pace, Falla found his work satisfying. In April 1944, he commented that "although [*Atlántida*] is going at a snail's pace, it continues, and not at all badly";[40] in June, he told Juan José Castro that he had gratefully returned to *Atlántida*, which had been calling him with "desperate cries."[41] In December 1944, he excitedly wrote Nin-Culmell that "thanks to the great kindness of God and the help of Our Lady (*Auxilium christianorum!*)" he had overcome his various illnesses and was maintaining "a strong and serene spirit . . . with undying hope for that poor *Atlántida*, which is what has suffered most (along with María del Carmen) from these ailments."[42]

This "strong and serene spirit" emerges in the seventh and final version of "La salve en el mar," which dates from the Argentine years.[43] Having experimented with

36. Letter, María del Carmen to Ernesto Halffter, 29 September 1940, cited in Budwig, "Manuel de Falla's *Atlántida*," 217.

37. Letter, Falla to Salazar, 29 April 1942, cited in Budwig, "Manuel de Falla's *Atlántida*," 221.

38. Antonio Gallego, "Nuevas Obras de Falla en América: 'El canto de la Estrella,' de *Los Pirineos* de Pedrell," *Inter-American Music Review* 11, no, 2 (1991): esp. 96–97.

39. Budwig, "Manuel de Falla's *Atlántida*," 8, 221.

40. "En cuanto a la *Atlántida*, aunque a paso de buey, sigue marchando y no por mal camino" (letter, Falla to José María Hernández Suárez, 9 April 1944, AMF correspondence file 7017).

41. Letter, Falla to Juan José Castro, 17 June 1944, AMF correspondence file 6835/2.

42. "[He podido soportarlo con] ánimo firme y sereno y con la ilusión siempre viva por esa pobre *Atlántida*, que es la que más viene sufriendo (en unión de María del Carmen) de estos males" (letter, Falla to Nin-Culmell, 11 December 1944, AMF correspondence file 7336).

43. The sketches are not precisely dated, but four sheets containing a continuity draft are on a type of paper manufactured in Argentina. See Budwig, "Manuel de Falla's *Atlántida*," 184.

Figure 21. Falla in a radio broadcast, Buenos Aires, 1942. (Reproduced from Jaime Pahissa, *Vida y obra de Manuel de Falla*, 2d ed., rev. and enl. Buenos Aires: Ricordi, 1956).

three-part imitative counterpoint for male voices, Falla now settled on a four-part mixed choir, although octave doublings in the upper voices (e.g., in mm. 14–21), which reduce the contrapuntal texture to three independent lines, recall the earlier conception, as do some passages of loosely imitative counterpoint (mm. 5–8). Subtle shifts in texture include homorhythmic declamation reminiscent of *falso-bordone* style, as in mm. 29–30, which are answered with cries of "Salve" in all four parts (see musical example 28). With "A" confirmed throughout as tonic, perfect balance between triadic, modally inflected harmony (as in the A minor, E minor, and D major chords at rehearsal 48) and cautious dissonance prevails. As the only Spanish-language number in the midst of this sonorous Catalan epic, the "Salve" is strikingly direct, and its lofty spirituality cuts across whatever evangelizing tone or bombast we might otherwise detect in *Atlántida*.

Even a performance seemed imminent, for at one point Falla announced to the press, "I hope that the principal parts of this symphonic poem can be premiered in the not too distant future in the Teatro Colón of Buenos Aires."[44] Evidently he had overcome his reluctance to a partial performance, perhaps having sensed that his own time was limited—and that perfection might ultimately elude him. Meanwhile, the international musical community continued to speculate over *Atlántida*. In the first edition of *The Music of Spain*, published in 1941, author Gilbert Chase stated that the composer was "still seeking that ultimate perfection which, like the vision

44. "Espero que las partes principales de este poema sinfónico puedan ser estrenadas no muy tarde en el Teatro Colón de Buenos Aires" (Iñigo de Santiago, "Manuel de Falla, desde la Argentina habla para *Arriba*," *Arriba*, 8 October 1944, AMF press file).

Musical Example 28. Falla, *Atlántida*, "La Salve en el mar," mm. 29–35. (Reprinted by kind permission of Ricordi/BMG Publications)

that drew Columbus onward, beckons him toward an illusive ideal," explaining that "*Atlántida* must remain a mystery until Falla sees fit to disclose it to the world."[45] Best situated to obtain firsthand information on the work was Pahissa, who visited Falla in Alta Gracia in 1944 and thus began the long series of interviews that eventually became the biography *Vida y obra de Manuel de Falla*, to which all subsequent studies are indebted.

One preoccupation of Falla's during the Argentine years was his ambiguous relationship with his native land. As we have seen, the Franco regime attempted to woo Falla even before he set foot on American soil. But the offer of the lifetime pension that he received aboard the *Neptunia* was not all: a decree of 24 November 1939 named him a member of the Consejo Superior de Investigaciones Científicas (Superior Council of Scientific Investigation), a new agency created to draw attention to "the classic and Christian unity of the sciences" and to enhance the regime's still dubious intellectual image.[46] A similar organization was the Patronato Marcelino Menéndez y Pelayo, to which Falla was appointed honorary president on 14 March 1940, along with the literary scholar Francisco Rodríguez Marín.[47] Another honor was finalized on 13 July 1940, when Falla was named Caballero de la Orden de Alfonso X el Sabio (Knight of the Order of Alfonso X, "the Wise"). Then a decree of 7 January 1941 named him a member of the Consejo de la Hispanidad (Hispanic Council), which promoted a traditionalist view of Hispanic identity by drawing on the regime's nostalgia for empire and the spirit of the Counter-Reformation.[48] In contrast to his previous resistance to officialdom, Falla barely reacted to these honors: despite his fear of "deformation" and his aversion to honorary titles, he seems neither to have sought clarification on the nature of these appointments nor to have officially rejected them. After his experience with the Instituto de España, he was probably unwilling to face a protracted bureaucratic battle. Ill health and genuine lack of interest in such honors also contributed to his apathy.

Falla's indifference to the promise of a lifetime pension is especially significant in light of his bleak financial circumstances. Besides his creative standstill during the Republic and war years, during which he composed no income-generating work on the level of, say, *The Three-Cornered Hat*, in the confusion of the postwar period, the Sociedad General de Autores Españoles (SGAE) failed to send him his royalties, which it normally distributed after collecting fees from Chester and Eschig, Falla's principal publishers. The European war impeded this process as well. Nor had

45. Gilbert Chase, *The Music of Spain* (New York: Norton, 1941), 197. Falla commented favorably on *The Music of Spain* in his letter to Nin-Culmell of 11 December 1944 (AMF correspondence file 7336).

46. The text of the decree is reproduced in Pérez Zalduondo, "El nacionalismo como eje de la política," 258.

47. Pérez Zalduondo, "El nacionalismo como eje de la política," 258–59.

48. On Hispanism under Franco, see Raúl Morodo, *Los orígenes ideológicos del franquismo: Acción Española* (Madrid: Alianza Editorial, 1985), 148–61.

Falla succeeded in collecting mechanical (recording) rights. Even before leaving for Argentina he had complained about this to R. D. Gibson, the successor at Chester of Otto Kling, with whom Falla had optimistically signed a contract in December 1919. Now Falla complained about the "problem of [his] rights in America," especially with regard to radio broadcasts, and emphasized the need to find a solution as soon as possible.[49] Gibson's response reflects the fruitless relationships among composer, publisher, and the various representative societies that tormented Falla in his final years:

> I must tell you that these affairs are neither under my authority nor my responsibility, and it is impossible for me to do more than what I have done in the past. The question of rights concerns entirely the Societies. These Societies receive the rights, and you must know that I do not have the right to intervene or occupy myself with arrangements made between you and the societies. I very much regret not being able to help you in this circumstance, and I can only advise you to act energetically toward the Spanish Society of Authors. It is their duty to put themselves in communication with the American Society, ASCAP [American Society of Composers, Authors, and Publishers], and to transmit to you the result, being one of their members. It's possible that because of the terrible conditions in your country during recent years, the payments were interrupted.[50]

A solution seemed imminent in August 1941, when a compatriot and friend of the Lorca family, Pedro Sanjuan, told Falla of Associated Music, Eschig's representative in New York.[51] In early February 1942, Associated Music's vice president, Ernest Voigt, wrote Falla a cordial letter, expressing interest both in publishing future works and in helping him collect from Eschig, with whom, Voigt added, it had been impossible to communicate since the beginning of the war. Voigt also noted that "certain funds charged for performances and rentals have been accumulating," a portion of which belonged to Falla. To collect, the composer would first need to "obtain the permission of the United States government to pay out that money, which

49. Letter, Falla to Gibson, 20 March 1939, AMF correspondence file 9138.

50. "Je dois vous dire que ces affaires ne sont nullement sous mon autorité ni sous ma responsabilité et il m'est totalement impossible de faire davantage à ce que j'ai fait dans le passé. La question de ces droits concerne entièrement les Sociétés. Ces Sociétés reçoivent les droits et vous devez savoir que je n'ai ni le droit d'intervenir ni de m'occuper des arrangements faits entre vous et les sociétés. Je regrette vivement de ne pouvoir vous aider en cette circonstance et je ne puis que vous conseiller d'agir enérgiquement envers la Société espagnole des droits d'Auteurs. Il est de leur devoir de se mettre en communication avec la Société américaine, ASCAP, et de vous transmetter le résultat, étant un de leurs membres. Il est possible qu'à cause des conditions terribles dans votre pays durant ces dernières années, les paiements aient été interrompus" (letter, Gibson to Falla, 11 April 1939, AMF correspondence file 9138).

51. Letter, Sanjuan to Falla, 29 August 1941, AMF correspondence file 7593.

requires time," Voigt noted, "even though we are sure of getting the permission."[52] Voigt gave no further information on this governmental technicality. Responding on 7 April, Falla attempted to list from memory the various conditions of his contract with Eschig (surprisingly, his contracts were still in Spain). He made no inquiry about the government permission.

By the end of 1942, however, Falla was as frustrated with Associated Music as with Chester and Eschig. He took the step of engaging lawyers from the firm of Mayer, Lobos, and Clusellas of Buenos Aires, who drafted a strongly worded letter to Voigt claiming that Falla had never been paid any royalties for performances of his works in the United States.[53] Finally, in May 1943, Associated Music sent him a royalty statement, a check for $80.47, and a list of recently reprinted arrangements of his works.[54] Another communication (22 May 1944) informed Falla that since Associated Music was not the sole agent for Eschig in the United States he should approach other companies, such as Carl Fischer of New York and Elkan and Vogel of Philadelphia. Chester, on the other hand, was represented by Galaxy Music Corporation, also of New York.

Falla was so distressed by all of this that he even swallowed his pride and prevailed upon his old friend Gregorio Martínez Sierra, with whom he had probably not communicated since the *Don Juan de España* episode. Falla informed his former collaborator that recent performances of *El amor brujo* and *The Three-Cornered Hat* at the Teatro Colón had yielded 20 percent for the librettist, rather than the 15 "fixed by the Society of Authors for its distributions."[55] Would Gregorio not consider, Falla wondered, reducing his percentage for scenic representations of their works?

> I will also allow myself to beg that you direct your attention and your good-will to the disproportionate amount of the percentage reserved for you, considering these are scenarios for *ballets* and not opera librettos, in which case [your percentage] would indeed be within generally established norms. Certainly with reason you can tell me that this is the way it's been since the pre-

52. "Se han venido acumulando ciertos fondos cobrados por ejecuciones y arrendamientos. . . . Tendrá que obtenerse el permiso del Gobierno de los Estados Unidos para pagar ese dinero, lo cual requiere tiempo, aunque estamos seguros de obtener el permiso" (letter, Ernest Voigt [vice president, Associated Music] to Falla, 28 February 1942, AMF correspondence file 9162).

53. Letter (draft copy with Falla's emendations), Mayer, Lobos, and Clusellas to Associated Music, 28 December 1942, AMF correspondence file 9162.

54. Letter, Hugo Winter to Falla, 20 May 1943, AMF correspondence file 9162. Voigt died on 31 March 1943.

55. Letter, Falla to Martínez Sierra, 14 September 1943, AMF correspondence file 7251/3. When the contracts were drawn up, it was agreed that Martínez Sierra would receive the normal rate for an opera libretto rather than what a ballet scenario normally commanded. See Budwig, "Manuel de Falla's *Atlántida*," 223; and "Summary of Contracts (the Late) Manuel de Falla," drawn up by Chester and presently uncataloged in the AMF.

mieres of *El amor brujo* and *The Three-Cornered Hat*, but if you think back you'll remember that *El amor brujo* had at its premiere a good deal of text and that later, revising it by mutual and congenial consent into a *ballet*, the text was reduced to the songs. And concerning the scenario of the new version, part of that was done by me (as you will surely recall as well), as with the *mise-en-scène*, which, based on your plot, I had to set for the performances of the *ballet*. I would say the same regarding the titles of some of the scenes and dances, as, for example, that of the *Ritual Fire Dance*, and above all my work in expanding the instrumental score to adjust it to the orchestral format for the *ballet* that we intended for (and succeeded in) representing in important theaters. As for *The Three-Cornered Hat* . . . I beg you to remember that the ballet has only two brief *coplas* as sung text.[56]

As in some of his letters to political organizations or leaders, Falla's courteous tone masks deeper frustrations:

> I have always felt great distaste toward any kind of discussion of this nature between true friends, and you may believe that if I'm letting myself talk about such things now, I do so thinking not only of the many years this arrangement has been going on, but most especially of the very unusual *economic* circumstances in which I now find myself, being unable to receive anything from Spain nor even benefit in the smallest way from the rights my own music generates. . . . In resolution (as Don Quijote would say): you decide what you believe to be just and equitable, and I will await this decision with full confidence. Meanwhile, receive the affectionate greeting that I send you, with the memory of our long friendship.[57]

56. "Voy a permitirme también rogar a usted que fije su atención y buena voluntad en la desproporción del porcentaje que se le reserva, tratándose de escenarios para *ballets* y no de libretos de ópera, en cuyo caso sí estaría dentro de las normas generalmente establecidas. Claro está que Vd., con razón, podrá decirme que así se ha venido haciendo desde que se estrenaron el *Amor brujo* y el *Sombrero*, pero si hace Vd. memoria recordará que el *Amor brujo* tenía cuando se estrenó bastante texto, el que luego, al convertirlo, de común y feliz acuerdo, en *ballet*, quedó reducido al de las canciones. Y por lo que concierne al escenario de la nueva versión, parte del mismo fué hecho por mí (como Vd. tambien recordará), así como la *mise-en-scène*, que, basada en su argumento, debí establecer para las representaciones del *ballet*. Lo mismo digo respecto a los títulos de algunas de las escenas y danzas como, por ejemplo, el de la *Ritual del Fuego*, y, sobre todo, mi labor de ampliación de toda la partitura instrumental para ajustarla al plan orquestal de un *ballet* que pretendíamos (como se ha conseguido) fuese representado en grandes teatros. En cuanto al *Sombrero de tres picos* . . . ruego a Vd. recuerde que sólo tiene el ballet dos breves coplas como texto cantado" (letter, Falla to Martínez Sierra, 14 September 1943, AMF correspondence file 7251/3).

57. "Siempre he sentido gran antipatía entre toda posible discusión de ese carácter entre verdaderos amigos, y puede Vd. creer que si ahora me permito hablarle de estas cosas, no sólo es pensando en los muchos años que ya lleva rigiendo esa norma de reparto, sino,

Of course, there was no mention of María in this frank discussion of author's rights. After witnessing the demise of the Republican government she had served, María had retreated to the south of France; as Falla was hopefully appealing to Gregorio, she was suffering the twin despair of material deprivation and encroaching blindness, all against the grim backdrop of Vichy. She, too, was having difficulty pinning down Gregorio, who occasionally sent her a bit of money (from New York). Only in June 1945 did she learn that he was in Buenos Aires. He attributed his long silence to health problems and responded to her queries about author's rights by shamelessly contending that although she was his "constant preoccupation," there was no money in their accounts. According to María's biographer, Antonina Rodrigo, this was when she finally saw Gregorio's true colors.[58] Falla was similarly disappointed, and despite his entreaty, there is no record of any response from Gregorio.

On another front, Falla was seeking remuneration for recordings of his music. After finding out that RCA Victor had recorded several of his works without his authorization, the composer complained to Bernardo Iriberri, a concert promoter based in Buenos Aires. "I haven't collected a cent since I've been in Argentina," he told him, in reference to the recordings, mainly of the "Ritual Fire Dance" but also of "all the rest" of what that formidable enterprise was producing.[59] (By October 1944, RCA Victor had recorded the "Ritual Fire Dance" three times; "all the rest" included *Noches*, *La vida breve*, various selections from *The Three-Cornered Hat*, and "Cubana" from *Cuatro piezas españolas*.[60]) Ironically, it was "thanks" to RCA Victor that Falla finally grasped the root of his problems. On 31 July 1944, H. C. Darnell, the company's manager of artistic rights, wrote Falla's lawyers that "we have known for some time that the works of the composer de Falla have been released by different publishers and that the question of who is their owner has been rather confusing throughout the world."[61] The situation was somewhat clearer when it came to

---

muy especialmente, en razón a las tan especiales circunstancias *económicas* en que ahora me hallo, sin poder recibir nada de España ni tampoco benificiarme más que de una mínima parte de los derechos que produce mi música. . . . En resolución (como diría Don Quijote): usted decide lo que crea justo y equitativo, ya esa decisión le espero con toda confianza. Mientras, reciba el afectuoso saludo que le envío con el recuerdo de nuestra vieja amistad" (letter, Falla to Martínez Sierra, 14 September 1943, AMF correspondence file 7251/3).

58. Rodrigo, *María Lejárraga*, 315.

59. "No he cobrado un solo centavo desde que estoy en la Argentina" (letter, Falla to Iriberri, 16 June 1944, AMF correspondence file 7124).

60. RCA recordings 12160, 2214, and 1596 ("Ritual Fire Dance"). Other works and catalog numbers are listed in a letter from H. C. Darnell of RCA Victor to Mayer, Lobos, and Clusellas, 12 October 1944, AMF correspondence file 7106.

61. "Hemos sabido por algún tiempo que las obras del compositor de Falla han sido publicadas por diferentes casas editoriales y que la cuestión de quién es su propietario ha sido algo confusa por todas partes del mundo" (letter, Darnell to Mayer, Lobos, and Clusellas, 31 July 1944, AMF correspondence file 7106).

mechanical rights: according to Darnell, Falla, a Spanish citizen, could not have enjoyed copyright protection in the United States until 10 October 1934, when, thanks to Franklin D. Roosevelt's Presidential Proclamation, works by "nationals of Spain" would thereafter be protected.[62] "Protection," however, applied only to works composed after 1 July 1909, works registered in the United States, or works not previously recorded in the United States. As Darnell concluded, "this practically eliminates all the best-known compositions of Mr. de Falla, which have been published many years ago and the majority, if not all, reproduced in the form of records before the day of the Proclamation."[63] To the composer's inquiry about radio performances, Darnell could only advise Falla to approach ASCAP.

We can easily imagine Falla's reaction to this news. Having suffered the trauma of the Civil War, it could not have been easy for a man of his age to establish himself in a new life on another continent, especially when burdened with ill health and precarious finances. Add to this the indignity of being swindled by the grasping—yet entirely legal—practices of the music industry, which now undermined his well-being while eating into whatever time he might otherwise spend on *Atlántida*. The situation seemed hopeless, Kafkaesque. A stroke of luck, however, came his way in the person of José M. Hernández Suárez. This generous young engineer of Spanish parentage directed the Argentine-Spanish Cultural Association and perhaps for this reason took a personal interest in the expatriate composer and his sister. For years, Hernández Suárez patiently assisted them with legal matters and all manner of household concerns, such as what type of air conditioner to buy, for example. Astonished that a composer's citizenship could impede payment of his royalties, Hernández Suárez worked closely with Falla's lawyers to challenge this arbitrary law. But between Falla's ill health, which occasioned long lapses in his struggle, ongoing communication problems with Eschig, and the endless cycle of

62. Darnell enclosed a copy of Roosevelt's text, along with a translation, in his letter of 31 July. For a contemporaneous view of the United States' role in international copyright agreements and the cumbersome practice of establishing separate conventions with individual countries (which, according to the author, often involved "national resentment and racial discrimination"), see Alfred M. Shafter, *Musical Copyright*, 2d ed. (Chicago: Callaghan, 1939), 447–58.

63. "Esto prácticamente elimina todas las composiciones más conocidas del Sr. de Falla, las cuales han sido publicadas muchos años antes de ahora y la mayoría, si no todas, han sido reproducidas en forma de discos antes del día de la Proclamación" (letter, Darnell to Mayer, Lobos, and Clusellas, 31 July 1944, AMF correspondence file 7106). Darnell also listed those countries in which Spanish composers *did* enjoy mechanical rights (Argentina, Brazil, Colombia, Costa Rica, Cuba, Mexico, and Peru, among others). Acknowledging that RCA's sales were limited in these countries, Darnell informed Falla that those royalties were paid by the French society BIEM (Bureau International des Sociétés Gérant les Droits d'Enregistrement et de Reproduction Mécanique), which he advised Falla to contact.

buck passing between various representative societies—in addition now to the "problem" that Falla was a Spanish national—prospects for success seemed dim. A letter of 30 October 1944 to Mayer, Lobos, and Clusellas from Hermann Finkelstein of ASCAP is only one indication of how hopelessly complicated the situation was. Finkelstein noted that ASCAP had been "endeavoring to make payment to the Spanish Society for some time . . . [but it had] not accounted to us since 1936 largely because of the civil war in Spain."[64] (Here, in his copy, Falla scrawled in the margin "ni antes tampoco"—"not before, either"). Stressing the importance of Falla's works in "the symphonic field," Finkelstein suggested that he contact ASCAP's New York representative and "communicate directly" with SGAE—as if the composer had never attempted to do precisely that. Adding to Falla's anxieties were some unpleasant rumors: from New York, Iriberri wrote Falla about "a Mr. Kramer [who] says he's your representative and charges for the performance of your works. This gentleman seems to belong to Galaxy Music Corp."[65] His success could be measured by the fact at least one dance company, the popular Chabalillos Sevillanos, "have for some time given up performing your works because in each instance Mr. Kramer was asking 150 to 200 dollars."[66] There was also discouraging news from Spain: Falla heard that it now cost a hefty 1,500 pesetas to rent the parts for *La vida breve*, which, in the difficult postwar economy, was a sure guarantee of fewer performances. Thus, Falla had to stomach "the scandalous disproportion," as he joylessly put it, "between the author's rights . . . and what the editor takes in."[67]

In the midst of these legal headaches, Falla continued to vacillate over his relationship with Spain. He was unperturbed, for example, when he learned that his *carmen* had been vandalized, and, although his silverware and some other items were stolen, he refused to press charges against the thieves. (His remaining belongings were moved to the nearby Convento de Santa Inés for safekeeping.)[68] If indifferent to material concerns, Falla kept at least minimally abreast of certain aspects of the political situation in Spain. He also advocated on behalf of former Republican friends and colleagues caught in the sinister grip of Franco's retributive campaign, which

64. Letter, Hermann Finkelstein to Mayer, Lobos, and Clusellas, 30 October 1944, AMF correspondence file 7106.

65. "Un señor Kramer se dice representante suyo y cobra por la ejecución de sus obras. Ese señor párece ser perteneciente a Galaxy Music Corp" (letter, Iriberri to Falla, 8 January 1946, AMF correspondence file 7124). An A. Walter Kramer was in fact Galaxy's managing director (see letter, Kramer to Mayer, Lobos, and Clusella, 28 July 1944, AMF correspondence file 7106).

66. "Han suspendido hace tiempo toda obra suya porque el señor Kramer pedía por cada vez 150 hasta 200 dólares" (letter, Iriberri to Falla, 8 January 1944, AMF correspondence file 7124).

67. Letter, Falla to Hernández Suárez, 11 July 1946, AMF correspondence file 7017.

68. Budwig, "Manuel de Falla's *Atlántida*," 249.

Preston has aptly described as a "politics of revenge."[69] In other words, the composer now challenged the policies of the regime toward which he had halfheartedly
leaned during the war. One case was that of Miguel Salvador, with whom Falla had
optimistically collaborated in the Sociedad Nacional de Música almost three decades
earlier. As a former minister in the Republic, Salvador was now scheduled to die.
After Falla appealed to Eduardo Becerra, the consul general of Spain in Buenos Aires,
however, Salvador's sentence was reduced to thirty years' imprisonment.[70] Falla's
entreaties were not always successful: although he intervened on behalf of the son
of his second cousin, María Luzuriaga, the young man died by firing squad.[71] In
addition, Falla's lifelong habit of giving to the poor now assumed a political dimension in that he began contributing to a Republican refugee camp near Toulouse,
one of many that had sprung up since the fall of Catalonia in early 1939 and in which
disease and death often greeted the refugees who swarmed across the border. We
will never know the extent of Falla's charity (certainly he could afford to give very
little), for he modestly kept such things secret. But there was also a deeper reason
for his secrecy. As María del Carmen told the Luzuriaga family: "We trust you
completely that our remittance will appear to be anonymous, since you already
know how Manolo has had to battle to maintain his independence from politics
(without this we would lack for nothing, *but he greatly prefers his liberty*) . . . [I]f
publicity about our remittance were forthcoming, *the other side* could require that
Manolo make statements and things that he has never wanted to do" (emphasis
added).[72]

"Liberty" in genteel poverty or material comfort with political "independence"
as its price? Falla weighed these possibilities during the second half of 1944, the only
time he seems to have seriously considered returning to Spain. This is shown in a
memo of 8 July of that year from Hernández Suárez to the Spanish ambassador to
Argentina (the Count de Bulnes). Entitled "Estado de Don Manuel de Falla" (Estate of Don Manuel de Falla), the memo notes that, although Falla's health had recently improved, it was nonetheless "always precarious . . . so that he could not go
to Spain except by a comfortable and direct trip lasting no more than fifteen or six-

69. Preston, *Politics of Revenge*, 42–43.

70. Letter, Becerra to Falla, 28 October 1940, AMF correspondence file 6755.

71. Interview, Andrew Budwig and Isabel Luzuriaga (sister of the victim), Madrid,
25 December 1981. See Budwig, "Manuel de Falla's *Atlántida*," 235.

72. "Confiamos completamente en vosotras para que aparezca como anónimo nuestro
envío, pues ya sabéis lo que tiene que batallar Manolo para conservar su independencia
de toda política (sin esto nada nos faltaría nunca, pero él prefiere con mucho su libertad)
. . . si se diera publicidad a nuestro envío podrían exigir *del otro lado* que hiciera Manolo
manifestaciones y cosas que él nunca ha querido hacer" (letter, María del Carmen to
Maruja and Isabelita Luzuriaga, 10 January 1946, AMF correspondence file 7218).

teen days."[73] Pending such a voyage, the memo continued, Falla would prefer to live not in Granada, where he would be haunted by unhappy memories, but in Huerta Chica, a village in Córdoba Province that belonged to "the Vallejo family, some members of which presently reside in Buenos Aires." The attentive Hernández Suárez urged the ambassador to decide quickly or "our admired maestro will again find himself short of funds."

Evidently the memo was never sent, for on page 1 of the draft copy in the AMF "no enviado" is scrawled in a hand other than Falla's. A roughly contemporaneous interview, however, with the *franquista* daily *Arriba* echoes some of the same desires, including the name of Falla's intended destination. In it, the composer is quoted as saying that he would "like to pass by unnoticed. I don't want to be an actor any more. I only want to return to Spain when the [European] war ends, when means of travel will be quicker and more secure, and stay there to quietly live out my last days in a Spanish village. . . . I'd like to go live in a village called Huerta Chica, where my sister and I looked at a little house when we passed by there."[74] Do Falla's words, filtered through the interviewer for the *franquista* daily, betray fatigue, homesickness, or resignation? He did order a guidebook of the Córdoba region, so the prospect of monklike solitude in Huerta Chica may have been more than a whim.[75] But he probably realized that it was naive to imagine he could could "pass unnoticed" in Franco's Spain, given the government's eagerness to claim him as one of their own. As he had done previously, he let health—and the passage of time—decide the matter. In the fall of 1944, he suffered another bout of iritis, along with high blood pressure and fevers.[76] Abandoning any thought of travel, Falla continued his self-imposed exile into what must have seemed an increasingly indefinite future.

In more optimistic moments, Falla revived his hopes of filming *El retablo de Maese Pedro*. As he explained to Juan José Castro's mother-in-law, Margarita Aguirre, "it's so difficult to obtain an entirely satisfactory scenic representation with the means available in a theater," an experience he knew firsthand.[77] Accordingly, Falla drew

73. "[Está] siempre precaria . . . así que no podría de ningún modo ir a España, sino en un viaje cómodo y directo que no durase más que 15 a 16 días" (draft of memo, 8 July 1944, AMF correspondence file 7106).

74. "Quisiera pasar ya inadvertido. No deseo ser más actor. Sólo aspiro a regresar a España cuando la guerra termine, que serán más rápidos y seguros los medios de viaje, y quedarme a vivir oscuramente los últimos días de mi vida en un pueblecito español. . . . Quisiera irme a vivir a un pueblecito que se llama Huerta Chica, donde hemos echado el ojo a una casita mi hermana y yo cuando pasamos por allí" (Santiago, "Manuel de Falla, desde la Argentina habla para *Arriba*").

75. Budwig, "Manuel de Falla's *Atlántida*," 233n2.

76. Letter, Falla to Nin-Culmell, 11 December 1944, AMF correspondence file 7336.

77. "Ya que tan difícil es obtener una representación escénica enteramente satisfactoria con los medios de que en un teatro se pueden disponer" (letter, draft copy Falla to Aguirre, 22 December 1941, AMF correspondence file 6680).

up a contract with a fellow Spaniard, Miguel Machinandiarena. This new associate had helped establish the Estudios San Miguel in Buenos Aires, a highly regarded studio that produced movies such as Ibsen's *Casa de muñecas* (A Doll's House, 1943), directed by Ernesto Arancibia, and *La pródiga* (The Prodigal, 1945), directed by Mario Soffici and featuring one Eva Duarte, who, that same year married Juan Perón, then on his way to becoming the most powerful man in Argentina. The contract, which probably dates from 1943, may never have been finalized, however. (Clause 7 reads that "The Estudios . . . San Miguel in its own name and in that of Maestro Falla, will make a donation of 5,000 pesos" to charity, surely the composer's emendation.)[78]

Regardless, Falla set to work, composing new music so as to extend the thirty-minute *Retablo* to a length suitable for film and drafting a partial screenplay of additional scenes. But two years later Machinandiarena was still stringing the composer along. He claimed to be unsure about whether the *Retablo* was filmworthy and proposed that it be paired with *The Three-Cornered Hat*. Falla, however, refused to use one work as a mere "curtain-raiser" for another, and the relationship deteriorated markedly.[79] This conflict affected progress on *Atlántida*: at one point in the course of their sterile debates, Falla accused Machinandiarena of callousness and pointedly called attention to the "great sacrifice it implies . . . to have had to abandon a project that forms a part of my own life (the composition of *Atlántida*)."[80] After two years, Falla gave up, disheartened and uncompensated.

Other cinematographic ventures had greater success, however, and in ways Falla never would have anticipated. In November 1943, Iriberri reported that Metro Goldwyn Mayer (MGM) wanted to use the "Ritual Fire Dance" in the forthcoming movie musical *Two Girls and a Sailor*. It would be interpreted by the Spanish pianist José Iturbi and his sister Amparo, José's unobtrusive duo-piano partner.[81] Like so many other "Latin" musicians, such as the bandleader Xavier Cugat, conga player Desi Arnaz, and tenor Carlos Ramírez, Iturbi found fame and fortune in Hollywood. In his movies, he invariably he played himself, that is, the classically trained musician who makes "serious" music accessible to the popular audience.

In principle, Falla agreed with Iriberri that the Iturbis would lend dignity to the project.[82] And after so many years of unsuccessfully wrangling with publishers and

---

78. A copy of this sloppily redacted contract, possibly a draft, mentions *"El retablo del* [*sic*] *Maese Pedro,* [*El*] *Amor Brujo, y El Sobrero* [*sic*] *de Tres Picos."* It does not bear Falla's signature, and several letters, such as Machinandiarena's to Falla of 8 June 1945 (AMF correspondence file 7226), refer to the eventual closing of the deal ("para cerrar definitivamente nuestro convenio").

79. Letter, Falla to Machinandiarena, 27 August 1945, AMF correspondence file 7226.

80. "No se dé usted perfecta cuenta . . . del gran sacrificio que supone . . . el haber tenido que abandonar un trabajo que forma parte de mi vida misma (la composición de la *Atlántida*)" (letter, Falla to Machinandiarena, 27 August 1945, AMF correspondence file 7226).

81. Telegram, Iriberri to Falla, 10 November 1943, AMF correspondence file 7124.

82. Letter, Iriberri to Falla, 11 November 1943, AMF correspondence file 7124.

their representatives Falla was probably staggered by the news that he would receive a minimum of 1,000 dollars "only to concede the authorization" (beyond this he collected 2,000 dollars). But he was not so dazzled that he overlooked the moral and artistic compromises Hollywood might exact. As he explained to Iriberri:

> At present, amorality enters into the normality of life so that, at times, almost unconsciously, our sense of responsibility is lulled. For that reason, I allow myself to insist on what I wrote you about the scenic part as a precondition. Certainly it surprises me that they indicate only three minutes as the duration of the dance . . . [and] this makes me suppose—and lament—that they are thinking of giving it a lively pace, contrary to its character of a ritual dance, which is one reason more to ask for exact details on the visual realization of the scene.[83]

Falla needn't have worried. The Iturbis' performance of the "Ritual Fire Dance" took place in the most tasteful of scenarios, and the strictures of Hollywood's Production Code Administration (PCA), which worked closely with the Catholic Legion of Decency, corresponded closely to Falla's own principles.[84] When PCA head Joseph I. Breen, an active lay Catholic, detected a few improprieties in the script, for example, he promptly warned Louis B. Mayer of MGM that a "pinching gag between the two sisters" be kept "away from the posterior" and reiterated the need for tasteful costuming.[85] The relentlessly upbeat *Two Girls and a Sailor* is an example of that anomalous subgenre the "war musical," to which audiences in the United States flocked in the early 1940s.[86] In it, two sisters (June Allyson and Gloria De Haven) open a canteen for military men, among them a sailor (Van Johnson), who awakens the romantic interest of both. The slim plot is but a pretext for a cascade of musical numbers, including Gracie Allen's "Concerto for the Index Finger," Agustín Lara's "Granada," rendered by tenor Carlos Ramírez and accompanied by Xavier Cugat and his orchestra, and Jimmy Durante performing "Inky-Dinky-Doo" backed

83. "En los tiempos presentes va entrando lo amoral en la normalidad de la vida, que, a veces, casi inconscientemente, se nos adormece el sentido de la responsabilidad. Por esa razón me permito insistir en lo que escribí a Vd. sobre la parte escénica como condición previa. Por cierto que me extraña indiquen sólo tres minutos como duración de la danza, y esto me hace suponer—y lamentar—que piensan darle un movimiento vivo, contrariamente a su carácter de danza ritual, lo que es una razón de más para que pidamos detalles exactos sobre la realización visual de la escena" (letter, Falla to Iriberri, 14 November 1943, AMF correspondence file 7124).

84. Gregory D. Black, *The Catholic Crusade against the Movies, 1940–1975* (Cambridge: Cambridge University Press, 1997), 23–28.

85. Letter, Joseph I. Breen to L. B. Mayer, 5 August 1943, Margaret Herrick Library, Academy of Motion Picture Arts and Sciences (hereafter MHL clippings file, unnumbered).

86. See Jennifer R. Jenkins, "'Say It with Firecrackers': Defining the 'War Musical' of the 1940s," *American Music* 19 (2001): 315–39.

by trumpeter Harry James and his band. Announced by James, the Iturbis play "the spectacular 'Ritual Fire Dance'" in formal attire on two concert grands against a backdrop of tall, stately windows, which temporarily conceal the canteen atmosphere. After Iturbi and his sister "whip out their de Falla on two pianos,"[87] the curtains close and the camera pans the enthusiastic expressions of the wholesome-looking military men. Here, the viewer understands that the "Ritual Fire Dance" was as gratefully applauded as any of the pop or gag numbers organized by the indefatigable sisters. One reviewer even admiringly noted the Iturbis' contribution of "a splendid de Falla piece for those who want their good music straight."[88]

With its frothy combination of escapism and morale building, *Two Girls and a Sailor* was a top-grossing film of 1944. Encouraged, Iriberri began negotiating the use of the "Ritual Fire Dance" for another Iturbi movie, *Holiday in Mexico*. According to none other than Harry Fox, it would be sung by Jane Powell with "no essential changes in the music and [in a manner] ethical and esthetically acceptable to de Falla."[89] In that era, cloying voices like Powell's made for brisk box office sales and fitting English words to "Latin" songs was common: we need only recall Gerardo Matos Rodríguez's "La Cumparsita," known in the United States as "The Masked One," or Julio César Sanders's "Adiós muchachos," reincarnated as "I Get Ideas." When Falla learned that he would receive $4,000 up front, he insisted that Iriberri take 5 percent.[90] Although Iriberri refused, he did travel to Rockefeller Center to discuss prospects for Falla's music with Fox, since, as he put it, Fox was "an exceedingly kind and correct person, very different from the majority of North Americans, who are only out for *business*."[91] As if this were not enough, Fox thought it likely that Falla could "make a fortune" and spoke to Iriberri of "many thousands of dollars."[92] The idea of suddenly becoming a millionaire—through Hollywood yet—must have come as a shock to Falla at this stage of his life.

Although it was eventually decided not to use the "Ritual Fire Dance" for *Holiday in Mexico*, Falla still collected a fee.[93] Neither did a plan for Iturbi to play the "Ritual Fire Dance" for Walt Disney, who was then making movies in the Good

87. Edwin Schallert, "*Two Girls and Sailor* Okay Musical," *Los Angeles Times*, 23 June 1944, MHL clippings file, unnumbered.

88. Red Kann, "Review: *Two Girls and a Sailor*," *Motion Picture Daily*, 25 April 1944, MHL clippings file, unnumbered.

89. Telegram from Harry Fox to Iriberri, quoted in a letter from Iriberri to Falla, 11 July 1945, AMF correspondence file 7124.

90. Letter, Falla to Iriberri, 12 July 1945, AMF correspondence file 7124.

91. "[He encontrado en] el señor Fox . . . una persona sumamente amable y correcta, muy distinta a la generalidad de los norteamericanos que solo buscan los *bussines*" [*sic*] (letter, Iriberri to Falla, 28 December 1945, AMF correspondence file 7124).

92. "Cree que podría sacar para Ud. una fortuna . . . [Fox] me ha hablado de muchos miles de dólares" (letter, Iriberri to Falla, 28 December 1945, AMF correspondence file 7124).

93. Letter, Iriberri to Falla, 15 October 1946, AMF correspondence file 7124.

Neighbor style such as *Saludos amigos* and *The Three Caballeros*, come to fruition.[94] But negotiations for *Carnegie Hall*, a lightweight "classical" variant of the movie musical, were soon under way. This overly long film, shot on location, features Walter Damrosch, Bruno Walter, Lily Pons, and a galaxy of other artists, including Grigor Piatigorsky playing Saint-Saëns's "The Swan" with a bevy of toga-draped female harpists. Also participating was Artur Rubinstein, who, not yet suffering from the "'Ritual Fire Dance' syndrome," offered the work on a dimly lit stage as an encore for a riveting performance of Chopin's Polonaise in Ab op. 53. As we shall see, the "Ritual Fire Dance" would bring Falla posthumous glory as well.

As *Two Girls and a Sailor* was attracting crowds at the box office, the Franco government stepped up its efforts to court Falla. In November 1944, he was appointed *consejero de honor* (honorary adviser) to the Consejo Superior de Investigaciones Científicas.[95] In January 1945 Bulnes asked him about it, which suggests that Falla had not officially accepted the invitation.[96] Instead of refusing outright, however, Falla questioned Bulnes on the political implications such an appointment might carry; predictably, Bulnes assured him that "this entity can at no point act corporately in favor of a given political tendency," a rather disingenuous account given the totalitarian government under which the commission operated.[97] When Falla again did not respond, Bulnes wrote back with additional enticements:

> The City Hall of Barcelona is showing great desire and interest in giving the first performance of your poem *Atlántida* if you finish it in the course of this year, in which the centenary of Verdaguer is being celebrated. . . . The government is offering you an official trip with all comforts, with as much money for the move as for your stay there. What do you say to all this? Consider that Spain is calling you and wants to receive you with open arms to pay tribute to all the honors due a national glory.[98]

94. Iriberri initially informed Falla of Disney's interest in a telegram on 25 July 1946 (AMF correspondence file 7124).

95. Letter, José María Albareda (general secretary, Ministry of National Education) to Falla, 27 October 1944, AMF correspondence file 7349.

96. Letter, Bulnes to Falla, 18 January 1945, AMF correspondence file 7804.

97. "Este organismo en ningún momento puede actuar corporativamente a favor de una tendencia política" (letter, Bulnes to Falla, 23 February 1945, AMF correspondence file 7804). Falla wrote Bulnes back on 28 January 1945 (AMF correspondence file 7804).

98. "El Ayuntamiento de Barcelona muestra un gran deseo e interés en dar la primera audición de su poema *Atlántida* si lo tuviera ultimado durante el curso de este año en que se celebra el centenario de Verdaguer. . . . El Gobierno le ofrece viaje oficial, con todas las comodidades, tanto para trasladarse como para su residencia allí. ¿Qué me dice de todo esto? Piense que España le llama y quiere recibirle con los brazos abiertos para tributarle todos los honores que corresponden a una gloria nacional" (letter, Bulnes to Falla, 25 April 1945, AMF correspondence file 7804).

A few days later Falla, now less optimistic about *Atlántida*'s viability, told Bulnes that he doubted it would be finished for the Verdaguer year. Evasive as ever, he bypassed any mention of the appointment from the Consejo, interest that he may well have feigned politely in his previous letter.[99]

In the summer of 1946, the question of returning to Spain arose again, this time through Francisco Cambó, Falla's provider of "divine gifts." He put it directly to the composer:

> The Spanish government has a great interest in your going to Spain, not for a visit but to stay there to live, and it offers you all you might want: travel costs, a comfortable house . . . a pension, and whatever you might need to live in peace and to be able to work as you like. . . . Naturally if you were to decide to accept, it would be best to detail everything very carefully to avoid the possibility that having left this corner of the world, in which things haven't been all that bad, you wouldn't encounter difficulties and headaches in Spain for things not having been well clarified.[100]

Three days later Falla refused Cambó, with his now customary explanation: "Although I am as honored as I am grateful for your offers on behalf of the government, I continue to think as I have until now about my return to Spain, that is, for the tranquility required by the delicate state of my health and the optimum realization of my musical projects, I must wait . . . until things at least begin to stablize in Europe."[101] Since World War II had ended the previous year, it is hard to know what sort of instability Falla meant. Perhaps he was tired of the government's importuning. Perhaps he was reluctant to leave his tranquil outpost in the Córdoba Sierra. Perhaps he was simply tired. Whatever lay behind this courteous explanation—if

99. Letter, Falla to Bulnes, 30 April 1945, AMF correspondence file 7804. The matter of the appointment arose again in July, with Falla merely promising Bulnes to write the secretary of the Consejo (letter, Falla to Bulnes, 9 July 1945, AMF correspondence file 7804). It is not clear that he did so.

100. "El Gobierno español tiene gran interés en que vaya usted a España, no para una visita, sino para quedarse a residir allí, y le ofrece todo lo que usted quiera: gastos de viaje, casa confortable . . . una pensión y cuanto usted necesite para vivir en paz y poder trabajar a sus anchas. . . . Naturalmente que si usted se decidiera a aceptar, convendría precisar mucho las cosas para evitar que después de haber dejado este rincón en que no lo pasa usted del todo mal, no se encontrara en España con dificultades y molestias por no haber puesto muy en claro las cosas" (letter, Cambó to Falla, 6 July 1946, AMF correspondence file 6813).

101. "Aunque tan honrado como agradecido por sus ofrecimientos en nombre del gobierno, sigo pensando como hasta ahora he pensado en cuanto se relaciona con mi regreso a España, o sea que por la tranquilidad que exigen el delicado estado de mi salud y la posible eficacia de mis trabajos de música, debo esperar . . . a que en Europa comiencen siquiera a estabilizarse las cosas" (letter, Falla to Cambó, 9 July 1946, AMF correspondence file 6813).

anything other than sheer force of habit—his dodging of the regime's invitation in 1946, the last year of his life, was his final interaction with the victors in the Spanish Civil War.

In that last year, Falla's inner light grew ever more faint. Sert's death in November 1945 came as a shock, and in early 1946 he lamented to his collaborator's family, "Of course I was left alone with the work, and what sorrow it causes me to think that, if God is willing that my health should permit me to finish it, [Sert] won't be with me to realize so many of the beautiful and admirable things he once planned!"[102] Even though Falla's correspondence with Sert had lapsed during the Argentine years, evidently the composer had never considered collaborating with anyone else on *Atlántida*. Completing it seemed more hopeless than ever, and perhaps it is not surprising that Falla became increasingly given to apocalyptic statements. In such troubled and irrational times, he even questioned the value of his music, confiding in the Luzuriagas: "It seems as though a vast mystery were passing over the earth, causing us at times to fear that . . . mankind is destroying itself. . . . I assure you that as I work I frequently ask myself if my time could be better spent doing something else . . . something more spiritual."[103] To Enrique Bullrich, of the prominent Buenos Aires family, Falla wrote: "I'm beginning to believe that we're approaching the end of the second generation of humans, and when I'm working at my craft many times I ask myself to what end I do it. But in the end: God above everything, and always go forward, as if we were in the best of all worlds! Besides, there's always the hope that one of these days they'll invent a way to travel to another planet, although when we arrive perhaps we wouldn't be admitted."[104]

As always, Falla's delicate health responded to these anxieties. On 18 July 1946, the tenth anniversary of the outbreak of the Spanish Civil War, María del Carmen offered a young friend of the family, Sergio de Castro (no relation to Juan José), a

102. "¡Ya me quedé solo con la obra, y qué pena me da pensar que, si Dios quiere que la salud me permita terminarla, [Sert] no estará conmigo para realizar tantas cosas hermosas y admirables como para entonces proyectaba!" (letter [carbon copy], Falla to Dolores and Carmen Sert, January [no day] 1946, AMF correspondence file 7682/1–7682–2).

103. "Parece que pasa sobre el mundo un tan inmenso misterio que a veces llega hasta hacernos temer que . . . la humanidad se destruye a sí misma. . . . Os aseguro que cuando trabajo en mi oficio, muchas veces me pregunto si no valdría más que me ocupara en otras cosas . . . que se refieren a las fuerzas del espíritu" (letter, Falla to Maruja and Isabelita Luzuriaga, 25 January 1946, AMF correspondence file 7218).

104. "Yo empiezo a creer que estamos acercándonos al final de la segunda generación humana, y cuando estoy trabajando en mi oficio, muchas veces me pregunto para qué lo hago. Pero en fin: Dios sobre todo, y siempre adelante, como si estuviéramos en el mejor de los mundos! Además nos queda la esperanza de que cualquier día de estos se invente la manera de trasladarse a otro planeta, aunque cuando llegáramos, acaso no quisieran admitirnos en él" (letter, Falla to Bullrich, 26 December 1945, AMF correspondence file 7803).

touching yet disturbing glimpse of Falla's health, referring to the high blood pressure that would cause his death shortly thereafter. We can imagine her thinking tenderly of her brother as she wrote: "I'm writing to you from both of us, for Manuel is on a strict regimen of rest ordered by Dr. Ferrer because of a burst blood vessel in the eye and high blood pressure. Since they don't let him work, yesterday he began reading in the gallery and fell fast asleep, undoubtedly because he's so weak, what with the little food they allow him and the strong medications he takes to lower his blood pressure."[105] Falla's good fortune in Hollywood aside, the U.S. music industry continued to aggravate him. In the spring of 1946, he received a long-delayed letter from Associated Music (in English) containing a series of questions on citizenship and residency, by means of which the U.S. Alien Property Custodian would effect "a prompt disposition and payment of the monies due" him.[106] Months later, Falla still had no word on the status of this disposition, and in October he informed Associated Music that Hernández Suárez would soon be visiting New York on his behalf.[107] Well might Falla have appreciated additional protection: that same fall he learned from Paco Aguilar, lutenist and founder of the Cuarteto Aguilar (see figure 22), that the North American publisher Edward B. Marks had pirated Falla's early *Serenata andaluza*. It is not clear through which of Marks's predatory strategies the *Serenata* had been ensnared. (According to John Storm Roberts, Milton Cohen, a part-time salesman for the firm, habitually traveled throughout South America buying up whatever local sheet music he could amass for publication.)[108] In any case, the work had been circulating since 1935 in Marks's *Collection Moderne* (see figure 23), and, to add insult to injury, extensive alterations had been made by the editor, Luis Sucra. Falla was furious. As he told Aguilar:

> Certainly, having seen the thing in print, I've recognized measures 18 to 22 of the third page as my own . . . but from the next measure on, that smart-aleck Mr. Sucra goes back to doing things *his own way* and in the most shameless manner. Then he completely cuts those measures that . . . are precisely those

105. "Le escribo en nombre de los dos, porque Manuel está con un régimen de reposo severísimo mandado por el Dr. Ferrer a causa de un derrame a la vista y la tensión alta. Como no le dejan trabajar, ayer se puso a leer en la galería y se quedó dormido, sin duda por lo débil que está con el poco alimento que le permiten y los fuertes medicamentos para rebajar la tensión" (letter, María del Carmen to de Castro, 18 July 1946, AMF correspondence file 6838).

106. The letter from John R. Andrus, vice president of Associated Music, to Falla is dated 19 March 1946, but Falla wrote in the margin "correo ordinario, recibido el 8 de mayo" (regular mail, received 8 May) (AMF correspondence file 9162).

107. Letter, Falla to Andrus, 24 October 1946, AMF correspondence file 9162.

108. John Storm Roberts, *The Latin Tinge: The Impact of Latin American Music on the United States*, 2d ed. (New York: Oxford University Press, 1999), 47. See also Gallego, *Catálogo*, 26–27.

Figure 22. Paco Aguilar and Falla in
Los Espinillos (Alta Gracia, Córdoba,
1945). (Reprinted by kind permission
of the Archivo Manuel de Falla)

I recall as having some interest. Then he uses others of mine and ends with five unfortunate measures of his own invention.[109]

It was worse than that. Sucra's "adjustments" included rewriting various passages (in mm. 37–40 he added an extra measure to this four-bar transitional section, which now alternates meter signatures, a strategy replicated in mm. 144–47), extensive cutting (mm. 41–64, 148–75, 186–94), changing harmonies (beginning of the bolero section, m. 174), eliminating expression marks (he strikes Falla's "sentido" in m. 68), eliminating ornaments (mm. 66, 74), adding ornaments (sixteenth-note triplets in m. 177 and scalar embellishments in mm. 179–80), and incorporating hand crossings, (m. 181ff.). As Falla complained, the new coda was particularly egregious. Here Sucra altered the rhythm of the alto voice (it now appears as a dotted half note instead of three quarters) and changed pitches in the same (adding an F# in m. 196). He inserted a "poco stringendo al fine," and instead of Falla's quiet, modally colored final cadence, which resolves in a bare *pp* octave, "that smart-aleck" Sucra

109. "Por cierto que, al verla impresa, he reconocido como míos los compases 18 al 22 de la tercera página . . . pero desde el compás siguiente vuelve el fresco Sr. Sucra a hacer *de las suyas* y del modo más descarado. Luego suprime en absoluto aquellos compases que . . . son los que precisamente recuerdo como de algún interés. Utiliza después otros míos, y termina con cinco desgraciados compases de su invención" (letter, Falla to Aguilar, 9 October 1946, AMF correspondence file 6678).

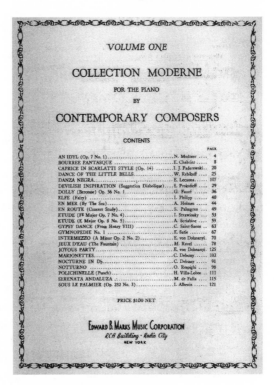

VOLUME ONE

COLLECTION MODERNE

FOR THE PIANO

BY

CONTEMPORARY COMPOSERS

CONTENTS

PRICE $1.00 NET

EDWARD B. MARKS MUSIC CORPORATION
RCA Building · Radio City
NEW YORK

Figure 23. Cover, *Collection Moderne*, E. B. Marks, which pirated Falla's *Serenata andaluza.*

inserted flashy scales with chromatic inflections and a *ff* cadence preceded by added-note dominant harmonies.

As noted, Falla disparaged his works prior to *La vida breve*, considering that "among [his] published works, there [was] nothing, nothing." But he was livid over the dismembering of his *Serenata*, which, moreover, had been perpetrated on account of that ominous loophole in U.S. copyright law so unfavorable to "Spanish nationals." For Falla, however, abuse by that law was less galling than Sucra's heavy hand. He told Hernández Suárez that the *Serenata*

> was . . . published in Madrid by Fuentes and Asenjo but without securing a copyright in the United States. Consequently, it's not strange that they've published it there; but what is really serious is that they've done so by omitting and adding measures however they like, and thus disfiguring a good part of the music. Is there any way to demand an indemnization for this *monstrosity*, moreover, to prevent them from continuing to publish it in this form?[110]

110. "[La *Serenata*] se publicó . . . en Madrid por los editores Fuentes y Asenjo, pero sin hacer el Copyright en Estados Unidos. Por consiguiente no es de extrañar que la hayan editado allí; pero lo que sí es grave es que lo hayan hecho quitando y poniendo compases

Falla, who twenty years earlier had laughed off the idea that anyone would want to pirate the song "Tus Ojillos Negros," now belatedly remembered that it had been circulating in the United States for decades. On 24 October 1946, he asked Hernández Suárez to obtain a copy in New York to see if "they've also made capricious messes (caprichosos desarreglos) in the song."[111] It is not clear what sort of success Hernández Suárez had, if any.

On 14 November 1946, Falla died quietly in his sleep of heart failure brought on by high blood pressure. The night before, after eating his habitually modest supper, he had been "very animated"; perhaps this was the burst of energy that sometimes precedes death.[112] Upon finding him the next morning, María del Carmen undoubtedly prayed for her brother's soul passing through the narrow gate to eternal life, where, she would have silently affirmed, the perfection that had eluded Manolo on earth now greeted him. In the coming days, the conscientious María del Carmen also visited a more pragmatic realm: making funeral arrangements, receiving visitors, and answering letters of condolence. There was also the usual business correspondence. The very day Falla died, Associated Music wrote with the latest installment in the legal runaround still sabotaging his royalties: the Alien Property Custodian had rejected his claim but, as the vice president of Associated Music explained, legislation had been passed by the U.S. Congress "permitting the Alien Property Custodian to return the property which he has vested, after the submission of a proper claim by Eschig,"[113] María del Carmen simply filed the letter, leaving its numbing details to be unraveled later. There was also a note of sympathy from Iriberri, who expressed regret that illness prevented him from visiting her.[114] Ever solicitous, he also mentioned that proceeds from *Carnegie Hall* were on the way. Sure enough, a few days later Falla's fee of 2,000 dollars (less Federal Films Incorporated's commission of 10 percent) arrived. Accompanying the check (for which the composer would have been so grateful) was a note from Harry Fox, who pre-

---

a su antojo, y desfigurando asi una buena parte de la música. ¿Hay manera de exigir una indemnización por esta *barrabasada*, impidiendo además que sigan editando en esa forma?" (letter, Falla to Hernández Suárez, 24 October 1946, AMF correspondence file 7017). This was not the first time the *Serenata* had been abused. It is not clear whether Falla knew of the 1931 recording (Odéon 188.755) for castanets and orchestra, which cuts mm. 107–74; that it had been made by his admired colleague La Argentina, who had danced the Paris premiere of the 1925 *El amor brujo*, would surely have distressed him. See *Manuel de Falla: Grabaciones Históricas* (Documentos Sonoros del Patrimonio de Andalucia), DS–0121.

111. Letter, Falla to Hernández Suarez, 24 October 1946, AMF carpeta 7017.

112. L. A., "Dolor de España: El cadáver de Falla—la hermana del maestro cuenta los últimos momentos del músico genial," *Fotos*, 11 January 1947, AMF press file.

113. Letter, Urban to Falla, 14 November 1946, AMF correspondence file 9162.

114. Letter, Iriberri to María del Carmen, 18 November 1946, AMF correspondence file 7124.

dicted that Falla's "works will [now] be more important."[115] As we shall see, Fox's intuition would be borne out in some surprising ways.

THE AFTERMATH: *ATLÁNTIDA*

Immediately, the *franquista* press was covering Falla's death. Alongside diatribes against the "foreign treachery" that was keeping Axis-friendly Spain out of the United Nations, headlines such as "Falla: Musician, Ascetic, Patriot" or "Falla, Knight of the Faith" appeared in papers throughout Spain.[116] Other headlines explicitly linked the composer to the *franquista* cause: one in *Arriba* read "A Letter from Falla Expressing His Joy at the Liberation of Madrid from the 'Reds,'" and reprinted a 1939 letter from Falla to music critic Carlos Bosch.[117] Journalists also emphasized Falla's loyalty to Spain, the "beloved country" he had never really wanted to leave, and his moral rigor, sometimes in the same breath. *Ya*, for example, reported that Falla had left France in 1914 because he "disparaged the worldly life in the great city of Paris," as if the outbreak of World War I had no bearing on his decision.[118] The papers also exalted Falla's will, with any number of headlines quoting its most memorable line: "I require that in the execution of my works the purest Christian morality be observed."[119]

Funeral services were held on 18 November in the Córdoba cathedral, the baroque edifice Argentine historian Luis Roberto Altamira called a "stone flower in the heart of the homeland." On María del Carmen's insistence there were no speeches, for she feared that any nonliturgical element could turn political.[120] Dr. Pedro Ara of the Spanish embassy in Buenos Aires embalmed Falla's body, preparing it for travel to Spain. But was it right to bury Falla in Spain, as the Franco government wished? Even the international press commented on the political dimension of this quandary, with *Time* noting "squabbles over where to bury him—in Argentina, said his anti-Franco friends; in Spain, said the Spanish embassy. The Franco government won."[121] (Among his staunchest "anti-Franco friends" was Juan José Castro.) The

115. Quoted in letter, Iriberri to María del Carmen, 6 December 1946, AMF correspondence file 7124.

116. Juan Hispaleto, "Falla: músico, asceta, patriota," *Sevilla*, 16 November 1946; "Falla, caballero de la Fe," unidentified press clipping from Extremadura, AMF press file.

117. Carlos Bosch, "Una carta de Falla expresando su alegría por la liberación del Madrid rojo," *Arriba*, 27 December 1946, AMF press file.

118. "Menospreció la vida mundana del gran París" ("Fallece en Argentina don Manuel de Falla: Su cadáver será trasladado a España a bordo del *Cabo de Hornos*," *Ya*, 15 November 1946, 1).

119. "Exijo que en la ejecución de mis obras se observe siempre la más límpia moral cristiana," *Pueblo*, 22 November 1946, 5.

120. Letter, María del Carmen to Germán, 3 December 1946, AMF correspondence file 7816.

121. "Mystery in Madrid," *Time*, 7 March 1949, 85.

obituary in the *New York Times* asserted that "during the Civil War in Spain [Falla] allied himself with the Franco forces and in 1939 [*sic*] was named president of the Institute of Spain,"[122] surely an incomplete picture given his nearly total indifference to the regime during the Argentine years. Isabel Luzuriaga, who was living in Buenos Aires at the time of the composer's death, later described to Andrew Budwig the following *coup de théâtre*: according to her, the conflict was resolved only when the casket was wrested from the Argentine authorities and hoisted with a loading hook onto the deck of a Spanish ship.[123] The event, fantastic as it sounds, did not appear in major newspapers in Buenos Aires, and it is by no means clear that Luzuriaga witnessed the episode herself. That she would be convinced of its validity so many years after the fact suggests that, at least for some, the events of Falla's burial and the questions it raised had passed into the realm of legend.

On 8 January 1947, Falla's body was returned to Spain on the warship *Marte*, having been transferred in Tenerife (Canary Islands) from the steamer *Cabo de Buena Esperanza*.[124] Thanks to special permission from Pius XII, who named Falla "a favorite son of the Church," the composer would be interred in the crypt of the Cádiz cathedral.[125] The day of the service, the cathedral was hung with funeral wreaths and black banners; outside a light rain fell. Numerous dignitaries were present, with Franco represented by the minister of justice, Raimundo Fernández Cuesta. Also paying their last respects were Padre Nemesio Otaño, director of the Madrid conservatory; Jesús Rubio, subsecretary of the Ministry of Education; Antonio de las Heras, head of the Music Section of the same ministry; José Cubiles, who thirty years earlier had premiered *Noches en los jardines de España*, representing the Real Academia de San Fernando; and Armando Corarelo representing the Instituto de España and various members of the Sociedad General de Autores Españoles, two entities that had so aggravated Falla in his later years. The Capella Clàssica of Mallorca, which Falla had mesmerized with his spiritual presence back in 1933, performed a mass by Victoria. Especially eloquent was the sepulcher marker, a simple stone with the inscription "Sólo a Dios el honor y la gloria" (To God alone honor and glory), which tourists seek out to this day.

Naturally, María del Carmen accompanied her brother's body from Argentina. The press portrayed her grief as "quiet, submissive, obedient to the designs of the Almighty"; in effect, equating her character with that of her brother and acknowl-

122. "Manuel de Falla, Composer, 70, Dies," *New York Times*, 15 November 1946, 23.

123. Interview, 25 December 1981, Madrid, cited in Budwig, "Manuel de Falla's *Atlántida*," 250n2.

124. "Santa Cruz de Tenerife, a la llegada de los restos de Falla," *ABC*, 7 January 1947, 17; Luis Calvo, "Hoy serán enterrados en la catedral de Cádiz los restos mortales de Falla," *ABC*, 9 January 1947, 1.

125. See "Falla, hijo predilecto de la Iglesia," *Arriba*, 23 December 1946, AMF press file.

edging her role in his life.[126] Now back in her native country after an absence of seven years, the "sister of the great composer," as one headline described her, was suddenly without an immediate purpose in life. After the burial, she went to San Fernando to visit her brother Germán and his family and then retired to a convent in Jeréz de la Frontera, where she lived out the rest of her days. Sadly, her mind declined. Whether mental deterioration had been building since the Civil War, whether something went awry as a result of her brother's sudden absence from her life, or whether some other cause precipitated her muddled state is unknown. Nin-Culmell visited her in the late 1950s, and to his dismay found that the once lively María del Carmen failed to recognize her erstwhile dining companion and coconspirator in mischief.[127]

It was Pemán who received by diplomatic mail all the materials for *Atlántida*, ten folders of autographs that he passed on to Germán.[128] Now that its author was dead, *Atlántida* was no longer an intensely guarded work in progress but an international curiosity. Almost immediately government officials and other interested parties approached Germán, even though he had not yet been declared the legal heir to the autographs. In mid-1947, Norberto Almandoz, director of the Seville Conservatory, insisted on copying portions of the work. In April of the same year, Padre Otaño visited Germán, intending to take the score back to Madrid for photostating. Germán initially refused, but Otaño returned to San Fernando in November to demand the autographs, which he then proceeded to hoard until March 1948.[129] Also traveling to San Fernando was Stokowski, who visited Germán in October 1951 to satisfy his decades-long curiosity about *Atlántida* by at least seeing fragments of the score he had probably given up on ever conducting. In 1953, José de las Heras, Franco's delegate of finance, culture, and public activities, tried to tempt Germán with the possibility of a concert performance of *Atlántida* in Madrid.[130] Of course, all the while Germán was receiving this steady stream of visitors the work was no closer to completion. Germán, however, who had last helped with one of his brother's compositions in 1905, the first version of *La vida breve*, set about transcribing what Falla had left of the libretto and even finalized its unfinished sections. After all, Falla had been constantly altering Verdaguer's text to suit the evolving score and had left no definitive libretto—even after twenty years of work.[131]

In 1953, seven years after Falla's death, it was decided that Ernesto Halffter would finish *Atlántida*. Many have questioned this choice. As we have seen, some friction had accumulated between Halffter and Falla, as in the misunderstanding over the

126. "Su pena es callada, sumisa, obediente a los designios del Todopoderoso" (L. A., "Dolor de España").

127. Interview with Joaquín Nin-Culmell, January 2000.

128. Sánchez García, *La correspondencia inédita*, 44.

129. Budwig, "Manuel de Falla's *Atlántida*," 266.

130. Budwig, "Manuel de Falla's *Atlántida*," 8n3, 275.

131. Budwig, "Manuel de Falla's *Atlántida*," 264–67.

Barcelona premiere of the Harpsichord Concerto and conflicts over Halffter's orchestration of the *Siete canciones populares españolas*. Other tensions had centered on Halffter's role in the Orquesta Bética de Cámera: Falla had initially favored Eduardo Torres, not Halffter, for the directorship, and when Halffter assumed that role (Torres being unavailable), Falla found some of his former student's decisions so imprudent that he told Halffter he had "absolutely no confidence in his abilities as an administrator," strong language for the painstakingly courteous Falla. At one point, Falla even told Halffter to step down temporarily.[132] Of course, we will never know whom Falla would have chosen to complete *Atlántida*, and at least some of his tangles with Halffter concern the latter's personality and administrative skills rather than his ability as a composer, which Falla genuinely admired. Perhaps the strongest argument against Halffter's candidacy, however, is the fact that in the more than four hundred letters he and Falla exchanged (most of which are three to eight pages long) Falla mentioned *Atlántida* exactly once.[133]

Once having agreed to finish "poor *Atlántida*," Halffter went about his task almost as slowly as Falla, despite a projected three-year timetable. One reason for this was that Halffter, undoubtedly disoriented in the aftermath of the Civil War, was often in debt and sometimes devoted himself to more lucrative projects.[134] Frustrated, in June 1955, Germán signed a contract with Ricordi that gave the Italian publisher the rights both to *Atlántida*'s publication and to the first performance.[135] Later that year Halffter promised Ricordi in writing that he would work exclusively on *Atlántida*. The Spanish press sarcastically registered these delays. An especially hardhitting piece by Antonio Fernández-Cid appeared in *ABC* in January 1958, almost twelve years after Falla's death. Noting Halffter's now invalid declaration that he would finish *Atlántida* by the previous summer, Fernández-Cid devoted half his column to lambasting this "unusual delay" and the other half to bemoaning the fact that the premiere was likely to take place outside Spain. This Fernández-Cid considered "an inconceivable monstrosity, an artistic crime"; after all, he declared, "the most beloved work, which occupied the greatest amount of time of our foremost musician, has to be given in Spain."[136]

132. Budwig, "Manuel de Falla's *Atlántida*," 254. See also letter, Falla to Halffter, 26 November 1930, cited on page 255; and letter, Falla to Segismundo Romero, 5 April 1926, cited in *Cartas a Segismundo Romero*, 231–32.

133. Budwig, "Manuel de Falla's *Atlántida*," 262.

134. Halffter's debts are detailed in Budwig, "Manuel de Falla's *Atlántida*," 284–85.

135. Germán had also removed 65 sheets from the total of 217 (distributed in the ten folders handed him by Pemán) that he believed to be duplicates, ensuring that Ricordi received only 152 sheets, each of which was labeled with a number indicating probable ordering. The remaining 65 sheets surfaced only after Germán died on 29 July 1959. Budwig, "Manuel de Falla's *Atlántida*," 265–67.

136. "La obra más querida, la que más horas ocupó del primero de nuestros músicos, tiene que darse en España" (Antonio Fernández-Cid, "Sobre la *Atlántida*," *ABC*, 29 January 1958, AMF press file).

Another obstacle to *Atlántida*'s completion came from within Falla's own family. Under the influence of her confessor in Jeréz de la Frontera, the mentally fragile María del Carmen underwent a fit of scrupulosity not unlike those her brother had suffered. In October 1960, she decided that it was her moral duty to uphold the codicil in Falla's will that forbade scenic representations of his works. María del Carmen's sudden intervention in her brother's artistic legacy could have been disastrous in any number of ways had Germán's daughter Maribel not intervened. Aware that only a higher Church authority could relieve her aunt's fears, Maribel took the matter to the cardinal archbishop of Seville. With the aid of his professor of moral theology, who examined the text, and his *maestro de capilla*, who studied the score, the cardinal archbishop decided that *Atlántida* merited scenic representation.[137] Not only was María del Carmen persuaded, but she also surrendered to her niece her status as executor of Falla's now famous will.

Meanwhile, rumors of a possible Spanish premiere were circulating. But where would it take place? The three-thousandth anniversary of the founding of Cádiz had come and gone in 1955, and in Madrid the Real was temporarily shut down. The strongest *Atlántida* lobby was gaining momentum in Barcelona. Some of its advocates even argued that Falla had composed the cantata's vocal passages expressly for the Orfeó Català, which continued performing during the postwar period despite Franco's prohibition on the official use of Catalan and on overt manifestations of Catalan culture, such as performing the *sardana*, the emblematic regional dance.[138] A provocatively titled article, "Does *L'Atlàntida* Run the Risk of Sinking Again before It Can Be Premiered in Barcelona?" rather heatedly cites witnesses to Falla's "promise" to uphold Barcelona's "moral rights" to the work even as it referred to others who doubted the work's very existence.[139] Soprano Victoria de los Ángeles, herself a Catalan, joined in by tagging *Atlántida* "the Catalan *Parsifal*." In doing so, she invoked her region's identification with Wagner's last opera, which is set in the craggy peaks of Montsalvat/Montserrat, that is, a mere forty kilometers from downtown Barcelona.[140] Of course, the discussion about *Atlántida*'s special significance to Catalans took place in an environment of fear, for Franco was convinced that regional identities would attempt to assert themselves and thus threaten the regime's inflexible vision of "one Spain."

137. Correspondence on the matter is cited in Budwig, "Manuel de Falla's *Atlántida*," 312–13.

138. See Stanley Brandes, "The Sardana: Catalan Dance and Catalan National Identity," *Journal of American Folklore* 103, no. 407 (1990): 24–41.

139. "¿L'Atlàntida corre el peligro de sumergirse otra vez, antes de llegar a estrenarse a Barcelona?" (*Destino*, 19 December 1959, AMF press file).

140. Cited in Antonio Fernández-Cid, "La Atlántida se estrenará en 1960," *ABC* (Seville), 1 July 1959, 34, AMF press file. On the significance of *Parsifal* in Spain, see Hess, *Manuel de Falla and Modernism in Spain*, 19–21.

Finally, Barcelona won out, and on 24 November 1961, fifteen years after Falla's death, *Atlántida* premiered at that city's Teatre Liceu in a sixty-five-minute version without scenery or movement. Through a variety of political machinations, Eduardo Toldrá rather than Halffter conducted. Unfortunately, Toldrá had only three months to prepare and was mailed the proofs page by page (rather the way Falla had treated Landowska on the eve of the Harpsichord Concerto's premiere). An audience of around three thousand gave the work a warm ovation, as the national and international press noted. Victoria de los Ángeles's "Dream of Isabella" made an especially strong impression, and at the conclusion Halffter appeared onstage holding aloft the score as a tribute to the late composer. In that first audience were several of Franco's ministers, as well as Juan Carlos de Borbón, the claimant to the Spanish throne, who would eventually see Spain through to democracy after Franco's death. Indeed, the premiere of *Atlántida* in Barcelona had its political significance, striking some as a loosening of Franco's anti-Catalan policies. As the *New York Times* pointed out, the Spanish minister of education himself "not only authorized [the performance] but insisted that the . . . work be sung in Catalan and have a Catalan setting." The reporter concluded that this was "a gesture of political significance in Spain, where Catalans have complained that the regime of Generalísimo Francisco Franco has been suppressing their cultural heritage."[141] Still, one must be realistic. Trying to inhibit a performance of *Atlántida* would have been a very stupid move indeed (even for Franco's censors), given Falla's stature and the regime's tireless courting of him. Quite possibly the Ministry of Education saw the premiere as a sop to Catalan nationalism that would cost the government nothing and perhaps even foment some regional support for the regime.

More of a Pandora's box was the staged version, which premiered at Milan's La Scala on 18 June 1962 under Thomas Schippers. In this format, *Atlántida* ran for close to three hours and was full of Halffter's music. This was because after Germán's death in 1959 Halffter managed to persuade Ricordi that "Els jocs de les Pleiades" needed a new text, which he secured—some 156 verses in all—from the Catalan poet Josep María Sagarra.[142] (As Budwig argues, Halffter had in fact already been thinking along these lines, for he habitually overlooked Falla's continuous draft for the whole work, instead completing every unfinished scene, even those Falla had abandoned as early as 1931.) Critics noted the undue length, which they felt was heightened by the fact that soloists Teresa Stratas (Isabel) and Giuletta Simoniato (Pyrene) sang only a few minutes each (Lino Puglisi sang the Corrifeo, that is, the narrator who comments on the action in the fashion of a Greek chorus). Likewise, the public registered its objections; at least one newspaper described "whistles and boos . . . from the upper galleries, traditionally the seats of the most ardent opera lovers."[143]

141. "World Premiere for Falla Work," *New York Times*, 25 November 1961, 27.
142. Budwig, "Manuel de Falla's *Atlántida*," 301–2.
143. "Premiere in Milan for Falla Cantata," *New York Times*, 19 June 1962, 28.

Opinion was also divided over *Atlántida*'s stylistic unity. One reviewer found "no evident discrepancies of style," while Nin-Culmell, whose opinion surely counts more than anyone else's, recalls that Halffter's passages "jumped out at [him]," so jarringly different were they from Falla's.[144] Entering the fray was Falla's old friend Segismundo Romero, who in the Spanish press lashed out at the incomprehension of international critics, some of whose reactions had been tepid, to say the least. Romero thundered that "the concept of 'semifailure' applied to the Milan premiere of *Atlántida* was totally inadmissible, and the idea that the work was 'wounded' even more inadmissible."[145] *Franquista* critics, of course, persisted in seeing the work as a symbol of *hispanidad*, echoing a tradition established by Regino Sainz de la Maza, who as long ago as 1939 had called *Atlántida* "the perennial voice of Spain."[146]

Not surprisingly, conductors did not exactly leap at the opportunity to program *Atlántida*. In the decade after the La Scala premiere, it received only a handful of performances. One of these took place in New York on 29 September 1962, where Falla's longtime admirer Ernest Ansermet conducted the Metropolitan Opera Orchestra and Chorus.[147] There was no staging or scenery, and unfortunately only a portion of the work was given, presumably because preparation time had been scant. Harold Schonberg complained: "Alas! . . . the Metropolitan Opera cut not only the entire second part but also a section of the first. There are 346 pages in the Ricordi vocal score. The Metropolitan went up to page 66 and jumped to 267, thus omitting about 60 per cent of the score."[148] There was, however, time on the program for the more familiar *El amor brujo*, which was performed by Jean Madeira and described in the press as a "curtain raiser."[149] Madeira also sang in *Atlántida*, along with Eileen Farrell and George London. Joseph Machlis's translation, although "clear, singable and indispensable," was deemed insufficient to "this radiant tribute to Catholic Spain."[150] Additional stature was conferred on *Atlántida* on 30 Sep-

144. Fedele d'Amico, "Italy: A Revival and a Premiere," *Musical America* 82, no. 9 (September 1962): 102; Joaquín Nin-Culmell, personal interview with author, January 2000.

145. "Es totalmente inadmisible el concepto de semi-fracaso que aplica al estreno de *Atlántida* en Milan y más inadmisible que la obra esté herida" ("Más sobre *Atlántida*: Segismundo Romero contesta a Jackes Lonchampt [*sic*]," unidentified press clipping, AMF press file).

146. Regino Sainz de la Maza, "Manuel de Falla," *Vértice* 21 (April 1939), cited in Pérez Zalduondo, "El nacionalismo como eje de la política musical," 261.

147. Ernest Ansermet, "Falla's *Atlántida*," *Opera News* 27, no. 1 (29 September 1962): 8–13.

148. Harold C. Schonberg, "Music: Met Gives *Atlántida* Premiere," *New York Times*, 1 October 1962, 36.

149. F. M. [Frank Merkling?], "Falla in Philharmonic Hall," *Opera News* 27, no. 3 (10 November 1962): 27.

150. F. M., "Falla in Philharmonic Hall," 27.

tember, when more than 250 officials from the United Nations attended a repeat performance, including Acting Secretary U Thant and various members of the Security Council. John D. Rockefeller III, chairman of the board of the newly opened Philharmonic Hall, greeted the audience.[151]

In 1972, Ricordi tried to address some of *Atlántida*'s problems. It was decided that Halffter's 1962 edition would be suppressed; accordingly, Ricordi asked him to remove all the newly composed music it contained. To be sure, Halffter pared down *Atlántida* to eighty-two minutes for a performance at Lucerne in 1976, the centennial of Falla's birth. But he refused to publish the so-called Lucerne *Atlántida* right away, for he wanted to expand it—but only slightly. This was the version recorded for the record label EMI by Rafael Frühbeck de Burgos in 1978; when Ricordi published a new vocal score, however, it was the Lucerne version that appeared.[152]

Is there a definitive version of *Atlántida*? Like *Turandot*, Mahler's Tenth Symphony, Bartók's Viola Concerto, and other posthumously completed twentieth-century masterpieces, *Atlántida* raises more questions than it answers. In addition to whatever conclusions we may draw about Falla's creative process from the work's tortured history, *Atlántida* throws up significant barriers for the listening public. One is the language, for the international audience is likely to be unfamiliar with Catalan. Also, as Andrew Thompson has pointed out in a review of Edmon Colomer's 1993 recording of the "flawed masterpiece," Verdaguer's poem is so loaded with symbols as to be "intractable."[153] An even more significant obstacle is *Atlántida*'s depiction of Spanish Catholicism evangelizing the planet. Even if Falla sincerely believed that this was "the only definitely glorious thing" Spain had ever done, the theme of Christianizing indigenous peoples, with its attendant implications of oppression and conquest, has limited appeal in a postcolonial era, however luminous the work's peak moments.

While the music of *Atlántida* may suggest more than one stylistic label—hieratic monumentalism, modernist traditionalism, or even eclecticism—the work's compositional history is a microcosm of Falla's personal tragedy. Why did the inspired creator of the spare, economical Concerto and the terse and witty *Retablo* persist for twenty years in a medium largely uncongenial to him? Why did he publicly affirm his desire to finish a project for which there was clearly no end in sight? *Atlántida* became a compulsion, a distancing mechanism through which Falla could remove himself from the horrors of twentieth-century Europe and fashion an inspiring narrative of past glories. But as disillusioned as he was by the world around him he

151. Schonberg, "Music," 36.

152. Another pioneering recording is that by the Orchestre de la Suisse Romande, conducted by Ansermet and featuring Monserrat Caballé (CD VEL 2005), although only excerpts are given and it is sung in Italian. See Ronald Crichton, "Opera on Disc, *Atlántida*, Falla-Halffter," *Opera*, September 1993, 1128–29.

153. Andrew Thomson, "CD: Manuel de Falla/Ernesto Halffter—*Atlántida*," *Musical Times* 132 (October 1993): 594.

was also incapable of vanquishing his old enemy, scrupulosity. Fear that he would produce something less than perfect stymied him to the point that *not* finishing *Atlántida* became part of Falla's very existence, a condition his unsteady health only exacerbated. As one writer put it, it is "understandable that he would never finish the work. It wasn't only the pressing anguish, the dreadful struggle . . . produced by an illness in irreversible process, together with a compulsive neurosis. It's that, deep down, he wasn't able to finish it. It was his compensation, his pretext and his viaticum, in a world in which he felt radically alienated."[154] If *Atlántida*'s place in Falla's legacy has yet to be completely resolved, other works of his have left their mark on musical culture in ways that reflect an array of thought-provoking social and aesthetic issues, as the next chapter will explore.

154. "Se comprende que no terminara su obra. No era sólo la premiosa angustia, la atroz lucha . . . producido doblemente por una enfermedad de proceso irreversible y por la neu-rosis compulsiva. Es que, en el fondo, no la podía terminar. Era su compensación, su asidero y su viático, en un mundo en que el que se experimentaba radicalmente alienado" (Luis Jiménez, "Mi recuerdo humano de Manuel de Falla," paper presented at a conference of the Comisón Pro-Centenario de la Muerte de Manuel de Falla, 28 April 1976, University of Granada, 1980, 66; cited in Budwig, "Manuel de Falla's *Atlántida*," 246).

Chapter 10

Falla's Legacy

In the reception of Falla's works in Spain, self, circumstance, and music intersect in compelling patterns that expose the innate idiosyncrasies in what I referred to above as the "narrative urge." It also reinforces the idea that music cannot exist as "the score itself," reified in some utopian preserve where "aesthetics alone" holds sway, but as an utterance whose meaning will shift depending on the premises of a particular environment. As we have seen, the political Right promoted both Falla's music and his character, emphasizing the period from 1932 on. Ironically, these were Falla's least productive years. Nonetheless, in concentrating on this period, the Franco government was able to find the most powerful ammunition for its propaganda machine, so that, with censorship wiping out all other points of view, *franquismo* singlehandedly laid the foundation for Falla's legacy in Spain.

FALLA AND SPAIN

There were, of course, some major discrepancies between this rightist orientation, with its fustian diction and warped nostalgias, and the reality of Falla's life. Commentators closely allied to the regime, such as Pemán, who continued to discuss Falla in the press as late as the 1960s, would hardly have been likely to acknowledge that the composer initially embraced much of the Republic's agenda. Yet, whatever his personal misgivings about "freethinking," "eclecticism," or "Robespierrean ideas," there is nothing to suggest that Falla actively opposed the *principle* of religious freedom (recall the delicacy with which he dealt with Lorca's "Ode" and his friendships with atheists and liberals). He was as willing to criticize the administration and practices of the Spanish Church as he was the vandalism against holy sites. The latter Falla saw not so much as an attack on a corrupt temporal power as a direct assault on God, and he feared that the Republic was bent on destroying not only the external trappings of the Spanish Church but the religious impulse itself.

Was this impression exaggerated or was the anonymous author of "Catholic Incongruence," the editorial that reproached Falla for overreacting to the significance of the Seville homage, closer to the mark? Nowadays there is a consensus among historians that the Republic "dug its own grave" through its inaction against rabid anticlericalism.[1] Certainly it was the "single issue" that ignited the passions of many who would have otherwise remained uninvolved. Thus, it is safe to say that had "circumstance" been different—had the Republic's religious policies been promulgated more gradually, had fewer inflammatory statements such as Azaña's circulated, or had antireligious violence been less maniacal—Falla might have stayed loyal to the government he initially favored.

As argued here, the composer's efforts to remain apolitical failed even more resoundingly once the war broke out. In treating that period, rightists have overlooked significant flaws in his loyalties while leftists have failed to acknowledge certain realities. Weeks after intervening on Lorca's behalf, Falla was availing himself of the twisted power of Nationalist rhetoric; the tone and volume of his correspondence with Pemán, Orgaz, Queipo de Llano, and Sainz Rodrigo, moreover, imply more than a resigned acceptance of the Nationalist effort or the mere desire to protect himself and his friends. To suggest this, however, is not to overlook the element of fear: considered a *rojillo* in some circles, Falla was mindful of the mortal risk for anyone suspected of Republican sympathies during the repression of Granada. But even if many of Falla's letters were dictated by fear—of the sort most of us can barely imagine—it is still impossible to affirm that *fear alone* motivated him. Falla may have been afraid *not* to compose the *Himno marcial,* for example. But it does not necessarily follow that he was unmoved by Orgaz's exhortations to serve a Nationalist vision of the *patria,* which, of course, included protection of the Church. (His friend Maritain, on the other hand, argued passionately against the very concept of a "holy war," holding that "in its essence war is of the things that belong to Caesar.")[2] Nor could fear have been the sole impetus behind his guarded but voluntary declaration to the magazine *Spain.* Although he may have issued the statement to put an end to pressure from the Right, the fact that he shared his views with Roland-Manuel (and perhaps others) confirms his sincerity. As for the Instituto de España, it would seem that anyone truly fearful would have silently accepted the honorary title and

1. Mitchell, *Betrayal of the Innocents,* 22.

2. Jacques Maritain, "From 'The Idea of Holy War,'" in Sperber, *And I Remember Spain,* 240.

kept a low profile. Instead, Falla undertook an extensive letter-writing campaign to correct "deformation" and arrive at a position he could defend once his role in the organization was properly explicated.

We do not know the composer's understanding of the darker aspects of the Nationalist enterprise, namely, the role of its German and Italian allies, the effects of fascism throughout Europe, and Hitler's designs. Nor could Falla have had fore-knowledge of the virulence of Franco's postwar reprisals. His support for the Na-tionalists *during the conflict itself*, therefore, must be counterbalanced by his polite indifference to the Franco government's overtures during the Argentine years. Hav-ing gone to Latin America for professional reasons and with every intention of re-turning, he was *not* a political exile, as is sometimes suggested.[3] His rejection of Franco's enticements no more indicates opposition to the regime than his dona-tions to Republican camps and advocacy for friends on the "wrong" side in Spain imply support for the vanquished Republic. Rather, in Argentina Falla pursued *self-imposed* exile—from the pettiness of public life and from the horrors of a war that surely echoed in his memory until the day he died. As María del Carmen put it, he sought "liberty." And in those final years he actually found it, for his desire to re-main "above the workings of politics" was fulfilled in Argentina as in no other pe-riod of his life.

And now? Since Franco's death in 1975, many Spaniards have tried to put the Civil War and the dictatorship behind them.[4] Spain's young democracy seems as-sured: as this book was being written sitcoms about the Franco period appeared on the television channel operated by the Right-leaning Aznar government; and books such as Andres Sopeña Monsalve's *El florido pensil* (1994), a spoof-memoir of Catho-lic-Nationalist education in the Franco period, have made the best-seller list.[5] The relationship between Franco and the Church is a focus of open debate, and in 2000 it was even proposed that the Spanish Church formally apologize for its alliance with

3. Demarquez, for example, refers to acceptance of Falla's "liberalism" as a factor in "his exile overseas" (Demarquez, *Manuel de Falla*, 5). The sixth chapter of Budwig's "Manuel de Falla's *Atlántida*" is entitled "Exile in Argentina"; on page 215 the author states: "Although Falla was not driven out of Spain, he considered himself . . . an exile."

4. A 1983 poll confirmed that "far from seeing the Civil War as a glorious crusade to defend the true religion . . . 73% of Spaniards regard it as 'a shameful period of Spanish history that it is better to forget'" (cited in Paul Preston, "The Legacy of the Spanish Civil War," in *"¡No Pasarán!" Art, Literature and the Spanish Civil War*, edited by Stephen M. Hart [London: Tamesis, 1988], 14).

5. The sitcom *Cuéntame cómo pasó* (Tell Me How It Happened) draws on various *tipos* (character types) of the period: the fortune-seeking uncle who makes good in Argentina after the Civil War, the young man fulfilling his military service, the harmlessly icono-clastic beatnik priest, and the women who work as seamstresses or secretaries. Occasional footage of the *caudillo* (Franco) completes the ambiance.

the dictatorship.[6] It is easy (and perhaps part of memory's natural defense mechanism) to let Falla's praise for Franco's "undefeated soldiers" and his professions of "complete respect for and loyalty to his Excellency the Generalísimo" slide into collective oblivion. As we review them here, we must ask to what extent we ought to condemn a sickly old man whose faith, although it blinded him to many realities, caused him to make remarks that now seem tragically flawed. Unlike Picasso, who refused to exhibit *Guernica* in Franco's Spain, or Casals, who turned down invitations to play there as long as Franco remained in power, Falla could have spoken out after the war. That he did not do so may make us uneasy today. But one who sees God before all else may become curiously tongue-tied over temporal matters.

Of course, it is Falla's music that prompts our reflections on his self and circumstance. Having already considered the obstacles *Atlántida* encountered, we now turn to other practical details of Falla's legacy in Spain. Unfortunately, deficiencies in the postwar musical infrastructure, coupled with the requirements of the works themselves, caused Falla's music to suffer in the immediate postwar period. Few Madrid- or Barcelona-based dance companies could produce *The Three-Cornered Hat*.[7] Similarly, staging requirements for the thirty-minute *Retablo* involve a huge investment. Neither did the unusual instrumentation of the Harpsichord Concerto lend itself to frequent performances, although it was played fairly regularly during the early Franco period, with portions broadcast on Radio Nacional prior to the news.[8] Performances of the more conventionally scored *Noches en los jardines de España* were certainly more common. As for *La vida breve*, as in Falla's lifetime, productions during the Franco period were infrequent, although the Teatro María

6. In the past decade, many Spaniards have confronted the realities of the war and dictatorship with candor and dignity. Other matters, which range from the issue of the beatification of clergy killed during the war to the Church's need for self-criticism, are addressed in a special issue of the general readership magazine *La Aventura de la Historia* (2, no. 17 [March 2000]). Since the 1950s, individual priests had been criticizing the regime; in 1971, after the Second Vatican Council, an assembly of Spanish clerics rejected the dictatorship's ideology. See Preston, *Politics of Revenge*, 40.

7. See Hess, "Manuel de Falla's *The Three Cornered Hat* and the Advent of Modernism in Spain," Ph.D. diss., University of California, Davis, 1994, 5–7. For decades, *The Three-Cornered Hat* held a central place in the international dance repertory, prompting the *New York Times* dance critic Clive Barnes to call it a "20th-century masterpiece" in his review of the 1969 revival by the Joffrey Ballet (Clive Barnes, "Dance: Falla's *Three-Cornered Hat*," *New York Times*, 26 September 1969, New York Public Library clippings file). Other dance critics have been less sanguine about its status in recent decades: apropos the Joffrey production, Arlene Croce wondered if *The Three-Cornered Hat* represented "a diminished aesthetic tradition beyond hope of revival" (Arlene Croce, "New York Newsletter: From *Tricorne* to Twyla Tharp," *Dancing Times* 40, no. 710 [November 1969]: 73). See also Deborah Jowitt on the ballet's "quaintness" in "Dance: 1919 Revisited," *Village Voice*, 2 October 1969, 27–28.

8. I wish to thank Michael Christoforidis for this information.

Guerrero in Madrid mounted it in 1945. As mentioned above, the Real remained closed until 1997. Would Falla have felt bemused or vindicated by the program for the reopening? For that gala occasion, the Real offered *La vida breve* and *The Three-Cornered Hat*, the former selected after a seventy-two year delay and the latter tagged as inferior to "a chapter out of the Black Legend" when it premiered at the same theater in 1921. As memories of *franquismo* recede (or become increasingly selective), new relationships and relevancies present themselves. An especially telling paradox is the Archivo Manuel de Falla itself: although it preserves the memory of a public figure lionized by the Right, and even houses his letters to Nationalist officials, it was built during the tenure of the liberal socialist government of the 1980s.

What of Falla's influence on Spanish music? Despite his reluctance to impose his outlook on others, he remains a point of reference in the scholarship of twentieth-century Spanish music. In his well-known survey, Tomás Marco devotes an entire chapter to Falla, declaring him "the most important composer Spain has produced in the twentieth century" largely for having substituted the neoclassical vocabulary of universalism for nationalism, so rooted in *andalucismo*.[9] Specific stylistic influences, whether nationalist or universalist, are harder to detect in subsequent generations, however. Some of this lack of continuity is due to political upheaval. From Falla's "class" of students, García Ascot and her husband left Spain for Mexico, as did Salazar and Rodolfo Halffter (Ernesto's brother) on account of the war. Other members of the same generation, such as Bacarisse and Bautista, also dispersed themselves, rendering impossible the notion of a Falla school, or even a Spanish one. Others were tragically silenced by the war: Fernando Remacha, for example, did not compose at all during that three-year period and afterward had to run the family business in Tudela. This considerably reduced his output, although his 1964 cantata *Jesucristo en la Cruz* (Jesus Christ on the Cross) has been said to recapture Falla's austere neoclassicism.[10] Other composers active in Spain after the Civil War revived *andalucismo*, the style Falla rejected. Noteworthy here is Joaquín Rodrigo, whose *Concierto de Aranjuez*, finished in 1939, put Spanish music back on the international map, albeit largely as a "picture postcard" of "sunny Spain." Joaquín Turina, who has been rather harshly accused of both excessive regionalism and kneejerk formalism (the latter presumably attributable to his studies at the Schola Cantorum), composed nothing during the war. Burdened with financial pressures throughout his life, from 1940 until his death in 1949 he held a high position in the *franquista* musical infrastructure; several of his prewar works, such as the orchestral *La procesión del Rocío* and *La oración del torero* (The Bullfighter's Prayer) have enjoyed a certain afterlife. Cristóbal Halffter, nephew of Ernesto and Rodolfo, took on themes of national significance in his opera *Don Quijote* of 1970 and *Elegía a la muerte de tres poetas españoles* (Elegy on the Death of Three Spanish Poets) of 1975; he also experi-

9. Marco, *Siglo XX*, 31–42.
10. Marco, *Siglo XX*, 138.

mented with electronic media such as tape, as in his *Espejos* (Mirrors) of 1964. Composers of Halffter's generation, moreover, represent the musical dimension of the gradual relaxation of *franquismo*: as the Spanish economy began to prosper (thanks in large part to the tourist industry), the regime's rabidly isolationist stance weakened. Thus, a composer like Juan Hidalgo, for example, could explore integral serialism, as in his *Cuarteto 1958* (Quartet 1958), while absorbing the influence of John Cage, whose experimentalism changed Hidalgo's outlook completely, and which prompted the aleatoric works *Offenes-Trio* and *Ciu-quartet Music* of the same year.

In all of this, Falla's stylistic influence remains elusive. It is tempting—even worthwhile—to speculate on what might have been, however. How, for example, might successive generations have realized Falla's interest in medieval and Golden Age sources? This tendency emerges only in isolated cases, such as Remacha's cantata *Jesucristo en la cruz* mentioned above, which draws on Barbieri's *Cancionero del palacio*. A corollary question is even more intriguing: what if more than a handful of European neoclassical composers had followed Falla's lead and drawn on medieval and Renaissance models instead of confining themselves to ironic treatments of sonata form and common-practice harmony? One of the major polemics in twentieth-century music, Stravinskian neoclassicism versus Schoenbergian serialism, might have taken on some significant new dimensions.

A more concrete aspect of Falla's legacy is the considerable number of compositions that either use his themes or take his memory as a point of departure. It is not only Spanish composers who have been so inspired: Poulenc's Three Novelettes, Lennox Berkeley's *Improvisation on a Theme of Manuel de Falla*, Malipiero's *Variations on the Pantomime from El amor brujo*, and, perhaps best known, Miles Davis's *Sketches of Spain* all use Falla's themes, while Juan José Castro's *El llanto de las sierras* (*En recuerdo de Manuel de Falla muerto en las sierras de Córdoba*) (Mourning of the Sierra: In Memory of Manuel de Falla Dead in the Córdoba Sierra) and Gonzalo de Olavide's *Sinfonía* (*Homenaje a Falla*) pay homage less directly.[11] These compositions also confirm the Spanish musical-academic world's estimation of Falla as the musical representative of the *vanguardia*. As noted, this position, which is still vociferously advocated, has it roots in the reception of the *Retablo* and the Harpsichord Concerto, seen as compelling examples of modernist universalism since the 1920s.

Perhaps the most paradoxical aspect of Falla the composer is this: as much as he struggled with indecision, he slipped from one style to another with almost disconcerting ease. After the conventional *zarzuelas* and salon pieces of the turn of the

---

11. The most complete catalog of such works is found in Yvan Nommick, "Des Hommages de Falla aux 'Homages' à Falla," in *Manuel de Falla: Latinité et Universalité—Actes du Colloque International tenu en Sorbonne, 18–21 novembre 1996*, edited by Louis Jambou (Paris: Presses de l'Université de Paris-Sorbonne, 1999), 515–41.

century, he experimented with *wagnerismo* in *La vida breve*. Then, rejecting late romantic strategies, he embraced in the *Cuatro piezas españolas* traits of Albéniz's harmonic vocabulary even as he was digesting the language of French impressionism in the *Trois mélodies*, which belatedly resurfaced in *Psyché*. His finesse with the miniature took shape with the *Siete canciones populares españolas*, with their modernized—some would say Frenchified—harmonization of traditional Spanish materials, a strategy he also pursued in *Noches en los jardines de España*. With *El amor brujo*, *The Three-Cornered Hat*, and the *Fantasía bética*, on the other hand, he adopted full-blown *andalucismo* only to make a complete about-face with the neoclassical *Retablo* and Harpsichord Concerto. Even as Falla was exploring this latter style, described here as "his true voice," however, he was beginning his work on *Atlántida*. There he embarked on new paths again, some hinted at in *Pour le Tombeau de Paul Dukas* (a jewel in the pianist's repertory that deserves greater exposure), others suggested by Renaissance counterpoint. Unlike Stravinsky, Falla pursued these new directions without fanfare or proselytizing. We can only guess at what might have resulted had he not stalled on *Atlántida* and continued his journey of stylistic variety. We know, for example, that he was fascinated by Webern and owned several of that composer's scores.[12] Might he have taken up serialism had *Atlántida* not consumed him? Or was it mainly Webern's finely chiseled orchestration that attracted him? Given his creative flexibility—and willingness to reinvent himself musically—the possibility is not entirely remote.

THE OTHER FALLA

If in Spain Falla's works exemplify restraint, purity, and understatement, and if the heterogeneous timbres and sharp-edged concision of the *Retablo* and the Harpsichord Concerto confirm his status as the musical leader of the *vanguardia*, a rather different picture emerges when we consider his reception in the United States. Crucial here is that country's monolithic commercial music industry ("the culture industry," as Adorno would have it).[13] Given its overwhelming power, both then and now, no picture of Falla can be complete unless we take this phenomenon into account, even if questions raised along these lines are provocative and can only be touched on here. For example, if we agree that the phenomenon of popularization is related to culturally based and ultimately arbitrary constructions of "popular" and "high" art, terms Lawrence W. Levine has roundly described as "crude labels," what exactly is implied when we acknowledge that Falla's music has been popular-

12. Sergio de Castro, public lecture, Granada, July 1992. See also letter, Falla to Iriberri, 12 July 1945 (AMF correspondence file 7124).

13. Theodor Adorno, *The Culture Industry: Selected Essays on Mass Culture*, edited by J. M. Bernstein (London and New York: Routledge, 1991).

ized?[14] How is it possible that a work such as *El amor brujo*, which was criticized in Spain in 1915 for being too close to the "foreign modernism" of Debussy and Ravel, was so overwhelmingly approved as a "light classic" in the United States just a few decades later?[15] In short, what consumer needs in the United States have been satisfied by Falla's music?

We have seen that in "serious" musical circles in the United States during the 1920s the archmodernism of the *Retablo* openly conflicted with Falla's more overtly nationalist works, with his modernist style the more highly regarded of the two. The unimpressive performance history of *La vida breve* in U.S. opera houses bears this out. After the Metropolitan Opera dropped it in 1926, Bori performed it several times at Ravinia (near Chicago), and productions in Philadelphia, New York (the City Opera), Aspen, Santa Fe, and Boston followed.[16] As always, programming was a vital consideration: sometimes Falla's own music was used to fill out the program, as in the New York City Opera performance, where Iturbi conducted *La vida breve* and *El amor brujo*; or in Sarah Caldwell's performance in Boston, which coupled *La vida breve* with a less than successful *Retablo*.[17] (Santa Fe's solution, pairing *La vida breve* with Ravel's *L'Enfant et les Sortilèges*, set a promising precedent but was never continued.) Perhaps the most apt summation of this state of affairs came just before Alicia de Larrocha's all Granados program at Carnegie Hall in December 1967, when Harold Schonberg made a pointed suggestion. Commenting on the lack of opportunity to hear the opera version of *Goyescas*, he proposed: "Here is a double bill for somebody: *Goyescas* and Manuel de Falla's *La vida breve*. Anybody listening?" Directors have hardly embraced the possibility.[18]

Then there is Leopold Stokowski, one of the central protagonists in the reception of Falla's music in the United States. Although that media star never fulfilled his dream of being the first to conduct *Atlántida*, his premiere of *El amor brujo* in

14. Lawrence W. Levine, *Highbrow/Lowbrow: The Emergence of Cultural Hierarchy in America* (Cambridge and London: Harvard University Press, 1988), 3.

15. Critic Michael Steinberg wryly described Falla as a "high-class pops composer" in his *Nights in the Gardens of Spain: Symphonic Impressions for Piano and Orchestra*, program booklet, New York Philharmonic, 4 November 1995, 19. This assessment is further explored in Hess, *Manuel de Falla and Modernism in Spain*, 2.

16. The dates of these performances are Philadelphia (Co-Opera Company, 17 and 19 May 1952), New York (New York City Opera, October 1957), Aspen (Aspen Music Festival, 2 August 1969), Santa Fe (Santa Fe Opera, July–August 1975), and Boston (Opera Company of Boston, April 1979). See Benny Gene Rackard, "A Directorial Analysis and Production Guide to Three Musical Theatre Forms for High School Production: *La vida breve*, *The Sound of Music*, and *The Chocolate Soldier*," Ph.D. diss., University of Southern Mississippi, 1980, 76–82.

17. See Lloyd Schwartz, "A Pair of Failed de Fallas," *Boston Sunday Globe*, 8 April 1979, 9. In January 2004, the Dallas Opera also paired *La vida breve* with *El amor brujo*.

18. Harold C. Schonberg, "Goya Captured in Music," *New York Times*, 26 November 1967, cited in Hess, *Enrique Granados*, 86.

the United States thrust Falla before the North American public, as did his programming of the same work with Nan Merriman in the famous Hollywood Bowl concerts, which some critics categorically dismissed as "sunkist" or "Hollywoodized."[19] We should note, however, that Stokowski's 1949 recording with William Kapell of *Noches en los jardines de España* also contains a children's concert rendition of Herman Hupfeld's "When Yuba Plays the Rhumba on the Tuba Down in Cuba," a tune made famous by Rudy Vallee and the Connecticut Yankees.[20] This programming decision is clearly related to the image of "Latin" music in the United States during the 1930s and 1940s. The infinitely flexible term *Latin* referred not only to South and Central American genres and styles—the tango's thrusting downbeat or the mambo's flashy sax riffs—but also to an attitude that became enshrined through lyrics, music, and the performer's persona. Songs such as Peggy Lee's "Mañana (Is Good Enough for Me)," Marion Sunshine's "Hot Tamales," and "All Dressed up Spic and Spanish" (the latter sung by the conga-toting Cuban Desi Arnaz in the Rodgers and Hart musical *Too Many Girls*) "reinforced an image of Latin music as 'fun,' lightweight, and essentially trivial," as John Storm Roberts has observed, an image, moreover, that has become "a crushing stereotype."[21] At the same time, classically trained Latin artists such Xavier Cugat, Agustín Lara, the Iturbis, and Bori crossed over from the popular realm with what we might call "Latin light classics." Cugat, for example, who was trained as a violinist, formed an orchestra dedicated to tangos, a genre to which Stravinsky crossed over more than once. The popularity of such artists (Cugat is said to have taken up "more film footage than any other American bandleader") and their crossover tendencies shows just how permeable the boundary line between concert hall and jukebox could be.[22]

We have seen that in *Two Girls and a Sailor* MGM conferred on Falla's "Ritual Fire Dance" the ambiguous status of "light classic." "Highbrow" trappings (two concert grands, potted plants, formal attire) created in that sequence a markedly different atmosphere for the Iturbis' performance than, say, that for Durante's "Inky-Dinky-Doo." But the next filmic use of the "Ritual Fire Dance," *Carnegie Hall*, which first appeared in theaters nine months after Falla's death, is more complicated. Unlike *Two Girls*, with its cheery rapprochement between "high" and "low" art, in *Carnegie Hall* aesthetic agendas butt heads. The plot centers on the recital hall's cleaning lady (Marsha Hunt), who, hell-bent on edification, raises her son (William Prince) to be a concert pianist only to be devastated when he favors jazz. This plotline resulted in a juxtaposition of musical tastes that some found problematic: as Mildred Norton complained in the *Daily News*, "lovers of serious music, attracted by the chance to hear it performed by Bruno Walter, Jan Peerce, Jascha Heifetz and Artur

19. William Ander Smith, *The Mystery of Leopold Stokowski* (London and Toronto: Associated University Presses, 1990), 188.

20. Roberts, *The Latin Tinge*, 83.

21. Roberts, *The Latin Tinge*, 84.

22. Roberts, *The Latin Tinge*, 85.

Rubinstein, among a host of others, will be alienated by the sharp gambit to the jazz camp," while "swing addicts . . . will have to sit through a probably exhausting session, for them, of longhair stuff."[23] For at least one critic, however, Falla's "Ritual Fire Dance" hinted at mediation between high and low art. Edwin Schallert noted that Rubinstein "probably can be credited with providing the most colorful interpretation [in the movie] . . . and exhibited particular *discretion* in proffering the De Falla 'Ritual Fire Dance'" (emphasis added).[24] "Discretion," in other words, subtly hinted at finer things, and the "Ritual Fire Dance" had redeemed this musical omni-umgatherum through refined persuasion. In light of the overwhelmingly negative reactions to *Carnegie Hall*, Schallert's approbation was anything but trivial.[25]

Two years after Falla's death, the "Ritual Fire Dance" appeared again—in Technicolor—in MGM's *Three Daring Daughters*.[26] José Iturbi, playing himself as usual, meets divorcée Louise Morgan, played by a middle-aged Jeanette MacDonald, on a Caribbean cruise. Art alone does not satisfy Iturbi, and he pursues Mrs. Morgan over the objections of her three daughters (one of them the ever-chirpy Jane Powell), who are ignorant of the unpleasant details of their mother's divorce. Cuba provides the sultry tropical backdrop for the "Ritual Fire Dance," introduced by a crooning chorus, and which Iturbi conducts for a nightclub audience. As Iturbi begins, he notices Jeanette MacDonald's empty seat, and stares at it morosely as he abandons the podium for the keyboard. Against the opening measures of the "Ritual Fire Dance," she rushes breathlessly in, and Iturbi, MacDonald, and Amparo Iturbi (as is often the case, she appears out of nowhere to play the second piano part) exchange knowing glances. All the while, the music surges forward. Unlike the reasonably faithful performance in *Two Girls and a Sailor*, however, this "Ritual Fire Dance" involves interpolated cadenzas, a question and answer section in broken octaves, choral interjections, and a chromatic descant for Amparo. The crowd goes wild, and afterward Iturbi's agent confesses, "I've never seen him shake up an audience like he did tonight."

Unlike *Carnegie Hall*, *Three Daring Daughters* emphasized the exoticism of the "Ritual Fire Dance" through both the tropical setting and the musical arrangement itself. Some critics, such as Leo Mishkin, complained about the latter. Mishkin wrote: "In one sequence, José Iturbi, not satisfied with playing the de Falla "Ritual Fire Dance"

23. Mildred Norton, Film Review, *Daily News*, 14 August 1947, MHL clippings file, unnumbered.

24. Edwin Schallert, "*Carnegie Hall*, Musical Victory," *Los Angeles Times*, 14 August 1947, MHL clippings file, unnumbered.

25. See, for example, Bosley Crowther, "'The Music Is Good': A Familiar Justification for *Carnegie Hall*," *New York Times*, 4 May 1947, MHL clippings file, unnumbered. He considered the movie "trite and artificial . . . a miserable device for . . . bringing before the camera such eminent musical lights."

26. The movie's vivid colors are described as "a riot of rich and tasty pastels" in Archer Winsten, "New York Views," *New York Post*, February[?] 1948, MHL clippings file.

on the piano as it should be played, is constrained to lead a full symphony orchestra, and what looks like the entire ensemble of the Phil Spitalny All-Girl Chorus, in a rendition that takes place in little short of the Hanging Gardens of Babylon."[27]

To be sure, like *Carnegie Hall* and *Two Girls and a Sailor*, *Three Daring Daughters* proposes a meeting ground for popular and classical idioms. Iturbi and MacDonald toss off one of Richard Strauss's *Rosenkavalier* waltzes fitted with Earl Brent's lyrics ("Where There's Love"); we are also treated to Enesco's *Roumanian Rhapsody* played by the Iturbis on two pianos and Larry Adler on the harmonica. These "classical" selections peacefully coexist with "The Dickey-Bird Song," by Walter Donaldson and Harold Adamson, and Bobby Troup's "Route 66," a boogie-woogie number played by Iturbi to win over the three brats.[28] So if the "Ritual Fire Dance" is one more routine in this series, the arrangement used is at least compatible with the rest of the movie. What is striking here is that the freer arrangement appeared only after Falla's death.

In addition, the Catholic Legion of Decency came down hard on *Three Daring Daughters*, deeming its treatment of divorce to be cavalier and contrary to Church teachings. Joseph Breen warned MGM head Louis Mayer that, although the script was "technically" acceptable under the Production Code, the film's essential meaning was "anti-social." Alluding to one of Paul's better-known epistles (II Cor. 3:6), Breen argued:

> This is exactly the type of story which thinking men and women in all parts of the world, who are concerned for the preservation of family life and the institution of marriage, will single out for serious criticism on the grounds that it treats of a very serious social question in a light and airy vein, and makes its solution appear to be thoroughly acceptable. It may be that such a treatment of this particular subject is not specifically forbidden by the Production Code, but it is our thought that it is in conflict with *the spirit* of the Code and its attitude toward marriage in general.[29]

Shades of the Spanish Catholic press's attacks on *El corregidor y la molinera*? The Legion of Decency rated *Three Daring Daughters* "morally objectionable in part for all" since "it tends to justify as well as reflect the acceptability of divorce."[30] For Falla,

27. Leo Mishkin in the *Morning Telegraph*, cited in *Keynote*, 17 February 1948, MHL clippings file, unnumbered. The Spitalny *Hour of Charm* All-Girl Chorus and Orchestra specialized in hymns and sentimental songs.

28. As with *Carnegie Hall*, critics were not persuaded. One complained that "boogie woogie is balanced by the classics . . . that hackneyed little trick of putting a concert artist 'in the groove' is exploited in the usual manner" (Virgina Wright, "Film Review: *Three Daring Daughters*," *Daily News*, 3 March 1948, MHL clippings file, unnumbered). See also Edwin Schallert, "Silly Story Well Glossed in *Daughters*," *Los Angeles Times*, 3 March 1948, MHL clippings file, unnumbered.

29. Letter, Breen to Mayer, 22 October 1946, MHL correspondence file, unnumbered.

30. The quotation is from the Web site <www.dandugan.com/maytime/f-3darin.hrml>, accessed on 2 October 2002.

of course, there would have been no middle ground. Although others—not he—
had designated the "Ritual Fire Dance" as a suitable accompaniment for lusting after
a divorced woman, the composer, who had long considered *El amor brujo* ripe for
employment "in the service of sin," fully accepted St. Thomas Aquinas's dictum:
"If an art produces objects which men cannot use without sinning, the artist who
makes such works himself commits sin, because he directly offers to others the occasion of sin."[31]

The multiple meanings of the "Ritual Fire Dance," reinforced by constructions
of Latin popular music, continued to attract popular artists in the 1950s and 1960s.
Dick Stewart, who is described on the record jacket of his *Dick Stewart Sings* (Hi Fi
Record R–401) as "fast on the up-take and with lots of S. A. [sex appeal]," offered
selections such as "Falling Leaves" and "The Glory of Love" along with "specialty
[instrumental] numbers adding to entertainment," one of which was the "Ritual
Fire Dance." Also linking the piece to romance and passion was Tommy Dorsey:
the "Sentimental Gentleman of Swing" presented it alongside Irving Berlin's "Cheek
to Cheek" (Vocalion VL–3613). The Harmonicats, an all-harmonica ensemble, recorded it twice, once with "Tea for Two" (RKO) and later with "I'm Confessin' That
I Love You" (International Award AKS–261).[32] Some recording companies, such as
Decca, marketed the "Ritual Fire Dance" as a "light classic." In *Seated One Day at
the Organ* (Hi Fi Decca DL–78902) the wasp-waisted organist Ethel Smith performed the "Ritual Fire Dance" with Sir Arthur Sullivan's *The Lost Chord*, Rimsky-
Korsakov's *Flight of the Bumble Bee*, and Ernesto Lecuona's *Malagueña*. Another
marketing category was "novelties," which is how Ernie Felice's *Accordion Power-*

31. Saint Thomas Aquinas, *Summa Theologica*, II–II, 169, 2. ad.4, cited in Maritain,
Art and Scholasticism, 71, which, as noted, Falla admired. Subsequent film uses of the
"Ritual Fire Dance" included *El amor brujo* of 1949, directed by Antonio Román and featuring Pastora Imperio; it and a 1967 version directed by Francisco Rovira Beleta essentially reproduce *El amor brujo*. The best-known *El amor brujo* on film is Carlos Saura's
version of 1986, with Antonio Gades, Laura del Sol, and Cristina Hoyos. Aside from incorporating several plot changes, Saura's *El amor brujo* mixes Falla's score with "authentic" flamenco interpolations, pop music, and traditional songs. For example, there is a
sudden transition from an *albolea* (a wedding song celebrating the bride's virginity) to
the music of a wedding reception, "barrio disco sung by a pair of señorita Supremes," as
a critic for the *Washington Post* put it. Elsewhere, the "Canción del amor dolido" silences
a traditional *villancico*. As for the "Ritual Fire Dance," Saura conceived it as a stagey group
number in which Candelas (Cristina Hoyos) dances *against* the members of the community, who employ prominent hand motions and impassively watch her collapse on the
final cadence. Unlike the organizers of the *cante jondo* contest of 1922, who earnestly believed they were preserving flamenco's "purity," Saura simply registers flamenco's proximity to outside styles without comment. See Rita Kempley, "*El amor brujo*," *Washington
Post*, 13 February 1987, <http://www.washingtonpost.com>, accessed on 1 August 2003.

32. Another harmonica version is Stan Fisher's (Epic, 1955).

house (Capitol L–307) was advertised and on which the "Ritual Fire Dance" appeared alongside "Oodles of Noodles" and "Just One of Those Things." Not surprisingly, supershowman Liberace recorded the "Ritual Fire Dance" several times: in mid-1947, on the Souvenir label (on the flip side of "Begin the Beguine"); then with Daytone, when the "Ritual Fire Dance" joined Addinsell's "Warsaw Concerto," "12th Street Rag," and "Tea for Two"; and again in 1948 with Signature.[33] Other artists capitalized on the exotic or ethnic element in Latin music. In *Jungle Drums: Morton Gould and His Orchestra* (RCA Victor LSC–1994), we find a reasonably faithful rendition of Falla's score, along with Noble and Leleiohaku's *Hawaiian War Chant* and other works said to form "a kind of stereophonic travelogue." A similar travelogue was *Safari*, recorded in 1958 (Somerset) by Edmond de Luca and the Trans-World Symphony, which included De Luca's own multimovement "Safari" (the movements are entitled "Mt. Kilimanjaro," "The Trek," and "Bantu Village"), with the composer of the "Ritual Fire Dance" listed as Emanuel de Falla.

The most bizarre pop arrangement of the "Ritual Fire Dance" may well be that by Fred Waring, that tireless defender of popular taste. Side B of the album *Fred Waring and His Pennsylvanians in Concert* (Columbia, Harmony HS–11363) opens with applause against the opening motif of the Prelude to *Die Meistersinger*. "Now we're getting into the high-class music!" Waring exults. He introduces the next number by playing directly into prevailing notions of Latin music: "Now the next is a real exciting transformation of the famed de Falla 'Ritual Fire Dance.' I'm sure Mr. de Falla would . . . uh . . . probably burn . . . uh . . . when he heard this. He never realized how much arson was involved in his composition [laughter]. This is a real gasser and I hope you enjoy it—'the Ritual Fire Dance.'" What follows recalls one of Adorno's more energetic—and controversial—diatribes, namely, his insistence that the "darkest secret" of arrangements is "the compulsion not to leave anything as it is."[34] Waring's "Ritual Fire Dance" mixes pseudojazz, Broadway pit orchestration, gestures reminiscent of Stan Kenton's big band album *Cuban Fire*, stop-on-a-dime cartoon music à la Raymond Scott, and the schizophrenic style of Juan García Esquivel's *Space Age Bachelor Pad Music*. Salient points include the prominence of the Cordovox (an accordionlike instrument) in the melody line of the A section, the four-bar rock fill leading to the B section, the use of the solo-tone mute (with which the trombonist jabs out only one note), the brass smears and glissandi, the "primitive" drumming, and a shout chorus straight off a big band chart. Thus, Fred Waring and his squeaky clean ensemble of young people rescued the "Ritual Fire Dance" from the indignity of "longhair" status. As we have seen, the work had already challenged the "crude labels" that traditionally inform debates over "high"

33. Darden Asbury Pyron, *Liberace* (Chicago and London: University of Chicago Press, 2000), 120.

34. "On the Fetish Character in Music," in Adorno, *The Culture Industry*, 43.

and "popular" art in the arrangements and contexts discussed above.[35] It is not surprising that the "Ritual Fire Dance" has also entered that most emblematic of U.S. institutions, the football game, where it has accompanied the exuberant movements of many a leggy majorette as halftime entertainment.

A final consideration in this afterword is "self" and the contradictions Falla's presents in the biographical tapestry, laid out here with all its knotted textures, backstitching, and irregularities. The numerous testimonials about Falla, whether conflicting or consistent, whether proffered by others or by himself, are constant reminders of the difficulty of isolating certain attitudes as representative when they may in fact be only transient. The charge that Falla was a misogynist is a case in point. If "morbid violence" (rather than artistic vigilance) actually compelled him to upbraid "La Argentinita" during a rehearsal of *El amor brujo*, as María Martínez Sierra rather heatedly contends, or if he publicly repelled a woman who expressed to him her admiration for the same work because "he could not tolerate . . . physical contact, the woman's hand-clasp," as Raquel de Castro claims, there are plenty of counterbalancing accounts of his kindness to women (Tamara Karsavina, Marie André) and of his professional encouragement to them (Rosa García Ascot, Bárbara Giuranna) to call into question this accusation.[36] There were also his friendships with Wanda Landowska, Concepción Badia, Emilia Llanos, Aga Lahowska; the wives of his colleagues, such as Raquel de Castro; and of course María Martínez Sierra. With María, after all, he worked, socialized, and traveled. He lived in her household and at various intervals maintained an extensive correspondence filled with gentle private jokes. There is nothing to suggest that their eventual falling-out was due to anything other than conflicting work habits and artistic disagreements, however much she may have emphasized his rigid moral code (by then an *idée fixe* in Falla scholarship) in her memoirs. It was also in collaboration with María that Falla immortalized two strong and independent female characters. But even before Candelas and Frasquita, he had sympathetically treated another female character in the person of Salud. Although lacking the wherewithal of María's "idealized female archetype," the protagonist of *La vida breve* elicits our sympathy in her struggle against social inequities and the tyranny of male domination, however dramatically unsatisfying her end.

35. Such principles had long been dear to Waring. See, for example, a 1928 interview, "His Art Is Harder Than Symphonies," in which he held that neither Koussevitsky nor Stokowski could "hold a theatre audience five minutes" and that it made him "mad" when "they" say "there is no art" in popular music" (Boston interview, 1928, Penn State Archives, book 3, cited in Virginia Waring, *Fred Waring and the Pennsylvanians* [Urbana and Champaign: University of Illinois Press, 1997], 79).

36. Martínez Sierra, *Gregorio y yo*, 132. "Comprendimos que no pudo soportar el contacto físico y el apretón de la señora" (Raquel de Castro [widow of Juan José Castro], Weinstein, *Fuego y agua: vida y música de Manuel de Falla*) [video]. In the same video, Juan Ignacio Ramos, a colleague of the composer's, explicitly refers to Falla as a misogynist.

To be sure, Falla's own romantic frustrations from around the time of *La vida breve* may have compelled him to try to sublimate his pain through the innocent Salud. This raises the question of whether Falla's single state, an atypical condition for a nonreligious in the Spain of his times, should also be seen as a manifestation of misogyny, as some have suggested.[37] Certainly he could have put his feelings for María Prieto Ledesma behind him and courted other women, especially after 1913, when his works were attracting international attention and financial stability seemed to be within his grasp. But the unlucky situation with his cousin brought to light more starkly than any prior episode the composer's natural timidity, which Padre Fedriani's blunt criticisms surely aggravated. The cleric's two-pronged critique, both of Falla's handling of matters of the heart and artistic decisions, presents the following paradox: however much we may recoil from Fedriani's supercilious tone and however problematic we may find the traditional Catholic concept of self-love, we must acknowledge that his assessment of Falla's doubting ways was largely correct. At the time of the thwarted affair, Falla doubted himself as a candidate for marriage; as a mature composer, he doubted his capacity to avoid offending God through his music. Unlike Salud, Falla did not die at his beloved's feet. But he did confess more frequently than Fedriani thought was healthy, he did agonize over practically every note he committed to paper, and he did develop a lifelong fear of romantic involvement. Thus, it is simplistic to blame Falla's failure to marry on misogyny. To be sure, his "self" *may* have harbored some misogynistic tendencies, and the "circumstance" of his day-to-day habits *could* have nurtured these. Yet we cannot attach to Falla the facile label of misogynist— hater of women—simply because he remained single, occasionally lost his temper with the opposite sex, and eschewed intimacy.

A similar anticonclusion arises with regard to Falla's possible homosexuality. This rumor, which has been whispered for decades, arose mainly because he remained single in a marriage-oriented society and was close friends with Lorca and Salazar. Although many of Falla's contemporaries would have been perfectly capable of viewing his friendship with these two important figures in a neutral light, others in that homophobic ambiance were not. Those who pegged Falla as a *rojillo*, that is, the inhabitant of some political no-man's land, would have found it easy enough to connect this ostensible lack of political focus to a lack of "appropriate" virility. Others have undoubtedly reasoned that since Falla was unmarried he had to be gay, especially given the artistic circles in which he moved. Is there hard evidence on the matter? There is none, at least not yet. But in its absence, Nin-Culmell's view seems the most sensible: at some point in his life, Falla *may* have had homosexual experiences or inclinations.[38] And while this is all that can be said for now, the possibility

---

37. See Marco, *Siglo XX*, 41.
38. Joaquín Nin-Culmell, interview with author, January 2000.

of homosexuality, latent or active, need not be excluded from our ongoing reflections on the composer. Recall, for example, his statement to Emilia Llanos that being rejected by María Prieto Ledesma caused him to contemplate the mortal sin of suicide. Many might interpret this surprising confession as, if not outright melodrama, a desperate expression of unrequited heterosexual love. But it also could have arisen from awareness of latent homosexuality, that is, the hopelessness and confusion any gay man who was also a devout Catholic in that intolerant society would feel on realizing that an intimate relationship, with a woman *or* a man, was forever closed to him.

Others have concluded that if Falla were neither married nor gay, he was celibate and therefore a "saint." Biographers who refer to Falla's "monklike"existence, however, are in effect implying that celibacy is inherently weird or aberrant; else why would it be worthy of comment? In fact, those who look askance at celibacy (or see it as a breeding ground for other neuroses, such as misogyny) are as misguided as those who unthinkingly condemn homosexuality. As for elevation to sainthood, although this extravagant description would have riled Falla, it is by no means unfounded. We have seen that Falla gave to charity even when in straitened circumstances himself; that he repudiated worldly goods such as property; that he often sought seclusion from the world; and that his tone was customarily gentle, with references to spiritual matters often surfacing in his everyday conversation. (We should also note a frequently animated tone: Sergio de Castro has described Falla as an animated conversationalist who enjoyed mimicking regional accents.) Even those with whom Falla ultimately parted company, such as Bergamín or de los Ríos, have consistently tagged his behavior as saintly. That these characteristics were transferred, rightly or wrongly, to criticism of his music created a neat alliance between self and circumstance: Falla, the purest of human beings, was seen along with his music, as the ideal vessel for the ideology of neoclassicism. This compatibility between the person and his artistic utterances, along with fervor for Catholic identity in various artistic, intellectual, and of course political factions, helps explain why many have felt compelled to sanctify Falla. In sum, many agendas are satisfied.

The distance between the continental views of "purity" and "abstemiousness" in Falla's music and its flashy packaging in the United States, just detailed, seems utterly unbridgeable. The questions it raises, however, can be explored in relation to Falla and in numerous other contexts as well. Are there such things as high and popular art, good and bad taste? [39] Is, as the anthropologist Clifford Geertz has as-

---

39. See Umberto Eco, "The Structure of Bad Taste," which defines *kitsch* as lacking "any standard but popularity," in *The Open Work*, translated from the Italian by Anna Cancogni (Cambridge: Harvard University Press, 1989), 180–216.

serted, "the giving to art objects a cultural significance . . . always a local matter?"[40] In short, that the name of a composer whose existence was narrowly circumscribed by perfectionism—by sacred passions—and who endlessly agonized over offending God should appear on the pop charts is one more irony encountered in tracing the porous boundary between self and circumstance in the life and music of Don Manuel de Falla.

40. Clifford Geertz, "Art as a Cultural System," *Modern Language Notes* 91 (1978): 1475.

Appendix 1

Works and First Performances

STAGE

(Listed by Date of Completion)

El conde de Villamediana (opera, Duque de Rivas), ca. 1891; unpublished, lost.
La Juana y la Petra, o La Casa de Tócame Roque (zarzuela, Javier Santero after Ramón
   de la Cruz), ca. 1900; score lost (libretto in ms.), unperformed, unpublished.
Los amores de la Inés (zarzuela, Emilio Dugi), 1901–2; Madrid, Teatro Cómico,
   12 April 1902.
Limosna de amor (zarzuela, José Jackson Veyán), 1901–2, unperformed, publication
   forthcoming.
El cornetín de órdenes (zarzuela, with Amadeu Vives i Roig, librettist unknown), ca.
   1903, unperformed, unpublished, lost.
La cruz de Malta (zarzuela, with Amadeu Vives i Roig, librettist unknown), ca. 1903,
   unperformed, unpublished, lost.
Prisionero de guerra (zarzuela, with Amadeu Vives i Roig, librettist unknown), ca.
   1903–4, unperformed, unpublished.
La vida breve (lyric drama, Carlos Fernández Shaw, French adaptation Paul Milliet),
   1904–5, unperformed; revised version 1905–13; Nice, Casino Municipal, 1 April 1913.
La pasión (incidental music, Gregorio Martínez Sierra,[1] possibly including a "Soleá"
   for guitar), 1914, unpublished, ms.; Madrid, Teatro Lara, 30 November 1914.

   1. It has been shown that the great majority of the librettos, scenarios, and texts signed
by Gregorio Martínez Sierra are in fact by his wife, María O Lejárraga, who, adapting the
English custom, used her husband's last name.

Amanecer (incidental music, Martínez Sierra), 1914–15, unpublished, lost; Madrid, Teatro Lara, 7 April 1915.

El amor brujo (gypsy ballet, Martínez Sierra), 1915; Madrid, Teatro Lara, 15 April 1915 (original version); ballet version (rev.) in one act, Paris, Trianon Lyrique, 22 May 1925.

Otelo (*Tragedia de una noche de verano*) (incidental music, Martínez Sierra), 1915, unpublished, lost; Barcelona, Teatro de Novedades, October (?) 1915.

El corregidor y la molinera (pantomime, Martínez Sierra, after Pedro Antonio de Alarcón), 1916–17; Madrid, Teatro Eslava, 7 April 1917.

Fuego fatuo (comic opera, Martínez Sierra), after Chopin (Waltz in A♭ op. 64 no. 2; Scherzo in B♭ Minor op. 31; Scherzo in E op. 54 (middle section); Mazurka in C op. 24 no. 2; *Bolero* op. 19; Mazurka in B Minor op. 33 no. 4; *Polish Songs* op. 74 nos. 1 and 2; Étude in E major op. 10 no. 3; Mazurka in A♭ op. 7 no. 4; Ballade in G Minor op. 23; Waltz in A♭ op. 42; Mazurka in B♭ no. 51 (no opus number); Étude in C Minor op. 10 no. 12; Tarantella op. 43; *Berceuse* op. 57; Ballade in F Minor op. 52; Barcarolle op. 60); 1918–19; unperformed, unpublished as opera, revised orchestration (by Antonio Ros Marbá) of acts 1 and 3 performed in Granada, 1 July 1976.

El sombrero de tres picos (ballet, Martínez Sierra, after Pedro Antonio de Alarcón, based on *El corregidor y la molinera*), 1917–19; London, Alhambra Theatre, 22 July 1919.

El corazón ciego (incidental music, Martínez Sierra), 1919, lost; San Sebastián, November 1919.

La niña que riega la albahaca y el príncipe preguntón (incidental music, Federico García Lorca), Españoleta, after transcription by Pedrell, 1922, unpublished; Granada, 6 January 1923.

Misterio de los reyes magos (incidental music, arrangement of *cantigas* and music from *Llibre Vermell*, arrangement of folk song "Cançó de Nadal," arranged by L. Romeu in ms.), 1922, unpublished; Granada, 6 January 1923.

El retablo de Maese Pedro (marionette opera, Falla, after Miguel de Cervantes), 1919–23; Seville (concert performance), Teatro San Fernando, 23 March 1923; Paris (staged), home of Princess Edmond de Polignac, 25 June 1923.

El gran teatro del mundo (incidental music, Pedro Calderón de la Barca), 1927; Granada, 27 June 1927, unpublished.

La vuelta de Egipto (incidental music, Félix Lope de Vega), 1935, unpublished; Granada, 9 June 1935.

La moza del cántaro (incidental music, Félix Lope de Vega), 1935, unpublished.

Atlántida (scenic cantata, Falla, after Jacint Verdaguer), 1926–46; completed by Ernesto Halffter; Barcelona, Teatre Liceu, 24 November 1961 (concert version); Milan, Teatro alla Scala, 18 June 1962 (scenic version).

ORCHESTRAL

Noches en los jardines de España, piano, orchestra, 1909–16, 1. "En el Generalife," 2. "Danza lejana," 3. "En los jardines de la Sierra de Córdoba"; Madrid, Teatro Real, 9 April 1916.

El amor brujo, concert version, 1915–16; Madrid, Sociedad Nacional de Música,
   28 March 1916 (concert version, revision of 1915 score), unpublished.
Orchestral Suites from *El sombrero de tres picos*, 1916–21; Scenes and Dances from
   part 1, Three Dances from part 2; Madrid, Teatro Eslava, 17 June 1919 (selections).
Overture to Rossini's *Barber of Seville*, revised orchestration, ca. 1924; Seville, Teatro
   de San Fernando, 11 November 1925.
Prélude a l'après-midi d'un faune (Debussy), revised orchestration, 1924; Seville,
   Teatro de San Fernando, 10 December 1924.
Fanfare sobre el nombre de E. F. Arbós, trumpets, trombones, percussion, 1934;
   Madrid, Teatro Calderón, 28 March 1934.
Homenajes, 1920–41: "Fanfare sobre el nombre de E. F. Arbós"; "A Claude Debussy:
   Elegía de la guitarra" (after guitar piece of 1920); "A Paul Dukas: Spes Vitae"
   (after piano piece of 1935); "Pedrelliana" (after Pedrell, *La celestina*), 1938–39;
   some reworking of "Pedrelliana" in 1941; Buenos Aires, Teatro Colón,
   18 November 1939.

CHAMBER AND INSTRUMENTAL

Melodía, cello, piano, 1897; Cádiz, Salón Quirell, 16 August 1899.
Romanza, cello, piano, ca. 1898; Cádiz, 14 August 1899.
Pieza en Do Mayor, cello, piano, 1898.
Quartet in G, violin, viola, cello, piano, 1898–99, lost; Cádiz, Salón Quirell, 16 August
   1899 (two movements).
Mireya (*Poema*): 1. "Muerte de Elzear," 2. "Danza fantástica," violin, viola, cello,
   flute, piano, 1898–99, unpublished, lost; Cádiz, Teatro Cómico, 10 September
   1899. Piano transcription by composer ca. 1899; Madrid, Ateneo, 6 May 1900.
Serenata andaluza, violin, piano, ca. 1899, lost; Cádiz, Salón Quirell, 16 August
   1899.
El amor brujo, 2 violins, viola, cello, bass, piano ("Pantomima," "Danza ritual del
   fuego"), 1914–15; Lisbon, Casino Espagnol, September 1915; revised 1926,
   unpublished; Cádiz, Real Academia Filarmónica de Santa Cecilia, 1 May 1926.
Homenaje: Pièce de Guitare Écrite pour "Le Tombeau de Claude Debussy," guitar, 1920;
   Madrid, Teatro de la Comedia, 8 March 1921 (premiered on harp-lute by Marie-
   Louise Casadesus, Paris, Salle des Agricultures, 24 January 1921).
Fanfare pour une fête, two trumpets, timpani, bass drum, 1921; London, 22 October 1921.
Concerto, harpsichord (or piano), flute, oboe, clarinet, violin, cello, 1923–26;
   Barcelona, Associació de Música "da Camera," Palau de la Música Catalana,
   5 November 1926.

VOCAL

"Preludio: Madre, todas las noches" (Antonio de Trueba), voice, piano, ca. 1900.
Rimas (Gustavo Adolfo Bécquer), voice, piano, ca. 1900; "Olas gigantes," "¡Dios mío,
   qué solos se quedan los muertos!"

"Tus ojillos negros" (Cristóbal de Castro), voice, piano, ca. 1903.

Cantares de nochebuena, arranged by Falla, (popular texts), violin, guitar, zambomba (friction drum), rebec. ca. 1903–4; "Pastores venir," "Maravilla nunca vista," "Esta noche ha de nacer," "Un pastor lleva un pavo," "Venga la bota," "En el portal de Belen," "Por la calle abajito," "La leche de viejas," "Un zapatero aburrío."

Con afectos de jubilo y gozo (author unknown), soprano, women's chorus, piano, 1908, unpublished.

Trois mélodies (Théophile Gautier), voice, piano, 1909–10; "Les colombes," "Chinoiserie," "Séguidille"; Paris, Société Musicale Indépendante, 4 May 1910.

Siete canciones populares españolas (popular texts), voice, piano, 1914; "El paño moruno," "Seguidilla murciana," "Asturiana," "Jota," "Nana," "Canción," "Polo"; Madrid, Ateneo, 14 January 1915.

"Oración de las madres que tienen a sus hijos en brazos" (Martínez Sierra), voice, piano, 1914; Madrid, Sociedad Nacional de Música, 8 February 1915.

"El pan de Ronda que sabe a verdad" (Martínez Sierra), voice, piano, 1915.

Psyché (G. Jean-Aubry), voice, flute, harp, violin, viola, cello, 1924; Barcelona, Associació de Música "da Camera," Palau de la Música Catalana, 9 February 1925.

"Soneto a Córdoba" (Luis de Góngora), voice, harp or piano, 1927; Paris, Salle Pleyel, 14 May 1927.

"Jesus ait," three-part children's chorus, 1932, unpublished.

Balada de Mallorca (Jacint Verdaguer), after Chopin (Ballade in F Major op. 38), 1933; Mallorca, Monasterio de Valldemosa, 21 May 1933.

"Invocatio ad individuam trinitatem," four-part chorus, 1935, unpublished (part of *La vuelta de Egipto*).

Himno marcial (José María Pemán), after Pedrell, "Canto de los almogávares," chorus, piano, drums, 1937, unpublished.

Canción de la estrella, soprano and orchestra, arranged from Pedrell's *Los Pirineos*, revised orchestration, 1941–42.

PIANO

Gavotte and Musette, ca. 1892; unpublished, lost.

Scherzo in C Major, ca. 1898.

Nocturno, 1897–99; Cádiz, Salón Quirell, 16 August 1899.

Mazurka in C Minor, ca. 1899.

Canción, 1900.

Serenata andaluza, ca. 1900; Madrid, Ateneo, 6 May 1900.

Vals-capricho, 1900; Madrid, Ateneo, 6 May 1900.

Cortejo de gnomos, 1901.

Segunda serenata andaluza, ca. 1901, lost; Cádiz, Teatro del Parque Genovés, 22 September 1901.

Serenata, 1901.

Suite Fantástica, ca. 1901, unpublished, lost (two movements, "En la rueca" and "Hadas"); Cádiz, Teatro del Parque Genovés, 22 September 1901.

Allegro de concierto, ca. 1903; Madrid, Ateneo, 15 May 1905.

Cuatro piezas españolas; "Aragonesa," "Cubana," "Montañesa," and "Andaluza," ca. 1906–9; Paris, Salle Érard, 27 March 1909.

Fantasía Bética, 1919; New York, 8 February 1920.

Homenaje: Pièce de Guitare Écrite pour "Le Tombeau de Claude Debussy," arrangement for piano, 1920; Paris, Société Indépendante de Musique, 24 January 1921 (harp-lute).

El sombrero de tres picos, arrangement for pianola, 1921–26.

Canto de los remeros del Volga, 1922

Pour le tombeau de Paul Dukas, 1935; Paris; Salle de l'École Normale, 1936.

Numerous "expressive versions" of vocal works by Victoria, Morales, Guerrero, Juan del Encina, Vecchi; other arrangements, transcriptions, and unfinished sketches.

Principal publishers: Chester, Eschig, Unión Musical Española, Ricordi, and Ediciones Manuel de Falla.

Appendix 2

Overview of Spanish History, 1874–1981

1874 Bourbon Restoration; Alfonso XII proclaimed king.

1875 *Turno pacífico*, or alternation of two main political parties, initiated under Antonio Cánovas de Castillo (Conservative) and Práxedes Sagasta (Liberal).

1876 New constitution proclaims "the Apostolic Roman Catholic religion [to be] that of the State"; other religions are tolerated.

1898 Spanish-American War. Defeated by the United States, Spain loses Cuba, Puerto Rico, and the Philippines.

1899 Alfonso XIII ascends to the throne.

1909 "Tragic Week" in Barcelona; strikes and anticlerical riots paralyze city.

1914 Thousands of Spaniards living abroad return to neutral Spain upon the outbreak of World War I (August).

1917 Military uprisings, new government formed under Eduardo Dato (June), workers' strikes (August).

1923 Coup d'état of Gen. Miguel Primo de Rivera.

1930 Resignation of Primo de Rivera, Berenguer government established.

1931 Monarchy collapses, Alfonso XIII leaves Spain, founding of the Second Republic (April).

Convents burned in Madrid (May).

Manuel Azaña declares before the Cortes (Parliament) that "Spain has ceased to be a Catholic country" (October).

Founding of fascist party, Juntas de Ofensiva Nacional-Sindicalista (JONS) (October).

1933   José Antonio Primo de Rivera founds Falange Española (October).

Conservative coalition is voted in (November).

1934   Merger of JONS and Falange Española (February).

Uprising, general strike in Asturias, put down by army (October).

1936   Presidency of Manuel Azaña (February).

Spanish Civil War breaks out (July).

Hitler and Mussolini decide to aid the rebel uprising (July).

International Brigades arrive in Spain on behalf of the Republic (starting in August).

Lorca executed by Nationalists (August).

Soviet Union confirms support for the Republic (October).

Republican government moves from Madrid to Valencia (November).

1938   Instituto de España established by the Burgos government (January).

1939   Civil War ends (April); dictatorship of Francisco Franco begins.

World War II begins; Spain declares neutrality, later nonbelligerency.

1940   Franco and Hitler meet at Hendaye.

1975   Death of Francisco Franco; dictatorship ends.

1977   Democratic elections held in Spain for the first time since 1936.

1981   Failed military coup of Colonel Antonio Tejero.

Bibliography

A. B. "Crónica teatral: Estreno de *La vida breve* en Madrid." *La Esfera,* n.d.

Abram, Paul. "Opéra Comique." *Le Petite République.* 2 January 1914.

Acker, Yolanda. "Ernesto Halffter: A Study of the Years 1905–46." *Revista de Musicología* 17 (1994): 97–172.

Addessi, Anna Rita. *Claude Debussy e Manuel de Falla: Un caso di influenza stilistica.* Bologna: Cooperativa Libraria Universitaria Editrice Bologna, 2000.

Adorno, Theodor. *The Culture Industry: Selected Essays on Mass Culture.* Edited by J. M. Bernstein. London and New York: Routledge, 1991.

Alarcón, Pedro Antonio de. *The Three-Cornered Hat.* Translated by Martin Armstrong. London: Gerald Howe, 1933.

Alonso, Miguel. *Catálogo de obras de Conrado del Campo.* Madrid: Fundación Juan March, Centro de Documentación de la Música Española Contemporánea, 1986.

Alted Vigil, Alicia. *Política del Nuevo Estado sobre el patrimonio cultural y la educación durante la guerra civil española.* Madrid: Ministerio de Cultura, 1994.

d'Amico, Fedele. "Italy: A Revival and a Premiere." *Musical America* 82, no. 9 (September 1962): 100–102.

Ansermet, Ernest. "Falla's *Atlántida.*" *Opera News* 27, no. 1 (29 September 1962): 8–13.

Arregui, Vicente. *Revista Musical Hispano-Americana,* 2d ser., 6, no. 1 (January 1914): 4–6.

"La Asociación Wagneriana efectuará un homenaje al compositor Manuel de Falla." *La Nación.* 20 November 1939.

Astrana Marín, Luis. "*La vida breve.*" *El Radical.* 14 November 1914.

"¿*L'Atlàntida* corre el peligro de sumergirse otra vez, antes de llegar a estrenarse a Barcelona?" *Destino.* 19 December 1959.

Aviñoa, Xosé. *La música i el modernisme.* Barcelona: Curial, 1985.

Avril, Georges. "Au Casino Municipal de Nice: *La vie brève.*" *Comoedia* (Paris). 3 April 1913.

Azaña, Manuel. *Obras completas.* Mexico City: Ediciones Oasis, 1966.

B. "Música de Cámara: Festival Manuel de Falla." *Correo Catalan.* 9 November 1926, 6.

Bal y Gay, Jesús, "La música en la Residencia."*Residencia* (Mexico) (December 1963): 77–80.

Bal y Gay, Jesús, and Rosita García Ascot. *Nuestros trabajos y nuestros días.* Madrid: Fundación Banco Exterior, 1990.

Balfour, Sebastian. "'The Lion and the Pig': Nationalism and National Identity in *Fin-de-Siècle* Spain." In *Nationalism and the Nation in the Iberian Peninsula.* Edited by Clare Mar-Milinero and Ángel Smith. Oxford and Washington, D.C.: Berg, 1996.

Barga, Corpus. "El Retablo de Maese Falla." *El Sol.* 20 June 1923, 1.

Barnes, Clive. "Dance: Falla's *Three-Cornered Hat.*" *New York Times.* 26 September 1969, New York Public Library clippings file.

Barr, Cyrilla. *Elizabeth Sprague Coolidge: American Patron of Music.* New York: Schirmer Books, 1998.

———. "A Style of Her Own: The Patronage of Elizabeth Sprague Coolidge." In *Cultivating Music in America: Women Patrons and Activists since 1860.* Edited by Ralph Locke and Cyrilla Barr. Berkeley: University of California Press, 1997.

Beardsley, Theodore. "Manuel de Falla's Sources for Calderón's *Gran teatro del mundo*: The Autograph Manuscripts." *Kentucky Romance Quarterly* 16 (1969): 63–74.

Ben-Ami, Shlomo. *The Origins of the Second Republic in Spain.* Oxford: Oxford University Press, 1978.

Bergadà, Montserrat. "La relación de Falla con Italia: Crónica de un diálogo." In *Manuel de Falla e Italia.* Edited by Yvan Nommick. Granada: Publicaciones del Archivo Manuel de Falla, 2000.

Bergamín, José. "La importancia del Demonio." *Cruz y Raya.* 15 August 1933, 9–51.

Bergamini, John. *The Spanish Bourbons.* New York: Putnam, 1974.

Binding, Paul. *Lorca: The Gay Imagination.* London: GMP Publishers, 1985.

Black, Gregory D. *The Catholic Crusade against the Movies, 1940–1975.* Cambridge: Cambridge University Press, 1997.

Blair, Deirdre. *Anaïs Nin: A Biography.* New York: Putnam, 1995.

Blas Vega, José. "Falla y el flamenco." *La Caña* 14–15 (fall-winter 1996): 5–19.

Blasco Ibáñez, Vicente. *The Four Horsemen of the Apocalypse.* Translated by Charlotte Brewster Jordan. New York: Dutton, 1918.

B. L. D. "Two Novelties Repeated." *Musical America* 43, no. 23 (27 March 1926): 9.

Blinkhorn, Martin. *Carlism and Crisis in Spain, 1931–1939.* Cambridge: Cambridge University Press, 1975.

[Blom, Eric]. *Manuel de Falla: Miniature Essays.* London: Chester, 1922.

Bonastre Bertran, Francesc. *Felipe Pedrell: Acotaciones a una idea.* Tarragona: Caja de Ahorros Provincial de Tarragona, 1977.

Borrás, Tomás. "Eslava: *El corregidor y la molinera.*" *La Tribuna.* 8 April 1917, 7–8.

Bosch, Carlos. "Una carta de Falla expresando su alegría por la liberación del Madrid rojo." *Arriba.* 27 December 1946.

Boyd, Carolyn P. *Historia Patria: Politics, History, and National Identity in Spain, 1875–1975.* Princeton: Princeton University Press, 1997.

Brandes, Stanley. *Metaphors of Masculinity: Sex and Status in Andalusian Folklore.* Philadelphia: University of Pennsylvania Press, 1980.

———. "The Sardana: Catalan Dance and Catalan National Identity." *Journal of American Folklore* 103, no. 407 (1990): 24–41.

Braun, Emily. "Political Rhetoric and Poetic Irony: The Uses of Classicism in the Art of Fascist Italy." In *On Classic Ground: Picasso, Léger, de Chirico, and the New Classicism, 1910–1930.* Edited by Elizabeth Cowling and Jennifer Mundy. London: Tate Gallery, 1990.

Brenan, Gerald. *The Spanish Labyrinth: An Account of the Social and Political Background of the Spanish Civil War.* 1950. Reprint, Cambridge: Cambridge University Press, 1990.

Brody, Elaine. "Viñes in Paris: New Light on Twentieth-Century Performance Practice." In *A Musical Offering: Essays in Honor of Martin Bernstein.* Edited by Edward H. Clinkscale and Claire Brook. New York: Pendragon, 1977.

Brooks, Jeanice. "Nadia Boulanger and the Salon of the Princesse de Polignac." *Journal of the American Musicological Society* 46, no. 3 (1993): 15–68.

Brown, G. G. *A Literary History of Spain: The Twentieth Century.* London, E. Benn; New York: Barnes and Noble, 1972.

Buckle, Richard. *Diaghilev.* New York: Atheneum, 1984.

Budwig, Andrew. "The Evolution of Manuel de Falla's *The Three-Cornered Hat,* 1916–1920." *Journal of Musicological Research* 5 (1984): 191–212.

———. "Manuel de Falla's *Atlántida*: A Historical and Analytical Study." Ph.D. diss. University of Chicago, 1984.

Budwig, Andrew, and Gilbert Chase. *Manuel de Falla: A Bibliography and Research Guide.* New York and London: Garland, 1986.

Buxton, Angela, trans. *Manuel de Falla, Ernesto Halffter: Atlántida.* Liner notes, Auvidis Valois, AD 4685, 1993.

Caamaño, Roberto. *La historia del Teatro Colón, 1908–1968.* Buenos Aires: Editorial Cinetea, 1979.

Caballero, Carlo. "Patriotism or Nationalism? Fauré and the Great War." *Journal of the American Musicological Society* 52 (1999): 593–625.

Cadenas, Juan José. "Impresiones de París." *ABC.* 8 August 1914, 9–10.

———. "Impresiones de París: Dos jornadas." *ABC.* 9 August 1914, 11–12.

Calvo, Luis. "Hoy serán enterrados en la catedral de Cádiz los restos mortales de Falla." *ABC.* 9 January 1947, 1.

Calvocoressi, M. D. "Nice." *Musica*, April 1913.

Campoamor Gonzalo, Antonio. *Manuel de Falla, 1876–1946*. Madrid: Sedmay Ediciones, 1976.

Campodónico, Luis. *Falla*. Translated by Françoise Avila. Collections microcosme, solfèges, no. 13. Paris: Éditions du Seuil, 1959.

El 'cante jondo' (cante primitivo andaluz): Sus orígenes, sus valores musicales, su influencia en el arte musical europeo. 1922. Reprint, Granada: Archivo Manuel de Falla, 1997.

Carr, Raymond. *Spain, 1808–1975*. 2d ed. Oxford: Clarendon, 1982.

Carreira, Xoan M. "García Ascot, Rosa." In *Diccionario de la música española e hispanoamericana*. Edited by Emilio Casares. 5:426. Madrid: Sociedad General de Autores, 1999.

"Carta al ilustre maestro gaditano Manuel de Falla." *Diario de Cádiz*. 26 June 1932.

"Carta del ilustre gaditano Don Manuel de Falla." *Diario de Cádiz*. 3 July 1932.

Casal Chapí, Enrique. "Música en la Guerra: Manuel de Falla." *Hora de España* 3, nos. 11–15 (1938): 491–92.

Casanovas, José. *Manuel de Falla, cien años*. Barcelona: Ediciones de Nuevo Arte Thor, 1976.

Casares, Emilio. "Música y músicos de la generación del 27." In *La música en la generación del 27: Homenaje a Lorca, 1915–1939*. Edited by Emilio Casares. Madrid: Ministerio de Cultura, 1986.

———, ed., *La música en la generacíon del 27: Homenaje a Lorca, 1915–1939*. Madrid: Ministerio de Cultura, 1986.

Casella, Alfredo. *Music in My Time*. Translated and edited by Spencer Norton. Norman: University of Oklahoma Press, 1955.

A Catechism of Christian Doctrine. New York: Paulist Press, 1929.

Chase, Gilbert. "Falla's Music for Piano Solo." *Chesterian* 21 (1940): 41–46.

———. *The Music of Spain*. New York: Norton, 1941.

———. *The Music of Spain*. 2d rev. ed., New York: Dover, 1959.

Chasins, Abram. *Leopold Stokowski: A Profile*. New York: Hawthorn, 1979.

Checa Puerta, Julio Enrique. "Los Teatros de Gregorio Martínez Sierra." In *El teatro en España entre la tradición y la vanguardia, 1918–1939*. Edited by Dru Dougherty and María Francisca Vilches de Frutos. Madrid: Consejo Superior de Investigaciones Científicas, Fundación Federico García Lorca, and Tabacalera, 1992.

Chinchilla, Concha. "Cronología de Manuel de Falla." In *Manuel de Falla en Granada*. Edited by Yvan Nommick. Granada: Publicaciones del Archivo Manuel de Falla, 2001.

Christoforidis, Michael. "Aspects of the Creative Process in Manuel de Falla's *El Retablo de Maese Pedro* and *Concerto*." Ph.D. diss. University of Melbourne, 1997.

———. "A Composer's Annotations to his Personal Library: An Introduction to the Manuel de Falla Collection." *Context* 17 (1999): 33–68.

———. "Constructions of Manuel de Falla's Political Identity and Musical Nation-

alism in the 1930s." Paper presented at the conference "Music in the 1930s:
Nation, Myth, and Reality," Royal Holloway College, London, October 1998.

———. "De *La vida breve* a *Atlántida*: Algunos aspectos del magisterio de Claude
Debussy sobre Manuel de Falla." *Cuadernos de música iberoamericana* 4 (1997):
15–32.

———. "Falla, Manuel de." In *Diccionario de la música española e hispanoamericana*.
Edited by Emilio Casares. 10 vols. Madrid: Sociedad General de Autores y
Editores, 1999–2002.

———. "Manuel de Falla, Debussy, and *La vida breve*." *Musicology Australia* 18
(1995): 1–10.

———. "Manuel de Falla and Romanticism: Insights into an Uncited Text." *Context*
6 (summer 1993–94): 26–31.

———. "Folksong Models and Their Sources: Manuel de Falla's *Siete canciones
populares españolas*." *Context* 9 (1995): 13–21.

———. *Un acercamiento a la postura de Manuel de Falla en el* cante jondo (*canto
primitivo andaluz*). Granada: Archivo Manuel de Falla, 1997.

Ciarrochi, Joseph W. *The Doubting Disease*. New York and Mahwah, N.J.: Paulist
Press, 1995.

Cirlot, J. E. *A Dictionary of Symbols*. Translated from the Spanish by Jack Sage. 2d ed.
London: Routledge and Kegan Paul, 1971.

Clark, Walter Aaron. "Doing the Samba on Sunset Boulevard: Carmen Miranda and
the Hollywoodization of Latin American Music." In *From Tejano to Tango*.
Edited by Walter Aaron Clark. New York and London: Routledge, 2002.

———. *Isaac Albéniz: A Guide to Research*. New York and London: Garland, 1998.

———. *Isaac Albéniz: Portrait of a Romantic*. Oxford: Oxford University Press, 1999.

Clément, Catherine. *Opera, or the Undoing of Women*. Translated by Betsy Wing.
Minneapolis: University of Minnesota Press, 1988.

"Cock-tail sevillano: Ahí va eso." *La Unión* (Seville). 31 May 1932.

Collet, Henri. *Victoria*. Paris: Librairie Félix Alcan, 1914.

Collins, Chris. "Manuel de Falla and *L'Acoustique Nouvelle*: A Myth Exposed."
Journal of the Royal Music Association 128, no. 1 (2003): 71–97.

Comellas i Barri, Montserrat. *El romanticisme musical a Barcelona: Els concerts*.
Barcelona: Els Llibres de la Frontera, 2000.

"El complot monárquico: El general Orgaz, deportado en Tenerife, fue detenido ayer
en Las Palmas y quedó incomunicado." *El Sol*. 17 June 1932, 8.

"Concert of Spanish Music." *Times* (London). 26 May 1911, 10.

"Concierto a beneficio de Auxilio Social." *El Diario Montañes*. 27 April 1938.

Cooper, Douglas. *Picasso Théâtre*. Paris: Éditions Cercle d'Art, 1967.

Cortes-Cavanillas, Julián. *Alfonso XIII y la guerra del 14*. Madrid: Alce, 1976.

Craft, Robert, ed. *Stravinsky: Selected Correspondence*. 3 vols. New York: Knopf,
1984.

Cramer, Eugene Casjen. *Tomás Luis de Victoria: A Guide to Research*. New York and
London: Garland, 1998.

"Creation of the Spanish Institute." *Spain* 1, no. 19 (8 February 1938): 13.

Crichton, Ronald. *Falla: BBC Music Guides*. London: British Broadcasting Corporation, 1982.

———. "Opera on Disc, *Atlántida*, Falla-Halffter." *Opera*. September 1993, 1128–30.

Croce, Arlene. "New York Newsletter: From *Tricorne* to Twyla Tharp." *Dancing Times* 40, no. 710 (November 1969): 73.

Crow, John A. *Spain: The Root and the Flower*. 3d ed. Berkeley: University of California Press, 1985.

Crowther, Bosley. "'The Music Is Good': A Familiar Justification for *Carnegie Hall*." *New York Times*. 4 May 1947.

C. S. S. "*Love the Sorcerer*." *Boston Evening Transcript*. 16 October 1924, 4.

Curtiss, Mina. *Bizet and His World*. New York: Knopf, 1958.

Curzon, Henri de. "*La vie brève* de Manuel de Falla." *Le Guide Musicale*. 4 January 1914, 6–7.

Daly, Emma. "Defenders of Spain's Masterpieces: A Prado Show Honors Civil War Rescue Effort." *New York Times*. 17 July 2003, B1, 5.

Dahlhaus, Carl. "Nationalism and Music." In *Between Romanticism and Modernism*. Translated by Mary Whittall. Berkeley: University of California Press, 1980.

Daniel. "Vida escénica en París." *Heraldo de Madrid*. 7 January 1914.

Daniel, Oliver. *Stokowski: A Counterpoint of View*. New York: Dodd, Mead, 1982.

Darío Pérez. "Figuras de España: Manuel de Falla." *La Libertad*. 2 October 1929, 3.

Delannoy, Marcel. *Chantecler*, 24 March 1928.

Demarquez, Suzanne. *Manuel de Falla*. Paris: Flammarion, 1963. Translated by Salvator Attanasio as *Manuel de Falla* (Philadelphia: Chilton, 1968).

Dennis, Nigel, ed. *El epistolario (1924–1935): José Bergamín–Manuel de Falla*. Valencia: Pre-Textos, 1995.

Dent, Edward. "Music: A Spanish Ballet." *Athenaeum*. 1 August 1919.

Díaz Martín, Emma. "Las echadoras de cartas en la provincia de Cádiz: Una actividad femenina marginal." In *Antropología cultural de Andalucía*. Edited by S. Rodríguez Becerra. Seville: Consejería de Cultura de la Junta de Andalucía, 1984.

Dietschy, Marcel. *A Portrait of Claude Debussy*. Oxford: Clarendon, 1990.

Domènech, Rafael. "La Danza Pantomima Rusa." *ABC*. 2 June 1916, 3–4.

Doreste Silva, Luis. "*Noches en los jardines de España*." Newspaper unidentified. 23 December 1937.

Downes, Olin. "American Premiere of Two Operas." *New York Times*. 8 March 1926, 9.

———. "Boston Symphony Orchestra." *New York Times*. 14 March 1926, 11.

———. "Music." *New York Times*. 7 January 1927, 14.

———. "Music: De Falla's Marionette Opera." *New York Times*. 30 December 1925, 10.

———. "Stravinsky Poem Wins at Premiere." *New York Times*. 27 March 1928, 27.

Duchesneau, Michel. "Maurice Ravel et la Société Musicale Indépendante: 'Projet mirifique de concerts scandaleux.'" *Revue de Musicologie* 80, no. 2 (1994): 251–81.

Durey, Philippe, and Brigitte Léal, eds. *Picasso: El sombrero de tres picos*. Paris: Spadem, 1993.

Easo, A. de. "Artistas españoles: Manuel de Falla en San Sebastián." *Vasconia.* 1 September 1932.

Eco, Umberto. "The Structue of Bad Taste." In *The Open Work.* Translated from the Italian by Anna Cancogni. Cambridge: Harvard University Press, 1989.

Eliade, Mircea. *The Sacred and the Profane.* Translated from the French by William Trask. New York: Harcourt, Brace and World, 1959.

"En la histórica Universidad de Salamanca." *Patria.* 7 January 1938, 7.

"Ernesto Halffter y el homenaje a Falla." *El Sol.* 24 March 1932, 1.

Ernst, Gerlinde. "Manuel de Falla (1876–1946): *El Retablo de Maese Pedro* (*Meister Pedros Puppenspiel*)." Ph.D. diss., University of Erlangen, 1994.

"España—dice 'Gaziel'—respira una atmósfera de guerra civil." *El Sol.* 16 May 1936, 3.

Espinós, Víctor. "El 'Te Deum' de Falla." *El Defensor de Córdoba.* 7 July 1932.

———. "Música: Falla va a América, el príncipe embajador." Newspaper unidentified. 4 October 1939.

"Esta noche se verificará en el Teatro Real el quinto y último concierto de la Orquesta Sinfónica." *ABC.* 16 April 1916, 15.

"Exijo que en la ejecución de mis obras se observe siempre la más límpia moral cristiana." *Pueblo.* 22 November 1946. 5.

Fala, Juan. "Los estrenos de anoche: *La vida breve.*" Newspaper unidentfied. 15 November 1914. "Falla con los 'facciosos.'" *Ideal.* 2 November 1937.

"Falla, hijo predilecto de la Iglesia." *Arriba.* 23 December 1946.

Falla, Manuel de. *Cartas a Segismundo Romero.* Transcribed and edited by Pascual Pascual Recuero. Granada: Excmo. Ayuntamiento de Granada, Patronato "Casa-Museo Manuel de Falla," 1976.

———. *Escritos sobre música y músicos.* Edited by Federico Sopeña. 4th ed. Madrid: Espasa Calpe, 1988.

———. "Felipe Pedrell," *La Revue Musicale* 4, no. 4 (February 1923): 1–11.

———. "My Hope." *Spain* 1, no. 18 (1 February 1938): 3.

———. "Notes sur Ravel." Translated by Roland-Manuel. *La Revue Musicale* 20, no. 189 (1939): 81–86.

———. "Una carta de Don Manuel de Falla." *La Unión.* 8 June 1932.

———. "Una carta de Falla." *El Ideal.* 4 November 1937.

"Falla puso fin a su actuación." *La Nación.* 24 November 1939.

"Fallece en Argentina don Manuel de Falla: Su cadáver será trasladado a España a bordo del *Cabo de Hornos.*" *Ya.* 15 November 1946, 1.

Fernández Ballesteros, A. *El Liberal.* 12 March 1932. Untitled article.

Fernández-Cid, Antonio. "La *Atlántida* se estrenará en 1960." *ABC* (Seville), 1 July 1959, 34.

———. "Sobre la *Atlántida.*" *ABC.* 29 January 1958.

Fernández-Montesinos, Manuel. *Federico García Lorca en la Residencia de Estudiantes.* Madrid: Fundación Federico García Lorca, Amigos de la Residencia de los Estudiantes, 1991.

Fernández Shaw, Guillermo. *Larga historia de La vida breve.* Madrid: Ediciones de Revista de Occidente, 1972.

F. G. "Rubinstein in New Music." *Musical America* 31 (14 February 1920): 51.

F. M. [Frank Merkling?]. "Falla in Philharmonic Hall." *Opera News* 27, no. 3 (10 November 1962): 27.

Foard, Douglas W. "A Chronology of the Spanish Civil War, 1930–1939." In *Historical Dictionary of the Spanish Civil War.* Edited by James W. Cortada. Westport, Conn.: Greenwood, 1982.

———. *The Revolt of the Aesthetes: Ernesto Giménez Caballero and the Origins of Spanish Fascism.* American University Studies, series 9, vol. 70. New York: Peter Lang, 1989.

Fontbona, Francesc. "The Art of *Noucentisme.*" In *Homage to Barcelona: The City and Its Art, 1888–1936.* Edited by Marilyn McCully and Michael Raeburn. London: Thames and Hudson, 1986.

Franco, Enrique. *Manuel de Falla y su obra.* Madrid: Publicaciones Españolas, 1976.

———. "El rey Arturo en la Corte de Madrid." In *Rubinstein y España: Esposición homenaje a Arturo Rubinstein.* Madrid: Turner, 1988.

Fulcher, Jane F. *French Cultural Politics and Music from the Dreyfus Affair to the First World War.* New York and Oxford: Oxford University Press, 1999.

Gallego, Antonio. *Catálogo de obras de Manuel de Falla.* Madrid: Ministerio de Cultura, 1987.

———. *Conciertos de inauguración: Archivo Manuel de Falla.* Granada: Archivo Manuel de Falla, 1991.

———. "Dulcinea en el prado (verde y florido)." *Revista de Musicología* 10 (1987): 685–99.

———. *El amor brujo.* Madrid: Alianza Música, 1990.

———. "*La vida breve.*" In *Teatro Real.* Madrid: Fundación del Teatro Lírico, Temporada 1997–98. Program booklet.

———. "Nuevas Obras de Falla en América: "El canto de la Estrella," de *Los Pirineos* de Pedrell." *Inter-American Music Review* 11, no. 2 (1991): 85–101.

Gallego, Antonio, ed., *Manuel de Falla, El amor brujo, 1915 Version.* London: Chester Music, n.d.

Garafola, Lynn. "The Choreography of *Le Tricorne.*" In *Los Ballets Russes de Diaghilev en España.* Edited by Yvan Nommick and Antonio Álvarez Cañibano. Madrid: Instituto Nacional de las Artes, Escénicas y la Música, 2000.

García Matos, Manuel. "El folklore en *La vida breve* de Manuel de Falla." *Anuario Musical* 26 (1971): 173–97.

———. "Folklore en Falla, I." *Música* 2, nos. 3–4 (1953): 47–67.

———. "Folklore en Falla, II." *Música* 2, no. 6 (1953): 33–52.

G. B. "Teatro Cómico." *La Época.* 13 April 1902, 2.

Geertz, Clifford. "Art as a Cultural System." *Modern Language Notes* 91 (1978): 1473–99.

Geiger. "En Eslava: *El corregidor y la molinera.*" *La Nación.* 8 April 1917, 10.

Gibson, Ian. *The Death of Lorca.* Chicago: Philip O'Hare, 1973.

————. *Federico García Lorca: A Life*. New York: Pantheon, 1989.

————. *En Granada, su Granada* . . . Granada: Diputación Provincial de Granada, 1997.

————. *Vida, pasión y muerte de Federico García Lorca, 1898–1936*. Barcelona: Plaza and Janés, 1998.

Gide, André. *Defensa de la cultura*. Translated by Julio Gómez de la Serna. Madrid: S. Aguirre, 1936.

Gilman, Lawrence. "Music: Landowska Plays a Modern Concerto for Harpsichord." *New York Herald Tribune*. 7 January 1927, 18.

Glaser, Ph.-Emmanuel. *Le Figaro* (Paris). 4 April 1913. Untitled article.

Gómez Amat, Carlos. *Siglo XIX*. Historia de la música española, no. 5. Madrid: Alianza Música, 1984.

Goubault, Christian. *La critique musicale dans la presse française de 1870 à 1914*. Geneva and Paris: Éditions Slakine, 1984.

Gray, Rockwell. *The Imperative of Modernity: An Intellectual Biography of José Ortega y Gasset*. Berkeley: University of California Press, 1989.

Grimal, Pierre. *The Dictionary of Classical Mythology*. Translated by A. R. Maxwell-Hyslop. Oxford and New York: Blackwell, 1986.

Gubern, Román. *Proyector de luna: La generación del 27 y el cine*. Barcelona: Anagrama, 1999.

"La guerra de los fascismos contra la cultura." *Las Noticias*. 9 October 1937, 3.

Haley, George. "The Narrator in *Don Quijote*: Maese Pedro's Puppet Show." *Modern Language Notes* 80 (1965): 145–65.

Harper, Nancy Lee. *Manuel de Falla: A Bio-Bibliography*. Westport, Conn.: Greenwood, 1998.

Hart, Brian. "The Symphony in Theory and Practice in France, 1900–1914." Ph.D. diss., Indiana University, 1993.

Hart, Stephen M., ed. *"¡No Pasarán!" Art, Literature, and the Spanish Civil War*. London: Tamesis, 1988.

Haskell, Arnold, and Walter Nouvel. *Diaghileff: His Artistic and Private Life*. London: Gollancz, 1935.

Henderson, W. J. "The Boston Symphony Concert." *New York Sun*. 7 January 1927.

Henken, John Edwin. "Barbieri, Francisco Asenjo." In *The Revised New Grove Dictionary of Music and Musicians*. Edited by Stanley Sadie and John Tyrell. 29 vols. London: Macmillan, 2001.

Henry, Leigh. "The Russian Ballet: M. de Falla's Ovation." New York Public Library, Dance Division, clippings file.

Herce, Fernando. "Ante el estreno de *La vida breve*." *La Mañana*. 14 November 1914.

————. "Crónicas madrileñas." *La vida breve* November 1914. Day unknown.

Hernández, Prisco. "Décima, Seis, and the Puertorican Troubadour." *Latin American Music Review* 14 (1993): 20–51.

Herr, Richard. *An Historical Essay on Modern Spain*. Berkeley: University of California Press, 1971.

Hess, Carol A. *Enrique Granados: A Bio-Bibliography*. Westport, Conn.: Greenwood, 1991.

———. *Manuel de Falla and Modernism in Spain, 1898–1936*. Chicago and London: University of Chicago Press, 2001.

———. "Manuel de Falla's *The Three Cornered Hat* and the Advent of Modernism in Spain." Ph.D. diss. University of California, Davis, 1994.

———. "Manuel de Falla's *The Three-Cornered Hat* and the Spanish Right-Wing Press in Pre–Civil War Spain." *Journal of Musicological Research* 15 (1995): 55–80.

———. "Nin-Culmell, Joaquín." In *The Revised New Grove Dictionary of Music and Musicians*. Edited by Stanley Sadie and John Tyrell. 2d ed. 29 vols. London: Macmillan, 2001.

———. "Silvestre Revueltas in Republican Spain: Music as Political Utterance." *Latin American Music Review* 18, no. 2 (1997): 278–96.

Hispaleto, Juan. "Falla: músico, asceta, patriota." *Sevilla*. 16 November 1946.

"Hombres de España." *Patria*. 15 June 1937.

Hook, John. *Alarcón: El sombrero de tres picos*. Critical Guide to Spanish Texts, no. 41. London: Grant and Cutler, 1984.

H. T. P. [Henry Taylor Parker]. "Baffling Moderns, Stirring Classics, also Koussevitsky." *Boston Evening Transcript*. 18 October 1926, 8.

Hughey, John David. *Religious Freedom in Spain: Its Ebb and Flow*. 1955. Reprint, Freeport, N.Y.: Books for Libraries, 1970.

Iglesias de Souza, Luis. "Monasterio y Agüeros, Jesús de." In *Diccionario de la música española e hispanoamericana*. Edited by Emilio Casares. 10 vols. Madrid: Sociedad General de Autores y Editores, 1999–2002.

"Incongruencia católica." *El Socialista*. 14 June 1932.

Inman Fox, E. *Ideología y política en las letras de fin de siglo (1898)*. Madrid: Espasa Calpe, 1988.

"Instituto de España." *Unidad*. 21 April 1938.

"The Ishmaels of Europe." *Spain* 1, no. 19 (8 February 1938): 8.

Izquierdo, Fernando. "En Lara, hablando con Martínez Sierra." *La Patria*. 14 April 1915.

Jackson, Gabriel. *The Spanish Republic and the Civil War, 1931–1939*. Princeton: Princeton University Press, 1965.

Janés i Nadal, Alfonsina. *L'Obra de Richard Wagner a Barcelona*. Barcelona: Fundació Salvador Vives Casajuana, Ajuntament de Barcelona, Serveis de Cultura, Institut Municipal d'Historia, 1983.

Jean-Aubry, G. "De Falla Talks of His New Work Based on a Don Quijote Theme." *Christian Science Monitor*. 1 September 1923, 17.

———. *French Music of To-Day*. Translated by Edwin Evans. 1919. Reprint, Plainview, N.Y.: Books for Libraries Press, 1976.

———. "Manuel de Falla." *Revista Musical Hispano-Americana*. 30 April 1917, 1–5.

———. "*La vie brève* por M Manuel de Falla." *L'Art Moderne*. 11 January 1914.

Jenkins, Jennifer R. "'Say It with Firecrackers': Defining the 'War Musical' of the 1940s." *American Music* 19 (2001): 315–39.

Jiménez-Fraud, Alberto. "The 'Residencia de Estudiantes.'" *Texas Quarterly* 4 (1961): 48–54.

J. M. O. "*El corregidor y la molinera* en Eslava." *El Debate.* 8 April 1917, 3.

Jowitt Deborah. "Dance: 1919 Revisited." *Village Voice.* 2 October 1969, 27–28.

Jung, C. G. *Memories, Dreams, Reflections.* Recorded and edited by Aniela Jaffé. Translated from the German by Richard Winston and Clara Winston. New York: Random House, 1965.

Kann, Red. "Review: *Two Girls and a Sailor.*" *Motion Picture Daily.* 25 April 1944.

Karsavina, Tamara. *Theatre Street: The Reminiscences of Tamara Karsavina.* London: Dance Books, 1981.

Kellas, James G. *The Politics of Nationalism and Ethnicity.* 2d ed. New York: St. Martin's, 1998.

Kempley, Rita. "*El amor brujo.*" *Washington Post.* 13 February 1987.

King, John. *Sur: A Study of the Argentine Literary Journal and Its Role in the Development of a Culture, 1913–1970.* Cambridge: Cambridge University Press, 1986.

Koechlin, Charles. "Chronique musicale." *La Chronique des Arts.* 4 January 1914.

"Kreisler Has Big Audience." *New York Times.* 21 March 1926, 26.

L. A. "Dolor de España: El cadáver de Falla—la hermana del maestro cuenta los últimos momentos del músico genial." *Fotos.* 11 January 1947.

Landormy, Paul. "Le déclin de l'Impressionisme." *La Revue Musicale* 2, no. 4 (1921): 97–113.

"Landowska a Feature with Boston Band." *New York Evening Journal.* 7 January 1927, 38.

Lannon, Frances. *Privilege, Persecution, and Prophecy: The Catholic Church in Spain, 1875–1975.* Oxford: Clarendon, 1987.

Lara, Isidore de. "*La vie brève.*" *Gil Blas.* 1 January 1914.

L. D., "La matinée du 'Figaro.'" *L'Éclaireur de Nice.* 2 April 1913.

Ledesma, Dámaso. *Cancionero salmantino.* Madrid: Imprenta Alemana, 1907.

Lesure, François. "Manuel de Falla, Paris, et Claude Debussy." In *Manuel de Falla tra la Spagna e l'Europa.* Edited by Paolo Pinamonti. Florence: Olschki, 1989.

Lesure, François, and Roger Nichols, eds. *Debussy Letters.* Translated by Roger Nichols. Cambridge: Harvard University Press, 1987.

Levine, Lawrence W. *Highbrow/Lowbrow: The Emergence of Cultural Hierarchy in America.* Cambridge: Harvard University Press, 1988.

Levy, Beth. "'The White Hope of American Music'; or, How Roy Harris Became Western." *American Music* 19, no. 2 (2001): 131–67.

Little, Douglas. *Malevolent Neutrality: The United States, Great Britain, and the Origins of the Spanish Civil War.* Ithaca and London: Cornell University Press, 1985.

Llongueras, Joan. "Els programes del XIV Festival de la Societat Internacional per la Música Contemporánea." *Revista Musical Catalana* 33, no. 389 (1936): 180–84.

Lolo, Begoña. "Las relaciones Falla-Pedrell a través de *La vida breve.*" In *Manuel de Falla: La vida breve.* Granada: Publicaciones del Archivo Manuel de Falla, 1997.

Lorca, Federico García. "Deep Song," in *In Search of Duende*. Translated from the Spanish by Christopher Maurer. New York: New Directions, 1998.

———. *Federico García Lorca: Collected Poems, a Bilingual Edition*. Edited by Christopher Maurer. New York: Farrar, Straus, Giroux, 2001.

———. *Lola la comedianta*. Edited by Piero Menarini. Madrid: Alianza, 1981.

———. *Obras completas*, 5th ed. Madrid: Aguilar, 1963.

———. "Play and Theory in Duende," in *In Search of Duende*. Translated from the Spanish by Christopher Maurer. New York: New Directions, 1998.

———. *Poeta en Nueva York*. Edited by Piero Menarini. Madrid: Espasa Calpe, 2002.

Lorca, Francisco García. *Federico y su mundo*. Madrid: Alianza Tres, 1981.

Loza, Steven. *Tito Puente and the Making of Latin American Music*. Urbana and Chicago: University of Illinois Press, 1999.

MacDonald, Nesta. *Diaghilev Observed by Critics in England and the United States, 1911–1929*. New York: Dance Horizons, 1975.

Maestro Jacopetti. "La música y los músicos." *Ahora*. 24 June 1934.

Mainer, José-Carlos. *La edad de plata (1902–1939)*. 5th ed. Madrid: Cátedra, 1999.

Maltby, William S. *The Black Legend in England: The Development of Anti-Spanish Sentiment, 1558–1660*. Durham, N.C.: Duke University Press, 1971.

"Manuel de Falla, Composer, 70, Dies." *New York Times*. 15 November 1946, 23.

"Manuel de Falla par lui-même." *La Revue Musicale* 6, no. 9 (1 July 1925): 94–95.

Manzano Alonso, Miguel. "Fuentes populares en la música de *El sombrero de tres picos* de Manuel de Falla." *Nasarre* 9, no. 1 (1993): 119–44.

Marco, José María. *Manuel Azaña: Una biografía*. Barcelona: Planeta, 1998.

Marco, Tomás. *Siglo XX*. Historía de la música española, no. 6. Madrid: Alianza, 1989.

Maritain, Jacques. *Art and Scholasticism and the Frontiers of Poetry*. Translated by Joseph W. Evans. New York: Charles Scribner's Sons, 1962.

———. "From 'The Idea of Holy War.'" In *And I Remember Spain: A Spanish Civil War Anthology*. Edited by Murray A. Sperber. New York: Collier, 1974.

Marsh, William Sewall. *Musical Spain from A to Z*. Provincetown, R.I.: Campbell Music, 1929.

Martin, V. M. "Eclecticism." In *The New Catholic Encyclopedia*. 16 vols. New York: McGraw-Hill, 1967.

Martínez Sierra, María. *Gregorio y yo*. Mexico City: Biografías Gandesa, 1953.

"Más sobre *Atlántida*: Segismundo Romero contesta a Jackes Lonchampt [*sic*]." Unidentified press clipping.

Masciopinto, F. Adolfo. *El nacionalismo musical en Manuel de Falla*. Publicación de Extensión Universitaria, no. 75. Santa Fe: Ministerio de Educación de la Nación, Universidad Nacional del Litoral, 1952.

Massine, Leonid. *My Life in Ballet*. Edited by Phyllis Hartnoll and Robert Rubens. London: Macmillan, 1968.

Mauclair, Camille. *Histoire de la musique européene, 1850–1914*. Paris: Librairie Fischbacher, 1914.

May, Ernest. *Imperial Democracy: The Emergence of America as a Great Power.* New York: Harcourt, Brace, and World, 1961.

May, J-A. "Les avant-premières au Casino Municipal: *La vie brève.*" *Le Petit Niçoise.* 1 April 1913.

———. "La belle création de la *Vie brève.*" *Le Petit Niçoise.* 3 April 1913.

McClary, Susan. *Carmen.* Cambridge: Cambridge University Press, 1992.

Meaker, Gerald H. "A Civil War of Words: The Ideological Impact of the First World War on Spain, 1914–18." In *Neutral Europe between War and Revolution, 1917–23.* Edited by Hans A. Schmitt. Charlottesville: University Press of Virginia, 1988.

Messing, Scott. *Neoclassicism in Music from the Genesis of the Concept through the Schoenberg/Stravinsky Polemic.* 1988. Reprint, Rochester, N.Y.: University of Rochester Press, 1996.

Metzer, David. "The League of Composers: The Initial Years." *American Music* 15 (1997): 45–69.

Migel, Parmenia, ed. *Pablo Picasso: Designs for "The Three-Cornered Hat."* New York: Dover, 1978.

Miller, Jeffrey, ed. *In Touch: The Letters of Paul Bowles.* London: HarperCollins, 1994.

"El ministro de Instrucción Pública en San Sebastián." *El Sol.* 4 September 1932, 12.

Míquis, Alejandro. "En plena paradoja." *Nuevo Mundo.* N.d.

———. "Una ópera española en París: *La vida breve.*" *Diario* [?]. 3 January 1914.

Mitchell, Timothy. *The Betrayal of the Innocents: Desire, Power, and the Catholic Church in Spain.* Philadelphia: University of Pennsylvania Press, 1998.

———. *Flamenco Deep Song.* New Haven and London: Yale University Press, 1994.

———. *Passional Culture: Emotion, Religion, and Society in Southern Spain.* Philadelphia: University of Pennsylvania Press, 1990.

Molina Fajardo, Eduardo. *Manuel de Falla y el "cante jondo."* Granada: Editorial Universidad de Granada, 1962.

Montsalvat. "Casino Municipal: *La vie brève.*" *Le Phare du Litoral.* 3 April 1913.

Mora Guarnido, José. *Federico García Lorca y su mundo.* Buenos Aires: Losada, 1958.

Morgan, Robert P. *Twentieth-Century Music.* New York and London: Norton, 1991.

Morodo, Raúl. *Los orígenes ideológicos del franquismo: Acción Española.* Madrid: Alianza Editorial, 1985.

Morris, C. B. *A Generation of Spanish Poets, 1920–1936.* Cambridge: Cambridge University Press, 1969.

Motta, Luigi. "*Anima allegra,* Puccini e Cilea." *L'opera* 2, no. 2 (January-March 1966): 64–67.

"Music Here and Afield." *New York Times.* 25 March 1928, 9.

"Músicos y conciertos." *ABC.* 16 April 1916, 15.

"Músicos y conciertos: Orquesta Sinfónica." *ABC.* 11 April 1916, 16.

M. Y. "Eslava: *El corregidor y la molinera.*" *El Mundo.* 8 April 1917, 2.

"Mystery in Madrid." *Time.* 7 March 1949, 85–86.

Nash, Mary. *Defying Male Civilization: Women in the Spanish Civil War.* Women and Modern Revolution series. Denver: Arden, 1995.

Neruda, Pablo. *Confieso que he vivido.* Barcelona, Caracas, and Mexico City: Editorial Seix Barral, 1981.

Nietzsche, Friedrich. *The Case of Wagner.* Translated from the German by Walter Kaufmann. New York: Vintage, 1967.

Nin-Culmell, Joaquín. "Manuel de Falla, pedagogo." *Revista de Occidente,* no. 188 (1996): 37–46.

Nommick, Yvan. "De *La vida breve* de 1905 à *La vie brève* de 1913: Genèse et évolution d'une oeuvre." *Mélanges de la Casa de Velázquez* 30 (1994): 7–94.

———. "Des *Hommages* de Falla aux 'Hommages' à Falla." In *Manuel de Falla: Latinité et Universalité—Actes du Colloque International tenu en Sorbonne, 18–21 novembre 1996.* Edited by Louis Jambou. Paris: Presses de l'Université de Paris-Sorbonne, 1999.

———. "*El sombrero de tres picos* de Manuel de Falla: Una visión a partir de los documentos de su Archivo." In *Teatro Real.* Madrid: Fundación del Teatro Lírico, Temporada, 1997–98. Program book.

———. *Jardines de España: De Santiago Rusiñol a Manuel de Falla.* Granada: Ayuntamiento de Granada, 1996.

———. "*La vida breve* entre 1905 y 1914: Evolución formal y orquestal." In *Manuel de Falla: La vida breve.* Granada: Publicaciones del Archivo Manuel de Falla, 1997.

Nommick, Yvan, ed. *Manuel de Falla: Fuego fatuo—edición facsímil de los manuscritos 9017–1, LII, A2, A4, A6, A9, A10 del Archivo Manuel de Falla.* Granada: Publicaciones del Archivo Manuel de Falla, 1999.

———. *Manuel de Falla e Italia.* Granada: Publicaciones del Archivo Manuel de Falla, 2000.

———. "Un ejemplo de ambigüedad formal: El *Allegro* del *Concierto* de Manuel de Falla." *Revista de musicología* 21, no. 1 (1998): 11–35.

Nommick, Yvan, and Francesc Bonastre, eds. *Manuel de Falla: Apuntes de harmonía y dietario de Paris (1908).* Granada: Publicaciones del Archivo Manuel de Falla, 2001.

Northedge, F. S. *The League of Nations: Its Life and Times, 1920–1946.* New York: Holmes and Meier, 1986.

Norton, Mildred. Film Review. *Daily News.* 14 August 1947.

"Notas y comentarios musicales." *Radio Nacional: Revista Semanal de radiodifusión* 1, no. 11 (1938): 11.

"Nuestro arte en el extranjero." *La Correspondencia de España.* 12 May 1913.

Nugent, J. B. "Error." In *The New Catholic Encyclopedia.* 16 vols. New York: McGraw-Hill, 1967.

O'Connor, Patricia. *Gregorio and María Martínez Sierra.* Boston: Twayne, 1977.

Oja, Carol J. "Women Patrons and Crusaders for Modernist Music: New York in the 1920s." In *Cultivating Music in America: Women Patrons and Activists since 1860.* Edited by Ralph Locke and Cyrilla Barr. Berkeley: University of California Press, 1997.

————. *Making Music Modern: New York in the 1920s.* New York: Oxford University Press, 2000.

Opperby, Preben. *Leopold Stokowski.* New York: Hippocrene, 1982.

Orenstein, Arbie. *Ravel: Man and Musician.* New York: Columbia University Press, 1975.

————, comp. and ed. *A Ravel Reader: Correspondence, Articles, Interviews.* New York: Columbia University Press, 1990.

Orozco, Manuel. *Manuel de Falla: Historia de una derrota.* Barcelona: Ediciones Destino, 1985.

Ortega y Gasset, José. *Meditaciones del Quijote.* Edited by Julián Marías. 3d ed. Madrid: Cátedra, 1995.

Pahissa, Jaime. *Manuel de Falla: His Life and Works.* Translated by Jean Wagstaff. 1954. Reprint, Westport, Conn.: Hyperion, 1979.

————. *Vida y obra de Manuel de Falla.* 1947. Rev. and enl. ed. Buenos Aires: Ricordi, 1956.

Pasler, Jann. "*Pelléas* and Power: Forces behind the Reception of Debussy's Opera." *19th-Century Music* 10 (1987): 243–64.

————. "Stravinsky and the Apaches." *Musical Times* 123 (1982): 403–7.

Pedrell, Felipe. *Cancionero musical popular español.* 4 vols. Valls: E. Castells, 1917–21.

————. *Músicos contemporáneos y de otros tiempos.* Paris: Paul Ollendorf, 1910.

————. *Por nuestra música.* 2d ed. Barcelona: Henrich, 1891.

————. "Quincenas musicales: *La vida breve.*" *La Vanguardia.* 29 May 1913.

Pemán, José María. *Obras completas.* Cádiz: Escelicer, 1947.

"Pepe Cubiles con la Orquesta Bética en el 'Falla.'" *Diario de Cádiz.* 11 May 1938.

Pérez Castillo, Belén. "Spain: Art Music, Nineteenth Century." In *The Revised New Grove Dictionary of Music and Musicians.* Edited by Stanley Sadie and John Tyrell. 29 vols. London: Macmillan, 2001.

Pérez Zalduondo, Gemma. "El nacionalismo como eje de la política musical del primer gobierno regular de Franco (30 de enero de 1938–8 de agosto de 1939)." *Revista de Musicología* 18 (1995): 247–73.

Persia, Jorge de. *I Concurso de Cante Jondo, 1922–1992.* Granada: Archivo Manuel de Falla, 1992.

————. "Falla, Ortega, y la renovación musical." *Revista de Occidente* 156 (1994): 102–16.

————. *Los últimos años de Manuel de Falla.* Madrid: Sociedad General de Autores de España, 1989.

Persia, Jorge de, ed. *Manuel de Falla: His Life and Works.* London: Omnibus Press, 1999.

————. *Poesía.* Número monográfico dedicado a Manuel de Falla, nos. 36 and 37. Madrid: Ministerio de Cultura, 1991.

Petit, Jacques, annotator. *Correspondence Paul Claudel–Darius Milhaud, 1912–1953.* Cahiers Paul Claudel, no. 3. Paris: Gallimard, 1961.

Pilapil, Vicente R. "Azaña y Díaz, Manuel." In *Historical Dictionary of the Spanish Civil War, 1936–1939.* Edited by James W. Cortada. Westport, Conn.: Greenwood, 1982.

"El poema de la guerra: Letra de Pemán y música." *ABC.* 7 October 1937.

"Por los teatros: Los estrenos—Lara, *El amor brujo.*" *ABC.* 16 April 1915, 20.

Potter, Pamela M. *Most German of the Arts: Musicology and Society from the Weimar Republic to the End of Hitler's Reich.* New Haven and London: Yale University Press, 1998.

Powell, Linton E. *A History of Spanish Piano Music.* Bloomington: Indiana University Press, 1980.

Powell, Philip. *Tree of Hate.* New York and London: Basic Books, 1971.

"Premiere in Milan for Falla Cantata." *New York Times.* 19 June 1962, 28.

Preston, Paul. *The Coming of the Spanish Civil War: Reform, Reaction, and Revolution in the Second Republic.* 2d ed. London and New York: Routledge, 1994.

————. *A Concise History of the Spanish Civil War.* London: Fontana, 1996.

————. "The Legacy of the Spanish Civil War," in *"¡No Pasarán!" Art, Literature, and the Spanish Civil War,* edited by Stephen M. Hart. London: Tamesis, 1988.

————. *The Politics of Revenge: Fascism and the Military in Twentieth-Century Spain.* London: Unwin Hyman, 1990.

————. *Las tres Españas del 36.* Barcelona: Plaza & Janés, 1998.

Prudhomme, Jean. "Opéra Comique." *Comoedia.* 18 January 1914.

P. V. *The World.* 20 March 1926, 13. Untitled article.

Pyron, Darden Asbury. *Liberace.* Chicago and London: University of Chicago Press, 2000.

Quesada Dorador, Eduardo. "Imágenes de Manuel de Falla en Granada." In *Manuel de Falla en Granada.* Edited by Yvan Nommick and Eduardo Quesada Dorador. Granada: Publicaciones Manuel de Falla, 2001.

Quintanal Sánchez, Inmaculada. *Manuel de Falla y Asturias: Consideraciones sobre el nacionalismo musical.* Oviedo: Instituto de Estudios Asturianos, 1989.

Rackard, Benny Gene. "A Directorial Analysis and Production Guide to Three Musical Theatre Forms for High School Production: *La vida breve, The Sound of Music,* and *The Chocolate Soldier.*" Ph.D. diss. University of Southern Mississippi, 1980.

Ràfols, J. F. *Modernisme i modernistes.* Barcelona: Edicions Destino, 1982.

Ramsden, H. *The 1898 Movement in Spain: Towards a Reinterpretation with Special Reference to En torno al casticismo and Idearium español.* Manchester: Manchester University Press; Totowa, N.J. : Rowman and Littlefield, 1974.

Ravel, Maurice. "À l'Opéra-Comique: *Francesca da Rimini* et *La vida breve,*" *Comedia Ilustré.* 20 January 1914.

Restout, Denise, comp., ed., and trans., with Robert Hawkins. *Landowska on Music.* New York: Stein and Day, 1964.

Rey Hazas, Antonio, and Florencio Sevilla Arroyo, eds. *Pedro Calderón de la Barca: El gran teatro del mundo.* Barcelona: Planeta, 1991.

Reyes, Luis, and Peter Rubie. *Hispanics in Hollywood: A Celebration of 100 Years in Film and Television.* Hollywood: Lone Eagle, 2000.

Río, Ángel del. *Historia de la literatura española*. Rev. ed. 2 vols. New York: Holt, Reinhardt, and Winston, 1963.

Ríos, Fernando de los. *Obras completas*. Edited by Teresa Rodríguez de Lecca. Madrid: Fundación Caja de Madrid, Anthropos Editorial (Barcelona), 1997.

Roberts, John Storm. *The Latin Tinge: The Impact of Latin American Music on the United States*. 2d ed. New York: Oxford University Press, 1999.

Rock, David. *Argentina, 1516–1987: From Spanish Colonization to Alfonsín*. Rev. and exp. ed. Berkeley: University of California Press, 1987.

Rodrigo, Antonina. *María Lejárraga: Una mujer en la sombra*. Madrid: Vosa, 1994.

Rogers P. P., and F. A. Lapuente. *Diccionario de seudónimos literarios españoles, con algunas iniciales*. Madrid: Editorial Gredos, 1977.

Rojas, Fernando de. *La Celestina: Tragicomedia de Calisto y Melibea*. Madrid: Alianza Editorial, 1969.

Roland-Manuel [Alexis Levy]. *Manuel de Falla*. Paris: Cahiers d'Art, 1930.

———. "*Le Tricorne* à l'Opéra." *L'Eclair*. 26 January 1920.

Romero, Justo. *Falla: Discografía recomendada*. Barcelona: Ediciones Peninsula, 1999.

Romero, Segismundo. "El ilustre músico Don Manuel de Falla goza de buena salud." 13 March 1937. Newspaper unidentified.

Ros Fábregas, Emilio. "Historiografía de la música en las catedrales españolas: Nacionalismo y positivismo en la investigación musicológica." *Codex XXI* (1998): 68–135.

Rosenthal, Earl. "Plus Ultra, Non Plus Ultra, and the Columnar Device of Emperor Charles V." *Journal of the Warburg Institute* 34 (1971): 204–28.

Ross, Alex. "Deep Song: Lorca Inspires an Opera by Osvaldo Golijov." *New Yorker*. 1 September 2003, 128–29.

Rubinstein, Artur. *My Young Years*. New York: Knopf, 1973.

Rubinstein y España: Exposición homenaje a Arturo Rubinstein. Madrid: Turner, 1988.

Saary, Margarete. *Persönlichkeit und musikdramatische Kreativität Hugo Wolfs*. Tutzing: Schneider, 1984.

Sachs, Harvey. *Music in Fascist Italy*. London: Weidenfeld and Nicolson, 1987.

———. *Rubinstein: A Life*. New York: Grove, 1995.

"Sacrilegios, incendios y asaltos de iglesias." *Diario de Barcelona*. 18 April 1936, 1.

Sagardía, Ángel. "A torno a Manuel de Falla y al crítico Santiago Arimón, Tristan." *Radio Nacional*. September 1934.

———. *Manuel de Falla*. Madrid: Unión Musical Española, 1946.

———. *Vida y obra de Manuel de Falla*. Madrid: Escelicer, 1967.

Salazar, Adolfo. *El siglo romántico*. Madrid: J. M. Yagües, 1936.

———. "Espagne: L'Orquesta Betica de Camara." *La Revue Musicale* 7, no. 1 (1 November 1925): 79–81.

———. "La vida musical: El Retablo de Maese Pedro en Nueva York." *El Sol*. 28 January 1926.

———. "La vida musical: Una nueva visita de Strawinsky." *El Sol*. 23 November 1933, 4.

———. "Polichinela y Maese Pedro." *Revista de Occidente* 4 (1924): 229–37.

———. *"Pulcinella* and *Maese Pedro."* *Chesterian* 6 (1926): 119–25.

———. *Sinfonía y ballet.* Madrid: Editorial Mundo Latino, 1929.

Salter, Lionel. "A Nation in Turbulence." In *The Late Romantic Era.* Edited by Jim Samson. Englewood Cliffs, N.J.: Prentice Hall, 1991.

Salvador, Miguel. "La Semana teatral: Eslava, *El corregidor y la molinera." España, Semanario de la Vida Nacional* 3/116 (1917): 11–12.

Salvat, Joan. "El III Congrés de la Societat Internacional de Musicologia a Barcelona." *Revista Musical Catalana* 33, no. 389 (1936): 185–99.

Samaroff, Olga. "Boston Symphony Presents New De Falla Work." *Evening Post.* 7 January 1927.

Sánchez García, Fernando, ed. *La correspondencia inédita entre Falla y Pemán.* Seville: Alfar, 1991.

"Santa Cruz de Tenerife, a la llegada de los restos de Falla." *ABC.* 7 January 1947, 17.

Santiago, Iñigo de. "Manuel de Falla, desde la Argentina habla para *Arriba." Arriba.* 8 October 1944.

Scanlon, Geraldine M. *La polémica feminista en la España contemporánea, 1868–1974.* Translated by Rafael Mazarrasa. Madrid: Akal, 1986.

Schallert, Edwin. *"Carnegie Hall,* Musical Victory." *Los Angeles Times.* 14 August 1947.

———. "Silly Story Well Glossed in *Daughters." Los Angeles Times.* 3 March 1948.

———. *"Two Girls and Sailor* Okay Musical." *Los Angeles Times.* 23 June 1944.

Schepers, M. B. "Self-Love." In *The New Catholic Encyclopedia.* 16 vols. New York: McGraw-Hill, 1967.

Schindler, Kurt, ed., *Spanish Sacred Motets.* Boston: Oliver Ditson, 1919.

Schonberg, Harold C. "Goya Captured in Music," *New York Times,* 26 November 1967.

———. "Music: Met Gives *Atlántida* Premiere." *New York Times.* 1 October 1962, 36.

Schubert, Adrian. "The Asturian Revolution of October 1934." In *Revolution and War in Spain, 1931–1939.* Edited by Paul Preston. London and New York: Methuen, 1984.

———. *The Great Pianists.* New York: Simon and Schuster, 1963.

Schulte, Henry F. *The Spanish Press: 1470–1966.* Urbana and Chicago: University of Illinois Press, 1968.

Schwartz, Lloyd. "A Pair of Failed de Fallas." *Boston Sunday Globe.* 8 April 1979, 9.

Schwartz-Kates, Deborah. "The *Gauchesco* Tradition as a Source of National Identity in Argentine Art Music (ca. 1890–1955)." Ph.D. diss. University of Texas, Austin, 1997.

———. "Ginastera, Alberto (Evarista)." In *The Revised New Grove Dictionary of Music and Musicians.* Edited by Stanley Sadie and John Tyrell. 29 vols. London: Macmillan, 2001.

Sedwick, Frank. *The Tragedy of Manuel Azaña and the Fate of the Spanish Republic.* Columbus: Ohio State University Press, 1963.

Seitz, Elizabeth. "Manuel de Falla's Years in Paris, 1907–1914," Ph.D. diss. Boston University, 1995.

"Semaine théatrale." *La Comédie Niçoise*. 10–17 April 1913.

Shafter, Alfred M. *Musical Copyright*. 2d ed. Chicago: Callaghan, 1939.

Shaw, Donald Leslie. *The Generation of '98 in Spain*. London: E. Benn; New York: Barnes and Noble, 1975.

Shumway, Nicolas. *The Invention of Argentina*. Berkeley: University of California Press, 1991.

Sigmund, Paul E. *Liberation Theology at the Crossroads: Democracy or Revolution?* New York and Oxford: Oxford University Press, 1990.

Simms, Bryan R. *Music of the Twentieth Century: Style and Structure*. New York: Schirmer, 1986.

Skidmore, Thomas E., and Peter H. Smith. *Modern Latin America*. 5th ed. New York and Oxford: Oxford University Press, 2001.

Smith, William Ander. *The Mystery of Leopold Stokowski*. London: Associated University Presses, 1990.

"Sobre el homenaje a Falla." *El Liberal* (Seville). 17 April 1932.

Sobrino, Ramón. "Marqués García, Pedro Miguel." In *Diccionario de la música española e hispanoamericana*. Edited by Emilio Casares. 10 vols. Madrid: Sociedad General de Autores y Editores, 1999–2000.

Sopeña, Federico, "La Espiritualidad de Manuel de Falla." In *Manuel de Falla tra la Spagna e l'Europa*. Edited by Paolo Pinamonti. Florence: Olschki, 1989.

———. *Manuel de Falla y el mundo de la cultura española*. Madrid: Instituto de España, 1976.

———. "Pedrell en el Conservatorio de Madrid." *Anuario Musical* 27 (1972): 95–101.

———. *Vida y obra de Manuel de Falla*. Madrid: Turner Música, 1988.

———. *Correspondencia entre Falla y Zuloaga, 1915–1942*. Granada: Ayuntamiento de Granada, 1982.

———. *Correspondencia Gerardo Diego–Manuel de Falla*. Santander: Fundación Marcelino Botín-Sanz de Sautolay López, 1988.

Sperber, Murray A., ed. *And I Remember Spain: A Spanish Civil War Anthology*. New York: Collier, 1974.

Steinberg, Michael. "Nights in the Gardens of Spain: Symphonic Impressions for Piano and Orchestra." Program booklet, New York Philharmonic, 4 November 1995.

Stevenson, Robert M. "Haydn's Iberian World Connections." *Inter-American Music Review* 4, no. 2 (1982): 3–31.

———. "Liszt in the Iberian Peninsula." *Inter-American Music Review* 7, no. 2 (1986), 3–22.

———. "Liszt at Madrid and Lisbon (1844–1845)." *Musical Quarterly* 65, no. 4 (1979): 493–512.

———. "Musical Remembrances of Columbus's Voyages." *Inter-American Music Review* 15, no. 2 (1996): 1–71.

———. "Tomás Luis de Victoria: Unique Spanish Genius." *Inter-American Music Review* 12, no. 1 (1991): 1–100.

Stokes, Richard L."Realm of Music." *Evening World.* 7 January 1927.

Stravinsky, Igor. *An Autobiography.* New York: Norton, 1962. Originally published as *Chroniques de ma vie* (Paris: Donoël et Steele, 1935).

Stravinsky, Igor, and Robert Craft. *Expositions and Developments.* Garden City, N.Y.: Doubleday, 1962.

———. *Memories and Commentaries.* New York: Doubleday, 1960.

Sturman, Janet. *Spanish Operetta, American Stage.* Urbana and Chicago: University of Illinois Press, 2000.

Suárez-Pajares, Javier, ed. *Icongrafía/Iconography: Manuel de Falla, 1876–1946—La imagen de un músico/the Image of a Musician.* Translated by Yolanda Acker. Madrid: Sociedad General de Autores de España, 1995.

Subirá, José. *Historia y anecdotario del Teatro Real.* Madrid: Editorial Plus-Ultra, 1949.

Tannenbaum, Edward R. *The Action Française: Die-Hard Reactionaries in Twentieth-Century France.* New York: Wiley, 1962.

Taruskin, Richard. "Russian Folk Melodies in *The Rite of Spring.*" *Journal of the American Musicological Society* 33 (1980): 501–43.

———. *Stravinksy and the Russian Traditions: A Biography of the Works through Mavra.* 2 vols. Berkeley: University of California Press, 1996.

Terry, Arthur. *A Literary History of Spain: Catalan Literature.* London: E. Benn; New York: Barnes and Noble, 1972.

"Théâtre National de l'Opéra Comique: Répétition générale de *La vie brève.*" *Autorité.* 31 December 1913.

Thomas, Hugh. *The Spanish Civil War.* 3d ed. New York: Simon and Schuster, 1986.

Thomas, Juan María. *Manuel de Falla en la isla.* Palma de Mallorca: Ediciones Capella Clasica, 1946.

Thompson, Oscar. "*El Retablo* Delights at American Premiere." *Musical America* 47 (9 January 1926): 7, 37.

———. "Spanish Novelty Introduced with Stravinsky Opera." *Musical America* 43, no. 21 (13 March 1926): 1, 4–5.

Thomson, Andrew. "CDs: Manuel de Falla/Ernesto Halffter—*Atlántida.*" *Musical Times* 132 (October 1993): 594.

Thurston, Herbert, and Donald Attwater, eds. *Butler's Lives of the Saints.* Rev. and suppl. ed. 4 vols. New York: P. J. Kennedy & Sons, 1956.

Todd, Larry. "Mendelssohn." In *The Nineteenth-Century Symphony.* Edited by D. Kern Holoman. New York: Schirmer, 1997.

Torres Clemente, Elena. "La presencia de Scarlatti en la trayectoria musical de Manuel de Falla." In *Manuel de Falla e Italia.* Edited by Yvan Nommick. Granada: Publicaciones del Archivo Manuel de Falla, 2000.

———. *Manuel de Falla y las Cantigas de Alfonso X El Sabio.* Granada: Universidad de Granada, 2002.

Torres Mulas, Jacinto. "Efemérides: Cien años de concurso de piano del Conservatorio: Los *Allegros de Concierto* de Granados y Falla." *Música: Revista del Real Conservatorio Superior de Música de Madrid* 10 (2003): 277–86.

———. *Las publicaciones periódicas musicales en España (1812–1990): Estudio crítico/ bibliográfico, repertorio general.* Madrid: Instituto de Bibliografía Musical, 1991.

Trask, David F. *The War with Spain in 1898.* New York and London: Macmillan, 1981.

Trend, John Brande. *Manuel de Falla and Spanish Music.* 1929. Reprint, New York: Knopf, 1934.

———. *A Picture of Modern Spain.* London: Constable, 1921.

Tristan. "*El corregidor y la molinera*: Teatro Eslava." *El Liberal.* 8 April 1917, 2.

Trueba, Antonio. *Arte de hacer versos, al alcance de todo el que sepa leer.* Barcelona: Librería de Juan y Atonio Bastinos, 1881.

Ullman, Joan Connelly. *The Tragic Week: A Study of Anticlericalism in Spain, 1875– 1912.* Cambridge: Harvard University Press, 1968.

"Última charla del General Queipo de Llano." February 1938. Newspaper unidentified.

"Una ópera española: *La vida breve.*" *ABC.* 14 November 1914.

"Una ópera española: *La vida breve.*" *La Época.* 14 November 1914.

Urman, David, and J. M. Thomson. *On Music and Musicians.* London and Boston: Marion Boyars, 1979.

Valverde, Alfredo. "Música en la Residencia de Estudiantes: Federico García Lorca." *Tutti música* 3, no. 7 (1998): 11–13.

Verdaguer, Mario. *Medio siglo de vida barcelonesa.* Barcelona: Editorial Barna, 1957.

Viault, Birdsall S. *Modern European History.* New York: McGraw-Hill, 1990.

"La Vie Théâtrale et Artistique." *Courrier del Argentine.* 15 January 1914.

Vilches de Frutos, María Francisca, and Dru Dougherty. *Los estrenos teatrales de Federico García Lorca (1920–1945).* Madrid: Tabapress and Fundación García Lorca, 1992.

Vinay, Gianfranco. "Scarlatti e Stravinsky nel *Concerto* per clavicembalo." In *Manuel de Falla tra la Spagna e l'Europa.* Edited by Paolo Pinamonti. Florence: Olschki, 1989.

Viniegra, Juan J. *Vida íntima de Manuel de Falla.* Cadiz: Diputación Provincial, 1966.

Vuillermoz, Émile. "La Musique: Le 'Concerto' de Manuel de Falla." *Excelsior.* 12 June 1927.

Wallace, W. A. "Form." In *The New Catholic Encyclopedia.* 16 vols. New York: McGraw-Hill, 1967.

Walters, F. P. *A History of the League of Nations.* London: Oxford University Press, 1952.

Ward, Philip. *The Oxford Companion to Spanish Literature.* Oxford: Clarendon, 1978.

Waring, Virginia. *Fred Waring and the Pennsylvanians.* Urbana and Chicago: University of Illinois Press, 1997.

Watkins, Glenn. *Pyramids at the Louvre: Music, Culture, and Collage from Stravinsky to the Postmodernists.* Cambridge: Harvard University Press, 1994.

Weill, Irving. "*Soldier* Given with Pantomimic Rite." *Musical America* 47 (31 March 1928): 1, 7.

Weinstein, Larry, dir. *Fuego y agua: Vida y música de Manuel de Falla*. Madrid: Rhombus RTVE, 1991. Video.

White, Eric Walter. *Stravinsky: The Composer and His Works*. 2d ed. Berkeley: University of California Press, 1979.

White, Hayden. *The Content of the Form: Narrative Discourse and Historical Representation*. Baltimore, Md.: Johns Hopkins University Press, 1986.

White, R. *"El corregidor y la molinera."* *El Universo*. 8 April 1917.

Wilson, Ann, ed. *The Spanish Civil War: A History in Pictures*. New York and London: Norton, 1986.

Winsten, Archer. "New York Views." *New York Post*. February[?] 1948.

"World Premiere for Falla Work." *New York Times*. 25 November 1961, 27.

Wright, Virgina. "Film Review: *Three Daring Daughters*." *Daily News*. 3 March 1948.

Z. "De Música: Festival Manuel de Falla." *El Liberal*. 6 November 1926, 3.

Zapatero, Virgilio. *Fernando de los Rios: Biografía intelectual*. Granada: Pre-Textos, Diputación de Granada, 1999.

Zubailde, Ignacio. *"La vida breve."* *Revista Musical* (Bilbao) 5, no. 9 (September 1913): 201–4.

Index